COLONIALIZATION OF ISLAM
Dissolution of Traditional
Institutions in Pakistan

COLONIALIZATION OF ISLAM
Dissolution of Traditional
Institutions in Pakistan

JAMAL MALIK

MANOHAR
1996

ISBN: 81-7304-148-2

First Published 1996

Published by
Ajay Kumar Jain for
Manohar Publishers & Distributors
2/6 Ansari Road, Daryaganj,
New Delhi - 110 002

Lasertypeset by
AJ Software Publishing Co. Pvt. Ltd.
305, Durga Chambers
1333, D.B. Gupta Road,
Karol Bagh, New Delhi - 110 005

Printed at
P.L. Printers
Rana Pratap Bagh, Delhi

CONTENTS

ACKNOWLEDGEMENTS   xiii

INTRODUCTION   1

I. TOWARDS A THEORETICAL APPROACH TO ISLAMIZATION   15
   The Politicization of Islam (15); The Making of a
   Colonial Sector (17); Social Paths of Transition and
   Intermediary Sectors (21).

II. LEGITIMIZING ISLAMIZATION: THE COUNCIL FOR
    ISLAMIC IDEOLOGY   33
    Introduction (33); History and Activities (33); Under
    Ayub Khan (34); Under Bhutto (37); The CII since 1977
    (38); Integrationist Islam policy (39); Resignations and
    opposition (44); The Budgets of the CII (46); Conclusion
    (47).

III. ISLAMIC ENDOWMENTS   55
     Introduction (55); Historical Outline (55); The position
     of the shrine-saints (56); The Auqaf Department (59);
     Reactions (64); Auqaf Department and Education (66);
     The 'Ulamâ' Akademî (67); Accounts (69); The structure
     of income and expenditure (70); Conclusion (73).

IV. THE ZAKAT SYSTEM   85
    Introduction (85); History of Zakat in Pakistan (86); An
    Integrationist Zakat System: The Panel and CII (87);
    The Problems of the Ministry of Finance (89); CII's
    Criticism (91); Structure of the Zakat System (92); Flow
    of Zakat Fund (95); Personnel (95); Zakat in Relation to
    Federal Receipts and Expenditure (96); Zakat Receipts
    and Expenditure at Different Levels (99); Voluntary

Zakat (102); Refunding and evasion of Zakat (102); The
District Level (107); Mean Value Deviations (108);
Zakat Receipts and Level of Development (109);
Correlations with Population (110); Receipts and Ex-
penditure (110); Conclusion (112).

V. THE ISLAMIC SYSTEM OF EDUCATION   120
    Introduction (120); Before and after Colonialization
    (121); Under Ayub Khan (123); The Organization of
    Dînî Madâris (123); Curricular Affiliation (125); Islam
    and Dînî Madâris under Bhutto (128); Since Zia ul Haq
    (130); The *Sargodha Report* (130); Ittihâd al-Madâris
    (132); A National Survey (132); A National Committee
    for Dînî Madâris (133); The *Halepota Report* (133);
    Reaction of the Dînî Madâris (136); The Dînî Madâris
    Regulation (139); Formal Recognition of Religious
    Schools (140); Their Economic Situation (142); Zakat
    for Dînî Madâris (143); Criteria for Zakat distribution
    (144); Disbursement at Provincial Level (149); Contri-
    bution of PZC-Zakat to the Annual Budget of Dînî
    Madâris (152); Political Impact via the Zakat system
    (152).

VI. REACTION OF RELIGIOUS SCHOLARS AND DÎNÎ MADÂRIS   164
    TO THE OFFICIAL POLICIES
    The Curricula and Integrationism (164); Traditionali-
    zation of the Reform (167); Divergence among Deobandis
    (169); The Brelwi Tanzîm (172); Pakistan Studies in
    Religious Schools (174); Overview on Different Curri-
    cula (175); Increase of Students, Teachers and Madâris
    (177); "Mushroom-Growth" (179); Different Levels
    (187); The Budget of Dînî Madâris (190); The Provincial
    and District Distribution (192); The Political Dimensions
    of Religious Schools (202); Dâr al-'Ulûm Haqqâniyyah
    and *Jihâd* (202); Origin of the Graduates (208); *Jihâd*
    and Jamâ'at-e Islâmî (208); Regional Nationalism (210);
    The Boycott of the Zakat System (210).

VII. TRADITIONALISTS ON THE ADVANCE?   227
    The Boom in examinations in Religious Schools (227);

Identification of the Districts of origin of the Graduates
(232); The Deobandis (235); Regional Centres for
Graduation (239); Family Background (241); The Brelwi
Graduates (244); Regional Centres of Graduation (246);
The Shia (247); The Ahl-e Hadith (249); Summary
(250).

VIII. The Problem of the Labour Market   265
The socio-economic conditions in the areas of origin of
the Graduates (265); The NWFP and the Tribal Areas
(265); The Agrarian Punjab (267); Industry in the Punjab
(269); Quo vadis, oh *mullâ*? (270); Arabic as an
Employment Scheme (271); Study of Koran in Formal
Institutions (273); LAMEC (274); Mosque Schools (275);
The Army as Saviour? (278); Summary (278).

IX. Concluding Remarks   289

Epilogue   297

Appendix A   310

Appendix B   320

Appendix C   321

Appendix D   324

Abbreviations and Glossary   326

Bibliography   337

Index   355

TABLES, GRAPHS, DIAGRAMS
AND MAPS

Table 1:   Social Basis of Islamization   20

Table 2:   Receipts and Expenditure of the Auqaf Department, Punjab, 1960-1985 (in Rs.)   71

Table 3:   Zakat in proportion to other federal receipts and expenditure   97

Table 4:   Proportion of Zakat as compared to the social expenditure of the provinces   99

Table 5:   Zakat receipts and expenditure at different levels   99

Table 6:   Reasons for refunding, number of cases and amounts refunded   103

Table 7:   Savings Accounts and Term Deposits Exempted from Zakat   105

Table 8:   Zakat evasion 1981-1985, Current Accounts and Savings Accounts in Rs. million   107

Table 9:   Movement of amounts on accounts at weekly intervals   107

Table 10:   Correlation-coefficients of the ranking of Zakat received per district per 1,000 inhabitants and the ranking according to stages of development in the district   110

Table 11:   Proposals and changes of the Committee of 1960/61   127

Table 12:   Income (I) and Expenditure (E) of the Dînî Madâris   142

Table 13:   Categorization of the Dînî Madâris for the receipt of Zakat   146

Table 14:   Disbursement of Zakat to the Dînî Madâris in the Punjab, 1982-1983, 1984-1985   148

Table 15:   Zakat disbursements from the Provincial Zakat Fund to the Dînî Madâris   150

Table 15(A): Zakat funds disbursed in 1,000 Rs.   150

Table 15(B): Number of Dînî Madâris   150

Table 15(C): Number of students   150

Table 15(D): Average annual amount per student in Rs.   150

Table 15(E): Proportion of funds disbursed in Dînî Madâris   150
              out of Zakat funds passed on to the provinces by
              the CZC, 1980-1985

Table 16:   Subdivision and categorization of different   165
              levels of education

Table 17:   Subjects suggested by the Dînî Madâris Committee,   168
              by the Wafâq and the Tanzîm at the Primary Level

Table 18:   The curriculum proposed by the Dînî Madâris   170
              Committee for the intermediate and higher stage

Table 19:   Curriculum of the Tanzîm al-Madâris for grades 1-8   173

Table 20:   The curriculum proposed by the Tanzîm for   174
              grades 9-16

Table 21:   Different Curricula at a Glance   175

Table 22:   Number of students and teachers of Dînî Madâris in   178
              different years

Table 23:   Quantitative Development of Dînî Madâris in   180
              Pakistan (formerly West Pakistan)

Table 24:   Registered Dînî Madâris and private schools in   181
              Punjab,1974-85

Table 25:   "Mushroom-Growth", figures for the NWFP   182

Table 26:   "Mushroom-Growth" in Karachi   182

Table 27:   Registered Institutions in Punjab according to   185
              Divisions: 1984 and 1985

Table 28:   Registered Institutions in selected districts of the 187
              Punjab,1984-85

Table 29:   Education in Dînî Madâris according to Levels   188
              offered, 1979

Table 30:   Education in Dînî Madâris according to Levels   189
              offered, 1982

Table 31:   Comparison of Levels of education in formal   189
              schools and in Dînî Madâris

Table 32:   Growth rates of the receipts and expenditure of the 190
              Jâm'iah Nizâmiyyah Ridwiyyah, Lahore

Table 33:   Budgets of the Jâmi'ah Nizâmiyyah, Lahore   193

Table 34(A): Dînî Madâris according to their school of thought   198
              and their affiliation to an umbrella organization in
              Pakistan

Table 34(B): Dînî Madâris according to their school of thought   198
              and their affiliation to an umbrella organization in
              Punjab

Table 34(C): Dînî Madâris according to their school of thought   198

and their affiliation to an umbrella organization in
Sindh

Table 34(D): Dînî Madâris according to their school of thought   199
and their affiliation to an umbrella organization in
NWFP

Table 34(E): Dînî Madâris according to their school of thought   199
and their affiliation to an umbrella organization in
Baluchistan

Table 34(F): Dînî Madâris according to their school of thought   199
and their affiliation to an umbrella organization in
Kashmir (Pak.) and in the Northern Areas

Table 35:   Candidates for Graduation of the Wafâq over the   203
years and the proportion of the Dâr al-'Ulûm
Haqqâniyyah

Table 36:   Budgets of Dâr al-'Ulûm Haqqâniyyah in selected   205
years

Table 37:   Amount of Zakat for the Dâr al-'Ulûm Haqqâniyyah 206

Table 38:   Areas of origin of the Graduates of the Dâr al-'Ulûm   209

Table 39:   Inhabitants per Deobandi candidate for Graduation   237
and per M.A. candidate for Graduation (formal
system of education)

Table 40:   Order of ranking of the candidates for Graduation   237
per 10,000 inhabitants per district

Table 41:   Number of candidates of Graduation of schools in   239
Peshawar and Karachi

Table 42:   Distribution of the candidates for Graduation within   244
the Tanzîm al-Madâris according to Provinces
and Years

Table 43:   Districts and towns of graduation of the Brelwis   246
from the Punjab, 1974 to 1979/80

Table 44:   Distribution of the candidates for Graduation of the   248
Wafâq al-Madâris Shia according to districts of origin,
1984 and 1985

Table 45:   Distribution of the candidates for Graduation of the   249
Wafâq al-Madâris al-Salafiyyah according to numbers,
districts of origin and the religious tradition, 1978-1985

Table 46:   Districts of Graduation of the Deobandis in selected   321
years (1963, 1965, 1974, 1975 and 1984)

Table 47:   Titles of Fathers of Deobandi candidates for   322
Graduation in selected years (1963, 1965, 1974,
1975 and 1984)

GRAPHS

Graph 1: Registrations according to the Societies Act 1860   183
          for particular years in the Province of Punjab
Graph 2: Number of candidates for Graduation of different   231
          schools of thought
Graph 3: Development of Graduates in Pakistan   233
Graph 4: Development of the *mawlânâs* in Pakistan, 1960-1995   234

DIAGRAMS

Diagram 1: CII Members according to type of education 1962-1981   40
Diagram 2: Collection and Disbursement of Zakat and Ushr Funds   93
Diagram 3: Administrative units of Zakat and their composition   94
Diagram 4: Number of candidates for Graduation of the different   228
           schools of thought
Diagram 5: Titles of Fathers, classified by groups   323

MAPS

Map 1: Spatial distribution of schools of thought in Pakistan,   204
        according to the number of their respective institutions,
        as of 1983
Map 2: Areas of origin of the *Mawlânâs*   254
Map 3: Administrative boundaries of Pakistan, 1973   324
Map 4: Administrative boundaries of Pakistan, 1982   325

ACKNOWLEDGEMENTS

The book in hand was submitted in April 1988 as a Ph.D. thesis at the Southasia Institute, University of Heidelberg and was published in 1989 in Stuttgart by Franz Steiner. The major part of this translation was done by Dr. Christine Gieraths. I am greatly indebted to her enduring work.

The present version has not been changed drastically, albeit suggested shortenings of the anonymous editors of the Indian Publisher—especially in regard to statistical data—have, as far as possible, been taken into consideration. I wish to thank them for their painstaking elaborations and for their persevering labour. I would like to express my thanks to Mr. Ramesh Jain for encouraging me to submit the English version to Manohar Publishers and Distributors. Nevertheless, I found it quite difficult during the process of revision to bring the thesis into the shape of a book, firstly, because of the vast amount of data contained in the original thesis and, secondly, because I have been out of touch with this topic for quite some time. However, I have tried in an Epilogue to bring together some new material and shed some light on the developments of the last couple of years. This part is grounded, however, on the basics of the thesis.

Before embarking on the text I would like to express my deepest respect and thanks to the many people who gave me valuable assistance during the preparation of the work.

I could never have undertaken this research without the financial aid provided by the German Konrad-Adenauer Foundation. It is a pleasure to thank the Foundation and their members for their long assistance, particularly Mr. K.S. Krieger and Mrs. R. Düchting, and to Dr. R. Backhaus.

The text could not been finalized without the innumerable discussions with informants, professors and friends in Pakistan as well as at the Southasia Institute in Heidelberg. Particularly I am grateful to the respectable muftis and maulanas as well as the numerous principals of the religious schools. Without their manifold support and obliging cooperation this enquiry would have remained much more incomplete than it is now. Special thanks go to Mufti Naimi, Mufti Anwar Shah, Maulana

Yusuf Talal and the late Maulana Hamid Miyan. I am pleased to mention Professor Dr. A.W.J. Halepota, who opened his valuable bookcase and who did not stop supporting me morally and intellectually during my field research in Pakistan from 1984 to 1986. Innumerable university professors and librarians, the staff of the Ministry of Education and representatives of Provincial Ministries kindly provided me with valuable data. The members of the Zakat Administration, Islamabad and Peshawar deserve special mention, to all of whom I would like to express my thanks. Indeed, what their bookselves contain provides this book's documentary basis.

Similarly, without the promotion of friends in Islamabad, Peshawar, Lahore, Multan and Karachi many a door would have remained shut for this enquiry. From them I also benefitted in nonacademic ways. For small and great help and provision of material as well as academic stimulations I am indebted to the staff of the Southasia Institute, Heidelberg, especially to Dr. Wolfgang-Peter Zingel, Dr. Inayatullah Baloch and Professor Fateh Muhammad Malik. Particularly my supervisor Professor Dr. Dietmar Rothermund made crucial suggestions and his academic help and support have contributed to the finalization of this work. To him I acknowledge my sincere gratitude.

I must also thank my parents for their help towards solving transcription problems and for their moral relief during the whole time, and I am grateful to Benjamin who always had a much realistic approach towards this topic.

Bonn   **JAMAL MALIK**
May 1995

INTRODUCTION

Western scholars working on Islam as a social, political and economic force have recognized their limited knowledge about Islamic institutions, such as Auqâf (religious endowments), Tarîqah (mystical association), Dînî Madâris (religious schools), and K̲h̲ânqâh (hospice). They have argued in favour of making such institutions the object of scientific inquiry in order to gain an insight into their organizational structures as well as their diverse cultural and religious articulations. Such studies were expected to lead towards understanding the traditional structures of Muslim societies.[1]

The aim of these inquiries was not questioned originally. Was it really a matter of gaining a better understanding of other cultures? Or was it a heuristic interest aimed at understanding one's *own* culture better through studying other cultures, comparable to anthropological studies? Or, was the central objective of oriental studies quite different having economic or even geo-strategic motivations? What was the appropriate epistemological framework into which facts and findings were to be put? Was there anything beyond heuristic interest of mere accumulation of data, were the scholars presenting data as purely practical, technical products of research, without considering the way in which their research would be made use of in specific contemporary circumstances?[2]

In an inquiry of an analytical character undertaken to put empirical data into a theoretical frame, one could quite often assume heuristic as well as normative euro-centrism. Frequently, so it would seem, the perception of backwardness of the orient from colonial times was reproduced and thus perpetuated and strengthened.[3] It is plausible that Muslim intellectuals picked up this concept of backwardness, accepted it as a fact, and finally attempted to stop the supposed decay of Islam by adopting western values and forms. This perception today serves to lend support to the "Third world" modernization strategies. The precondition for this was to create a division of the world into modern and non-modern. This visualization was based on a common assumption among reform-minded representatives of "developing countries" on the one hand, and among scholars of "developed countries" on the other. The common assumption was that not only "tradition" existed next to "modernity" but especially that tradition had to be substituted by modernity, and thus the society had to be transformed. Thus, a teleological tendency to dissolve tradition is part of this conception. In this context, it is necessary to look at Islamic institutions, i.e. endowments, mystical orders, traditional institutions of education and traditional social systems. These are, in fact, still autonomous institutions, representing, in most cases, the autochthonous character of precolonial societies. The majority of these institutions, to be sure, had been pushed aside in recent times and attracted little attention in contemporary politics. They served as a refuge in case of social crises and as sources of enrichment for elites and representatives of the colonial society who usually reflected colonial western thought, alienated from the traditional culture.

The rediscovery of autochthonous structures, especially in the recent past, has given rise to academic interest in them. It was not the traditionalists, the guardians of autochthonous culture and institutions, who brought tradition and its institutions into limelight, but the modernist and largely secularist forces. These forces turned towards these structures with the intention of reforming them. The guardians of traditional institutions reacted to this imposed modernization either by closing ranks against the modern, colonial sector or by opening up and assimilation (see chapter I). These forces who wished to "reconstruct" traditional institutions, like the Dînî Madâris, organized conferences in western metropolises, such as the seminar on "Traditional Forms of Education whithin a Diversified Educational Field: The Case of the Coranic Schools."[4] The declared aim was ". . . to make religious teachers aware that modernity, properly understood, does not pose a threat to Islamic identity."[5]

Divergences of interest among representatives of traditional institutions as well as among western scholars engaged in research on such institutions are not unusual.[6] In these seminars most participants nevertheless agreed on the necessity of modernizing such institutions. In the long run, an approach of this kind might lead to an integration and a close tie-up of autochthonous structures with the state. Even if Osterloh stresses the singularity of traditional education,[7] representatives of non-governmental organizations, multinational trusts and state institutions held the opinion that traditional education needed to be de-romanticized and de-mystified[8] in order to put it into the service of development[9]—assuming that developing countries are either non-developed or at least under-developed.

The main difficulty in overcoming problems of heterogeneous social structures is that those coming forward with strategies are rarely part of the traditional culture and therefore usually represent external interests. They are mostly integrated completely into the modern (colonial) sector, a sector which in our concept is to be understood as one part of a complex society,[10] a sector enjoying comprehensive political power. Suggestions and visualizations of this sector, as of any other sector of society, are to be understood as projections of a particular social microcosm. This microcosm is propagated as a macrocosmic pattern calling for its realization throughout society. Understandably, this results in divergences between pretensions on the one hand and the actual realization on the other. At first sight, this seems rather like a banality. If, however, a contradiction of this kind manifests itself in society and leads to social eruptions, that may cause considerable social and political change. Such divergences can be traced in the areas dealt with in this book, especially the now institutionalized Islamic ideology (Council of Islamic Ideology, CII), the traditional social system [Waqf and Zakat (arab. zakâ)] and the religious schools (Dînî Madâris).

We can now anticipate the aim of the indigenous reformers—be they representatives of the state or other products of colonial rule—to abolish their primarily self-perceived backwardness by uncompromising modern strategies of development. They may sometimes be assisted by Western scholars who provide the legitimation for the compulsory reforms with which the Islamic *avant-garde* has burdened them.

Certainly, such a movement for reform carries with it the need for a considerable degree of universalization in an indigenous, heterogenous society. This universalization is meant to remove or at least to diminish the autochthonous character of local cultures so as to bring about a standardized culture, a culture which takes its bearings from the values of western societies. This goes along with the growing centrifugal force of the state sector and the state's interests. A tendency towards universalization proceeds through institutional and normative reforms basically oriented towards the structures of an exogenous society.

In a complex society like Pakistan, the assimilation of various social sectors is, however, highly problematic. The complexity does not only stem from geographic diversity; it is increased by the introduction of a colonial—now politically dominant—sector of society. Furthermore, ethnical, linguistic and religious affiliations and conflicts result in a broad social diversification. Even though the essentials of a pluralistic society thus exist, the emergence of a uniform overall social and normative order is hampered as there is no homologous orientation.

This book concentrates primarily on the diverse religious groups and points out how the nation-state as an incarnation of colonial values, consolidates its power through traditional and non-traditional institutions by incorporating formerly untouched parts of society. To a great extent, the integration policy towards autochthonous cultures, as is evident in the Islamization process, is positively influenced by exogenous interests, sometimes of a geo-strategic nature. Reactions of local cultures to state expansion are also influenced by these interests, this time negatively, as they try to resist the state's universalizing "world-culture".

At this point it seems appropriate to briefly deal with the various religious groups in Pakistan in order to prepare the ground for a discussion and analysis of the empirically researched and systematically arranged data.[11] While presenting the different religious groups this book limits itself to the most widespread and popular forms of articulation within the Pakistani Islamic culture.

Constitutionally, Pakistan is an Islamic state. Its legislative foundation supposedly is based on the Hanafi interpretation (Abû Hanîfah, 699-767) of Islam but till today the colonial legal system, such as the Pakistan Penal Law, is widely applicable. Besides these two legal systems, officially recognized since the Islamization drive of 1977, customary law (*'urf*) is popular in most areas of Pakistan, subject to regional variations.[12] Beyond these three legal systems there is the legal system of the Shia (shî'ah) which accounts for 10-15 per cent of the population and the "legal perception" of the so-called fundamentalists who basically reject any orientation towards the major legal schools. They consider Koran and Sunnah as the only binding sources for the interpretation of law.

Broadly speaking, the Hanafi legal school is represented by the theologians and doctors of Islamic law (*'ulamâ'* and *fuqahâ'*), belonging to two groups opposed to each other. One group calls itself Deobandi as they feel connected in one way or the other with the theological seminary founded in 1867 in Deoband near Delhi.[13] The Deoband seminary was aimed at revitalizing and promoting traditional Islamic sciences (*manqûlât*). The founding fathers of the seminary stressed the orthodox teachings of Islamic law to be realized through a theologically oriented curriculum. As a reaction to British imperialism, the school was not of a purely academic or theological character but also claimed political leadership among the Muslims of British India. Their catchment area stretched from Bengal to Iran. The core of affiliation comprised civil servants and merchants, while the students of the seminary basically originated from urban retail merchant families, small landowners, and also from the poorer strata of society.

The role of the Prophet and the widespread cult of hereditary saints (*pîr*) were de-mystified among the Deobandis. They do not project the solution of contemporary problems into the hereafter as other groups did.

In this sense, they were vividly interested in the actual conditions of life, *hic et nunc*. Thus they were politicized to a considerable degree, as manifested in their political party, the Jam'iyyat al 'Ulama'-e Hind.[14] The political union of the Deobandis in Pakistan is presented in the Jam'iyyat-e 'Ulama'-e Islam (JUI); their mystical divines are mainly represented in the *Naqshbandiyyah* order.[15]

Besides this large group, there are the Brelwis [Brêlwî], named after the abode of origin of their founder, Ahmad Rida Khan (1855-1919) from Bareilly (between Delhi and Lucknow).[16] They also represent the Hanafi legal school but differ from the Deobandis in their affiliation to different social groups–mostly of peasant provenance–and in their adherence to a pronounced cult of saints and shrines. They are also distinguished by their membership in *Sûfî* orders, mainly the Qâdiriyyah. For the Brelwis, the Prophet is the pivotal figure, but the Muslim, according to the Brelwis, communicates with the Prophet only through a saint. Therefore, obedience towards the leader-saint as well as towards the existing system seems to be a crucial element of this school of thought. The acceptance of the existing structures of power has, however, sometimes put the Brelwis in line with loyalists. They are said to have held a pro-British position.[17] Their political organization in Pakistan is the Jam'iyyat-e 'Ulama'-e Pakistan; their mystical organization is the Jam'iyyat al Mashâ'ikh Pakistan.[18]

Both Deobandis and Brelwis consider themselves *ahl-e sunnah wa'l jama'ah,* people of the tradition of the Prophet and the community of believers, thus recognizing the legal schools of thought, especially that of Abû Hanîfah. They therefore call themselves *muqallidûn* (follower of the historical law schools), who practised *taqlîd* (adherence to the views of a legal school). Among the Deobandis, one may also find *salafî* (salafiyyah)–tendencies. They practise *ijtihâd* (individual reasoning) within their legal school.[19]

In Pakistan today there is a strong rivalry between the two groups as evident in the vehement polemics in a Brelwi pamphlet, "Views and Principles of Deobandi *'ulamâ',*"[20] pointing out the differences between the two schools of thought. In it, the Brelwis list seventeen quotations of renowned Deobandi scholars, frequently citing them completely out of context.

The opponents of the Brelwis resort to similar polemics. The bone of contention seems to be the attack on the Prophet's pivotal role. Only such a central position would legitimize the existence of saints, as the salvation through the Prophet can only be achieved via the saint. And only the Prophet can be the doorway to God. It is against this background that the

1985 dispute of the two groups on dûrûd _sharîf_ is intelligible.[21]

Besides these two groups, the Ahl-e Hadith (the people of the Prophet's tradition) have to be considered. They reject the authority of any school of law whatsoever. Their representatives therefore consider themselves _ghair muqallidûn_. This predominantly merchant-based group stresses Koran and Hadith to be the only sources of law and regards any kind of innovation as harmful, following the motto: "_kullu bid'a dalâlatun_", any innovation is a disgrace.[22] The Ahl-e Hadith is said to have practised earlier (and, at times, still today) a pietist quietism, while at the same time being opposed to the colonial rulers. In contrast to the Jama'at-e Islami, a group with similar fundamentalist tendencies, which came up in the forties of this century, the Ahl-e Hadith do not claim political leadership.[23]

What all three movements—the Deobandis, Ahl-e Hadith, Brelwis—have in common is that they are rooted in specific areas and specific social groups. They perceive themselves against the background of colonial penetration and are oriented towards Western patterns of cultural articulation. The Deobandis and the Ahl-e Hadith can be considered as scripturalists[24] while the Brelwis adhere to traditional modes of communication. The majority of their representatives in today's Pakistan are, however, associated with the traditional sector.[25]

The Shia are divided into at least two major groups. The Ismailis[26] under the chairmanship of Agha Khan Karim comprise on the one hand the important and influential Karachi caste of merchants and, on the other, inhabitants of the northern areas of Pakistan, especially in Hunza and Gilgit. The latter belong to the socially weaker groups. As the Northern area is politically sensitive the Ismailis living there have of late become an object of public interest.

The other Shia group in Pakistan is the _ithnâ 'ashar_. They are followers of the twelfth _imâm_, in contrast to the Ismailis, who are followers of the sixth _imâm_. The "twelver"-Shia[27] maintain that they have refrained from any political activity whatsoever, and have only organized themselves as a political movement in reaction to the pressures of the Islamization drive under the regime of Zia ul Haq. Their connection with Iran and their internal solidarity has, however, made them a political factor not to be neglected in today's Pakistan, especially when it comes to activities beyond the boundaries of the state. Being venerators of Ali, the fourth caliph and cousin and son-in-law of the Prophet, as well as devout celebrators of the cult around Husain, the son of Ali, they are inclined towards the cult of saints and in this respect are comparable to the Brelwis.

Last but not least, the Jama'at-e Islami is an influential and organized group on Pakistan's Islamic scene, recruiting its members predominantly from the urban middle strata. They are eagerly trying to develop political programmes and put them into action, claiming to represent the interests of the society as a whole.[28] Its founder Abul Ala Mawdudi (1903-1979), who was not an Islamic scholar in the classical sense ('ālim), tried to elaborate a theory of Islam as a social ideology. It is necessary to note that he almost entirely adopted all the values recognized as universal in the Western world. The precondition for introducing his reforms is the unconditional acceptance of *ijtihâd*, in contrast to the position held by most of the Deobandis and the Brelwis who adhere to *taqlîd* . The Jama'at-e Islami thus does not follow any school of law. In matters of everyday life, however, they seek guidance from the Hanafîs.[29] The revitalization of the fundamentals of Islam puts the Jama'at-e Islami in opposition to the Brelwis and the Shia, also because of the cult of saints. This they consider to be un-Islamic and a pagan innovation (*bid'ah*).

While all the other groups mentioned above have their own institutions to educate traditional religious scholars ('ulamâ'), the Jama'at-e Islami does not. On the contrary, it was the aim of Mawdudi to merge traditional and modern education with special emphasis on the latter.[30] Thus, the Jama'at-e Islami cannot be put in the same category as the traditional scholars but it should rather be categorised as a reformist *avant-garde*. They emerged, similar to the other Sunni mainstreams, in the course of confrontation with colonial rule. In contrast to the previous three groups, the Jama'at-e Islami is structured according to highly modern patterns of organization, and not on the basis of traditional institutions like Auqâf, madâris and khânqah. Furthermore, their teaching has dispensed with any form of esoterics and instead stresses an ideological Islamic discourse. Hence, they aspire to objectives quite different from the traditionalists. One can actually speak of a rupture of tradition.[31] Lately, however, a re-activation of traditional institutions is noticeable even in the Jama'at-e Islami.

All these groups not only hold different ideological and theological positions; as will be elaborated later, they recruit their members from different social strata and can be identified with different regions.

Besides these groups, the representatives of popular Islam have to be mentioned. They are inclined towards popular piety and have absorbed many elements from outside Islam into their teachings. The so-called Tarîqah-Islam (tarîqah meaning path, of a saint) is based on the cult of saints and on mystical associations depicting a strict hierarchical system. This manifestation of Islam often appeared in the course of Islamic history as an egalitarian, peasant-liberating movement, with a charismatic leader heading it.[32] The mystical orders[33]–there are four major ones in today's Pakistan–have organizations similar to guilds[34] and often represent separate professions. The leader of a mystical order is the *pîr*, the saint, often represented today by his descendants. Depending on his authority and charisma, the *pîr* has authority over a network of shrines and khânqâhs and also of Dînî Madâris. State politics cannot function without integrating or limiting the power of the *pîrs* in Pakistan.[35] Besides being organized in diverse orders,[36] their representatives in Pakistan are loosely organized in the Jam'iyyat al Mashâ'ikh Pakistan.[37]

Apart from popular Islam, there is the Sharî'a-Islam, whose representatives are scholars of law. Many among them (with the exception of the Brelwis) reject the excessive cult of saints as well as other syncretist influences and point towards Islamic law in its pure form.[38] Therefore, disputes between representatives of esoteric and exoteric Islam are frequent. Sometimes they act as two separate social groups.[39] The rupture between these two groups came about only in the last two hundred years. It began with modernism as represented by Sayyid Ahmad Khan and culminated with Mawdudi[40] who overemphasized Islamic ideology.

The diverse tendencies of Islam in Pakistan suggest that a single uniform policy of Islamization as envisaged under the regime of Zia ul Haq in collaboration with fundamentalist forces was doomed to failure from the very start.[41]

Failure being inherent in the Islamization policy, the question arises as to the purpose in trying to bring it about. Islamization really appears to be a means of legitimation for the regime. It is, in fact, "Islam from the cantonment" far from a visualization of the needs of the overwhelming majority of the population. It is this aspect which this book seeks to investigate.

I have attempted to put the data collected, reviewed and evaluated into a larger theoretical context. I do not refer to the theory of dualism, which reduces the formation of society in Pakistan to a mere polarity of modernity and tradition, and, at the same time, declares as immanently necessary the transformation of the traditional sector of society. The principles underlying modernization theories not only testify to an eurocentric view but also obscure the increasingly complex social circumstances in Pakistan. They project merely the strategies of action of a small, mostly alienated minority, making its particular suggestions for change according to maxims of generalized social action. The representatives of this reformism draw on their personal microcosm for a pattern for macrocosmic realization;

through these patterns Pakistan's society is supposed to undergo a healing process.

I have leaned towards a heuristic model, one developed against the background of increasing social complexity. The perception is of a new social group, injected into traditional society, which tries to legitimize itself as a new social type in its political and economic positions and simultaneously to expand its power.

In this sense, the book intends to elucidate the conditions of practicability for realizing "Islamization" as a political programme, either by preference or by compulsion if necessary. I wish to explain neither the conditions nor the Islamization itself in a monocausal way, but rather intend to elaborate on the whole spectrum of causes, factors of influence and consequences. I proceed historico-empirically as well as on a theoretical and systematic basis. Such a theoretical arrangement is of special significance for the further interpretation and understanding of the different measures of Islamization described here. Therefore, I will relate the respective social bases and ideological alignments of the religious groups named in chapter I to a socio-historical theoretical context. This classificatory relationing will be extended in the course of further discussion to the contemporary conditions of Pakistan.

As any other epistemological model, this model is of reductionary character, more specifically in a two-fold manner, there is a tendency to move exclusively within the model's theorems, and all empirical data is analysed and evaluated exclusively within its specific boundaries. Consequently other perspectives are taken into account rarely. Thus, the personal heuristic interest is narrowed down, possibly carrying with it a distorted interpretation of the historical process. The interpretation is inherent to the system. A certain confinement cannot be avoided, as every analysis is subjectively determined.

In order to diminish, if not to eliminate, the charge of reductionism, I have applied a number of methodological procedures. They are not rooted exclusively in the classical humanistic methods, as for example hermeneutics and history of ideas, but also in the more recently developed interest of historians in science and cognition. They thus cover elements from social psychology, prosopography and methodology of modern social science. The latter includes statistical evaluation or "cliometrics", thus allowing for quantitative statements on events as well as the use of interviews and questionnaires.

While discussing contemporary socio-economic issues, I have referred to social science inquiries already available. Admittedly, they often use parameters of the type developed by modernization theories. This, no doubt, is in contrast to the general approach chosen in this book, but it sometimes assists the purpose of demonstrating the social and economic conditions that are the background to different streams of thought and to the governmental measures of Islamization.

On the basis of the first chapter, further areas of the Islamization policy are described and analysed, referring naturally to the historical context as well.

This general theoretical chapter is followed by an analysis of the Council of Islamic Ideology (CII), which is a forum of legitimation for state policies and reflects in its composition the various policies of the state. The Council's proposals demonstrate the divergence between ideal Islamic action (as understood by the theological elite, parts of the Islamic *avant-garde* and the intelligentsia), and the actual steps of Islamization and their realization by the representatives of the state. This chapter further points out the interests of the Islamizing agents and of the state as well as the degree of integration of theological dignitaries within the governmental sector. The integration of these dignitaries and their institutions is the subject of the next chapter dealing with the endowments system. It also discusses Islamic mysticism, its forms of organization and its manifestation against state expansionism. Specifically mystical aspects are, however, dealt with only marginally. The chapter on endowments focuses on how the traditional sectors of society are brought under governmental influence and thus are de-traditionalized and bureaucratized. The chapter on Zakat (*Zakât*), in contrast, points out how the state undertakes to legitimize colonial values and concepts—as for example secular taxation—by applying Islamic nomenclature. Not only that: the Zakat system seems to be an appropriate means to consolidate the areas of governmental influence and to extend them. In this way, traditional security systems in case of illness and poverty are increasingly substituted by the governmental (formal) sector, without bringing about the ideal and propagated "social welfare system". The following chapters further elaborate on the theorem of state expansion. The investigation there focuses on how the traditional, autonomous institutions of Dînî Madâris (religious schools) attract the attention of different regimes, especially in the course of the Islamization drive; on how the state tries to tie these entities to itself; on the means used and the effects of these reformist measures. All sectors touched by Islamization, the institutions involved and responsible authorities are identified socially and put into a systematic order.

Given the complexity of events and circumstances, and with an ever-changing basis of information, this endeavour may sometimes seem to be rather disconnected or influenced by coincidences. I have continued to search for causal connections. It is up to the reader to judge whether the data and conclusions are plausible.

In the transcription of Arabic, Persion and Urdu terms I have preferred to adopt the current usage in the English version of the *Encyclopedia of Islam*. Names of areas and locations as well as those of administrative entities have been adopted from the current English spelling.

NOTES

1. D. Rothermund, ed., *Islàm in South Asia*, Heidelberg, 1975. Similar problems were discussed during the Dissertation Workshop on Contemporary Muslim Societies in July 1987 in Tanger, Marocco (held by the American Social Science Research Council).
2. In this context one may recall the critical remarks by J. Habermas on Popper; cf. Th. Adorno *et al., Der Positivismusstreit in der deutschen Soziologie*, Darmstadt, 1982; there the contribution by Habermas, *Gegen einen positivistisch halbierten Rationalismus*, p. 235.
3. Edward Said, *Orientalism*, London, 1979 as well as the contribution by Brian S. Turner, "Accounting for the Orient", in D. Maceoin and A. Al-Shahi (eds.), *Islam in the Modern World*, Canberra, 1983, pp. 9-26.
4. Dec. 10th-12th, 1984 in Paris, organized by the International Institute for Educational Planning (UNESCO).
5. D. Eickelman, op.cit., "Working document", dated 17.6.1986 (mimeo.), p. 5.
6. This became evident at the conference, "The Impact on Peasantry of Education and Community Development in Indonesia", July 9th-13th, 1987, Berlin (West), organized by the Technische Universität (TU), Berlin and the Friedrich Naumann Foundation.
7. K.H. Osterloh, "Traditionelle Lernweisen und europäischer Bildungstransfer. Zur Begründung einer adaptierten Pädagogik in den Entwicklungsländern", in T. Schöfthaler and D. Goldschmidt, eds., *Soziale Struktur und Vernunft*, Frankfurt a.M., 1984, pp. 440-460.
8. These terms certainly recall Weber's sociology of religion. Some decent contributions on this topic and on Weber's de-mystification are now available in Wolfgang Schluchter, ed., *Max Webers Sicht des Islams*, Frankfurt a.M., 1987.
9. This very imprecise term could not be defined clearly even during the cited conference.
10. Say, in the sense of J. Habermas, *Zur Rekonstruktion des Historischen Materialismus*, Frankfurt a.M., 1982, esp. pp. 144-199.
11. A short presentation of different currents of Islam in Pakistan is Duran

Khalid, "Pakistan and Bangladesh", in W. Ende and U. Steinbach (eds.), *Der Islam in der Gegenwart*, Munich, 1984, pp. 274-307.

12. Like the "Codes of honour" among Pakhtun tribes.

13. Concerning the Deobandis in India prior to independence cf. the contributions by Ziya-ul-Hassan Faruqi, *The Deoband School and the Demand for Pakistan*, Lahore, 1963; Yohannan Friedman, "The attitude of the Jam'iyyat al-'Ulama'-i Hind to the Indian national movement and the establishment of Pakistan", in *African and Asian Studies (AAS)* 7, 1971, pp. 157-180; "The Jam'iyyat al-'Ulama'-i Hind in the Wake of Partition" in *AAS* 11, 1976, pp. 181-211; Muhammad Abd Allah Chughtai, *Qîâm dâr al-'ulûm dêôband*, Lahore,1980; Sayyid Mahbub Ridwi: *Tarîkh dâr al-'ulûm dêôband*, vols. I and II, Delhi, 1977; Barbara D. Metcalf, *Islamic Revival in British India: Deoband, 1860-1900*, New Jersey, 1982 (henceforth *Revival*).

14. Friedman, op.cit.

15. At present there is no literature on the role of the Deobandis in Pakistan; see also the manifesto of the JUI, *Islâmî Manshûr, Kull Pâkistân Jam'iyyat-e 'Ulamâ'-e Islâm*, 1969.

16. At present no monographs on the Brelwi movement are available. Mrs. Usha Sanyal of the University of Columbia, New York, is currently preparing her dissertation on the Brelwis. See also Metcalf, *Revival*, pp. 296-314 et passim; S.M. Ikram, *Modern Muslim India*, Oxford, 1968, pp. 119-121; also Francis Robinson, *Separatism among Indian Muslims: The Politics of the United Provinces' Muslims, 1860-1923*, Cambridge, 1974, passim (henceforth *Separatism*).

17. Robinson, *Separatism*, pp. 266ff, 325 and 422; also *Majalla*, Râbitat al-'âlam al-islâmî (Makka), 23 (1405) 5/6, p. 1.

18. No research on either of these institutions is as yet available. See, however, the manifesto of the JUP: *Dastûr Jam'iyyat-e 'Ulamâ'-e Pâkistân*, 1979 s.l. as well as *Qandîl*, vol. 4/53, Lahore, 1979 (Urdu).

19. Metcalf, *Revival*, p. 143.

20. *'Ulamâ'-e dêôband kê 'aqâ'id o nazariyyât*, n.d. (Urdu).

21. Chapter III.

22. They are also critical of the Brelwis and the Shia. Their leading functionary, Mawlana Zuhur Illahi, in the magazine *Majalla* published by the Islamic World League consequently demands that the Brelwis be declared non-muslims. See *Majalla*, op.cit.

23. At present no monograph on this movement is available. See, however, Muhammad Hanif Yazdani, *Hindustân men Ahl-e Hadîth kî 'ilmî khidmat* (compiled by Abu Yahya Imam Khan Naushehrwi), maktabah nadhariyyah, Chichawatni 1970; Metcalf, *Revival*, pp. 268-96 et passim; A. Ahmad, *Islamic Modernism in India and Pakistan*, Oxford, 1967, pp. 113-122 (henceforth *Modernism*). See also the manifesto of the Ahl-e Hadith Pakistan, *Dastûr Markazî Jam'iyyat Ahl-e Hadîth Maghribî Pâkistân*, Lahore, 1955 (Urdu) as well as *Manshûr Markazî Jam'iyyat Ahl-e Hadîth*

Pâkistân, Lahore, 1971 (Urdu).
24. In the sense of Clifford Geertz, *Islam Observed,* London, 1968.
25. For a detailed discussion and social classification cf. chapter I.
26. For the *Ismailis* cf. Werner Schmucker, "Sekten und Sondergruppen", in W. Ende, and U. Steinbach, eds., *Der Islam in der Gegenwart,* p. 505.
27. For Shia Islam see op.cit., p. 70 and Moojan Momen, *An Introduction to Shi'i Islam: The History and Doctrines of Twelver Shi'ism,* New Haven and London, 1985. No monograph on the Shia in Pakistan is available at present. Cf., however, J.N. Hollister, *The Shi'a of India,* London, 1953 and M. Ahmed, "The Shi'ia of Pakistan", in Martin Kramer, ed., *Shi'ism, Resistance, and Revolution,* London, 1987, pp. 275-287. See also Cole, JRI, *Roots of North Indian Shiism in Iraq and Iran,* Berkeley, 1988. Wherever in this book I use the term Shia, I am referring to the Twelver Shia.
28. Literature on the Jama'at is easily available. Cf. the commemorative publication by Khurshid Ahmad and Zafar Ishaq Ansari, eds., *Islamic Perspectives: Studies in Honour of Mawlana Sayyid Abul A'la Mawdudi,* London, 1979, and the literature listed there as well as the bibliography by Asaf Hussain, in *Islamic Movements in Egypt, Pakistan and Iran: An annotated bibliography,* London, 1983.
29. Conversation between Shaikh al-Hadith Mawlana Abd al-Malik, Markiz al-'Ulûm al-Islamiyyah, Mansurah, Lahore, and Mawlana Hamid Miyan, *mohtamim* Jami'ah Madaniyyah, Karimpark, Lahore on Feb. 13th, 1986 in the Jami'ah Madaniyyah, Lahore.
30. Abul Ala Mawdudi, *Ta'lîmât,* Lahore, 1982 (Urdu). Similar tendencies are followed by the "International Institute of Islamic Education", in Mansurah Lahore; cf. the different curricula later on in this book, chapter VI.
31. According to Thomas Kuhn this could be compared to the change of paradigm; cf. Kuhn, *Die Strukturwissenschaftlicher Revolutionen,* Frankfurt a.M., 1973.
32. Examples for this in India are Pîr Pagârô and Faqîr Épî. Cf., chapter III.
33. Mostly identified as *silsilahs* (chain) by its members, as the uninterrupted genealogic lineage to a major saint or at best to the Prophet has an important function of legitimation of the order.
34. F. Taeschner, *Zünfte und Bruderschaften im Islam,* Munich, 1979. The orders thus contributed a common conscience in diverse social groups and were able to level out social discrepancies.
35. See chapter III.
36. J. S. Trimingham, *The Sufi Orders in Islam,* Oxford, 1971.
37. Concerning the political situation of the *Sûfîs* in Pakistan there is hardly any scholarly inquiry available. See also chapter III.
38. The Islamic *avant-garde* consider themselves part of these representatives.
39. There is, however, no academic study available on this issue.
40. This opinion is shared by Marc Gaboriau, *Horizons de pensée et pratiques sociales chez les intellectuels du monde musulman,* Paris, 1987.

41. The interpretation of Islam by different groups is the obstacle to the introduction of the Islamic system; to quote: The chairman of the CII on September 12th, 1980 to Zia ul Haq , in GoP, Council of Islamic Ideology (CII) in *Consolidated Recommendations on the Islamic Economic System*, Islamabad, 1983 (Urdu/English), p. 178. The existence of secular political groupings is not taken into account in the inquiry. It would further increase the complexity and heterogeneity of the society.

CHAPTER I

TOWARDS A THEORETICAL APPROACH
TO ISLAMIZATION

The theoretical treatment which now follows aims at grasping Islamization from a socio-historical point of view and putting it in the context of a social order. The only way to comprehend the policy of Islamization with its manifold ways of articulation is to put the supporters (sustainers) of Islamization into their specific social context. The theorems evolved in the course of this chapter will be referred to when dealing with single aspects further on;[1] in doing so I will proceed inductively as well as deductively.

Scholarly literature indicates clearly that Islam has undergone a change of function: from theology to ideology. Now it is no more the relationship of God to human beings which is in the foreground but rather the relationship of human beings to human beings;[2] this de-mystification seems to be influenced by the age of European enlightenment and of colonialism.

THE POLITICIZATION OF ISLAM

The politicization of Islam is closely linked to the emergence of an Islamic *avant-garde*, an intelligentsia educated in a European way. They are oriented towards European values and norms, following the description "Indians by blood, British in taste and thought" (Macaulay 1835). Being a product of the colonial society, this social class reproduced itself through the colonial system as it evolved in the course of the 19th and 20th centuries, and has now consolidated and expanded. Therefore, this class is also the guarantor of the post-colonial society, a society reflecting not only structures similar to their "Motherlands" but also a high degree of dependency on them.[3] Even though the colonial society evolved through political opposition to colonialism, its ideology evolved by adoption of a Western concept, i.e. nationalism.[4] This ideology, formed "under the law of the adversary" (D. Rothermund), at first conserved what had been achieved, i.e. the colonial *status quo*, and later served to extend it by means of Islamization into areas hitherto untouched by the colonial society.

The expansion of the colonial sector in the course of Western penetration led to a crisis of legitimation among the traditional representatives of Islam. Corresponding to the functional transformation of the Islamic society the role of Islam itself had to be transformed. Moreover, a Western critique of the Islamic society was voiced—a critique meant to legitimize colonialism. For the first time Islam was questioned: what so far went without saying was now on trial.[5] New movements among parts of the "clergy" reflected the Islamic self-statement by referring to concepts attuned to the structures of colonial society. Thus, the theory of caliphate had to provide an extended interpretation in order to legitimize power.[6] Islam was now meant to legitimize rulership in general and not merely the rule of a dynasty or a regime.[7] The self-statedness of the Islamic identity had to be transformed into an Islamic self-statement. This required a discussion on Islam in a cognitive approach.[8] Analogously, secular Western terms had to be assimilated into the colonial society. Hence the Islamic intelligentsia tried to enlarge Islam into a comprehensive system through integration of Western concepts, terms and values and thus to legitimize the existing (colonial) system. At this stage Islam no more represented only a form of rule vis-a-vis Western ideologies, but also a social ideology with the objective of being compatible and competitive. This implied an "integrationist"[9] understanding of Islam, whose most eminent representatives were Jamal ad-Din al-Afghani and Sayyid Ahmad Khan. Both tried to make use of Islam as a political counteracting force in the dispute with the West, without, however, taking recourse to traditional institutions of Islamic scholarship.[10] A precondition of the elevation of Islam to an ideological platform was the unconditional reintroduction of *ijtihâd* along with a limitation of or even aversion to *taqlîd*. Only through the institution of *ijtihâd*—according to the *avant-garde*—would the Islamic society be in a position to compete with Western nations and their ideologies. Now the timeless values which had developed in the course of Western civilization–universalities so-to-speak–were regarded as being Islamic[11] and immanent in Islam. In order to make themselves understood, the Islamic intellectuals had to employ the terms of the Western critique. Parallel to this adoption of Western terms the *avant-garde* often appropriated the media for propagating the cause of political exiles (mostly in the metropolis of the colonial motherlands).

The representatives of the traditional clergy, in contrast, tried to complete the revaluation of theology into ideology in their own way, so as not to lag behind completely.[12] Some of them tried, nevertheless, to keep the mystical elements of Islam and thus to create a symbiosis of esoteric and exoteric elements. The Islamic *avant-garde* in contrast was inclined to separate one from the other. Sayyid Ahmad Khan was the first to advocate this separation with his concept of rationalist deism.[13] Mawdudi completed this separation and rejected any kind of mystical experience. This separation of exoteric and esoteric elements not infrequently led to an alienation from Islam.[14]

The process of ideologization of Islam can therefore be understood as the intellectual response to the cultural domination of the Western world in the 18th and 19th centuries. But it was only during the time between the two world wars that Islamic intellectuals started to re-evaluate Islam as a political ideology analogous to that of the Western world and to extend it. Islam was now meant to cover all those areas which had been integrated into Muslim society in the course of colonialization as European structures.[15] In this sense, Islamization at first is a justification of the integration of Western values and norms and thus of the colonial structures and not the dissemination of Islam in hitherto virgin un-Islamic regions. Socio-historically the process of ideologization can be outlined as follows.

THE MAKING OF A COLONIAL SECTOR

Starting from the ideal type of the oriental society[16] the three existing segmental and hierarchically structured societies − urban, agrarian, nomadic−were extended by a further, externally induced sector of society.[17] This new sector was first represented by the intelligentsia and later on by the representatives of the colonial state. Its supporters can be considered as bridgeheads.[18]

Now tied to the world market, a tremendous upheaval of the society occurred. Parts of the traditional society were integrated into world market relations to an ever-increasing degree. This multi-layered process came about primarily through technical innovation,[19] investment of capital, privatization of landed property and, of course, through restructuring of the economic process.[20] Alongside the traditional agrarian sector (TAS)[21] a colonial agrarian sector (CAS) had developed. The nomadic sector was noticeably marginalized.[22] Parallel to the traditional urban sector (TUS) the colonial rulers set up a colonial urban sector (CUS), i.e. the colonial administrative and military sector.[23] It was partly related to the agrarian sector; visually it can be recognized in the construction of new settlements (Civil Lines and Cantonments).[24] The traditional educational system was of course replaced by a new formal European[25] one. The colonial sectors were connected via infrastructure and represented the colonial society.

This restructuring was accompanied by profound changes in the socio-psychological sphere. Traditional systems of society, values and relations[26] were now replaced by abstract, anonymous authorities of the state. A privatization of social and economic relations came about.

All these social sectors were, nevertheless, oriented towards the traditions of Islam: while the TUS was responsible for the traditional legitimation of the ruler (i.e. fraternities, clergy, systems of relationship), in the CUS Islam was predominant as a political ideology (i.e. representatives of the Islamic *avant-garde* and of religious-political parties). In contrast to this, in the TAS Islam prevailed as an egalitarian peasant culture (i.e. mystical associations and movements, especially in today's Sindh).

With increasing expansion of the colonial sector, the traditional forces broke down. Not all sectors and areas were, however, seized by the colonial sector, as their integration was not always profitable. Therefore, such areas were not integrated into the world market and were consequently "marginalized".[27] The consequence of this was to further weaken sections of the population, who continued to function as a permanently available reserve, as seasonal or migrant workers, easy to dispose of deliberately at any time. They served as a cheap and permanently available army of labour.[28]

The increasing complexity of society went along with a disintegration of formerly integrated areas of life. A new division of labour developed, characterized by a separation of the area of production (labour and ownership) from the area of reproduction (cultures and forms of living). When labour was part of the colonial sector (in modern industries or in the administration) the worker "lived" in the traditional area (of reproduction). Both sectors were, however, governed by specific, culturally determined systems of norms and reflected specific forms of economic and cultural types of organization and articulation.[29] This dual tension has a potential for conflict. Its way of articulation depends on the degree of material poverty of those working in the area of production. This tension can be discharged in at least three different ways:

1. To compensate for lack of resolution of prevailing conflict by some kind of substitute culture, such as urban crime, consumption of narcotics, or escape into the world of cinema, providing a temporary refuge from the sharp contrast between the areas.[30]

2. To integrate both areas through "traditionalizing" production. The traditional norms of behaviour (here of Islam) are inserted into the process

of production (as becomes evident in the integration of Islamic symbols and rites into the area of labour and ownership). There is, however, no integration beyond rituals.[31]

3. To colonize the area of reproduction and thus Islamize the everyday culture (as is evident in the adoption of Western culture and the excessive consumption of luxury goods).

The choice in favour of one way of resolution of conflict as against another depends on the one hand on the type of work and thus the material conditions for a possible colonization of everyday life and, on the other hand, on the relevance of such colonization for the individual. One may suppose that the degree of personal wealth is decisive for the pattern of resolution of the conflict: a poor worker will tend to traditionalize his area of production (due to objective material reasons), while a skilled worker would rather modernize his area of reproduction or de-traditionalize it.

One may now specify this model by applying it to the social structure of Islamization[32] according to professional fields as in Table 1.

These four main sectors differ as much in their supporters as in their orientations, primarily influenced by their respective economic and social organizations.

1. The TUS is ruled by local trade, small scale traffic of goods and local subsistence, embedded into traditional security systems. The latter are, however, increasingly weakened through the introduction of the Zakat and Ushr Ordinance 1980,[33] causing a disintegration of the traditional social support system. This sector is the centre of numerous articulations of local autochthonous Islamic culture, especially the shrines,[34] the clergy[35] and the religious schools.[36] One can, therefore, rightly suppose a traditional (Islamic) cultural identity. The pattern of organization of this hierarchically structured sector is often oriented towards the traditional patterns of fraternities and associations,[37] irrespective of whether they are of a mystical or confessional character, based on guilds or on kinship.[38]

2. The CUS sector consists of representatives of the (colonial) state, especially of large trade associations, representatives of Government, the higher grades of the bureaucracy, the police and the army, professionals and the self-employed, the intelligentsia and the higher formal sector of education.[39] We also find secular representatives of the traditional sector integrated into the CUS.[40] Quite often they are *Muhâjirs* from India or of Turkish, Afghan, Iranian or even European origin.

Both sectors are socially cohesive and hierarchical by internal structure,[41] with the consequence that conflicts can be resolved by working

TABLE I : SOCIAL BASIS OF ISLAMIZATION

TUS	Intermediary Sector I	Intermediary Sector II	CUS
street-economy subsistence traditional infrastructure (horse-coaches, mosques, waqf, madâris), traditional social and class systems (orders, tribe, kinship) and trad. profession (*pîrs*, *'ulamâ'*, *mullâ*, *hakîm*, soothsayer, etc.)	lower grades in the army, police administration and infrastructure. shrines, mosques trad. infrastructure state-sustained and trad. social system informal sector rel.-polit. parties unskilled, students *'ulamâ'*, *pîrs*, students	middle grades in the army, police administration and infrastructure. shrines, mosques state-sustained and trad. social system rel.-polit. parties skilled workers, students relig. elite intelligentsia	higher grades in the army, police, administration and infrastructure, *pîrs, sayyids,* shrines, waqf, universities, hotels, foreigners, capital, state-sustained social system polit. parties, free lance, self-employed, members of parliament intelligentsia
local trade	sectoral trade	inter-sector. trade	trans-urban trade
socially cohesive, as no separation of the areas of production and reproduction	not cohesive, as separation of the areas of production and reproduction	not cohesive, as separation of the areas of production and reproduction	socially cohesive, as no separation of the areas of production and reproduction

DWELLING

old town (preferably *mandîs*) own market	*kachâ âbâdîs* old settlements *sadr bazâr*	new settlements sattelite town *sadr bazâr*	cantonment, civil lines planned schemes own market

sadr bazâr as junction of TUS and CUS
here sectoral, inter-sectoral and trans-urban trade

traditionalization theological Islamization isolationism	colonialization ideological Islamization integrationism

out an "internal arrangement". Therefore, one rarely witnesses problems of identification.[42]

SOCIAL PATHS OF TRANSITION AND INTERMEDIARY SECTORS

Between these two opposite poles, at least two intermediary sectors have developed. They are oriented towards the traditional sector whenever their area of reproduction is concerned and towards the colonial sector whenever their area of production is concerned. Each of the extreme sectors can thus be associated with an intermediary sector:

1. The intermediary sector I comprises labour in industry and infrastructure, lower grades of the army, police, administration, local merchants controlling local trade as well as the traditional elite.

2. The intermediary sector II in contrast comprises skilled labour, representatives of the intermediate formal system of education, intermediate grades of the army, police, administration as well as merchants controlling intersectoral trade. The elite of the "clergy"[43] and some parts of the intelligentsia are of genuine importance for the mobilization of this sector.

Lack of hierarchical structures carries with it the absence of a stable internal mechanism to resolve conflicts. Against this background, one may suppose that intermediary sectors are inclined towards mechanisms of conflict-resolution prevalent in the pole to which each is oriented.[44] Their disintegration[45] is the cause of possible conflict.

The four sectors live in particular areas which can be identified within the topography of a town. It is striking that the representatives of intermediary sectors prefer to live in the so called "new indigenous communities" and "satellite towns", areas which have features of design demonstrating a symbiosis (or integration) of traditional and modern architecture.[46]

A look at the individual patterns of resolving conflicts (substitute-culture, traditionalization and colonialization) against the background of the intermediary sectors allows for the following assumption: The intermediary sector I is inclined to traditionalize (i.e. Islamize) its area of production; the intermediary sector II tends to colonialize (secularize) its area of reproduction. Islam in both cases provides the cultural framework, while it differs in TUS and CUS in the way it is interpreted.

The representatives of the intermediary sector I resolve their conflicts with reference to the TUS within the theological tradition, sometimes on an esoteric level. Representatives of the intermediary sector II are inclined towards a pattern of resolving conflicts with reference to the CUS in an ideological secular way. This pattern aims at resolving individual or (formal) general social conflicts in this world.

The *avant-garde* (intermediary sector II) is the one which lays down general social claims and presents these claims as a political concept.[47] When material conditions are evidently poor, parts of the intermediary sector I and even of the TUS may be mobilized to create a mass support base which is otherwise lacking.

Islam in its ideological version tries to develop concepts for *this* world (as opposed to the hereafter) in the tradition of its genesis. These concepts are meant to remove the conflicts of the urban colonial society. In doing so, this Islam differs from theological Islam. The elite holding these concepts is competing with representatives of the CUS through various political formations.[48] In times of crisis, however, the CUS tends to seclude itself from its traditional surroundings. The result is an interruption of the paths of transition from the intermediary sectors to the CUS.[49] In such a situation, the supporters of the intermediary sector II may easily present themselves as an integrative force. Their latent readiness to de-traditionalize or to secularize the area of reproduction becomes a political factor.

At first, Islamic intellectuals are not able to realize their claim of political power for lack of a mass support base.[50] This explains why in 1977 neither the members of the TUS nor members of the intermediary sectors were mobilized.[51] Only subsequently, could the traditional institutions[52] and the masses be pushed into action.[53] And even then it was merely a movement of the "middle class".[54] Only gradually the masses were integrated into political organizations. The leadership of these organizations firmly lay in the hands of Islamic intellectuals and the clerical elite, both considering themselves able to compete with the political intelligentsia.

The competition between the intermediary sector II and the CUS may have an integrating effect, whenever the Islamic elite considers itself an *avant-garde* and thus creates a new Islamic selfstatement, and whenever they develop political ideas which can serve to legitimize the programmes of the CUS.[55] Activities of this *avant-garde* are of a purely political nature and are exercised via the public media. In putting their programmes to work, the economic power gained through the colonial sector is of particular importance.[56]

To the outsider, i.e. the colonial public, this *avant-garde* argues ideologically, limiting the use of Islamic symbols to the indispensable. To the insider, i.e. the traditional society, they use the theological argument. The Islamic cult is reinforced, but the discussion is of disputable theological value.[57]

In its concept of values, this Islamic *avant-garde* is oriented in substance and form towards the colonial sector. It tries to interpret the colonial values and structures and its terms in an Islamic way. They thus guarantee them without questioning them. Therefore its supporters could be labelled integrationists, their ideology being integrationism.[58] They thus are concerned not with dissolving the colonial society[59] but rather with the integration of the traditional society into the colonial sector or with de-traditionalization. This is evident in the creation of neologisms and the nomenclatural change of colonial terms and values:

Form and style of propaganda and organization are mostly modelled according to those of the opponent and integrated with one's own ideas in a quite often amazing way.[60]

Accordingly, the central terms were reinterpreted. *Shûrâ*, originally meaning consultation, especially the counsel of influential personalities of the community, is taken as parliamentary democracy by Muhammad Abduh. *Ijmâ'*, which meant consensus, becomes public opinion.[61] *Dawla*, properly speaking the period of rulership of a single person or a dynasty, finally turns into nation-state. The same is true of the term constitution (*dastûr*); it is interpreted as something that always existed, and as if Islam harboured the best of all constitutions. Even political parties which did not exist in early Islam and thus contradict fundamentalist concepts,[62] are recognized as Islamic and admitted.

The integrationists are also capable of adopting Western institutions and developing them further without abandoning Islamic identity. Simultaneously, this "nativist" transfer of originally colonial concepts into Islamic history was helpful in rejecting the reproach of *bid'ah*, the heretic innovation condemned by traditionalists. In this manner, one could as well mobilize traditionalists for the legitimation of the colonial circumstances.[63] In other areas of society, such as the economy[64] or the formal system of education,[65] the integrationists tried to present models of solution without changing the given structures or extending them. On the Islamization of the legal system the "Summary for the Cabinet"[66] in 1978 thus revealingly reads:

2(c) "Law" includes any custom or usage having the force of law but does not include the Constitution, any fiscal law, personal law, any law relating to the procedure of any court or tribunal or any law relating to the levy and collection of taxes and fees or banking or insurance practice and procedure. . . .

To this day, the so called Federal Shariat Court has to yield to this injunction.[67]

Besides an integrationist *avant-garde*, one may also find an isolationist[68] *avant-garde*, mainly recruiting itself from the intermediary sector I. It rejects any kind of adoption of colonial values and concepts or organization and thus isolates itself from the CUS. It tends to traditionalize its area of production and thus to keep it apart from the national economy. It idealizes Islamic principles, deriving them mostly from socialist ideas,[69] and thus politicizes the Islamic concepts themselves. The isolation becomes evident in their principle of emigration (*hijra*)[70] or in their rejection of other central colonial-values.[71] This *avant-garde* is, however, not organized very strictly. It has easy access to broad strata of society and is rather inclined towards the TUS. It makes its presence felt through individual terrorist actions and seldom has a specific programme.[72] In Pakistan, the radical representatives of isolationism seem to exist among the Sindhi nationalists. The members of intermediary sector I can easily and effectively mobilize large masses. Such a mobilization is also certainly due to their infrastructure and that of the TUS, as movements in Iran and Pakistan have demonstrated. The frequency of isolationist activities leads towards increasing separation of the intermediary sectors from the extreme poles. Therefore, the integrationists finally identify increasingly with the colonial state. The state, uses this *avant-garde* as an instrument of legitimation for its own repressive measures against other sectors in order to pursue its own concept of the state. The representatives of the *avant-garde* in return receive political and economic power.[73] By now the Jama'at-e Islami and parts of the clerical elite from the Ahl-e Hadith, the Brelwis, the Shia and the Deobandis have been integrated into state power; in return they produced legitimation for Zia ul Haq.[74]

The manner in which the state now tries to cover further areas of the traditional sector and of the intermediary sectors via integrationist politics is the subject of this book. It shows that the regime not only expands into hitherto untouched areas and thus colonizes them, as, for example shrines and religious schools, but also aims at traditionalizing colonial structures such as the Council of Islamic Ideology (CII) and the Zakat system. Both strategies, traditionalization and colonialization, are, of course, put into action with the help of the integrationist *avant-garde*, who try to legitimize state intervention in an Islamic and fundamentalist manner. We can thus summarize that the integrationist *avant-garde* turns out to be the ultimate saviour of the colonial capitalist system. This reproach is also raised by the isolationists against the representatives of the intermediary sector II.

NOTES

1. The approach developed in the course of the academic year 1983-84 at the Oriental Seminar of the University of Bonn will be frequently referred to. Cf. Reinhard Schulze, "Islamische Kultur und soziale Bewegung", in *Peripherie*, no. 18/19, April 1985, pp. 60-84 (henceforth *Islamische Kultur*). The approach presented here calls for some modification of that approach, elaborated further down. Its basic statement is, however, valid, also when referring to Pakistan. It should explicitly be stated here that the argument is a model and must deviate in individual cases thus leading at times to overstraining the terms used in this chapter and in those following.

2. For the change of function from theology to ideology cf. Reinhard Schulze, "Die Politisierung des Islam im 19. Jahrhundert", in *Die Welt des Islams*, Leiden, 1982, vol. XXII, no. 1-4, pp. 103-116 as well as C.V. Findley, "The Advent of Ideology in the Islamic Middle East", in *Studia Islamica*, 1982, vol. 50, pp. 143-169 and 1982, vol. 51, pp. 147-180. For the region covering Indian Islam few publications of a similar kind are available. A conspicuous personality among the early Islamic intellectuals was Sir Sayyid Ahmad Khan; cf. C.W. Troll, *Sayyid Ahmad Khan: A Reinterpretation of Muslim Theology*, Oxford, 1978/79 (henceforth *Sayyid Ahmad Khan*); W.C. Smith, *Modern Islam in India*, Lahore, 1969, esp. chapters I and II; cf. Aziz Ahmad and Gustav v. Grunebaum, eds., *Muslim Self-statement in India and Pakistan, 1857-1968*, Wiesbaden, 1970.

3. See the contributions of Dieter Senghaas, ed., *Peripherer Kapitalismus: Analysen über Abhängigkeit und Unterentwicklung*, Frankfurt a.M., 1981; Senghaas, *Kapitalistische Weltökonomie, Kontroversen über ihren Ursprung und ihre Entwicklungsdynamik*, Frankfurt a.M., 1982; Senghaas, *Weltwirtschaft und Entwicklungspolitik, Plädoyer für Dissoziation*, Frankfurt a.M., 1978; for the regions of India and Pakistan cf. the contributions of Hamza Alavi, "State and Class under Peripheral Capitalism", in Hamza Alavi and Theodor Shanin, eds., *Introduction to the Sociology of "Developing Societies"*, London, 1982, pp. 289-307; Alavi, "Class and State", in H. Gardezi and J. Rashid, eds., *Pakistan: The Roots of Dictatorship*, London, 1983, pp. 40-93; Alavi, "The State in Postcolonial Societies: Pakistan and Bangladesh", in K. Gough and H.P. Sharma, eds., *Imperialism and Revolution in South Asia*, New York, 1973, pp. 145ff. and H.N. Gardezi, "Neocolonial Alliances and the Crisis of Pakistan", in Gough and Sharma, eds., op. cit., pp. 130-144. Cf. D. Rothermund, *Grundzüge der indischen Geschichte*, Darmstadt, 1976, pp. 83ff; see also *Europa und Indien im Zeitalter des Merkantilismus*, Darmstadt, 1978.

4. Thus the first large-scale congress of Arab nationalists was not convened until 1913, and then, in fact, in Paris! On the question of nationalism in the Indian subcontinent, its strategies and supporters see also D. Rothermund,

"Nationalismus und Sozialer Wandel in der Dritten Welt: Zwölf Thesen", in Otto Dann, ed., *Nationalismus und Sozialer Wandel*, Hamburg, 1978, pp. 187-208; esp. p. 189.

5. There are numerous records on the Western critique toward the "barbarious orientals"; see Ahmad, *Modernism*; Troll, *Sayyid Ahmad Khan*. For the scientific point of view turn to Said, *Orientalismus*. See also Bryan S. Turner, "Accounting for the Orient", in D. Maceoin and A. al-Shahi, eds., *Islam in the Modern World*, Canberra, 1983, pp. 9-26.

6. On the theory of Khalifat and its expansion cf. Tilman Nagel, *Staat und Glaubensgemeinschaft im Islam; Geschichte der politischen Ordnungsvorstellungen der Muslime*, Zürich and Munich, 1981, vol. II, pp. 172-223. The defensive position of the Islamic traditionalists became evident in India in the Deoband movement.

7. Analogous to this phenomenon, single terms would undergo alterations. Thus, the meaning of *dawla* was extended. Originally covering the period of rule of a dynasty or a regime the term now means nation-state or the territories in general.

8. This became evident in the rational deism of Sayyid Ahmad Khan as well as in the re-introduction of philosophy into the Islamic discussion by al-Afghani (cf. Nikki R. Keddie, *An Islamic Response to Imperialism*, Berkeley, 1983 (henceforth *Islamic Response*). In the course of this process of transformation the advocates of an Islamic ideology at times deviated from Islam; cf. Keddie, *Islamic Response*, esp. the dispute of al-Afghani with Ernest Renan, pp. 84-95 and 181-187. See also Elie Kedourie, *Afghani and 'Abduh: An Essay on Religious Unbelief and Political Activism in Modern Islam*, London, 1966 and W. Ende, "Waren Ğamâladdîn al-Afgânî und Muhammad 'Abduh Agnostiker?" in *Zeitschrift der Deutschen Morgenländischen Gesellschaft*, Supplement I, XVII, Deutscher Orientalistentag, Vorträge Teil 2, Wiesbaden, 1969, pp. 650-659.

9. It is close to recognizing a propensity to harmony in this concept. In the course of this study it will, however, become clear that the integrationist activities are not only an attempt to harmonize different social areas but also an attempt to dissolve all those entities opposed to integrationism, and intend to suppress or even destroy such interests.

10. They differ, of course, in the degree of their enthusiasm towards integration; cf. The dispute between al-Afghani and Ahmad Khan in Keddie, *Islamic Response*, pp. 73-84, 130-180; see also Aziz Ahmad, "The conflicting heritage of Sayyid Ahmed Khan and Jamal Ad-Din Afghani in the Muslim political thought of the Indian Subcontinent", in *Trudui XXV Mezdhunarod. Kongres Vostokovedov*, 1960, vol. IV (1963), pp. 147-152.

11. Thus, central concepts as nation, culture, freedom and justice were not transferred into the language of the Islamic cultural complex until the last century; cf. Albert Hourani, *Arabic Thought in the Liberal Age*, Oxford, 1962, p. 194.

12. Thus, say *Deoband, Farangî Mahall* and *Nadwat al-'Ulamâ'*; cf. Metcalf, *Revival*; Robinson, *Separatism;* Faruqi, *The Deoband School*; Friedman, "The attitude of the Jam'iyyat al-'Ulama'-i Hind"; Peter Hardy, *Partners in Freedom and True Muslims: Political Thought of some Muslim Scholars in British India, 1912-1947*, Lund, 1971; Peter Hardy, *The Muslims of British India,* Cambridge, 1972. All contributions listed here nevertheless hardly deal with the process of ideologization of Islam.

13. For the interpretation of the Koran by Ahmad Khan, cf. J.M.S. Baljon, *Modern Muslim Koran Interpretation 1880-1960*, Leiden, 1961.

14. This externalization often becomes obvious in an individual, cf. Michael Gilsenan, *Recognizing Islam*, London, 1982, pp. 9ff.

15. This is quite evident in Hasan al-Banna, Mustafa al-Sibai, Mahmud Shaltut, and Mawdudi. All of them state that the advantages of Western societies were also present in Islam, cf. Kemal H. Karpat, ed., *Political and Social Thought in the Contemporary Middle East*, New York, 1982, pp. 90-116, as well as R.P. Mitchell, *The Society of the Muslim Brothers*, London,1969. Similar positions were taken by Inayatullah Khan al-Mashriqi. He even held the opinion that true Islam was to be found in Europe, cf. Jamal Malik, "Al-Mashriqi und die Khaksar, Eine religiöse Sozialbewegung indischer Muslime", im 20. Jahrhundert. Master's Thesis, Bonn, 1982 (mimeo). This opinion is still held by some Muslim intellectuals.

16. In the geographic sense only.

17. In the sense of an increasing social complexity, manifesting itself socially, economically and politically.

18. With reference to the term used by D. Rothermund, who talks of European bridgeheads which were "primarily instrumentalized to procure the East-India Company's access to the trade of Asia" (see also *Europa und Indien*, p. 92, and see also *Grundzüge*, pp. 83ff). Here this term is meant to include the indigenous elite, also referred to by Hamza Alavi, "Class and State", pp. 40-93; Alavi, "The State in Postcolonial Societies", p. 145 and H.N. Gardezi, "Neocolonial Alliances", pp. 130-144.

19. This is especially true when it comes to cultivation methods, like, mono-cultures (cotton), which were only feasible with the alteration of irrigation methods (cf. Klaus Dettmann, "Agrarkolonisation im Rahmen von Kanalbewässerungsprojekten am Beispiel des Fünfstromlandes", in J. Hagedorn, J. Hovermann and H.J. Nitz, eds., *Landerschließung und Kulturlandschaftswandel an den Siedlungsgrenzen der Erde*, Göttingen, 1976, pp. 179-191; for further bibliographical sources cf. chapter 3 of my M.A. Thesis: Al-Mashriqi).

20. Cf. the contributions by D. Senghaas and Hamza Alavi, op. cit., and Rothermund, *Grundzüge,* pp. 64-87 and see also *Europa und Indien,* pp. 39ff.

21. The abbreviations TAS, CAS, TUS, and CUS are taken from Schulze, "Islamische Kultur", pp. 60-84.

22. On this, cf. Fred Scholz, "Detribalisierung und Marginalität. Eine empirische Fallstudie", in Wolfgang Köhler, ed., *Pakistan: Analysen-Berichte-Dokumentationen,* Hamburg, 1979, pp. 31-68. Because of its small numbers this sector is not dealt with later.

23. On the history of the army cf. the somewhat carefully worded contribution by Stephen P. Cohen, *The Pakistan Army,* Berkeley, 1984. On the administration cf. Charles H. Kennedy, *Bureaucracy in Pakistan,* Oxford, 1987; Rothermund, "Nationalismus und Sozialer Wandel", pp. 187-208, esp. Theses 4 and 9.

24. There is an excellent contribution on urban development by Mohammad A. Qadeer, *Lahore: Urban Development in the Third World,* Lahore, 1983. For further studies on urban geography see the standard study by A.D. King, *Colonial Urban Development: Culture, Social Power and Environment,* Boston, London, 1976; B.L.C. Johnson, *Pakistan,* London, 1979; Wolfgang-Peter Zingel, "Urbanisierung und regionale Wirtschaftsentwicklung in Pakistan", in Hermann Kulke, H.C. Rieger and L. Lutze, eds., *Städte in Südasien, Beiträge zur Süd-Asien Forschung,* vol. 60, Wiesbaden, 1982, pp. 233-267 and Fred Scholz, "Verstädterung in der Dritten Welt: Der Fall Pakistan", in W. Kreisch, W.D. Sick and J. Stadelbauer, eds., *Siedlungsgeographische Studien,* Berlin, New York, 1979, pp. 341-385.

25. Cf. the contributions in D. Goldschmidt, and H. Melber, eds., *Die Dritte Welt als Gegenstand erziehungswissenschaftlicher Forschung,* Weinheim, 1981 (Zeitschrift für Pädagogik 16. Beiheft). Zia ul Haq, "Muslim religious education in Indo-Pakistan", in *Islamic Studies,* vol. 14, no. 1, 1975, pp. 271-292 and Sayyid Muhammad Salim, *Hind o Pâkistân meñ musalmânôñ kâ nizâm-e ta'lîm o tarbiyyat,* Lahore, 1980 (Urdu).

26. Based on collective responsibility. A good contribution on this topic is made by Rosa Luxemburg, *Die Akkumulation des Kapitals,* Berlin, 1913. Reprinted in Luxemburg, *Gesammelte Werke,* vol. 5, East Berlin, 1975, pp. 600f; cf. chapter 3 of my M.A. Thesis: Al-Mashriqi.

27. In the sense of Senghaas. For other, broader interpretations of the term marginality cf. D. Rothermund, "Marginalität und Elite in Entwicklungsländern", in *Die Dritte Welt 1972,* vol. 1, no. 1, pp. 15-22.

28. On this cf. Senghaas, *Weltwirtschaft und Entwicklungspolitik,* pp. 193ff.

29. Schulze, "Islamische Kultur", pp. 67ff.

30. The consumption of drugs alien to the local culture such as heroin has increased markedly in the urban Pakistani society in the course of the last few years; see Pakistan Narcotics Control Board, *National Survey on Drug Abuse in Pakistan, 1986 (Highlights),* Islamabad, 1987. Cinemas usually convey images of harmony or of violence.

31. Into this category one may group the "humanization of the working place" in Western industrial nations.

32. Schulze, "Islamische Kultur", p. 73. Also refer to Qadeer, *Lahore,* op.cit., and Fred Scholz, *Verstädterung in der Dritten Welt,* pp. 341-385.

33. Cf. chapter IV on Zakat.
34. They are, however, increasingly brought under the control of CUS and are thus colonized (cf. chapter III on the Islamic endowments).
35. Their elite is integrated to a great extent into the colonial sector as well (cf. chapter II on the CII).
36. They have lately been subject to a strong integration policy by the state (cf. chapter V on the Islamic system of education).
37. This is evident in (today's) Sindh, especially in the traditional agrarian sector; cf. chapter VI.
38. This is evident from the boycott of the proposals in the *Halepota Report* and in the regulations on Zakat of the Deobandis and the Shia (see chapters IV, V and VI).
39. Here one must mention the secular judges, writers and scholars, who transmit colonial values.
40. Thus, the Pîr Pagârô in Sindh [chairman of the (Pagârô) Muslim League], the Governor of Sindh Sayyid Ghawth Ali Shah and the former Minister of Law and current chairman of the Islamic World Conference, Pirzadah. Even the Prime Minister under Zia ul Haq, Junejo Khan was said to foster a tendency towards the traditional sector (esp. the cult of shrines). The integration of the *pîrs* and of other dignitaries were of special interest to the colonial rulers. Cf. on this David Gilmartin, "Religious Leadership and the Pakistan Movement in the Punjab", in *MAS*, 13, 1979, pp. 485-517 and S.F.D. Ansari, "Sufi Saints, Society and State Power: The Pirs of Sind, 1843-1947", (Ph.D. dissertation, Royal Holloway and Bedford College, London, 1987), as well as Abdul Wali Khan, *Facts are Sacred,* Peshawar, n. d., chapters 10 and 11.
41. This becomes obvious in the high degree of organization and of the system of kinship and of politics, administration and economy.
42. Here as well, however, traditional principles of order are referred to. The cult of shrines or saints eventually found here implies a fluctuation within the social affiliation.
43. In the present case, these are the clerical members of the CII, as well as the representatives of the religio-political parties.
44. The integration of both sectors is obvious in the infrastructure, where verses of Koran, the affiliation to shrines and to religious schools are meant to traditionalize the area of production. Thus there are shrines and madâris especially for the drivers of taxis and rikshaws. This is also the line on which one may read the offer to low and medium range employees of banks to interrupt payment on credits during the two holy months of the year. There are fluctuations within these mixed sectors as well. The model therefore should not be regarded as static. It supplies, nevertheless, points of reference and thus elucidates the interests of different groups of supporters.
45. This is reinforced through migration and through the disintegration of the joint family system.
46. For these terms turn to Qadeer, *Lahore*, pp. 181ff et passim.

47. Actually it is a matter of self-interest of the representatives of this intermediary sector.

48. Schulze, "Islamische Kultur", pp. 75ff.

49. This was the case in Pakistan in 1977, when the Bhutto regime was no longer in a position to negotiate with the representatives of the mixed sectors. When finally there was a possibility to remove the deadlock between the PPP and the PNA in May 1977, the army under Zia ul Haq intervened in order to preserve the *status quo*.

50. This is primarily true of the representatives of the Jama'at-e Islami. However, also some top representatives of the Jam'iyyat-e 'Ulamâ'-e Islam and of the Jam'iyyat-e 'Ulamâ'-e Pakistan may also be counted among these intellectuals. "The hard-core organization of the movement (PNA) came from the religious parties..." (cf. Khalid B. Sayeed, *Politics in Pakistan: The nature and direction of change*, New York, 1980, pp. 157ff). Unfortunately Sayeed does not differentiate the traditional supporters from those already integrated into the colonial sector. The "hard-core" comprises primarily representatives of the intermediary sector II.

51. ". . . the industrial labour did not play as important a role as shopkeepers, small traders and merchants during the demonstrations against the Bhutto regime." The largest group among these were the "commercial traders"; this term refers to the representatives of the mixed sectors. (Sayeed, *Politics in Pakistan*, op. cit., p. 143.

52. Sayeed unfortunately does not focus on this relevant aspect in his analysis of the social basis of the PNA: "For cohesion and strength one should look at organizational units and cells like the madrasahs and mosques, commercial associations or federations, and some trade unions. . ." (Sayeed, *Politics in Pakistan*, op.cit., p. 158). The madâris only entered into the activities starting from March, cf. Muhammad Munsha Tabish Qasuri, *Tahrîk-e nizâm-e mustafâ aur Jâm'iah Nizâmiyyah Ridwiyyah Lâhawr*, Lahore, 1978 (Urdu).

53. J.S. Burki, *Pakistan under Bhutto, 1971-1977*, London, 1980, p. 171; cf. S. R. Ghauri, "How Streetwar and Strikes beat Bhutto", in *Far Eastern Economic Review*, July 1, 1977, pp. 10ff. For an analysis of the elections cf. Akhtar Rashid, *Elections '77 and Aftermath: A political appraisal*, Islamabad, 1981, chapters II-X; Shariful Mujahid, "The 1977 Pakistani Elections: An analysis," in Manzooruddin Ahmed, ed., *Contemporary Pakistan: Politics, Economy, and Society*, Karachi, 1982, pp. 63-91 and W.L. Richter, "From Electoral Politics to Martial Law: Alternative Perspectives on Pakistan's Political Crisis of 1977", in Manzooruddin Ahmed, ed., op.cit., pp. 92-113.

54. Burki, *Pakistan under Bhutto*, op.cit., pp. 137 and 184ff. Sayeed, *Politics in Pakistan*, op.cit., here pp. 143, 157 et passim.

55. The religio-political parties had been active since the sixties and had presented comprehensive party programmes. The PNA, in contrast, presented its constitution only on Oct. 10th, 1977.

56. The economic power of the Jama'at-e Islami should not be underestimated. An analysis of the literature relevant to the subject of the Jama'at, as in *ASIA* from Lahore (Urdu), reveals a deeper economic entanglement on their part.

57. This is demonstrated by the fact that the Jama'at-e Islami is not equipped with a classical theological or religious curriculum (state of affairs in 1986); cf. the discussion on curricula in chapter VI.

58. Schulze, "Islamische Kultur", p. 76.

59. This is true even if Mawdudi and al-Banna held this opinion. Ultimately they have adopted the universally accepted Western values.

60. Rothermund, "Nationalismus und Sozialer Wandel", pp. 190f.

61. Albert Hourani, *Arabic Thought in the Liberal Age*, op.cit., p. 144.

62. Fritz Steppat, "Der Muslim und die Obrigkeit", in *Gegenwartskunde*, vol. 28, 1979, pp. 319-332, Bassam Tibi, *Die Krise des moderen Islam*, Munich, 1981, pp. 137f and 145 et passim.

63. In Pakistan, this became evident in the 'Ulamâ'-Committee of 1951,which drafted the famous *22-Points*. One may find representatives of the traditional sector who had been won over in favour of the integrationist policy within the CII as well.

64. Christine Gieraths and Jamal Malik, *Die Islamisierung der Wirtschaft in Pakistan unter Zia ul Haq*, Bad Honnef, 1988.

65. Jamal Malik, "Islamisierung des Bildungswesens in Pakistan: zum Verständnis der Erziehungspolitik des Zia-Regimes", Heidelberg, 1987 (Research report for the Konrad-Adenauer-Foundation; unpublished).

66. GoP, Ministry of Law and Parliamentary Affairs (Law Division), *Draft Shariat Commission Order,* 1978 without author, Annex I.

67. "(c) Law includes any custom or usage having the force of law but does not include the Constitution, Muslim personal law, any law relating to the procedure of any court or tribunal or, until the expiration of ten years from the commencement of this chapter, any fiscal law or any law relating to the levy and collection of taxes and fees or banking or insurance practice and procedure" (author's underlining). Cited according to Comparative Statement of the Constitution as it stood before the March 20th, 1985 and as it stands after that date, GoP, Ministry of Justice and Parliamentary Affairs (Justice Division), p. 54, within "Provision, if any, as it stands after amendment".

68. This expression may carry with it too negative a connotation. As will become evident, the isolationists may be taken as representatives who quite legitimately defend their traditional ideas.

69. Rothermund in a similar context uses the term "culturally immanent socialism" cf. by the same author "Nationalismus und Sozialer Wandel", p. 203.

70. This becomes evident in Sayyid Qutb (Yvonne Y. Haddad, "Sayyid Qutb: Ideologue of Islamic Revival", in J.L. Esposito, ed., *Voices of Resurgent Islam*, Oxford, 1983, pp. 67-98) and later on in *Takfir wa'l hijra* in Egypt.

71. Thus, in Pakistan the Shia, just like parts of the traditional clergy, the

Deobandis (Fadl al-Rahman wing), repeatedly rejected the Sunni integrationist regime.

72. Especially evident with the assassins of A. Sadat (cf. the contribution by J.J.G. Jansen, "The Creed of Sadat's Assassins", in *Die Welt des Islams,* vol. 25, 1985, pp. 1-30). The underground organization of the Al-dhû al-fiqâr, formerly operating from Afghanistan, may also be put in this category.

73. Thus the representatives of the PNA were nominated for the federal cabinet of July 8th, 1978. They withdrew, however, on April 15th, 1979. A leading Jama'at-e Islami functionary was nominated chairman of the Planning Commission in 1978. To date the Jama'at-e Islami participates in the process of political decision making. For the process of integration, this is also true of the integrationist clergy, thus in the CII since 1977 (cf. chapter on the CII, Appendix A) and in the Majlis-e Shura (cf. *Directory Federal Councillors of Pakistan*, Karachi, n. d.; on the composition of the members of the Majlis cf. *Dawn Overseas Weekly,* January 15, 1982, p. 7).

74. Some '*ulamâ*' were even members of the Senate, as, for example, Sami al-Haq, the son of Abd al-Haq, the founder of the largest Dâr al-'Ulûm in Pakistan.

CHAPTER II

LEGITIMIZING ISLAMIZATION
THE CASE OF THE "COUNCIL OF ISLAMIC IDEOLOGY" IN PAKISTAN

INTRODUCTION

The Council for Islamic Ideology (CII) must be regarded as a vehicle of Islamic ideological discourse or anti-critique and, in the contemporary setting, as one of the most interesting and important institutions in the Islamization process in Pakistan. It started functioning even before the Zia ul Haq period. It is strange therefore that no detailed work has been done on it to this day. Neither social scientists and historians nor economists and legal scholars deemed it worth paying attention to it, although there is no scarcity of source material. Specially since 1977, the year of the announcement of "nizâm-e mustafâ" (the order of the Prophet Muhammad), much attention has been given to the Council in the vernacular press.

After giving a brief historical survey of the Council, the present chapter contrasts its activities with those of the Government, thus providing some instructive insights into the policies of different regimes as well as the interests of the members of this advisory body. In this way the divergence or conformity of the official policy with the principles of the Shari'a—as understood by the representatives of the CII—is set out.

HISTORY AND ACTIVITIES

It was to be expected that Islamic norms would be implemented in the young nation-state of Pakistan, in the face of the requirement that Muslims should live according to their religion. It is, therefore, strange that no attempt was made despite the Objectives Resolution[1] until 1950 to set up an institution or organization concerned with applying Islamic principles to the future of Pakistan. It is also very strange that the upholders of Islamic legal tradition, the 'ulamâ', were hardly considered when drawing up the policies on which the State was to be run. The Resolution did not envisage any Islamic institution which could help politicians.

After three years an 'Ulamâ' Board or a Board of Ta'limat-e Islamiyyah was set up,[2] comprising five 'ulamâ' and some modernists.[3] It had been proposed by Shabbir Ahmad Uthmani (1887-1949), a famous graduate from the Deoband seminary in India. The aim was to set up an institution which could deal with Islamic issues in Pakistan. According to its own proposals the Board was to be the body to look after these issues. A report prepared by the members of the Ta'limat-e Islamiyyah Board, was, however, never published and its proposals never implemented,[4] although the Board was affiliated to the Basic Principles Committee (BPC)[5] and, thus, involved in constitutional discussions. The members of the BPC were elected by the Constituent Assembly and had to develop basic principles for consideration in the Assembly. But the Board's proposals did not have any specifically Islamic features; Muslims were merely exhorted to learn and read the Holy Book. Nevertheless, the proposals were different in some respects from the perceptions of the BPC whose report would have undermined the Bengali majority in Pakistan.[6] The majority of Islamic scholars denied the authority of the BPC.[7]

According to the draft of the 'Ulamâ' Board it had the power to reject laws not in accordance with Koran and Sunna and thus to prevent their implementation.[8] Hence, the Board was more powerful than the CII which was recommended in the Constitution of 1956. It is probably because of this authority that the Board was dissolved.[9] Binder is of the view that the Board's proposals were more romantic than realistic in their approach to contemporary problems:

They [the members] became romantics in the sense of reading back institutions which are a product of their own imagination into the obscure period of the 'Rightly-Guided Caliphs'.

Also, the decisions of the Board "were not thought through as a rational whole".[10]

Besides this Board, the Islamic scholars tried to establish an independent platform in order to realize what they thought was Islamic. In 1951 they proclaimed the famous 22 basic points or the basic principles of an Islamic State. In principle, these suggestions aimed at establishing Islamic sovereignty, bringing national politics in line with Islamic laws, fostering Islamic internationalism and maintaining Islamic education, etc.,[11] without however mentioning an Islamic economic system.

UNDER AYUB KHAN

The demand for an Islamic institution as part of the Constitution came twelve years after the establishment of Pakistan in 1959. It was to participate in building up a policy oriented on Islamic principles and was to have a constitutional character. But it took another four years until an Islamic Advisory Council (or Advisory Council for Islamic Ideology: ACII) was set up in 1962.[12] As an authority established under Ayub Khan the ACII was meant to serve the reinterpretation of Islam according to "modernist" parameters and, thus, had to legitimize national policies in Islamic terms. With this step it was also envisaged that different sections of the Islamic elite would be integrated in an ideological State.

The President of Pakistan, however, wanted only limited rights for the Council. To give a right of veto to the 'ulamâ' would be "fatal" to Ayub Khan, because of the potential pressure of Islamic scholars on secular oriented forces.[13]

In the beginning the Council came under heavy criticism from the ranks of the 'ulamâ', who were provoked by their not being adequately represented in it. They did not see their interests being served, either by the Council or by the newly established Institute for Islamic Research (IIR), specially in view of their small numbers as compared to the advocates of administration, secular jurisdiction and economy in these newly established institutions.[14]

Because of the traditionalists' pressure some secular minded members had to resign.[15] However, strengthening of the 'ulamâ' in the Council did not occur for the time being.

The activities of the Council during the first two periods of its working up to 1969 were mainly concerned with clarification of interest (ribâ) and with general proposals on how to reform the social order. Clear directions on how to resolve these issues were, however, not developed.

In response to the Government's wishes, the advisory body published a questionnaire in 1963 on certain religious and social problems. On the basis of the replies some Islamization measures were to be worked out. The project had to be abandoned in the face of poor response from the public.[16]

The question of ribâ was certainly crucial for an Islamic Republic. Thus, the Council was asked to elaborate on it and in January 1964 stated that "'Riba' is forbidden" and there is "unanimity on the point that for the fulfilment of the Islamic concept of social justice and human brotherhood, a system of interest-free economy should be built up."[17] However, when this opinion was submitted to the Government it was not thought to be comprehensive and was again referred back to the Council for reconsideration.[18]

In December 1966 the Council was still of the view that most of the transactions prevalent in Pakistan involved ribâ. "As a matter of fact . . . the present banking system is fundamentally based on Riba and requires a complete scrutiny and thorough overhauling." It was agreed that a questionnaire be prepared by the Council [19] and circulated nation-wide as well as to 123 religious scholars in other Muslim countries. The questionnaire, was never dispatched; the Council instead made a "historical decision on Riba" on December 23, 1969, on its own, stating that all transactions resulting in more money than the actual debt be regarded as *ribâ*.[20] This was an answer to the Government's question on whether interest prevailed in the country.[21] No action was undertaken until 1979 when some steps were taken to resolve the problem, but as has been shown elsewhere, there has been no basic change.[22]

According to the Constitution the Council was to represent the various Muslim schools of thought, include two judges of the Supreme Court or High Court and not less than four members engaged in Islamic research and education for at least 15 years. One female member was allowed.[23] While other members were engaged part-time, the chairman, a judge of the Supreme Court, had to be a full-time member. The President of Pakistan was the final authority.[24] The membership was limited to three years, although this was hardly adhered to.

The working procedure was laid down by the Council of Islamic Ideology (Procedure) Rules 1974.[25] The proceedings and the reports were to be conducted and printed in Urdu and were to be kept confidential. Every three months a meeting with at least five members was to be held; five members were to form a quorum.

The IIR, set up in 1962, was to support the ACII in producing source material on certain issues and elaborate comments on them. In case of problems regarding personnel, the chairman of the Council was entitled to consult experts.[26]

Besides the IIR and the experts, three advisors could be consulted by the Council. They did not hail from religious institutions: a Civil Servant of Pakistan (CSP), a specialist in banking and a member of the Planning Commission.[27]

The subordination of a semi-religious advisory council to political and secular institutions was in line with Ayub's ideas. This becomes apparent from the following statement:

There was obviously no place for a supra-body of religious experts exercising a power of veto over the Legislature and the Judiciary. . . . A constitution could be regarded as Islamic only if it were drafted by the Ulama and conceded them the authority to judge and govern the people. This was a position which neither the people nor I (Ayub Khan) was prepared to accept.[28]

Thus, Ayub had confined the *'ulamâ'* to their limits. But in spite of limitations the Council had some impact both positive and negative on the politicians. On the one hand, the composition of its personnel reflected the policy of Government which was keen on nominating its own members, on the other, there were certain undoubted social pressures of some '*ulamâ*' on the Government via the Council.

UNDER BHUTTO

From 1965 to 1975 the Council received little public attention, but from 1975 onwards it became prominent again.[29]

The constitution of 1972 had not only enhanced the influence of the spokesmen of Islamic tradition but also the scope of Sharî'a norms for society, economy and culture. Until then it was up to the National Assembly to accept or reject the proposals of the Council. The constitution under Bhutto worked out a compromise between Pakistan People's Party (PPP), which, nevertheless, wanted to curb the influence of the traditionalists and the '*ulamâ*', who were demanding more rights for the Council with regard to its status in Parliament.[30] The Constitution gave new functions to the Council, providing for a total Islamization of Pakistan's society by the eighties. The Government had nine years to develop Sharî'a norms on the basis of which Pakistan was to be governed. In order to realize this target the Council was to produce annual interim reports as well as a final report within seven years of its appointment. The reports were to "be laid for discussion before both Houses and each Provincial Assembly within six months of their receipt", and "Parliament and the Assembly, after considering the report, were to enact laws based on it within a period of two years of the final report."[31] Thus, by the middle of 1980, Pakistan was to have witnessed total Islamization.[32]

Even the nomenclature of the institution was changed. The ACII was renamed the Council of Islamic Ideology. The number of members was increased from a minimum of eight to a maximum of fifteen[33] to ensure greater efficiency. However, this rendered a uniform Islamic norm more difficult, with the representatives of different schools of thought (*makâtib-e fikr*) pursuing their particular interpretations of Islamic law.[34]

From 1974 to 1977 the chairman was Justice Hamoodur Rahman (Hamud al-Rahman, d. 1981), member of the Mu'tamar al-'âlam al-Islâmî (Islamic World Congress) and later Adviser on Constitutional Affairs to the Central Martial Law Administrator (CMLA). During his time, 31 proposals were made aiming at what can be called an integration of the modern sector (including labour and political power) with the traditional sector (including culture and private life) without, however, initiating any change in the economic structures, laid down by the British. Their suggestions were concerned with ritualization of certain sectors of life, rather than any revolutionary changes.[35]

The official support to a particular section of the 'ulamâ' reflected the internal political struggle with which the Bhutto regime was increasingly confronted. Therefore, from 1975 onwards Islam was once again propagated by Government itself through the Council as well as through the then Minister of Religious Affairs, Kawthar Niyazi,[36] resulting in the expansion of the Council's suggestions of how to Islamize Pakistan. The Government on its part demanded that the Council should be swifter in finalizing its work as time was running short.[37]

THE CII SINCE 1977

When Zia ul Haq entered the political arena in 1977, the CII was restructured and under the chairmanship of Justice Muhammad Afzal Cheemah began, as expected, to launch an intensive Islamization campaign. Apparently, this meant an increase in the Council's prestige.[38] The newspapers gave considerable publicity to the members with biographical details and pictures.[39] The promotion of the Council was primarily done by the conformist *Pakistan Times*, while critical issues were raised by the Shiite daily *The Muslim*. Despite official support, the Constitution (Fourth Amendment) Order 1980 still contained Article 230, which had been in existence ever since the inception of the Council in 1962.[40] The article shows how little the Government was concerned about the Council's proposals. This was especially true in the case of any law which was in public interest; the Government could implement it without considering the Council's opinion.[41]

The proposals of former members were partly revised and additional suggestions made on daily prayers, Zakat, Sharî'a-courts,[42] hudûd-regulations, Islamic programmes in the media, etc. Besides these stress was laid on legal and educational reforms as well as on the Islamic banking system and Zakat.[43] For a theoretical elaboration of the "Islamic economic system", a panel was set up by the Council comprising secular scholars, economists and bankers.[44] The panel produced a questionnaire on an Islamic economic system which failed to get response from the public and was finally answered by the CII itself, namely by three *jayyid 'ulamâ'*.[45] For scrutiny and reform of law a panel of experts was likewise set up.[46] For the first time, the CII proposals were implemented to a certain extent, although in a modified way. This modification resulted in heavy criticism among the members, specially the religious scholars.[47]

With the help of the Constitution (Fourth Amendment) Order 1980[48] the number of the members was enhanced from 15 to 20.[49] In order to make the work more efficient the selection of five full-time members was deemed necessary. Also the number of working days and hours changed drastically.

The official support to the Council resulted in the enhancement of its work. Similary, visitors from important international Islamic organizations, specially Saudi Arabia, increased, underlining the CII's *salafî* character. There were representatives from other parts of the world as well, including the West,[50] which points to a more integrationist orientation of the body in line with neo-*salafî* Islam.[51]

The CII's aims and conceptions can be deduced from its composition and its members' functions as well as their professional affiliations.[52] This enables us to assess the activities of the Council and the policy of the Government.

INTEGRATIONIST ISLAM POLICY

Overtime, the composition of CII changed substantially. Those with westernized education decreased gradually through the years while the number of those traditionally educated increased correspondingly. The large number of the "seculars" till the mid-seventies changed drastically with the advent of Zia in 1977. This change of membership explains the differences of policies pursued by the CII. Thus, it was to be expected that with increase in their number Islamic scholars would project the norms and values represented by them.

Considering that the composition of the CII is decisive for its interpretation of Islam advocated by it, one can presume that during the first fifteen years of the Council's existence '*ulamâ*' had hardly any impact on its proposals. The large number of secular jurists, scholars and economists on it ruled out any reliance on classical elements of Islamic culture. But, even later, when the number of the '*ulamâ*' increased, their disagreement on several issues rendered it difficult for the Council to develop into an effective political platform of the traditionalists.

However, one has to bear in mind that the '*ulamâ*' and *pîrs* who coopted into the Council were representatives of a religious elite, which had already been integrated into State apparatus either via the Auqaf Department or through the subsequently installed Zakat 'Ulamâ'

Committees.[53] One can assume that they tended towards the colonial view and thus pursued an integrationist kind of Islamization.

Diagram 1 reflects a steady increase of Islamic scholars in the CII. The religious elite of the body was, however using political forms and methods as used by colonial societies, like political parties, parliaments, constitutions, etc., even if these norms and institutions were given Islamic nomenclature.

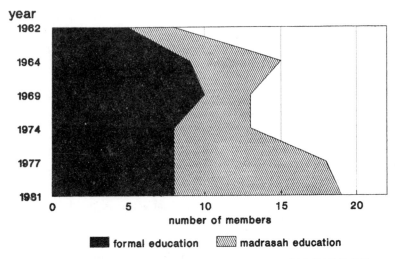

DIAGRAM 1: CII MEMBERS ACCORDING TO TYPE OF EDUCATION 1962-1981

Sources: Bujet Mahkamah Awqâf Punjâb barâ-e 1985-86, Lahore, 1986 (Urdu), p. 13; A.A. Khan: Paper presented at the seminar on the Management and Development of Awkaf properties at Jeddah, Saudi Arabia, 4.8.-18.8.1984 (mimeo), p. 13.

Around July 1979 Zia ul Haq ordered that CII elaborate on this issue, specially whether "the prevailing system of elections is un-Islamic".[54] A committee set up under the chairmanship of Zafar Ahmad Ansari, who had been a member of the Ta'limat-e Islamiyyah Board, was not able to examine the matter. Another committee set up in June 1981 again could not produce a report. The Council, under the chairmanship of Tanzil al-Rahman, started working on the subject and submitted its report on April 1, 1982.[55] However, Zia, meanwhile, decided to engage internationally reputed scholars to advise on this issue, though of the 285 specialists contacted, only 47 responded.[56]

The CII also elaborated on the procedures of voting. It recommended qualities which are prevalent in the colonial and urban society rather than those held by members of the traditional sector or rural groups as a voter's qualifications. One major recommendation of the report was that the President was to be subject to the discussions of the _Shûrâ_.[57] Zia refused to accept this report and set up another committee in February 1983 comprising members of the Federal Council to examine the issue. This time the members were of the opinion that the constitution of 1973 should by and large be the basis for any further elections. "The committee came to the conclusion that Parliamentary system of Government, which was in accordance with Islam, would be more appropriate for Pakistan."[58] The committee further stated that the Constitution of 1973 gave too much power to Prime Minister and should be amended. Some members were even of the view that the "post of the Prime Minister be done away with".[59] Concerning political parties, the committee concluded:

Islam believes in democracy and the development of democratic institutions and traditions through which it seeks to secure the welfare and well-being of the people. Without a political forum and political parties, no Government, believing in democracy, can properly function. Accordingly the committee felt that, in an Islamic State, Political parties could be allowed to function in order to protect and safeguard the rights of the people and to ensure checks and balances against the excesses and high-handedness of the Government in power.[60]

Following this, the CII once again started working on this subject and submitted its Report on Islamic System of Government and Elections, in May 1983. "The Presidential form of Government was nearer to Islamic concept" but the President was not allowed to dissolve Parliament and to amend the Constitution. He should either follow the resolutions of the Parliament or resign. Furthermore, the Parliament was empowered to remove him. A Supreme Council of Islamic Affairs was to be set up and followed by the courts. And, "in the light of the Qur'an and Sunnah elections on the basis of political parties are not valid".[61]

As with the CII's first report in 1982, there were some members of the advisory body who did not share this view. They were either members of the Shia group or sympathizers of the Jamâ'at-e Islâmî. The chairman, Dr. Tanzil, reserved his opinion, as he was not sure whether or not according to the Koran and Sunna, elections could be held on the basis of political parties.[62] Thus, the CII as a body supported elections on non-party basis, which, in fact, suited Zia and was a handsome gift from the CII members.

The last committee set up to go into this issue produced the famous

Ansari Report under the chairmanship of Zafar Ahmad Ansari. This committee was set up in July 1983 and submitted its report in August next.[63] Following the proposals of the Ta'limat-e Islamiyyah Board 1951, this committee proposed discarding both parliamentary as well as presidential system and instead "introduce the full-fledged Islamic system of Amarat corresponding with Islamic traditions which, though it may have some points in common with the presidential form, has a distinct character of its own".[64] The Head of State should also be Head of Government. An Islamic Consultative System of Government was recommended in which the Majlis-e Shûrâ had crucial functions. This institution was to elect the amîr al-mamlukat, who shall be ex-officio Commander-in-Chief of the Armed forces of Pakistan. He "shall be empowered to appoint, in his discretion, Ministers as needed in order to carry on the administration . . . and shall have the power to promulgate with the view to safeguarding vital national interests, an ordinance in cases of emergency". But he shall neither have "the power to suspend the constitution, either wholly or partially", nor "to dissolve the Majlis-e Shura in any circumstance whatsoever".[65] Hence, the country should change over to elections on a non-party basis[66] since "political parties are highly harmful for Pakistan".[67]

Under Zia the CII for the first time faced the problem of different schools of thought. Earlier the hegemony of one school of thought over the others was not visible. Rather, there had been a system of parity. In 1977 the Government nominated members according to their theological affiliations. Three or four Brelwis and Deobandis against one or two Shia and Ahl-e Hadith, were nominated which reflects to some extent the proportion of the *makâtib-e fikr* in Pakistan. In fact, some representatives of the Brelwis felt neglected.[68] The "seculars", on the other hand, still represented a sizeable number.

From 1977 the influence of the '*ulamâ*' in the Council was reduced through setting up of panels, whose proposals were articulated by those trained in the formal educational system, a colonial legacy. An ideological Islamization was demanded. Because a considerable number of CII '*ulamâ*' shared this approach, one may find corresponding suggestions even in regard to their own religious educational system. In this respect, the categorization of secular and religious or colonial and traditional have to be considered as indicative. However, they reveal the degree of integration, modernization and secularization of the Pakistani "clergy". These scholars have, for example, *shu'bah jadîdah* in their religious schools and curricula or syllabi offering modern subjects[69] while their respective seminaries (*Dâr al-'Ulûm*) are attached to umbrella-organizations.[70] One can presume that the majority of these '*ulamâ*' are secularized to some degree.

As can be seen in the "Consolidated Recommendations of the Council of Islamic Ideology Relating to Education System in Pakistan 1962-82",[71] the '*ulamâ*' not only emphasized Arabic and the study of Koran, but were also interested in integrating *fudalâ'* from Dînî Madâris (graduates from religious schools) into the formal educational system and to reform their own traditional madrasah system.

The integration of the traditional educational system was to be made possible through an "independent and autonomous institution" in which specialists of modern education (*jadîd ta'lîm kê mâhirîn*) would also participate. Moreover, degrees of religious schools were to be recognized and made equivalent to those of the formal educational sector. The precondition was an administrative tying up of religious schools under a central institution[72] and inclusion of new, formally recognized subjects like mathematics, social sciences, modern philology and primary education as a part of religious education. The central institution was also authorized to elaborate the curricula and to issue degrees, which was previously done by the umbrella-organizations of the respective schools of thought.

One can here recognize the willingness of the '*ulamâ*' to modernize their madrasah system and their implicit acceptance of reforms in their system of education. However, they believed that such reforms could be successful only through a high degree of centralization. These proposals were made by the CII in 1978, some months before the setting up of the National Committee on Dînî Madâris 1979.[73]

From 1980 there had been discussion in the CII on the recognition of degrees of religious schools. The University Grants Commission (UGC) and Establishment Division maintained that M.A. or B.A. degrees for '*ulamâ*' were possible only if certain changes were made in the theological curricula, specially the incorporation of "modern" subjects and the elimination of certain "old" subject. The '*ulamâ*' of the CII pressed for equivalence without these changes. It was the personal intervention of Zia ul Haq which made the recognition of theological degrees by the UGC and the Establishment Division finally possible. This decision recognized the value and enhanced the honour and prestige of religious knowledge for which the President was thanked.[74]

The main objective of the proposals of the Council was to integrate the madrasah students into the formal educational sector[75] rather than to change the system of formal education. Thus, we see a latent readiness among the religious elite to integrate Islam into the colonial system and to enrich it with Islamic norms and nomenclatures without aiming at revolutionizing inherited structures.

RESIGNATIONS AND OPPOSITION

The extent of disintegration of the CII in general and that of the *'ulamâ'* in particular can be measured by resignations of its members. Resignations during the period 1964 to 1969 were mostly from the Bengalis. I.H. Qureshi resigned because of his chairmanship of the IIR in 1965. By the end of the Ayub era (1969/70) the modernist Dr. Fadl al-Rahman had to resign and leave the country because of the pressure of some *'ulamâ'* who criticized his "heretic thinking".[76] He was also not acceptable to the traditional forces as chairman of the IIR.

Especially conspicuous was the number of resignations between 1977 and 1980, during which six members left the CII. Only three of them were *'ulamâ'*—two Shia and one representing the Brelwis. They left out of discontent with the Council's work which they either considered to be wasted effort or dominated by fundamentalist Sunni Islam. The remaining three were "seculars" nominated to higher posts in the Government.

During the next period (1981-84) five members resigned, two of them being Brelwis and the others Shia. All of them were disappointed by the policy of the Government and the Council.

Although the *'ulamâ'* of the Council were themselves secularized in the broadest sense, pursuing an integrationist Islamization, the high ratio of resignations of Islamic scholars reflects a growing opposition within the body. But the opposition hardly transcended their own individual positions—with regard to their own school of thought and the respective interpretation of Islam. This became specially apparent for the Shia on occasion of the Zakat and Ushr Ordinance 1980. The *shî'î* members Mujtahid Jafar Husain and Sayyid Muhammad Radi turned their backs on the Government because it was not recognizing the rights of the *Ja'farî fiqh* and because they did not agree with the Sunnite policy of Islamization.[77]

At the same time Mufti Muhammad Husain Naimi (Brelwi) left the CII. He declared that the work done in the Council was of no use and its proposals were not implemented.[78] He wanted to create a precedent and demonstrate to Zia ul Haq that the President could not do anything he liked with the *mawlânâs*, even if he offered them the facilities of international hotels.[79] During the 'Ulamâ' Convention 1980 Mufti Naimi had criticized that the Council's proposals had not been implemented faithfully and that the Zakat and Uṣhr Ordinance 1980 differed considerably from the one the CII had suggested.[80] 'Allamah Ahmad Said Kazimi (Brelwi) also resigned due to similar problems in 1981.[81]

While most Brelwi and Shia members of the Council resigned, those of Deobandis, Ahl-e Hadith and Jamā'at-e Islāmî stayed on.[82] Only a few "seculars" resigned. While the 'ulamâ' showed their disappointment with official policy through their resignation, the "seculars" manifested their support by accepting higher Government posts.[83]

Obviously, the chairmanship of Tanzil al-Rahman from May 1980 ushered in a new era of the CII, since the members were now more articulate and critical about official policy than had been the case under the chairmanship of Justice Muhammad Afdal Chimah (who was suggested as chairman of the Council by Mawlana Ansari, a close friend and advisor of President). Justice Chimah did not make any attempt to denounce or criticize publicly the policy of Islamization. It was different under Tanzil al-Rahman who, it is believed, was introduced to the Council by the then Minister of Justice A.K. Brohi.[84]

While the interests of the Council were not at variance with those of the Government during the sixties and seventies, if that was the case now. This became apparent in the divergence between the Council reports and the implementation of Islamic measures by Government. Only recommendations concerning ritualization of religion, such as prayers, parts of the penal law (although in a different way from what the Council had suggested), holidays, Zakat (also not implemented in the way the Council had proposed) and some changes were taken up. None were aimed at changing existing structures. Thus, including the Chimah period 1977-80, the Council had worked in line with the Government more or less in a conformist way, be it in the form of ijtihâd, or with the help of hiyal.

Chimah's detachment from the body had at least two reasons: his 3-year tenure had ended and he had the prospect of becoming a delegate to the Mu'tamar al-'âlam al-Islâmî.[85] Thus, it was not until the time of Tanzil al-Rahman that the Council became a kind of opposition to the Government. His position towards official policy is reflected in many speeches.

In 1982, on the occasion of the third Pakistan-French Colloquium in Islamabad, Tanzil al-Rahman expressed his fear that Islamization was not implementable due to different Islamic interpretations prevalent in Pakistan.[86] Moreover, in his speech during the 'Ulamâ' Convention 1984 he criticized the Government for its weak performance in the field of Islamic economics and the educational system. He maintained that the administration continued to neglect the Council's proposals, especially with reference to the un-Islamic economic reforms and the un-Islamic educational system.[87]

The criticism of some *'ulamâ'* during the 'Ulamâ' Convention 1980 had prompted Zia ul Haq to suggest in his final address the publication of the Council's reports so that everybody could consult them and discuss the issues raised. He stressed, however, the advisory character of the Council and said that its proposals were to be considered with reference to administrative, economic and political aspects. "If a proposal of the Council is not implemented immediately, it does not mean, for God's sake, that Government is not interested in its implementation. The reason for that lies rather in administrative or financial problems"[88] (he did not mention political problems). The Council itself also voiced its demand to publish its reports, often through the press.[89]

Despite the strong impact of secular forces on the Council, neither its reports nor the religious scholars seem to be really accepted in the secular political arena. Not only the Government and administration, but also the members of the then National Assembly, which was elected in 1985, did not agree with the Council's activities. At the time of discussing the annual reports of the Council in the National Assembly, the members did not seem to be interested and left the house after boycotting the house, and a quorum could not be maintained.[90]

THE BUDGETS OF THE CII

The support to the Council during the Bhutto regime after 1975, and specially during the Zia era after 1977 meant increasing financial provisions.[91] In 1975/76 the financial allocations for the Council increased by 68 per cent in comparison to the preceding year (from Rs. 258,100 to Rs. 433,500). The rate of increase from 1975/76 to 1976/77 was only 12.2 per cent. However, the Council remained more busy during 1975-76 as compared to the preceding year and immediately after that.

With the coming to power of Zia ul Haq, the budget of the Council increased 21-fold: from Rs. 486,600 in 1976/77 to Rs. 10,591,000 in 1977/78. A considerable amount was reserved for the setting up of the panel of Bankers and Economists which produced a report on Islamic economic system.

After this boom the allocations decreased gradually: from Rs. 5,965,000 in 1979/80 to Rs. 4,229,000 in 1980/81; and only Rs. 2,283,000 were shown as revised receipts in 1981-82.

It is remarkable that the main part of the Council's allocation went into "Commodities and Services" (1979/80: 83 per cent; 1980/81: 75.3 per cent; 1981/82: 44.8 per cent). Previously (until 1979), this part was claimed as "Miscellaneous Expenditure." Thus, the real Council receipts increased, but there seems to be enough money to finance different projects, experts and foreign visits, for which the money was spent out of "Commodities and Services".

CONCLUSION

Despite the permanent presence of '*ulamâ*' in the Council and their increasing ratio, and the fact that the CII spent more time on its work than in the preceding years, and also Government's strategy of coopting Islamic scholars according to their political power and influence, the fact remains that the '*ulamâ*' were merely tolerated by the State. This becomes evident in different speeches which Zia and other members of the Cabinet made at '*ulamâ*' and *mashâ'ikh* conventions and other official forums. It is said that even the President, not to speak of the bureaucracy becoming uneasy about the '*ulamâ*', was not prepared any more to appoint any divines and theologians to the Council.[92] He thought they were not concerned with contemporary issues but were only interested in being respected by their students. Moreover, the President is said to have expressed his utter disappointment regarding the '*ulamâ*' during the activities of the National Committee on Dînî Madâris 1979.[93]

The isolation of the '*ulamâ*' from the Council, however, was not possible since they enjoyed mass support. The Government depended on the collaboration of the '*ulamâ*' and tried to accommodate their main leaders.

Since there exist an integrationist version of Islamization in Pakistan, the '*ulamâ*' and divines coopted by the Government in order to legitimize its policies are affiliated to the modern sector or at least are oriented towards it. The impact of the few exceptions is confined to an individual level. Only in case of the Shia, as a reasonably organized minority, could the opposition mobilize mass support and develop into a kind of isolationist or counter-integrationist movement. A unified reaction in the Council, however, has not been developed yet.

A non-conformist CII could mean a strong Islamically (traditionalist) legitimized moral pressure to the de-Islamizing policy of Government. Apparently, members of the Council are alienated from each other to a high degree and are not able to transcend their different problems of interpretation of Islamic law. They cannot agree on a common platform and build up a common opposition in order to safeguard the interests of the traditional sector of society. The heterogeneity of Islam in Pakistan is apparent. Because the members of the CII are integrated to a certain degree, the administration has little difficulty in using it as an instrument for its own purposes.

NOTES

1. Leonard Binder, *Religion and Politics in Pakistan*, Berkeley, 1961, pp. 116-154.
2. See also Fadl Karim Shaikh/Asrar al-Rahman Bukhari, *Pâkistân kê idârê*, Lahore, n.d. about 1983, p. 66 (Urdu); this was meant for the Constitution of 1952. Contrary to this the Constitution of 1956 did not mention a body like the 'Ulamâ' Board (ibid.). For a discussion on the Islamic Constitution and the 'Ulamâ' Board cf. Leonard Binder, *Religion and Politics*, pp. 155-182.
3. The chairman, Shabbir Ahmad Uthmani (Deobandi), had been an active member in the Muslim League before partition. During the forties he was opposed to the anti-Pakistan policy of the Deoband seminary (cf. Ziya-ul-Hasan Faruqi, *The Deoband Seminar and the Demand for Pakistan*, Lahore, 1960, pp. 102f and p. 119; for the seminary cf. B.D. Metcalf, *Islamic Revival in British India, Deoband, 1860-1900*, New Jersey, 1982) and had been chairman of the pro-Pakistani Jam'îyat-e 'Ulamâ'-e Islâm, a kind of schism of the Jam'îyat-e 'Ulamâ'-e Hind. In Pakistan he became Shaikh al-Islâm (cf. L. Binder, *Religion and Politics*, pp. 156ff). Zafar Ahmad Ansari (b. 1905, Deobandi sympathiser)—former office secretary of the Muslim League—was the Board's secretary. He was not an *'âlim* in the strict sense. Other members were Mufti Shafi (Deobandi), likewise a member of the League and an important religious personality. He was given the title Muftî-e Azam-e Pâkistân. Mufti Jafar Husain was a prominent representative of the Shia, while Dr. Hamidullah was regarded to be an Islamic modernist. The East-Pakistani Muhammad Akram Khan was also committed to the Muslim League. Prof. Abd al-Khaliq, a Bengali, had to represent the Bengali interests. As the Board's highest authority Sayyid Sulaiman Nadawi (1884-1953) from Lucknow in India was to be invited [cf. Manzooruddin Ahmed, "Political Role of the Ulama in the Indo-Pakistan Sub-continent", in *Islamic Studies (IS)*, vol. 6, no. 4, Islamabad, 1967, p. 334 and L. Binder, *Religion and Politics*, pp. 155-182]. As an adabî, Nadawi was active in the Khilafat-movement and, as a supporter of the celebrated Shibli Numani (1857-1914), had been editor of *ma'ârif* from Azamgarh.
4. Muhammad Miyan Siddiqi, in *Fikr o Nazr, nifâz-e sharî'at nambar*, vol. 20, nos. 9-10, March-April, 1983, Islamabad, 1983, p. 164 (Urdu).
5. BPC, the members of which represented a Western oriented secular elite of the Constituent Assembly (mostly from the Muslim League), wanted to set up a state in line with Western democratic systems.

6. M. Ahmed, "Political Role" in *IS*, p. 335; Afzal Iqbal, *Islamization in Pakistan*, Lahore, 1986, pp. 58ff and Y.V. Gankovski and V.N. Moshalenku, *The Three Constitutions of Pakistan*, Lahore, 1978, pp. 20-26.

7. For the criticism of the '*ulamâ*' on the BPC-report cf. A.A. Maudoodi, *Islamic Law and Constitution*, Lahore, 1969, pp. 319-351. The majority of them were those Islamic scholars, who had elaborated the famous *22-Points*. For the role of '*ulamâ*' in Pakistani politics refer also Aziz Ahmad, "Activism of the Ulama in Pakistan", in N.R. Keddie, ed., *Scholars, Saints, and Sufis*, 1978, pp. 258-272.

8. Cf. G.W. Choudhury, *Constitutional Development in Pakistan*, Lahore, 1969, pp. 185f.

9. The Board, it is told, was dissolved because of the death of its chairman Sayyid Sulaiman Nadwi and because of Dr. Hamidullah's stay in Paris (cf. Siddiqi, in *Fikr o Nazr*, op. cit., p. 164).

10. Binder, *Religion and Politics*, p. 160. Thus, the solutions of conflicts were mere individual attempts, based on subjectivity, rather than built on a general consensus.

11. Riaz Ahmad Syed, *Pakistan on Road to Islamic Democracy, Referendum 1984*, Islamabad, 1986, pp. 21-27 and Iqbal, *Islamization*, pp. 51f; see also Maudoodi, *Islamic Law*, pp. 321-325 and Binder, *Religion and Politics*, pp. 219-232.

12. Tanzil al-Rahman, in *Hurmat, Nifâz-e nizâm-e Islâm nambar*, vol. 20, no. 25/26, Rawalpindi, August 1983, pp. 193ff (Urdu); Tanzil ur Rahman, *Islamization in Pakistan*, Council of Islamic Ideology, GoP, Islamabad, 1984, p. 2; Tanzil al-Rahman, in *Fikr o nazr, nifâz-e sharî'at nambar*, vol. 20, no. 9-10, March-April 1983, Islamabad, 1983, pp. 153-162 (Urdu), as well as Sh. Shaukat Mahmood, *The Constitution of Pakistan* (as amended up to date), Lahore, 1965, pp. 557ff. In Article 199 it is called "Advisory Council of Islamic Ideology", ACII; cf. *Pakistan Times*, 23.7.1962, "CII Eight persons were selected".

13. Choudhury, *Constitutional*, p. 184.

14. M. Ahmed, "Political Role", in *IS*, p. 339; the Urdu daily *Anjâm* (26.7.1962) gives an account of Abu al-Ala Mawdudi's opposition to the Council; with this institution the Government was planning to finally resolve the Islamic dream. For the Jamâ'at-e Islâmî's opinion on the CII cf. *Dawn*, 4.8.1962. Some members of the Jamîyat-e 'Ulamâ'-e Islâm (JUI) also criticized the composition of the Council and demanded an adequate "representation of ulamâ". The JUI even planned to set up an unofficial Council in August 1962, in order to scrutinize the ACII's proposals and recommendations; cf. *Dawn*, 6.8.1962 and *Nawâ'-e Waqt*, 6.8.1962 (Urdu).

15. This was the case with Dr. Fadl al-Rahman in 1969.

16. The population did not react to the 15 questions, which were published in the daily newspapers; for example *Dawn*, 7.9.1963.

17. GoP, *Annual Report of the Proceedings of the Advisory Council of Islamic Ideology for the year 1966*, n.p., n.d., p. 28 (henceforth *ARPACII* 19XX).

18. *ARPACII*, 1967, n.p., n.d., p. 16.

19. Op. cit., p. 17. The drafted questionnaire is published in *ARPACII*, 1966, n.p., n.d., pp. 65f.

20. GoP, CII, *Consolidated Recommendations on the Islamic Economic system*, Islamabad, 1983, pp. 4-10 (Urdu/English) (henceforth *CRIECS*).

21. *Morning News*, 3.3.1963 and *ARPACII*, 1966, pp. 27-30 and pp. 65-67.

22. Christine Gieraths and Jamal Malik, *Die Islamisierung der Wirtschaft in Pakistan unter Zia ul Haq*, Bad Honnef, 1988, pp. 9-29 and pp. 65-125.

23. *The Constitution of the Islamic Republic of Pakistan 1973*, Article 228 (3).

24. Mahmood, *The Constitution*, p. 558, Article 202 (3).

25. *The Gazette of Pakistan (TGoP)*, Islamabad, May 18, 1974, pp. 771ff.

26. Cf. ibid.; also Mahmood, op. cit., p. 560 and Muhammad Khalid Masud, "Islamic Research Institute: An historical analysis", in *IS*, Islamabad Supplement, 1976, pp. 38ff as well as *Handbook and Masterplan of Islamic Research Institute*, Islamabad, n.d.

27. *ARPACII, 1971*, n.p., n.d., p. 2.

28. Ayub Khan, *Friends not Masters*, Oxford, 1967, pp. 194-204.

29. Newspaper clippings looked at in the Press Information Department, Islamabad, in 1985 on the CII. Until 1972 the Council had "islamized" some volumes of the Pakistan Legal Code and suggested them to the Government. Besides this, 24 proposals were made concerning interest, Zakat, reform of the curricula in schools and observance of Ramadân, etc. Cf. Tanzil al-Rahman, in *Hurmat*, op. cit., p. 194.

30. Cf. Article 228 and 230 of the Constitution of 1973; see also Anwar Syed, *Pakistan, Islam, Politics and National Security*, Lahore, 1984, p. 146 and Tanzil ur Rahman, *Islamization*, pp. 2f.

31. *The Constitution of the Islamic Republic of Pakistan 1973*, article 230 (4) (henceforth *TCIRP* 1973).

32. Cf. also Tanzil al-Rahman, in *Hurmat*, op. cit., pp. 193f. Bearing this in mind, the Islamization under Zia was only the consequent policy laid down by the constitution of 1973.

33. Cf. *TCIRP 1973*, Article 228 (2).

34. This opinion is shared also by Syed, *Pakistan*, op. cit., p. 146.

35. As for example the introduction of the national dress, rules of prayers for the civil servants, annual secret reports on the Islamic conduct of civil servants, examinations in Islamic subjects for the public service, penalty in case of adultery (*zinâ*), prohibition, Friday to be holiday, Zakat and Ushr, interest-free banking as well as the elimination of prostitution, etc., see Tanzil al-Rahman, in *Hurmat*, op. cit., p. 194.

36. He himself stands for a more *fundamentalist* Islam with modernist tendencies. During the sixties he had been a leading member of the Jamâ'at-e Islâmî; see also his critique in *Jam'at-e Islâmî 'awâmî 'adâlat meñ*, Lahore, 1973 (Urdu).

37. See also the Urdu dailies *Jang, Mashriq* and *Nawâ'-e Waqt*, 6 and 8.4.1975 and *The Sun* and *New Times*, 6.4.1975.

38. Administratively, the Council is connected to the Ministry of Religious Affairs. In March 1978 it was constituted as an autonomous institution and only in regard to "conduct of Government business" was attached to the Ministry of Religious Affairs (cf. *Pakistan Times* and *Dawn*, 16.5.1978). The autonomy was based on the chairman's authority to appoint members at his own discretion, while nominations of officials were usually made by the Public Service Commission (interview with Abd al-Malik Irfani in Oct./Nov. 1984 in Islamabad). *De facto* and *de jure* it is the President who appoints both members and chairman, viz., Article 228 (2) of the Constitution. The merely formal autonomous character of the Council was once again pointed out by Zia ul Haq in 1981, when he declared, that "the Islamic Council was an advisory institution and the work of such an institution lies in advising us" [cf. Diya al-Haq, *Naw tashkîl-e islâmî nazariyâtî kawnsil, iftitâhî ijlâs*, Islamabad, 22.6.1981, GoP, Islamabad, n.d., p. 7 (Urdu)]. The central position of the President regarding the Council became apparent once more in 1982, when Zia ul Haq changed Article 228 (4) of the Constitution. Originally it is said that the chairman had to be a Justice of the Supreme Court or High Court. Zia now decided that "the President shall appoint one of the members of the Islamic Council to be the chairman thereof" (cf. *TGoP*, Extraordinary Part I, 22.9.1982; Constitution Fourth Amendment Order 1982). This most probably aimed at installing Mawlana Ansari as the new chairman, who, however, refused due to several reasons (Information by a former leading member of the International Islamic University, Islamabad in Oct. 1985).

39. For example *Mashriq*, 1.6.1981 (Urdu) and *Pakistan Times*, 23.6.1985 for Tanzil al-Rahman; *Pakistan Times*, 24.6.1981 for Syed Shams al Haqq Afghani; *Imrôz*, 21.6.1981 (Urdu), for Zafar Ahmad Ansari and Dr. Ashraf Ali Hashimi; *Imrôz*, 27.6.1981 (Urdu) and *Pakistan Times*, 1.7.1981 for Sayyid Muntakhib al-Haq and Qadi Said Allah (for the latter cf. also *Pakistan Times*, 1.6.1981); *Pakistan Times*, 24.6.1981, for Mawlana Hanif; *Pakistan Times*, 25.6.1981, for Dr. Ziauddin Ahmed; *Pakistan Times*, 29.6.1981, for Dr. A.W.J. Halepota; *Pakistan Times*, 2.7.1982, for Seyed Najmul Hasan Kararvi; this listing is by no means complete.

40. Mahmood, *The Constitution*, p. 559, Article 204 (3).

41. Provisional Constitution Order 1981, Article 230 (3) as well as *TCIRP 1973*, ibid.

42. Tanzil al-Rahman, in *Hurmat*, op. cit., pp. 194f.

43. *Pakistan Times*, 8.10.1977 and GoP, *Islâmî nazarîyâtî kawnsil kî sâlânah repôrt*, 1977-78, Islamabad, n.d., passim (Urdu) (henceforth *INKSR*, 19XX).

44. Cf. *Imrôz* 15.10.1977 (Urdu); *Jasârat* 16.10.1977 (Urdu) and *CRIECS*, pp. 19-21 (Urdu/English). The members of this Panel were usually trained abroad having degrees in economics, etc. Only a few of them had access to Islamic sources since they hardly knew Arabic. For a discussion on the results of the Panel cf. Gieraths and Jamal Malik, *Die Islamisierung der Wirtschaft*, pp. 65-70.

45. *CRIECS*, pp. 26-41 (Urdu); the three *'ulamâ'* were all inclined towards fundamentalism and reform—Mufti Sayyid Siyah al-Din Kakakhel (Deobandi/Jamâ'at), Muhammad Husain Naimi (Brelwi) and Taqi Uthmani (Deobandi). The reaction to the questionnaire was, however, not mentioned in the media. One has to bear in mind that even among the traditionalists of the Deobandi school of thought there is a *salafî* or fundamentalist branch. One major institution following on these principles is the Dâr al-'Ulûm Haqqânîyah in Akora Khattak, Peshawar; cf. chapter VI.

46. *Pakistan Times*, 7.2.1979. Saudi aid played a prominent part in this, financially as well as academically. Cf. *INKSR, 1978-79*, Islamabad, n.d., pp. 371-374 (Urdu). Besides these conceptual activities the CII warned the people to ". . . beg for forgiveness for 30 years' sins" (*Pakistan Times*, 14.11.1977).

47. Cf. *'Ulamâ' Kanwenshan 1980 and 1984, taqârîr o tajâwîz*; Islamabad, 1980 and 1984, pp. 11-21 and 127-138 respectively. Urdu (henceforth *UC*, 1980 and 1984). The conference proceedings are not available to the public, while for example "Hurmat", "Fikr o Nazr" and "Islamization in Pakistan" all by Tanzil al-Rahman are open to everybody. The criticism of the chairman of CII, Dr. Tanzil, who is not a religious scholar in the traditional sense is, however, not apparent in the latter three sources, while at the "Ulamâ' Kanwenshan" he severely criticized Government.

48. President's Order No. 16 from 1980 of 30.11.1980.

49. The All Pakistan Legal Decisions D.L.D. 1981, vol. XXXIII, Lahore, p. 332; *TGoP*, Extraordinary, Part I, Nov. 30th, 1980; Tanzil ur Rahman, *Islamization*, pp. 3ff and Provisional Constitution Order 1981, Article 228 (2).

50. For example a certain John Harsh, Counsellor to the American Embassy in Islamabad, on Nov. 24th, 1981. Cf. *INKSR*, 1981-82, Islamabad, n.d., p. 285 (Urdu).

51. For a discussion on salaffism and neo-salaffism see Reinhard Schulze, "Die Islamische Weltliga (Mekka) 1962-1987", in *Orient*, 29 (1988) 1, pp. 58-67.

52. A detailed analysis of the personnel has been made in Appendix A.

53. For the activities of the Auqaf Department set up in 1960 cf. chapter III. On the Zakat system in general and *'ulamâ'* in particular cf. chapters IV and V.

54. *INKSR, 1981-82*, Islamabad, n.d., p. 311 (Urdu).

55. Op. cit. p. 57 and pp. 312-317. The members of the committees under Ansari were mainly recruited from the colonial sector and from professional groups tending towards it. There seems to be a direct link between chairman Ansari and Saudi Arabian interests as they are propagated by the Râbitat al-'âlam al-Islâmî; he had been visiting this institution in Mecca frequently (cf. op. cit., p. 317).

56. Op. cit., p. 318.

57. Op. cit., pp. 332ff.

58. GoP, *Report of the Special Committee of the Federal Council on the Form*

and System of Government in Pakistan from the Islamic Point of View, Islamabad, n.d., pp. 8f (English/Urdu).

59. Op. cit., pp. 11 and 30.

60. Op. cit., pp. 17f.

61. GoP, CII, *Constitutional Recommendations for the Islamic System of Government,* Islambad, 1983, pp. 7, 11, 12, 21 (English/Urdu).

62. Op. cit. pp. 23 and 28ff.

63. Its members were either nominees of the CII or had been part of the Committee of Federal Council in spring 1983. See GoP, *Ansari Commission's Report on Form of Government,* Islamabad, 1983.

64. Op. cit., p. 12.

65. Op. cit., p. 66.

66. Op. cit., pp. 14ff and 24ff.

67. Op. cit., p. 36

68. Paradigmatically, the criticism of Mahmud Ahmad Ridwi (Brelwi), who was very much concerned about the Deobandis, specially in regard to the Waqfs (cf. *Ridwân,* Hizb al-Ahnaf, vol. 38, no. 4/5, Lahore, March 1984, pp. 22f (Urdu). In fact, there have been great controversies between the "puritans" (Deobandis, Jamâ'at-e Islâmî and Ahl-e Hadith) and the representatives of popular Islam (Brelwis and Shî'î) in India and Pakistan.

69. This has been elaborated on the basis of religious schools as well as curricula of the CII-*'ulamâ'* indicated, as given in Hafiz Nadhr Ahmad, *Jâ'izah-e Madâris-e 'Arabîyah Islâmîyah maghribî Pâkistân,* Liyalpur, 1960 (Urdu) and Hafiz Nadhr Ahmad, *Jâ'izah-e madâris-e 'arabîyah maghribî Pâkistân,* Lahore, 1972 (Urdu) as well as GoP, Ministry of Religious Affairs, *Repôrt qawmî kamîtî barâ-e dînî madâris Pâkistân,* Islamabad, 1979 (Urdu).

70. This has been discussed at some length in S.J. Malik, "Islamization of the Ulama and their places of learning in Pakistan 1977-1984", in *Asien,* no. 25, October 1987, pp. 41-63.

71. GoP, CII, *Consolidated Recommendations of the CII relating to Education in Pakistan, 1962 to 1982,* Islamabad, 1982, (Urdu/English), pp. 29, 31, 52ff et passim (Henceforth *Consolidated*).

72. *Consolidated,* pp. 34f.

73. The report is popularly known as the *Halepota Report.* Cf. chapter V.

74. *Consolidated,* pp. 44f here p. 46. "The fact is that the personal interest of the President eased the decision (i.e. to recognize degrees of Dînî Madâris as equivalent to B.A. and M.A. of the UGC" (op. cit., p. 45, Urdu).

75. *Consolidated,* p. 32 et passim.

76. *Al-Baiyanât,* "Binorî nambar", Jâmi'ah al-'Ulûm al-Islâmiyyah, Karachi, 1978, pp. 10f, 49, 51, 83 and pp. 318-323 (Urdu).

77. *Morning News,* 5.5.1980. Allamah Karrarwi, another Shî'î member of the CII, is said to have resigned due to failing eyesight in 1981. Cf. *INKSR, 1981-82,* Islamabad, n.d., p. 16 (Urdu).

78. *Nawâ'-e Waqt,* 13.5.1980 (Urdu).

79. Interview with Mufti Naimi in Lahore in December 1985.

80. *UC*, 1980, p. 165 (Urdu).

81. *Nawâ'-e Waqt*, 13.5.1981 (Urdu) and *INKSR, 1981-82*, Islamabad, n.d., p. 293 (Urdu).

82. This, however, does not imply that the Deobandis totally conform with Government's policy. We may observe different sections among the schools of thought. For instance, some Deobandis adhere to the non-conformist Fadl al-Rahman group, while others follow the Darkhwâstî wing. The majority of the Brelwis, on the other hand, do cooperate with Islamabad.

83. This is specially true in the case of Mr. A.K. Brohi, who in 1978 became Federal Minister for Religious Affairs and Mr. I.H. Imtiazi, who became Administrator General of Zakat in 1980.

84. Tanzil was to chair the Islamic Law Cell established under Law Ministry in October 1979 in order to scrutinize the somewhat unclear suggestion of the Council concerning Islamization. It is said that Tanzil was interested to do this job in his capacity as a judge, for which he was then nominated judge of the Sindh High Court and thus was authorized to chair the CII.

85. He was appointed to the post of President of the *Mu'tamar's* Asiatic Islamic Coordination Council, which was founded in January 1980 in Karachi. I am thankful to Prof. Reinhard Schulze for confirming this information.

86. *Jang*, January 1985, "Compilation of Islamic Law" (Urdu).

87. *UC*, 1984, pp. 131ff (Urdu).

88. *UC*, 1980, p. 236 (Urdu).

89. *The Muslim*, 15.1.1981; *The Muslim*, 11.7.1982, "CII report on Islamization of .banking ignored"; *The Muslim*, 20.7.1982. "Not a very complex PLS system", in which it is said, that the CII report on the economic system was not implemented. Also *The Muslim*, 13.8.1982, "Officialdom's obsession with secrecy". Here the secrecy and refusal of publishing the reports are heavily criticized.

90. National press in January and February 1986.

91. The sources for the following elaboration are different "Federal Budgets" from 1964 to 1982; the respective figures are given under "Ministry of Law and Parliamentary Affairs" and from 1976 under "Ministry of Religious Affairs".

92. Interview on 29.11.1984 in Islamabad with a member of the CII. This was also mentioned by the representatives of the Islamic *avant-garde* (in Dec. 1984 in the Islamic University, Islamabad).

93. According to a high official, Zia did this with the words, "*mêrê bâp awr mêrê bâp dâdê kî tawbah*", crossing his arms and holding his ears with the thumb and the index. *Tawbah* means repentance; here, apparently, a repentance is hinted at, which Zia felt after having committed a big sin, a sin which neither his grandfather nor his father had committed. Because of the gravity of the sin, even they were to show repentance. Thus, he promised to never commit such a grave sin again, namely to rely on religious scholars.

CHAPTER III

ISLAMIC ENDOWMENTS

INTRODUCTION

The position of Islamic endowments (Waqf, pl. Awqâf; property which cannot be transferred and which is therefore inalienable) in Islamization is an interesting topic, which is being obscured by those heading the Islamization campaign. After a short historical outline of Awqâf in British India, this chapter shows how the State policy of integration operates *vis-a-vis* religious endowments challenging the traditional social order and replacing it with agents of bureaucracy. One can argue that an Islamic movement which supports this policy is against Islamic traditions. Further, it is secular and even agnostic to some extent.

Nationalization of Awqâf has a long tradition in other Muslim countries, dating back to the last century in some cases.[1] In Pakistan the State started to take them over only from 1960. This nationalization had three aims: first, the State wanted to extend and protect its interest, since these endowments are often in the form of religious schools, estates and shrines. The shrines are meeting points for large contingents of people, because of the popular cults associated with them. Religious schools are the centres which produce both religious and political leaders. Secondly, the State was interested in the financial resources accruing from the shrines and schools. Thirdly, nationalization meant the bureaucratization of the shrine-culture and of endowments which, in association with *Folk*-Islam, was striving for autonomy.

State intervention or nationalization was followed by reaction on the part of those affected bringing about unions and consolidation of Islamic scholars, the hereditary saints (*pîr, murshid*), the enlightened and their descendants, the *sajjâdah-nashîns*, administrators (*mujâwirs*[2] and *mutawallîs*) and finally the owners of the shrines (*wâqif*). These people were alarmed by the growing influence of the bureaucracy in their material and spiritual life.

HISTORICAL OUTLINE

The regulation of Awqâf goes back to the initiative of Muhammad Ali Jinnah (1867-1948) in British India, although Sayyid Ahmad Khan (1817-1898) had argued on this issue in 1877 and Shibli Numani (1857-1914) had also taken up the matter.[3] In his opening address to the Indian National Congress in 1906, Jinnah pleaded for the restoration of the right of private ownership of Islamic endowments, which had come increasingly under the influence of the British authorities since 1887.[4] The Privy Council had ruled in 1894 that Islamic foundations were to be considered as religious and charitable institutions, and that they should nevertheless be public and not remain in private hands. Thus, they were regarded neither as purely religious nor as purely private, but rather as so-called "mixed endowments".[5] In this manner, the Awqâf were removed from the private ownership of Muslims.[6] Jinnah stated:

If a man cannot make a *wakf alalawlad* (a *waqf* in the name of his children),[7] as it is laid down in our law, then it comes to this, that he cannot make any provision for his family and children at all and the consequences are the breaking up of Mussalman families.[8]

Jinnah, presented a "private member's bill" relating to Waqf to the Imperial Legislative Council in 1909. By 1911 he succeeded in pushing things through, and two years later the Mussalman Wakf Validating Act, 1913 was passed. The Act restored private ownership of waqf.[9]

While Jinnah managed to win over an important section of '*ulamâ*' for pushing through this Validating Act, the majority of Islamic scholars were against his plan. Strangely enough, the traditional upholders of Islamic culture did not have much to say in this matter.[10] It is, therefore, somewhat unclear how the Islamic *avant-garde*, which was constituted by intellectuals, independent persons and traders rather than by the '*ulamâ*', could assert its interests under Jinnah's leadership.[11] Although the application of this law was very limited, its ratification was nevertheless a (legislative) victory of the Muslims over the British. However, as the Act was not retrospective, the Council could still consider endowments created before 1913 to be invalid.[12]

Jinnah's achievement won him the hearts of Muslims.[13] He thus received the support of a sizeable section of the '*ulamâ*' in the Muslim League during the forties.[14]

THE POSITION OF THE SHRINE-SAINTS

Until the intervention of the State in endowments in 1960, the '*ulamâ*' and *mashâ'ikh* (or *pîrs*) were very influential. Their power was religiously legitimized.

The political power of the *pîrs* was used before and during the

Pakistan movement in the thirties and forties by the British and the Muslim League. They were drawn into political events and converted into supporters of centralized politics.[15] There was only a partial political administration of the *sûfîs* and *mashâ'ikh*, although their followers were organized on the pattern of mystical brotherhoods (*turuq*).[16] In Pakistan, only the Jam'iyyat-e 'Ulamâ'-e Islâm (JUI) under the leadership of the Deobandi '*âlim* Shabbir Ahmad Uthmani could, to some extent, assert itself among the *pîrs*, due to its organizational structure, the pattern of which was taken from the Deobandi '*ulamâ*'. Another important institution was the Brelwi-dominated Jami'yyat-e 'Ulama'-e Pakistan (JUP).

Sociologically, the '*ulamâ*' and the leading representatives of *folk*-Islam can be conceptualized as groups with an exclusive life-style, and access to political power. The legal scholars tend to be representatives of urban culture. The representatives of mysticism tend to be mainly from the rural areas.[17] On an ideological plane there are many differences among them, as they do not have any homogeneous doctrine.

The legal scholars concentrate on the Holy Book of Islam. The *mashâ'ikh*, on the other hand, belong to those sections which seek the mystic element beyond all written knowledge.[18] Eighty per cent of the *mashâ'ikh* are, according to their own perceptions, men of knowledge and wisdom (*ahl-e 'ilm wa 'irfân*), while only five to six per cent of the '*ulamâ*' are modern (*jayyid 'ulamâ*').[19] In fact there is a great discrepancy between the representatives of legal- and *folk*-Islam: the '*ulamâ*' are said to have expressed their dissatisfaction over the lack of knowledge among *pîrs* during Ayub Khan's time. The polemics of the '*ulamâ*' against the saints continue even today.[20] Sometimes the animosity between the two groups leads to violent clashes.[21]

A *pîr* or his successor has great economic and social influence over his followers (*murîd*) which is also expressed as a political power.[22]

The prerequisites for becoming a *pîr* do not include theological studies. A *pîr* must have *ma'rifa* (gnosis) and be able to bestow blessings (*barakah*). Nowadays it appears that anyone can become a *sajjâdah-nashîn* (a holder of a shrine) for it apparently does not take much to be able to administer a shrine or waqf. If a person can show that a saint has been buried there or stayed at the very place for a while, or if he himself is a descendant of the Prophet[23] this often constitutes sufficient grounds to be a *pîr*. Due to this and also because the illiterates believing villagers are regarded as servants by the shrineholder (A. Schimmel calls it *pîrism*),[24] there has been a lot of criticism of this development from many quarters apart from the '*ulamâ*', i.e. from secularized quarters as well.[25]

The saint- and shrine-cult is predominant in rural areas, especially where big landholdings prevail. In many cases the local *pîr* is the local landlord or at least is close to him.[26] He guarantees the local villagers' participation in the *barakah*. This is tied to absolute obedience (*itâ'ath*) and the giving up of oneself in favour of the *pîr*.[27] This is manifested in the form of material gifts to the saint:

Reality is to follow the Holy Prophet. For this purpose the discipline of *mashâ'ikh* and *pîrs* is needed. The *shaikh* is the spiritual physician who heals the diseases of soul and body. The *pîr* is the gateway to absorption in the Holy Prophet. Through him we reach the congregation of the Prophet, and to reach this congregation is to become close to God....[28]

This order reminds one of the central position of the *guru* in the Hindu tradition. There also it was maintained that "only through him is the path to salvation accessible".[29] As the first Muslims in the subcontinent were mostly mystically inclined and syncretistically took over many local practices into Islam,[30] it is possible that the centrality of the saints and teachers rests partly on the old Hindu point of view.[31] It was these people who spread Islam in the subcontinent. The shrines often played an integrative function:

For it was through its rituals that a shrine made Islam accessible to nonlettered masses, providing them with vivid and concrete manifestations of the divine order, and integrating them into its ritualized drama both as participants and as sponsors.[32]

It is a well-known fact that the saints with their charisma were often leaders of millenaristic peasant movements[33] who gave the village or members of the mystical order a sense of social security and solidarity, thereby erasing social differences between them.[34]

The shrine cults were restored and caught on, especially in the Punjab,[35] under Moghul rule through the influence of the representatives of the *Chishtiyyah*.[36] Thus, in West Punjab the districts were

dotted with the shrines, tombs of the sainted dead ... and to the shrines of the saints, thousands upon thousands of devotees resort, in the hope of gaining something on the sacred soil. . . .[37]

The cult of saints and the associated folk-piety is especially evident in the countryside of Punjab and Sindh, which have very big landlords and where land-concentration is a crucial feature.[38] Even to this day nearly every Muslim in Pakistan is tied up in one way or the other to a mystical order and is a follower of a *pîr*.[39]

Religious authority of the kind the *pîrs* enjoy corresponds to the notions of the widespread Brelwi school of thought[40] which has a strong inclination towards the cults of saints. It is said that ever since its founding by Ahmad Rida Khan (1855-1919) the members of the Brelwi movement subordinated themselves to the contemporary authorities.[41] The Prophet was also of central importance to them. He is present and all-observant (*hâdir o nâzir*), as can be derived from the theory of *nur muhammadî*, the light of Muhammad. Love for the Prophet is also apparent from the fact that their founder called himself '*Abd al-Mustafâ*'. According to Islamist notions, only god's 99 names can follow the name '*Abd* (slave) and certainly not that of the Prophet. In the eyes of the Deobandis and other "puritans" the name '*Abd al-Mustafâ*' was, therefore, blasphemy (*shirk*) and an anti-Islamic innovation (*bid'a*).[42] This has caused tensions between "puritans" and Brelwis. In fact, the Auqaf Department was told to issue a circular according to which its employees would no longer be allowed to say *durud* (request for mercy upon the Prophet and praise) or *salâm*, which was regarded as *shirk* by puritans. The matter ended in a case before the Federal Shariat Court in 1985, but could not be resolved for good reasons. The circular was withdrawn.[43]

The implicit hierarchy of religious and political systems of authority signified an acceptance of local feudal or even patrimonial structures.[44] The Brelwis are still a symbol of peasant culture which is why they could gain control in the Punjab countryside so easily after Partition.[45] They are staunch followers of the shrine cult whereas the Deobandis, the largest group in Pakistan, who also came from the *Sûfî* orders, reject the developed form of the shrine cult.[46]

THE AUQAF DEPARTMENT

In 1950 a suggestion was made to introduce a Survey Act on Waqfs in order to know the number and quality of the endowments in Pakistan and to nationalize them.[47] This did not happen till the end of fifties, when Javed Iqbal in his book *Ideology of Pakistan* demanded, at the end of the fifties, the abolition of shrines and curbing the power of the *pîrs* and the *sajjâdah-nashîns*.[48] He followed the ideas of his father, the poet-philosopher Muhammad Iqbal (1873-1938), who had criticized the shrine cult and the lower ranks of Islamic scholars. This resulted in the passing of the Auqaf Ordinance 1960.[49]

The "West Pakistan Waqf Properties Rules" of 1960 aimed at curbing the power of the saints and "regulating" the endowments, which were being "exploited" by the *sajjâdah-nashîns*, the *mujâwirs* and the '*ulamâ*'.

According to the Rules, the endowments were to become State property apparently contrary to the Mussalman Wakf Validating Act, 1913. To prevent any kind of criticism by the shrine holders, etc. especially with reference to Jinnah's achievement in 1913, Section 3 of the Mussalman Wakf Validating Act was excluded:

'Waqf property' means property of any kind permanently dedicated by a person professing Islam for any purpose recognized by Islam as religious, pious or charitable, but does not include property of any Waqf such as is described under section 3 of the Mussalman Waqf for the time being claimable for himself by the person by whom the Waqf was created or by any member of his family or descendants.[50]

Hence, the endowments were no longer available for the economic well-being of a Muslim and the State was able to intervene in religious foundations legally without interfering with the Validating Act.

The Central and Provincial Governments were now empowered to look after the "neglected and misused" institutions. This new policy was even propagated in formal schools: "They (awqâf) caused anti-social wastage of national wealth. It was misused by pirs, mutawallis, sajjadanashins and other parasites."[51]

As a rule, however, only profitable endowments were nationalized. The Waqf Properties Ordinance 1961 enabled an administrator to take over a Waqf.

The position of the Administrator Auqaf was strengthened through the years by legislation. This was specially true after 1964.[52]

The bureaucratic character of the new Administrator Auqaf was evident from the fact that he was not required to have any special theological or religious knowledge, although it was clearly necessary in order to deal adequately with Islamic affairs. He only required such qualifications "as may be prescribed by Government" and had to be a Muslim.[53]

Any rejection of the authority of the Administrator was punishable.[54] The absolute authority of the saint or the holder was thus replaced, at least partly, by more or less omnipotent though anonymous governmental authority of the Administrator Auqaf. The difference, of course, was that his power was legitimized not theologically or religiously but only secularly and ideologically.

At first, the Government was not primarily interested in enriching itself through the income of the foundations. Most of the income which accrued to the Auqaf Department was ploughed back into the foundations in the form of salaries for those employed there in order to safeguard their ideological interests. There was otherwise the danger that the *'ulamâ'* would use their religiously legitimized influence among the masses to work against Government intervention. The *khutabâ* (preachers, especially the Friday preachers) and the *a'imma* (the prayer leaders) were also expected to hold the important Friday sermons (*khutbah*) in conformity with the interests of the State, and to ensure that these were supported by the social network of these foundations.[55]

The transformation of the traditional order was made possible through a demystification of those holding these offices.[56]

In the context of the nationalization of religious endowments, an attempt was made, both under Ayub and later under Bhutto, to reduce the traditional religious authority of the shrineholders, by formally propagating an emancipation of the pilgrims to the shrines. In order to do so it was necessary to play down the shrine or at least to represent it as a worldly institution and thus to take away its religious character. Up to this stage the ordinary *murîd* had no direct access to God. The saint was the mediator. The holder of the shrine had taken over the position of the saint and now functioned as the mediator between the pilgrim and the *pîr*. The saint, and therefore the *mujâwir* or *sajjâdah-nashîn,* "monopolized" access to God, and only through him was the path (*tarîqah*) to salvation experienced. This meditating role was now supposed to be rendered superfluous through the activities of the Auqaf Department.

From now on every citizen, provided only that he was a "good Muslim", was supposed to be able to enter directly into a dialogue with God. Thus the saints or shrine holders acquired more mundane features and their annual feasts (arabic *'urs'* literally "marriage", i.e. the union with God)[57] became public holidays and were consequently secularized. The miraculous healing power of the saints was replaced by the building of hospitals in the endowments. In this manner, shrines became catalysts of modernization and limits were placed on the unbridled power of the *'ulamâ'* and holders of shrines. There was to be no mediator between the state and the individual and also none between God and the individual.[58] A new philosophy was created which corresponded to the social and economic aims of the Government. The integration of land and of autochthonous institutions in the expanding capital sphere was necessary for the creation of markets. It reflected the politics of the "Green Revolution" of the sixties.[59]

Till Bhutto's time, nationalized endowments were organized at a provincial level. The nationalization after 1971 brought the foundations directly under the Central Government. The Administrator Auqaf was henceforth called Administrator General of Auqaf for Pakistan and had a greater sphere of influence. The newly introduced obligation of registering the endowments[60] and the power of the Administrator General or of anyone delegated by him "to issue directions for the management etc. of Waqf properties" served to bring the endowments further under the purview of the Government. This was also meant to prevent sectarian activities of the *khutabâ'* and the *a'imma*.[61] Bhutto's administration followed the policies laid down by Ayub.[62]

Under Zia ul Haq the endowments were once again put under the Provincial Governments.[63] As against the earlier Regulation, the Administrator Auqaf of a province had complete control on the endowments.[64] Despite Islamization under Zia, the Administrator was still not required to have any special knowledge of Islamic law.[65]

Yet his legal authority extended to the highest provincial court. He could take over any endowment as defined by section 7 of the Auqaf Federal Control (Repeal Ordinance 1979) through a declaration to that effect,[66] without being in any way legally answerable, thus encouraging arbitrariness. Moreover, Section 20 (2)[67] made it possible to intervene in the Waqf in order to preserve the "sovereignty and integrity of Pakistan" in case of any political agitations, whether in the form of sermons or whatsoever.

Since 1976, the Auqaf Administration has reserved the right to change the curricula of those religious schools which represent endowments.[68] This is an extension of the Jamiah Islamia Regulation of 1963. As is known, religious endowments sometimes take the form of religious schools and mosques. A nationwide control over these institutions was to be achieved through an extensive "clerical" net spreading from the district-*khatîb* and district-*mawlânâ* right to the village-*khatîb*, from province to village. Ayub had already introduced different *khatîb/imâm* schemes which, however, collapsed. Ever since the nationalization in 1960 there was a tendency for religious schools to join in umbrella organizations according to different schools of thought. This restricted the influence of State for the time being. Nevertheless, the Auqaf Department succeeded by 1962 in bringing 247 such schools in Punjab under its surveillance. Thereafter, it was only partially possible to halt State intervention through the formation of umbrella organizations. The network of State control was strengthened, taking over further autonomous institutions. Thus, for example, an Auqaf 'Ulamâ' Board was set up, which had the power to examine new *khutaba'* by any criterion whatsoever and to appoint or dismiss them. In this manner, a conformist Friday sermon was guaranteed in those mosques which were tied to the department.

The Islamization of the seventies led, among other things, to a Seminar on the management and development of Auqaf properties in August 1984 in Jeddah. It aimed at enhancing the number of nationalized endowments and to improve their quality and resources.[69]

One may observe an increase in receipts from the endowments in absolute terms during the last eight years. The reason for this probably lies in the authoritarian handling of shrines and other foundations by the Government. It could, however, also result from the fact that the Auqaf Department sold some of the nationalized endowments to State Development Authority (such as the Lahore Development Authority) or even returned some to former *mutawallîs*.[70] The return of Waqf could be regarded as a policy of reconciliation with respect to the politically restive former shrineholders, but it is also possible that these Awqâf were simply not profitable.[71]

The criticism of the '*ulamâ*' and the *sajjâdah-nashîns* was noticeable in the press. It reached a climax in 1960 and 1969,[72] and received a new spurt under Zia's regime. The Government reacted by mobilizing those sections of the '*ulamâ*' which conformed with its policies. More than 200 '*ulamâ*' from Hazara district (from where Ayub Khan originated) under the leadership of Abd al-Salam Hazarwi,[73] praised the activities of the Auqaf Department.[74]

The integrationist policy of the different regimes finally led to a "Mashâ'ikh-Convention" in 1980 in the Capital. This enabled the State to convince a large section of the *pîrs* to its strategies.[75]

In terms of basic content Ayub's secularization policy was carried on by Zia ul Haq. A booklet on shrines published by the Pakistan Tourist Development Corporation reads:

Human being is made of two entities, namely body and soul. Of these, the soul is more important. Islam has underlined the need to develop the soul by prayers and meditation. Those who train their souls in this manner are called 'Sufi'.[76]

Hence every citizen was able to become a *Sûfî*.

The Zia regime, in pursuance of the modernization of the earlier regimes, attempted to open the holy shrines to international tourism. The booklet listed 137 shrines,[77] out of which 100 are described in detail. The condition for the listing of the shrines in the pamphlet is that they would be in a moderate condition and accessible to foreign tourists. This presupposes an effective administration which in turn means that those shrines must be well integrated.

In the course of time the traditional, sacred and autochthonous character of the shrines is bound to suffer due to tourism, although many people still undertake a lot of difficulties in order to visit them, as they do especially at the time of *'urs*. Visits during *'urs* can be compared to a pilgrimage to Mecca (*hajj*), a mini-*hajj*,[78] so to speak. The loss of their exclusively sacred character will ultimately lead to further extensions of State control. In the short run, however, the *murîdîn* tend to look upon tourists as a sign of interest in their local shrine.

In spite of the policy of integration and attempts to curb the autonomy of shrines and other endowments, some of them still reflect a politically restive character. In the broadest sense of the word, "un-Islamic" activities taking place around these microcosms of local Islam represent merely the last refuge of the marginalized social groups.[79]

REACTIONS

It was only to be expected that many *'ulamâ'*, and those linked to and profiting from endowments, would protest against these developments.[80] The popular reactions took many forms[81] and resulted in the formation of organizations like the umbrella-organizations of the religious schools, the so called Anjuman-e sajjâdah-nashîn (Society for the heirs of shrine-saints) and the Qâdirî inclined Jam'iyyat al-Mashâ'ikh Pâkistân (JMP), Society of the Mashâ'ikh Pakistan.[82]

The latter was founded in 1963 under the chairmanship of Pîr Dewal Sharif in the context of growing nationalization. Apparently, Ayub Khan had regularly paid homage to this *pîr* who had also a great number of *murîdîn* in the army. Alongside this intertwining of Government and saints, there were also some relations between JMP and the Saudi Arabian Government,[83] which actually represented a more puritan, sober Islam and rejects all forms of saint cult and popular religion. Today, one can consider the JMP a largely conservative and conformist grouping.[84] It derives its strength from the fact that it accepts members of all other *silsilahs* or *turuq*, similar to the *Tarîqah Muhammadiyyah* of the 18th and 19th centuries.[85] However, the members of the JMP are affiliated mostly to the *Naqshbandiyyah* and *Qâdiriyyah*. And it is specially the latter which strongly represents the Brelwis. The apparently close connection of Pîr Dewal Sharif with Government could be seen as a political strategy, namely to work as closely as possible with the politically ruling classes in order to influence them.[86]

These organizations were, however, not strong enough to hinder nationalization. One would have imagined that Waqf-holders had sufficient following to prevent official intervention, specially when the Auqaf

Department took over endowments yielding high incomes[87] and those which did not have a *mujâwir*.[88]

According to the information of the legal adviser of the Auqaf Department, Punjab,[89] there were a dozen appeals against the interventions of the department, pursued up to the Supreme Court until the end of 1985. This indicates clearly the hostility of the foundation-holders to the Government policy. Of the 12 petitions, 9 were rejected and three taken up.[90]

The conflict with the Auqaf Department and the tendentious Court jurisdiction finally led to the condemnation of the Auqaf Department by the Council of Islamic Ideology (CII).[91] According to them, the confiscation of the Waqf by one or more persons or by the State was in contradiction to Shari'a and ought to be revoked. This was an answer to the enquiry of the Cabinet Division and the Ministry of Religious Affairs in May 1980 and in August 1981, with reference to the land reforms (Martial Law Regulation No 115) of 1972. The Waqf estates were to be exempted from the land reforms, according to the CII resolution.[92] This position corresponded to the Mussalman Wakf Validating Act, 1913.

In 1983, the CII put forward the same opinion once again: Waqf cannot be transferred or sold. This denied the handing over of the Waqf or its sale to a third person or institution.

Apparently, the position of the Council reflected public criticism, which was strong at that stage.[93] There were '*ulamâ*' and mystic divines in the CII as well, whose material well-being depended very much on the endowments. Thus, some representatives of the Islamic tradition, who were CII members, could defend their material position and legitimise it according to Islam. Their arguments, however, were not reflected in the Government policies, which tended to be more integrationist and fundamentalist. The Government wanted to limit the influence of Waqf-holders, or, even better, wipe it out wherever possible, in line with *salafî* Islam.

Apart from that, the Federal Shariat Court (FSC) set up in 1981,[94] examined the Waqf Ordinance of 1979 along with all other existing Acts and legitimized the nationalization. According to it, nationalization was not in contradiction with the Shari'a and, consequently, the Court did not suggest any basic changes in the ordinance. Section 16–the sale of Waqf-land–was considered justified as long as "the main purpose of the waqf is served and satisfied".[95] The authorities cited by the FSC often called for a redistribution of the land in favour of the peasants and delivered *fatwâs* to this effect. The fact that the passing of the judgement was carried through in a pragmatic manner, with many otherwise unpopular authors and sources quoted, was not surprising.[96] Thus, once more, the law of necessity prevailed.

The most visible reaction to the policy of integration can, however, be seen in the reduced donations of visitors to shrines. Such receipts decreased specially from 1982, two years after the introduction of the official Zakat and Ushr system. After all, why should the Pakistani Muslim contribute to the shrines when the Government was already taking money away from him via the new Zakat system? Similarly, the religious schools deplored that "since the introduction of the Zakat system ... their source of private donations has dried up".[97]

Apart from that, new shrines were being set up as "anti-shrines", mostly looked after by women.

AUQAF DEPARTMENT AND EDUCATION

The first aspect of eductaional system is the reform of the syllabus by the Auqaf Department according to which the "antique" and outdated curricula of the religious schools had to be modernized and their administration brought under the jurisdiction of the Islamic University Bahawalpur. Consequently, the Jamiah Islamia was founded in 1963 in Bahawalpur, with the object of harmonizing modern and traditional educational systems.

The erstwhile Jâmi'ah 'Abbâsiyyah (founded 1925) enjoyed a good reputation within a section of the 'ulamâ'. Their final examination was considered to be equivalent to a B.A. degree. In the wake of Ayub's "one unit" politics and the dissolution of the princely state of Bahawalpur in the mid-fifties, this school was linked to the Ministry of Education.[98] In 1963 it was brought under the Auqaf Department and it was resolved to merge the Jâmi'ah with other, hitherto private, theological schools.

By 1962, 247 of such schools had been nationalized and brought under the supervision of the department. Nationalization of more schools was hardly possible because of the creation of umbrella organizations of different schools of thought. Many of these schools were later denationalized. This was also the case with the shrines and centres of folk-Islam.

The West Pakistan Jamia Islamia (Delegation of Powers) Regulation, 1968[99] strengthened the position of the Auqaf Department further. Nevertheless, in 1969 only 35 religious schools had found entry into the Bahawalpur scheme.[100] In order to enhance the official sphere, a decree was passed[101] through which the Auqaf Department acquired access to other religious schools which had merged with the Jâmi'ah.[102] This was done through the nationalized Islamic University which revealed the hierarchical relation between the Department, the Jâmi'ah and other religious schools. For the State, however, this meant further success in their intervention into traditional social spheres.

In course of time, this integrated university was forgotten and at present for most of the *'ulamâ'* it represents a sign of warning to what the bureaucratization of traditional institutions can lead to.[103]

Out of the 24 religious schools in Punjab, which were run by the department in 1982, only one offered *dars-e nizâmî*–the classical curriculum in the subcontinent, while in 13, the Koran was read and learnt by heart. The syllabus was supposed to have been reformed.[104] This cannot, however, be confirmed, since the simple recitation of the Holy Book does not point to any reform.

In the Punjab, there were 55 such institutions in 1985 along with the 'Ulamâ' Akademî. With the exception of the Academy, all other institutions were small *hifz* (memorizing Koran) and *nâzirah* (reading Koran) schools, which were, or still are, attached to the shrines. The salaries in these religious schools–one or two teachers per school–are mainly paid by the Auqaf Department.[105]

The *khatîb/imâm* scheme was another means of ensuring that education in traditional institutions followed the requirements of modern, western norms.[106] The Auqaf Department was concerned with enforcing the official ideology in nationalized foundations by appointing correspondingly conformist *khutabâ'* and *a'imma*.

The clause in the Auqaf Legislation since 1976, which suggested a reform in the syllabus in formal and religious schools,[107] found its climax in the setting up of the 'Ulamâ' Akademî.

THE 'ULAMÂ' AKADEMÎ

The 'Ulamâ' Akademî was founded in 1970 in accordance with the demands of the Islamic *avant-garde* during the sixties. In this institution the *a'imma* and *khutabâ'* were to be educated and trained practically with modern ideas under directions of the Auqaf Department.[108] The actual work of the Academy did not, however, start until Zia took office.

The two-year study programme of the 'Ulamâ' Akademî was meant to unite new and old disciplines, i.e. to "enrich" the classical theological syllabus with modern subjects. The precondition for admission was a good grade in the *dars-e nizâmî* or a *fâdil 'arabî*,[109] matriculation or M.A.

Arabic/Islamiyyat or B.A. Arabic/Islamiyyat or the *darjah-e fawqâniyyah*[110] of the Tanzîm al-Madâris al-'Arabiyyah and/or the Wafâq al-Madâris al-'Arabiyyah.[111] The applicant ought not to be over 28 years and was to reside in the Akademi. This was considered to be an essential aspect of the education.[112]

Up to 1982 the 'Ulamâ' Akademî had conducted 10 courses of 6 months each (one course a year) and 233 *khutabâ/a'imma* qualified (i.e. maximum of 30 participants per course).[113]

Along with these courses, the 'Ulamâ' Akademî organized three-month courses for the *mu'adhdhins* (three courses per year). Up to 1982, in altogether 10 courses 79 participants were thus "educated".[114]

All participants were functionaries of the Auqaf Department and were given scholarships.[115] With such integration-courses the interests of the State were meant to reach right down to the local levels.

A committee of the University Grants Commission maintained that the level of education in the subjects of Politics, Economics, Biography of the Prophet, History of Islam, Comparative Religion and also English, Natural Sciences and Islamiyat corresponded to that of the formal colleges. The main reason for this was, it was thought, the lecturers' recruitment from the Government College Lahore and the Punjab University.[116] Through its lecturers, which either belonged to the colonial urban sector or at least to the sector oriented towards it in terms of norms and values integrationist, an attempt was made to modernise members of a traditional society.

The activities of the 'Ulamâ' Akademî were abruptly interrupted in 1982. The chairman of the Akademî, Dr. Yusuf Guraya, had published a book in 1976 which had served as the catalyst. *The History of Mysticism*[117] was presented to the '*ulamâ*' and to various traditional and secular educational institutions by the Islamic Research Institute, an advisory body set up under Ayub Khan. Until 1982, there were no negative reactions to the book.

In the beginning of 1980, a new institution was set up under the aegis of the Auqaf Department, called the markaz-e tahqîq-e awliyyah, which was to conduct studies on *Sûfîs* and mysticism. In the context of Islamization, this must be seen not merely as a concession of State-Islam to folk-Islam, but also as a further attempt to win over and thus integrate *pîrs* and shrineholders with the Central Government. Dr. Guraya was to administer the new institute as its chairman. This, was objected to by the chairman of the markaz. In order to weaken Guraya's authority, a campaign was launched against him and justified by referring to the "un-Islamic" passages in his book, which had so far never been criticized. No "un-Islamic" passages were evident to this present author while reading the book. Guraya merely pointed out to the so-called "un-Islamic" customs in Pakistan, which he connected with the widespread shrine cult; and this was the bone of contention. According to him, the shrine cult represented the feudal character of the country and the concomitant exploitation of the people and their alienation from true Islam. He himself had enjoyed both madrasah education as well as formal/secular education. As an academician previously employed by the Islamic Research Institute and now an administrator, he referred to the position of Ibn Taymiyya (1263-1328).[118] Today both "fundamentalists and even modern authors" refer to Ibn Taymiyya "especially to support their opinions in matters of legal methodology (e.g. the problem of *ijtihâd* and *taqlîd*), in their criticism of the practices of some of the mystical orders and the practice of saint-cults and generally in questions relating to mediators".[119]

Guraya held the view that "*tasawwuf* is one pillar of corruption", and that it guaranteed the *status quo* and lulled the masses. Data Sahib,[120] the saint of the biggest shrine in Lahore, was supposed to bestow *barakah* by which the solving of any problem would be transferred to the hereafter. This did not, however, correspond to the administrator's notion of true Islam. The polemic against him had a massive impact as he rejected the shrine cult and consequently the cult around Data Sahib, although he did not discredit the Saint himself. Thus Guraya's opponents were able to mobilize the masses and bring about a bloody conflict in the neighbourhood of the 'Ulamâ' Akademî between the Brelwis (supporters of the cult), and the Deobandis (opponents of the cult) and other groups. This at first led to the withdrawal of the book (which became available again only in 1985) and then to the removal of the chairman of the 'Ulamâ' Akademî.[121]

The manipulation of peoples' emotions through religious slogans was once again evident. The affair stemming from a personal conflict (the non-acceptance of the chairman), turned political due to the latent conflict between the two main streams of thought: the shrine followers and the "puritans".

ACCOUNTS

The receipts of the Auqaf Department are derived from the following sources:

1. Cash-boxes in shrines (about 50 per cent of the annual income).[122]

2. Income from *nadhrânah* (about 15 per cent).[123]
3. Income from attached businesses (about 5 per cent).
4. Income from rented shops/houses (about 15 per cent).
5. Income from rented agricultural land (about 10 per cent).

These are the general proportions, with some variations from year to year.

The apparently rapid increase in income of the Auqaf Department is due to the huge increase of the cash-box income. This means that compared to preceding years donations increased. At the beginning the growth doubled more or less every five years. The enormous real growth of Waqf incomes between 1960/61 and 1970/71 is, however, conspicuous and must be seen in connection with the increasing nationalization of endowments. During the Bhutto period the real growth fell, however, by nearly 100 per cent.

Since 1980, the data for each year are available. The growth rate has fluctuated between a minimum of 7.1 per cent and a maximum of 35 per cent. If inflation is taken into account this growth is very modest. In the years 1983/84 and 1985/86 even a stagnation of income can be noted.

Although nationalization advanced under Zia ul Haq—more than under Bhutto—and although the people were against these nationalizations, the shrine cult and the donations connected with it remained popular. The contributions in cash were specially high (1983/84: 42 per cent, 1984/85: 46 per cent). Part of the cash donations is remitted by overseas workers belonging mostly to the Punjab. The overall receipts, however, declined significantly.

Since the vast majority of Pakistanis are still "traditional" and a very small section can be considered as secular, shrines and cults around them will remain. The pilgrimage of the *murîdîn* to their chosen *darbars* will also continue and as changing shrines is socially condemned, profitable shrines will most probably remain a good investment for the Auqaf Department. From the decrease in receipts of the Auqaf Department which can be regarded as an indicator of public acceptance of the official policy, one may assume that there is a latent disapproval of the policy on the part of those visiting the shrines and other endowments.

THE STRUCTURE OF INCOME AND EXPENDITURE

The following conclusions regarding structure of income may be drawn taking into account detailed data of the Auqaf Department's budgets[124] as shown in Table 2.

TABLE 2: RECEIPTS AND EXPENDITURE OF THE AUQAF DEPARTMENT,
PUNJAB, 1960-1985 (IN RS.)

Year	Income	Inc. pre. Year	Infl. Rate	Real Increase	Expendit.	Thereof Exord. Expendit.
60-61	2,085,793				349,050	
65-66	3,969,925	90.3%	7.3%	83.0%	1,550,045	
70-71	8,814,284	122.0%	25.3%	96.7%	4,697,594	
75-76	16,378,334	85.8%	178.5%	-92.7%	12,993,226	
80-81	34,911,507	113.2%	63.7%	49.5%	27,311,422	
82-83	47,111,200	34.9%	18.6%	16.3%	46,066,800	
83-84	52,093,599	7.1%	19.1%	-12.0%	36,087,382	14,631,762
84-85	57,612,700	14.2%	9.1%	5.1%	45,977,500	11,140,900
85-86	54,649,400	-0.5%	n.a.	n.a.	40,990,700	13,031,100

Sources: Bujet Mahkamah Awqâf Punjâb barâ-e 1985-86, Lahore, 1986 (Urdu), p. 13;
A. A. Khan: Paper presented at the Seminar on the Management and Development of Awkaf properties at Jeddah, Saudi Arabia, 4.8.-18.8.1984 (mimeo),
p. 13.

Comments: The rate of inflation for "General Wholesale Prices" is calculated on the basis
of Pakistan Economic Survey 1975/76, Part II, p. 65 and Pakistan Economic
Survey 1984/85, Part II, p. 173; these are official rates.
The percentages refer to income only, not to expenditure. Rates for the year
1981-82 were not available.

In some regions, such as the Bahawalpur Zone[125] (districts of Rahim
Yar Khan and Bahawalpur), the percentage of income from cash boxes is
low (18.9 per cent) as compared to leasing land (42 per cent). The
percentage from rents is 27.5 per cent. In the Sargodha Zone (with the
districts of Sargodha, Faisalabad, Jhang and Chiniot tehsil) cash box
income is only 23.9 per cent, while 26.9 per cent comes from leasing and
43.3 per cent from rents.

In the Multan Zone (with the districts of Multan, Muzaffargarh and
Dera Ghazi Khan) the cash box income increases to 39.2 per cent. The
highest income from cash boxes of this zone comes, however, from the
Pakpattan shrine[126] (18.4 per cent = Rs. 1,563,000), whereas the income
from land leasing is even higher (18.8 per cent = Rs. 1,600,000).

Similarly the cash box income in the Central Zone of Punjab (with the
districts of Lahore, Qasur, Sheikhupura, Gujranwala, Sialkot and Okara)
is very high (the highest, 47.6 per cent = Rs. 5,090,750), whereas only 12.6
per cent comes from leasing of land and 31.8 per cent from rents.

In the Rawalpindi Zone (with the districts of Rawalpindi, Jhelum and

Gujrat) incomes from cash boxes go up to 45 per cent, the land-lease contributes only 6.9 per cent and the rents 24 per cent.

The income structure of the endowments reflects the social structure of their environment: in industrial and urban areas the cash box incomes tend to be high, whereas the income from land-leasing and rents tends to dominate in agrarian regions.[127]

The fact that the income from the Lahore Zone and from the Data Darbar in Lahore makes up half of the total Auqaf receipts (Rs. 27,606,900) of which Rs. 20,127,200 comes from the cash boxes, is very revealing. Thus the Auqaf Department receives most of its income from the Lahore region, in which cash box incomes are high. The analysis of the source of income reveals that most of the income is generated from the region itself because the pilgrims mostly hail from the region around the same shrine which means that there is very little transprovincial trade and migration connected with it.

In the analysis of the expenditure, we refer to the expenses of the Auqaf Department mainly (the salaries of the senior employees). This clearly shows that the bureaucracy benefited through the nationalization of traditional institutions.[128]

According to available data, administrative expenditure was Rs. 8,201,458 in 1983/84, Rs. 9,372,240 in 1984/85 and Rs. 10,254,100 in 1985/86 (exclusive of salaries of those directly employed in the endowments).

In 1985/86 the rent of the managers' offices amounted to Rs. 2,025,500, the rent of the district-_khutabâ_ was Rs. 586,700, and on the direct employees of the endowments themselves a sum of Rs. 10,731,740 was spent. The expenditure on administration of both categories of employees thus totalled Rs. 23,598,040, i.e. 57.6 per cent of the total expenditure, which was equal to 43.2 per cent of the total receipts.

The extraordinary expenditures, which on an average, amount to 49 per cent, 24 per cent and 32 per cent for the last three years respectively, were spent on development projects, repairs on endowments, Data Darbar construction and conservation of historically important endowments. One could question these expenditures since normally the Auqaf Department is supposed to repair/conserve the endowments under its control. One might, therefore, assume that very little was done as the maintenance of nationalized endowments was not profitable. It is clear that the expenditure for administration is on the increase while the total expenditure is far behind the receipts. Thus, the official policy is justifiably criticized by those affected by it.

According to the Auqaf Department, its financial resources are very limited and allocations for education and the Islamic mission meagre. Thus, the expenses for *ta'lîm o tablîgh-e dîn* (education and mission) was only Rs. 2.4 million in 1983/84; i.e. only 6.7 per cent of the Department's expenditure (since the mission is included here, the actual amount spent for education is even less than Rs. 2.4 million). This amount includes Rs. 382,500 for the religious schools affiliated to the Auqaf Department and Rs. 250,000 for those religious schools not connected to the Department, which, however, are contributed to by the Provincial Zakat Council.[129] The sum of Rs. 20,000 for the New Muslims (mission) paid by the Provincial Zakat Council is also to be included here. This means that the Auqaf Department had spent only Rs. 1.7 million for education, which is a very small amount compared to the costs for the Sîrat-conferences, the *'ulamâ'* conventions and other ceremonies, borne by the department.[130]

In the area of social welfare, the Auqaf Department helped the poor and needy financially. The percentage of the expenditure for health and social welfare was 20 per cent, i.e. Rs. 7,236,007 in 1983/84. A year later it was Rs. 7,322,900 (now only 15 per cent). One of the most important institutions of public health is the hospital in Data Darbar (Lahore). In 1985/86 Rs. 7,288,400 were invested in it. In the same year only Rs. 369,800 were spent on other hospitals attached to endowments outside Lahore.[131] Added to this was the money spent on the welfare of widows (Rs. 162,400), the handicapped (Rs. 50,000) and *"dahez"*[132] (Rs. 280,000). Apart from this there were other minor expenditures for which Rs. 1,780,00 were spent out of the Zakat Funds.[133] This means that the Auqaf Department itself spent only Rs. 6,410,600 (i.e. 11.7 per cent) for health and social welfare in 1985/86. In this area the Department has done very little. Rather it has tended to dissolve the traditional social formations without replacing them with others.

CONCLUSION

Contrary to the text of the Mussalman Wakf Validating Act, 1913, which the "father of the nation" had pushed through, the State nationalized profitable endowments in order to further its interests. Section 3 of this Act was excluded. It was therefore possible not merely to employ officials to administer Wakfs, but also to identify and neutralize "subversive" tendencies. The administrative control of autochthonous institutions was accompanied by a significant transformation of their foundations. Thus, the sacred shrine-holders (*pîr, mujâwir*, etc.) were, at least formally, replaced by the anonymous State and its agents. Similarly, the bureaucracy and the military attempted to transform religious education in the endowments through changes in the curricula.

These changes did alter the attitudes of the *murîdîn* to a certain extent, compensating for the official policy by a reduction of their contributions and by setting up of new private shrines. However, the rejection of State-power rarely takes any form other than individual protests. In the face of this, the State can afford to restrict its investments to those endowments which earn large incomes. For example, a modern hospital (with possibilities of eye-operations using laser-techniques!) was built in the Data Darbar and its mosque and shrine rebuilt, while other foundations, especially those in rural areas, decayed.

The installation of cash boxes in shrines proved very profitable for the Auqaf Department. Their contributions are almost 50 per cent of its annual receipts. The structure of income, however, differs from region to region, reflecting its social composition.

Sectarian conflicts increased during Zia regime. This gave the Government the excuse to nationalise more foundations and to strengthen its own control; all this with an "Islamically legitimized" goal of preserving Pakistan's integrity.

One can say that the colonial sector successfully absorbs autonomous institutions. It enriches itself, pushes through its ideology and legitimizes through religion. At the same time, traditional organizational structures are dissolved without being adequately replaced. As such, one may conclude that the policy with regard to traditional Islamic institutions actually reflects a high degree of secularism.

NOTES

1. Regarding the nationalization of religious endowments in Afghanistan cf., e.g. Ashraf Ghani, ''Islam and State-building in Afghanistan,'' in *Modern Asian Studies*, vol. 12, 1978, pp. 269-284. For Turkey cf. bibliography, p. 123 in Kemal A. Faruki, *The Evolution of Islamic Constitutional Theory and Practice*, Lahore, 1971. For the nationalization legislation in other Muslim countries see also J. Schacht, *An Introduction to Islamic Law*, Oxford, 1979, pp. 94ff.
2. For this institution cf. Werner Ende's article on *mujâwir* in the *Encyclopedia of Islam*.
3. G.C. Kozlowski, *Muslim Endowments and Society in British India*. Cambridge, 1985, pp. 158ff (*Endowments*).
4. Francis Robinson, *Separatism among Indian Muslims*, Cambridge, 1975, pp. 27 and 197; also S.Kh. Rashid, *Muslim Law*, Lucknow, 1973, p. 150. In

fact, educational system of the Muslims was very much connected with the religious endowments. Between 1828 and 1846, awqâf, was resumed to scholars during the Muslim rule. Thus, W. W. Hunter stated that a large sum "was derived from lands held rent free by Musulmans or Muhammadan foundations.... Hundreds of ancient families were ruined and the educational system of the Musulmans, which was almost entirely maintained by rentfree grants, received a deathblow." (Hunter, *The Indian Musulmans, Are they bound in conscience to rebel against the Queen*, London, 1871).

5. Kozlowski, *Endowments*, p. 60, for the historical development of Waqf cf. Rashid, *Muslim Law*, pp. 140-162.

6. Kozlowski, *Endowments*, pp. 5 and 131-155; also Rashid and S.A. Husain, *Wakf Laws and Administration in India*, Lucknow, 1973, p. 21.

7. A Muslim was authorized to create a Waqf, for among other purposes, the maintenance and support, wholly or partially, for himself, his family, children or descendants, provided it did not violate Islamic injunctions. "A Wakf-alal-aulad can be created for the maintenance and support of the family, children or descendants of the Wakif ....". Cf. Zia ul Islam Janjua, *The Manual of Auqaf Laws*, Lahore, n.d., Part II, p. 60, Section 3 and p. 61, "Validity of Wakf-alal-aulad". Beyond this private waqf there is "charitable" waqf "which is, however, the private *waqf* too, is considered a charity, and the same rules apply to both kinds of *wakf*". (Cf. J. Schacht, *Introduction*, p. 126, note 1.)

8. Jinnah cited in Kozlowski, *Endowments*, p. 187; see also p. 181.

9. Cf. the text of the Act printed in Janjua, *The Manual of Auqaf Laws*, Lahore, n.d., Part II, p. 59 and in Raja Abdul Ghafoor, *Manual of Waqf Laws*, Lahore, 1983, Part I, p. 142.

10. "When it came to the consideration of questions on *awqâf*, the initiative belonged to those most committed to working within the institutional framework established by the British rule", Kozlowski, *Endowments*, p. 177.

11. The divided reaction of British legislators was probably the reason for the passage of the Bill (Kozlowski, op. cit., p. 182.). Another reason could be that the British wished to win the goodwill of Muslims through this move, in consonance with their "divide et impera" strategy. A third possibility for the reprivatization of waqf could be that the British crown could in this manner create a new group of loyalists among the Muslims. This Thesis is elaborated by V.T. Oldenburg, *The Making of Colonial Lucknow, 1856-1877*, New Jersey, 1984. Compare chapter 6 "The city must be loyal", pp. 191-200.

12. Kozlowski, op. cit., p. 188.

13. Afzal Iqbal, *Islamization in Pakistan*, Lahore, 1986, p. 30. The reasons for his commitment were diverse. On the one hand, he probably hoped to save the Waqf of the Bombay magnate Qasim Ali Jairaybhai Pirbhai, on the other hand, he was interested in building up his career. Cf. Kozlowski, op. cit. pp. 152 and 179.

14. David Gilmartin, *Religious Leadership and the Pakistan Movement in the Punjab*, in *ModernAsianStudies*, 13, no. 3, 1979, pp. 485-517 (*Leadership*).

15. Cf. Gilmartin, *Leadership*. For Sindh see Sarah F.D. Ansari, "Sufi Saints, Society and State Power, The Pirs of Sind, 1843-1947" [Ph.D. Royal dissertation, London, 1987 (unpublished)].

16. For brotherhoods cf. J.S. Trimingham, *The Sufi Orders in Islam*, Oxford, 1971.

17. There has, however, been a change during the last two centuries. See Trimingham, *Sufi Orders*, pp. 248-251 et passim.

18. The splitting of esoteric and exoteric had evolved during the first centuries of Islamic rule but was integrated later by men like al-Ghazzali (d. 1111).

    In recent times only a few '*ulamâ*' attempted a symbiosis of esoteric and exoteric like those of Farangi Mahall in Lucknow, cf. F. Robinson, *Separatism*, e.g. p. 419 and also his article, "The 'Ulamâ' of Farangî Mahall and their Adab", in B.D. Metcalf, ed., *Moral Conduct and Authority*, Berkeley, 1984, pp. 152-183.

19. *Jam'iyyat al-Mashâ'ikh Pâkistân*, Islamabad, vol. II, Sept. 1984, p. 6.

20. The case is similar in Iran, cf. Richard Gramlich, "*Die schiitischen Derwischorden Persiens, part II*", in *Abhandlungen für die Kunde des Morgenlandes,* Wiesbaden, 1976, pp. 125, 148, 153, 301 et passim.

21. Cf. below "Ulama Academî".

22. David Gilmartin, "Shrines, Succession, and Sources of Moral Authority", in Metcalf, ed., *Moral Conduct*, pp. 221-240; Adrian C. Mayer, "Pir and Murshid", in *Middle Eastern Studies*, 3/1967, pp. 160-169 and Richard M. Eaton, "The Political and Religious Authority of the Shrine of Bâbâ Farid", in Metcalf, ed., *Moral Conduct* , pp. 333-356; also Eaton, *Sufis of Bijapur 1300-1700*, New Jersey, 1978.

    The saints and shrines played a predominant role in the 1977 elections in Pakistan (cf. *Viewpoint,* Lahore, vol. II, no. 2, p. 11). The *Pîr* of Sial Sharif had an enormous influence in the districts Sargodha and Jhang where the shrine-cult is very popular (cf. Katherine Ewing, "The Politics of Sufism, Redefining the Saints of Pakistan", in *Journal of Asian Studies,* vol. XLII, no. 2, February 1983, p. 257). The shrines played an important role in the Pakistan elections of 1985 as well.

23. Doris Buddenberg, "Islamization and shrines: An anthropological point of view", Paper read at the 9th European Conference on Modern South Asian Studies, July 9-12, 1986; on the *folk*-Islam, cf. Nikki Keddie, ed. *Scholars, Saints, and Sufis*, Berkeley, 1972; F. De Jong, "Die mystischen Bruderschaften und der Volksislam", in W. Ende and U. Steinbach, eds., *Der Islam in der Gegenwart*, Munich, 1984, pp. 487-504. For folk-belief and shrines cf. the anthropological studies in Imtiaz Ahmad, ed., *Ritual and Religion among Muslims in the Subcontinent,* Lahore, 1985.

24. Annemarie Schimmel, *Mystical Dimensions of Islam*, Chapel Hill, N.C., 1975, p. 22.

25. *Istiqlâl,* Lahore, vol. 11/40, 1982, *Mashâi'kh nambar* (Urdu) and the short story *"Bain"* (dirge) by Ahmad Nadim Qasimi, Lahore, 1985 (Urdu), where the saint-cult is strongly criticized. For a German translation of "dirge" see Jamal Malik, in *Sudasien* (Dortmund), no. 7, 1990. For Qasimi refer S.J. Malik, "Urdu Kurzgeschichten, Ahmed Nadim Qasimi, in *Pakistan Destabilisierung durch Kontinuitat? Eine Dokumentation des Sudasienburo,* Wuppertal, March 1989, pp. 86-91.

26. This is particularly evident in the case of the comtemporary Pîr Pagâro in Sindh. For the development of the *pîrs* in Sindh and their cooption by colonial powers see Sarah F.D. Ansari, op. cit.

27. Mubashshir Hasan, *Razm-e Zindagî,* Lahore, 1978, pp. 116-118 (Urdu); the relation between *pîr* and *murîd* is characterized there as feudal.

28. Abd al-Bari cited in F. Robinson "The 'Ulamâ' of Farangî Mahall" in Metcalf, ed. op. cit. p. 167. Or "The Novice should be like one who is totally blind. He should not have an opinion on anything, neither relating to things of everyday life, nor in matters of faith, morality or the mystical path. Whatever the Master says or does is for him infallibly correct, because he has given up his critical faculty towards him. As a result, his inner eye (i.e. faculty) which sees the transcendent, becomes open. The Novice must be like a corpse before being washed by the undertaker. He should not even refer to God's law. If the Master were to tell him to drink wine or to burn the Quran, he should do so; his obedience would be praiseworthy even in this case. Even if the Master were to deny the existence of God, the Novice should not doubt his word. For the Novice only one thing is wrong, to think or to act independently not in accordance with his master. The Shaikhs are not without mistakes, but even their mistakes lead the adept to salvation. The offence of the Pîr is the faith of the Novice" (transl. by J.M.), A Sufi Shaikh cited in R. Gramlich, *Derwischorden,* part II, p. 244.

29. For the functions and position of the guru in the old Hindu *Weltanschauung,* see Arun Kotenkar, *Grundlagen der hinduistischen Erziehung im alten Indien,* Frankfurt a.M, 1982, pp. 138-151.

30. Aziz Ahmad, *Studies in Islamic Culture in the Indian Environment,* Oxford, 1964, pp. 119-190.

31. There is no doubt that mystical concepts were developed in Islam elaborating on the perception of *qutb* and *al-insan al-kamil,* the perfect man, probably without having ever heard anything about the guru.

32. Eaton, "Bâbâ Farîd", p. 334.

33. In the sense of E.J. Hobsbawm, *Die Banditen,* Frankfurt a.M, 1972, and his *Sozialrebellionen,* Gießen, 1979. Pîr Pagâro of Sindh who was hanged by the British, can be considered as representative of millinaristic movements. Cf. H.T. Lambrick, *The Terrorist,* London, 1972. For the contemporary Pîr Pagâro cf. Azhar Suhail, *Pîr Pagâro kî kahânî,* Karachi, 1987 (Urdu). Faqir Epi can also be regarded as such a representative in the North West Frontier Province, cf. Abd al-Hamid Tarun, *Faqîr Epî,* Karachi, 1984.

34. Shrines were very important in this context. They "made a universal culture system available to local groups, enabling such groups to transcend their local microcosms". Eaton, "Bâbâ Farîd", p. 355. For the social role of *Sûfî* convents cf. S. Babs Mala, "The Sufi Convent and its Social Significance in the Medieval Period of Islam", in *Islamic Culture*, vol. LI, no. 1, Hayderabad, 1977, pp. 31-52.

35. Gilmartin, *Leadership*, p. 489 and Aziz Ahmad, *Studies*. The predominant existence of Saints in Punjab is especially evident through the numerous biographies in Punjab. In Sindh *Pîrism* was also widespread.

36. For the history of this order in the Indian environment cf. Sulaiman Siddiqi, "Origin and Development of the Chisti Order in the Deccan, A.D. 1300-1538", in *Islamic Culture*, vol. LI, no. 3, Hayderabad, 1977, pp. 209-219.

37. Major Aubrey O'Brien cited in Gilmartin, *Leadership*, p. 487.

38. For the patterns of land ownership in Pakistan cf. Mahmood Hasan Khan, *Underdevelopment and Agrarian Structure in Pakistan*, Lahore, 1981.

39. JMP, according to which 90 million Pakistani muslims were *murîdûn*, among them intellectuals and senior officers of the police and military. Even Benazir Bhutto's first political move, after many years of exile, in 1986, was to pay her respect to several saints and shrines in Punjab as well as Sindh.

40. There is still no definite work done on this school of thought. See however Metcalf, *Islamic Revival*, pp. 296ff. For Brelwi religious schools and the economic and social background of their *fudalâ'* in Pakistan cf. chapter VI et passim.

41. Thus, they are even regarded to be loyal to the British; cf. Francis Robinson, *Separatism*, op. cit., p. 266.

42. The subordination to the Prophet by the Brelwis has been a matter of strong criticism brought forward by Deobandis and specially by the Ahl-e Hadith and Jamâ'at-e Islâmî; cf. Majalla, *Râbitat al-'âlam al-islâmî* (Mecca) 23 1405 5/6, p. 1, *Al-Brelwiyyah ba'd al-Qâdîâniyyah* (Arabic).

43. The Ahl-e Hadith was particulary against *salâm* and *durûd* before the *adhân*. According to fundamentalists this "un-Islamic" practice had become popular only since 1966 under Ayub Khan. They opposed the opinion of Shah Ahmad Nurani, the leader of Brelwi Jam'iyyat-e 'Ulama'-e Pâkistân, according to whom the Auqaf Department was only executing the perceptions of Râbitat al-'âlam al-Islâmî and its Supreme Council of Masjid. Cf. *Ahl-e Hadith*, vol. 16/41, Lahore, Oct. 1985, pp. 2 and 8 (Urdu). Nurani rejected the Wahhabite Rabita's interference in internal affairs of Pakistan and said that the Supreme Council of Masjid set up in 1973, was merely an instrument to disseminate Wahhabism via mosques and that the former Amir of Jama'at-e Islami, Miyan Tufail, was its member (cf. *Sawâd-e 'Azam*, Lahore, vol. 9/3-4, Sept./Oct. 1985, p. 17). On Nurani cf. S.J. Malik, "The Luminous Nurani, Charisma and Political Mobilization among the Brelwis in Pakistan", in Pnina Werbner, ed., *Person, Myth and Society in South Asian Islam,* Social Analysis, no. 28, Adelaide, 1990.

44. Even Mughal emperors used similar structures for their own purposes; see Peter Hardy, "Islamischer Patrimonialismus, Die Moghulherrschaft", in W. Schluchter, ed., *Max Webers Sicht des Islam*, Frankfurt a.M, 1987, pp. 190-216 and Stephen P. Blake, "The Patrimonial-Bureaucratic Empire of the Mughals", in *Journal of Asian Studies*, vol. 39, no. 1, 1979, pp. 77-94.

45. In Sindh, Brelwis are represented in the townships, like Hayderabad and Karachi. Compare the distribution of the different schools of thought and their respective religious schools in Table 34(C), and the social and geographical background of the graduates in Table 43.

46. For the position of Brelwis and Deobandis on shrines and cults cf. B.D. Metcalf, *Islamic Revival*. An attempt to bring the Brelwis and Deobandis closer was undertaken by Muhammed Abd Allah from Bhakkar, *'ulamâ'-e Deoband awr Mashâ'ikh-e Punjâb* (Urdu), published by Sîrat Kamîtî, 1984. He maintained that Deobandis also visit shrines and like Brelwis speak out against the Wahhâbiyyah—in the sense of fundamentalism or *salafî* Islam. What Deobandis reject is, however, the exaggerated cult of saints and their shrines.

47. *Civil and Military Gazette* (L), 14.1.1960.

48. First published 1959 in Karachi, cf. p. 57.

49. Katherine Ewing, *Politics of Sufism*, p. 259.

50. Zia ul Islam Janjua, *The Manual*, Part II, p. 6.

51. Mazhar ul Haq, *Civics of Pakistan for Intermediate Classes*, Lahore, 1983, p. 141. This is, however, not a Government prescribed textbook, nevertheless, it is widely used as such.

52. Sec. 6 A-B of The Waqf Properties Ordinance 1961 (TWPO 1961); compare also Table 2, specially for the period 1965/66 to 1970/71.

53. TWPO 1961, Section 3.

54. See the instructions for the "Managers", printed in Zia ul Islam Janjua, *The Manual of Auqaf Laws*, op. cit., p. 43.

55. The West Pakistan Auqaf Department (*khatîbs* and *imâms*) Services Rules 1968, in Raja Abdul Ghafoor, *Manual*, pp. 108-113.

56. There is a clear parallel here between Ayub Khan' politics and that of Amir Abd al-Rahman (1880-1901) in Afghanistan , cf. Ashraf Ghani, "Islam and State-building", pp. 269-284.

57. For *'urs*, cf. e.g. Syed Shah Khusro Hussain, "Die Bedeutung des 'urs Festes im Sufitum und eine Beschreibung des 'urs des Gisudaraz", in *Asien* (Hamburg), no. 17, Oct. 1985, pp. 43-54.

58. Kathrine Ewing, "Malangs of the Punjab, Intoxication or Adab as the Path to God?" in Metcalf, ed., *Moral Conduct and Authority*, op. cit., pp. 357-371.

59. For a discussion on the Green Revolution cf. Keith Griffin, *The Political Economy of Agrarian Change*, London, 1979.

60. The Auqaf (Federal Control) Act 1976, Section 6 (TAFCA 1976).

61. Cf. TWPO 1961, Section 20 and TAFCA 1976, Section 24.

62. Cf. Ewing, *The Politics of Sufism*.

63. Cf. The Auqaf (Federal Control, Repeal Ordinance) 1979 (TAFCRO 1979).
64. Cf. TWPO 1961, Section 3; TAFCA 1976, Section 2, TAFCRO 1979, Section 3.
65. TAFCRO 1979, Section 4ff.
66. Op. cit., Section 13.
67. For the 1961 Regulation cf. Section 16; for 1976 and 1979 cf. Section 20.
68. TAFCRO 1979, Section 25
69. As was to be expected, very few of the *'ulamâ'* and *mashâ'ikh*, the traditional upholders of Islamic tradition, participated in this Seminar. The initiative came from the representatives of the colonial sector of the society and from the *avant-garde*, as well as from the religious elite, who tended to support *salafî* reformist Islam strongly.
70. The Auqaf Department acted in this instance in accordance with section 12 of the Regulation of 1961 and Section 16 of 1976 and 1979.
71. Cf. the position of the chairman of the Tanzîm al-Jihâd in Lahore; he names 15 Waqf which were returned to former shrine holders and several endowments sold to Development Authorities in 1985 (Urdu Pamphlet, Feb. 1986 at Data Darbar, Lahore). Cf. *Ridwân*, publ. by Hizb al-Ahnaf, Lahore, vol. 33, no. 4/5, May 1984 and vol. 38, no. 6, June 1984, p. 2 (Urdu), the Brelwis demand a separate Brelwi Auqaf Board. The Shias, similarly have demanded their own Shia Auqaf Board since 1985. Cf. the *Annual Report* of the Tanzîm al-Madâris (Brelwis umbrella-organization for religious schools), in which Tanzîm representatives pointed out illegal sales by the Auqaf Department whereupon the then Zakat Administrator, I.H. Imtiazi, warned Administrator General Auqaf to refrain from such sales [*sâlânah riport*, Lahore, 1984, pp. 14, 31 (Urdu)]. Similarly, the Brelwis criticise the way money is spent by the department which is not aimed at any real reconstruction of Waqf. The reason for this negligence was, that Auqaf employees were "secular and modern", cf. *Tarjumân-e Sawâd-e 'Azam*, Lahore, vol. 7/9, March 1985, pp. 17 and 32 (Urdu).
72. As a point of criticism, the interest drawn by the Auqaf Department was cited, cf. *Zindagî* (Lahore), 22.9.69, p. 35; *Hurriyat* (Karachi) (Urdu), 21.10.69. This prompted the Auqaf Department, "to withdraw all bank deposits-earning of interest". Instead, all shares of NIT were to be sold on PLS basis. The banks (UBL, HBL and NBL) however did not want to part with the Rs. 40 million [cf. *Nawâ'-e waqt* (Rawalpindi) (Urdu), 24.10.70 and *National News* (Lahore), 21.10.70 and 26.11.70, "Auqaf Department withdraws Bank Deposits"].
73. He was the President of the Islamic World Congress in Pakistan at that time; the representatives of this institution pursue a predominantly integrationist policy.
74. *Dawn* (Karachi), 24.11.69, "Allegations about accounts are false, says Auqaf Chief".
75. Naturally, only those mystic divines were invited who appeared to be conformist from the start. Those who were critical, specially those from

Sindh, were not called. The contributions of the saints were correspondingly favourable to Zia and his policy; cf. GoP, Ministry of Religious and Minorities Affairs, *Mashâ'ikh Kanwenshan 1980, taqârîr o tajâwîz,* Islamabad, n.d. (Urdu).

76. Cited from Pakistan Tourism Development Corporation, *Journey into light,* Islamabad, 1985, p. 3.

77. 65 in Sindh, 50 in Punjab, 10 in NWFP and 12 in Baluchistan.

78. The *'urs* is considered by many *murîdîn* as such a mini-*hajj.*

79. According to the "working paper" of the Ministry of Religious Affairs on shrines in Punjab and Sindh (Islamabad, October 1985; mimeo), in nearly all of the 24 shrines investigated, illegal activities were prevalent. Thus, the shrines are still a refuge for sub-cultures. As expected these shrines, of course, are not listed in the booklet of the Tourism Department.

80. Interestingly, nobody referred to the Mussalman Wakf Validating Act, 1913 when raising criticism.

81. For the reactions see *Civil and Military Gazette,* 6.5.1960, *Pakistan Observer* (Dacca), 12.5.1959 and 13.3.1968, *Times of India* (Bombay), 13.4.1961, *Jang* (Karachi), 29.9.1967 (Urdu), *Nawa-e waqt* (Rawalpindi), 12.11.1967 (Urdu), *Pakistan Times* (Lahore) 24.2.1968 and 26.2.1970, *Chitan* (Lahore), 16.2.1970 (Urdu), *Morning News* (Karachi), 29.4.1971.

82. Very little known about this organization.

83. See the photograph with Pîr Dewal Sharif and the Foreign Minister of Saudi Arabia in 1963, in *JMP,* vol. 2, Islamabad, Sept. 1984, p. 49 (Urdu).

84. See the photograph with Pîr Dewal Sharif with Zia ul Haq in *JMP,* vol. 4, Islamabad, Nov. 1984, p. 33.

85. For *silsilah* cf. Trimingham, *Orders,* passim.

86. Aziz Ahmad, *Studies,* p. 182, where he points to this strategy of the *Naqshbandis.* Cf. Hamid Algar, "The *Naqshbandi* order, a preliminary survey of its history and significance", in *Studia Islamica,* vol. XLIV, Paris 1977, pp. 123-152.

87. Mahkamah Awqâf Punjab, Lahore, n.d., (Urdu), p. 1.

88. D. Buddenberg, *Islamization of Shrines.*

89. In Lahore on 15.2.1986.

90. These petitions can be consulted in (1) *1964* SC (Supreme Court) 126, PLD (Pakistan Law Decisions) vol. XVI, p. 126; (2) *1969* SC 223, PLD vol. XXI, p. 223; (3) *1971* SC 401, PLD vol. XXIII, p. 401; (4) *1971* SCMR (Supreme Court Monthly Review) vol. IV, p. 713; (5) *1972* SCMR vol. V, p. 297; (6) *1975* SCMR vol. VIII, p. 104; (7) *1976* SCMR vol. IX, p. 450; (8) *1976* SCMR vol. IX, p. 500; (9) *1976* SC 501, PLD vol. XXVIII, p. 501; (10) *1977* SC 639, PLD vol. XXIX, p. 639; (11) *1981* SCMR vol. XIV, p. 620; (12) *1982* SCMR vol. XV, p. 160.

91. For this advisory body cf. chapter II.

92. GoP, *Nazariyyâtî Kawnsil kî sâlânah ripôrt, 1981/82,* Islamabad, 1982, pp. 136, 287 (Urdu).

93. According to the Urdu media.

94. Provisional Constitution Order, 203 A-J; the FSC can be considered basically as a legitimising example of the Zia-regime. Its competence does not extend beyond the province of Islamic criminal and personal law.

95. Judgement of 21.6.1984; the argumentation followed the premises put forward by A. A. Mawdudi, in the manifesto of the Jam'iyyat-e 'Ulama'-e Islam, by Hifz al-Rahman Seoharwi (*Islâm kâ iqtisâdî nizâm*, Lahore, 1981) and Rafi'ullah Shahab (*Islâmî rîâsat kâ iqtisâdî nizâm*, Islamabad, 1973). FSC judgements, made available to me on 18.2.1986 in Lahore, Auqaf Department.

96. The inquiry was carried out by Justice Aftab Hussain, B.G.N. Qazi, Ch. Muhammad Siddique, Mawlana Malik Ghulam Ali, Mawlana Abd al-Qaddus Qasim and Mufti Sayyid Shujja'at Ali Qadri. Only the latter spoke out against the right of the Government to acquire Waqfs. None of the judges referred to the Mussalman Wakf Validating Act, 1913.

97. *Morning News*, 27.2.82

98. Hafiz Nadhr Ahmad, *Jâ'izah-e Madâris-e 'arabiyyah Islâmiyyah maghribî Pâkistân*, Liyalpur, 1960 (Urdu), pp. 639-650. The extent of its integration can clearly be seen from the fact that its former pupils formed an Abbasia Old Boys Federation in 1953.

99. *Manual of Rules and Regulations of the Auqaf Department of West Pakistan*, Lahore, 1969, pp. 87-91 and the official circular of 17.5.1968, pp. 92-97.

100. Hafiz Nadhr Ahmad, *Jâ'izah-e madâris-e 'arabiyyah maghribî Pâkistân*, Lahore, 1972 (Urdu), pp. 66 and 603.

101. The West Pakistan Jamia Islamia (Bahawalpur) Ordinance, 1964, West Pakistan Ordinance, No. XVII of 1964.

102. *Manual of Rules and Regulations of the Auqaf Department of West Pakistan*, pp. 68-83.

103. Thus, e.g., the criticism of the Brelwis, c.f. *Tanzîm al-madâris, sâlânah ripôrt*, Lahore, April 1984, p. 20 (Urdu).

104. Mahkamah Awqâf Punjab, *Ta'âruf 'Ulamâ' Akademî*, Lahore, 1982, p. 35 (Urdu). Henceforth, *Ta'âruf*.

105. There are 10 such schools in Lahore. Along with these the Auqaf Department supported some other primary schools, which are also supposed to be endowments. Thus, the department in the Punjab has 75 employees in religious schools, 19 school-teachers, 11 employees of Grade 4, and one employee for each High-, Primary-, and Middle-School (information collected in the 'Ulamâ' Akademî in spring 1986).

106. Abdur Rauf, *Renaissance of Islamic Culture and Civilization in Pakistan*, Lahore, 1965, pp. 172-180, 243.

107. TAFCRO 1979, Section 25.

108. *Ta'âruf*; Mahkamah Awqâf Punjab, *Tarbiyyat*, Lahore, n.d. (Urdu), (henceforth *Tarbiyyat*); also *Dawn* (Karachi), 9.4.68; *Pakistan Times*, 12.5.68 and 3.11.68.

109. This was a secular language course with a final examination, introduced by the British administration; cf. here Sayyid Muhammad Salim, *Hind o Pâkistân mêñ musalmânôñ kâ nizâm-e ta'lîm o tarbiyyat*, Lahore, 1980, (Urdu), p. 243 and G.M.D. Sufi, *Al-Minhaj, Evolution of Curricula in the Muslim Educational Institutions*, Lahore, 1981 (first published in 1941), p. 115. The '*ulamâ*' in the CII called for the abolition of this secular language course, cf. GoP, CII, *Consolidated Recommendations of the CII relating to Education System in Pakistan, 1962 to 1982*, Islamabad, 1982 (Urdu/English), p. 35.

110. Then the highest degree of theological qualification.

111. Both umbrella organizations of religious schools of the Brelwis and Deobandis respectively.

112. Cf. *Tarbiyyat*, p. 17.

113. These were in-service courses. Annual courses before joining service were offered only after 1978 (twice) and had a capacity of 20 participants a year; cf. *Ta'âruf*, p. 11.

114. These participants had to be under 40 years; op. cit., p. 25. Out of every 10 *mu'adhdhins*, 5 came from Punjab, 2 from Sindh, 2 from the NWFP, 1 from Baluchistan; out of 30 *a'imma/khutabâ*', 18 from Punjab, 7 from Sindh, 4 from the NWFP and 1 from Baluchistan; cf. *Tarbiyyat*, op. cit., p. 12.

115. Cf. op. cit., p. 10.

116. Cf. *Ta'âruf*, p. 19.

117. *Târikh-e Tasawwuf*, Lahore, 1976 (Urdu).

118. The Syrian Hanbalite theologian had criticized all deviations from what he considered to be the original (Muhammadan) Islam, especially mysticism and folk-piety (cult of saints). Mysticism and syncreticism were considered by him to be *bid'a* (unjustified innovation and a deviation from the *Sunnah*). He was against the legal methods of consensus (*ijmâ'*), conclusion by analogy (*qiyâs*) and against philosophy, but supported, however, *ijtihâd*. His ideas were first realized through Muhammad Ibn Abd al-Wahab (1703-1792). For Ibn Taymiyyah's political notions cf. Qamaruddin Khan, *The Political Thought of Ibn Taymiyah*, Islamabad, 1985 and Tilman Nagel, *Staat und Glaubensgemeinschaft im Islam; Geschichte der politischen Ordnungsvorstellungen der Muslime*, vol. II, Zürich and Munich, 1981, p. 109 et passim.

119. Cited from R. Peters, "Erneuerungsbewegungen im Islam vom 18. bis zum 19. Jahrhundert und die Rolle des Islams in der neueren Geschichte, Antikolonialismus und Nationalismus", in W. Ende, and U. Steinbach, eds., *Der Islam in der Gegenwart*, p. 95 (Trans. by J.M.); see also Rudolph Peters, "Islamischer Fundamentalismus, Glaube, Handeln, Führung", in Wolfgang Schluchter, ed., *Max Webers Sicht des Islams*, pp. 217-241, specially p. 221.

120. Shaikh 'Al Bin 'Uthmân al-Hijwerî, died 1072, author of *Kashf al-Mahjub*.

121. Interview with Dr. Yusuf Guraiyyah on 24.11.1985 in Lahore, 'Ulamâ' Akademî. For the problems between Deobandis and Brelwis see also Ashraf Zafar, *Madhabi awr siyâsî firqah bandi,* Lahore, 1987, pp. 169ff (Urdu).

122. These are closed, green, metal urns placed at shrines and emptied weekly or monthly by functionaries of the Auqaf Department and "provided double locker system similar to those of bank lockers" (*Dawn,* 10.8.1967). In the shrine of 'Shaikh Ali ibn Uthman al-Hijweri alone 1 million rupees were collected in 1965; Rs. 15,834,573 in 1983/84, Rs. 17,100,000 in 1984/85 and Rs. 18,494,000 in 1985/86; which is a high percentage of the total cash collected; see below; calculated according to *Dawn,* 10.8.1967, and Mahkamah Awqâf, Punjab, *Bajet Mahkamah Awqâf Punjâb barâ-e 1985-86,* Lahore, 1986, p. 15 and 33 (Urdu) (henceforth *Bajet*).

123. These are mostly gifts given in connection with the vows taken.

124. *Bajet,* passim.

125. The Auqaf Department has divided its operation areas into different zones.

126. Pakpattan is a tehsil in the eastern part of the Sahiwal district without any industrial hinterland. The shrine is, however, very well known and its *sajjâdah-nashîn* very influential, so that pilgrims come from far to pay their homage and oblations. For a discussion of this shrine cf. Gilmartin, *Shrines, Succession, and Sources of Moral Authority,* pp. 228-236 and Mazhar al-Islâm, *Lok Panjâb,* Islamabad, 1978, pp. 118ff (Urdu).

127. These include traditional military recruitment areas, like the zones of Lahore and Rawalpindi. I have drawn on the following studies on social sciences in order to work out the extent of development of different districts, Ijaz Nabi, ed., *The Quality of Life in Pakistan,* Lahore, 1986; Wolfgang-Peter Zingel, *Die Problematik regionaler Entwicklungsunterschiede in Entwicklungsländern,* Wiesbaden, 1979, and M.H. Khan, *Agrarian Structure and Underdevelopment in Pakistan,* Lahore, 1985.

128. The following figures are based on *Bajet,* op. cit.

129. For the Zakat system cf. Christine Gieraths, "Social Welfare through Islamization in Pakistan Assessment and Evaluation (1979-1984)", in *Asien,* no. 31, April 1989, pp. 1-31 and below chapter IV. The financial allocations for the religious schools through the media of the Zakat system are discussed in chapter V.

130. Calculated on the basis of *Bajet,* p. 17.

131. *Bajet,* p. 11.

132. These are gifts of Rs. 2,000 for very poor families in order to render possible the marriages of their daughters.

133. Calculated on the basis of *Bajet,* p. 18.

CHAPTER IV

THE ZAKAT SYSTEM

INTRODUCTION

In this chapter, the official Zakat and Ushr system, as introduced in 1980, is presented and analysed. The implications of such a governmental social welfare system are critically evaluated. It will be shown that the colonial state enacts its policy of integration by traditionalizing colonial institutions (such as tax system) on the one hand and by colonializing the traditional institutions (such as the Zakat system) on the other. Such a policy brings about the disintegration of the traditional systems of social welfare and health insurance.

Zakat has its roots in pre-Muhammadan times. In early Islam there were directives for collecting and distributing Zakat alms. These alms are not merely duties collected in order to contribute to the welfare of the weaker social groups. The root of the term Zakat (from the arabic *zakâ*) means "purify" and "grow". What is meant to be purified is the accrued wealth (cf. sura 2/219).[1] Thus, giving Zakat is a pious act (*'ibâdah*).[2] It is prescribed for every Muslim. The required duty amounts to 2.5 per cent of annual savings.[3] Assets liable to Zakat are those in one's possession, be it money, gold, silver, jewellery or goods in stock, agricultural or maritime produce (cf. sura 9/103; 2/267; 6/141) as well as livestock (cf. sura 6/136). Duties on agricultural output are called Ushr, i.e. the tithe. It is not levied on landed property but only on agricultural output.

While those liable to pay Zakat are not specified in the Koran,[4] those entitled to receive Zakat are listed in sura 9/60:

The alms are only for the poor and the needy, and those who collect them, and those whose hearts are to be reconciled, and to free the captives and the debtors, and the cause of Allah, and (for) the wayfarers: a duty imposed by Allah. Allah is All-knowing, Wise.[5]

Furthermore one has to distinguish the visible goods (*amwâl-e zâhirah*)[6] on which the state may levy Zakat from the invisible goods (*amwâl-e bâtinah*)[7] on which Zakat should be paid voluntarily by its owner; this regulation was supposedly introduced by Khalif Umar ibn al-Khattab[8] (died 644) in order to prevent the state from intervening in the private affairs of the individual. The representatives of the Islamic *avant-garde* concede, however, the right of the state to levy even *bâtinah*-Zakat, in case the citizens do not do so themselves.[9]

The religious duty of paying Zakat is valid only if it is offered with proper inner attitude (*niyyat*). Without it, the payment of Zakat does not retain its pious, purifying value. The Islamic *avant-garde* holds the view that this attitude of the individual may be supposed to exist even if he pays Zakat not directly to the needy but via the state.[10]

HISTORY OF ZAKAT IN PAKISTAN

In 1950, under Prime Minister Liaqat Ali Khan a Zakat-Committee was founded and put under the supervision of the Ministry of Finance. This committee[11] was required to draw up suggestions for the introduction of Zakat in Pakistan, in order to collect it as a "pious duty" (*'ibâdah*) on a voluntary basis. In 1952, the report of the committee was finalized on the basis of a questionnaire. The committee took the view that *ijtihâd* was the proper method of interpretation: views of the doctors of Islamic law in the committee's opinion were not of ultimate validity and "all such practices (i.e. concerning the assessment and distribution of Zakat) should be re-examined in the light of the changing circumstances",[12] thereby stressing the fundamentalist character of the Zakat Regulation. The main interest of the *avant-garde* was to create a social welfare system comparable to that of Western welfare states. The *avant-garde,* of course, held the view that Islam had an effective system from early Muhammadan times. The introduction of a Zakat system relying on the Shari'a was thus meant to finally bring about an Islamic welfare state.

In order to avoid criticism from the supporters of traditional institutions, the Zakat-Committee stressed that it was not interested in creating another source of revenue for the state.[13]

According to the calculations of the committee, Rs. 200 million could be expected to be raized via Zakat.[14] The sum collected by a specially set up agency, did not however, even exceed Rs. 100,000. So this undertaking had to be suspended.[15]

THE SIXTIES

The issue of Zakat was again discussed in Pakistan during the International Islamic Conference 1968,[16] though the basis of an Islamic social system had already been laid down in the Constitution of 1962.[17] The discussion became heated when the then chairman of the CII, Alauddin Siddiqui proposed alterations in the tax system. A discussion on principles led to the statement of one participant–Professor Rafiullah Shahab–that Islam did not recognize any other tax apart from Zakat. Further he held that the whole region of Pakistan was "conquered land" in contrast to the genuine Islamic land of Arabia. Therefore, no Ushr but only *kharâj* could be levied in Pakistan.[18] He also declared that a standing army was unknown to Islam–an alarming declaration in the face of the Pakistani army swallowing up the lion's share of Pakistan's budget. If the standing army was abolished, an Islamic budget could be financed exclusively through Zakat. Shahab in fact presented an "Islamic" budget[19] in his book published by the Islamic Research Institute in 1972, but it did not receive much attention.

In 1969, the CII proposed to the Central Government the establishment of a separate Ministry for the collection and distribution of Zakat.[20] This proposal, however, got bogged down until a new questionnaire was drawn up by the CII in 1974.[21] The questions raized were:

(1) whether the Government was entitled to levy Zakat legally;
(2) on which assets Zakat would have to be deducted;
(3) whether enterprises and shareholders should be subject to the same Zakat rates;
(4) whether nationalized and semi-governmental institutions would be liable to pay Zakat;
(5) whether natural resources should be subject to Zakat;
(6) whether the tax system would have to be altered;
(7) what the limit of value would be;[22] and
(8) whether Zakat could be spent for defence purposes as well.[23]

The revived discussion on Zakat has to be considered in the light of Article 31 of the 1973 Constitution[24] according to which the Government was supposed to take measures for the levy of Zakat. One year later, the CII presented its proposal for the introduction of Zakat, stating that it was the duty of the Government to levy Zakat and to distribute it according to the regulations of the Shari'a.[25]

An Integrationist Zakat System: The Panel and CII

In November 1977, the CII was requested by Zia ul Haq to establish a Panel of economists[26] to prepare a report on Zakat as a basis for the introduction of an Islamic welfare system.[27] On 5 March 1978, the Panel presented its report with proposals which were taken up partly unaltered and partly supplemented:[28]

1. Zakat was to be made an obligatory measure by the state, with the approval of the CII.

2. The Government was to collect Zakat from every Muslim. Private and public enterprises were also liable to Zakat as were goods in stock, while industrial entities and trading companies[29] were exempted. The CII, however, was of the opinion that not only goods in stock but trading companies should also be subject to Zakat.

3. The proposal to levy a Special Welfare Tax on Non-Muslims was supported by the CII.

4. Zakat was due on all those goods on which there was a consensus among the different schools of law. The CII approved.

5. Zakat should be levied only in monetary units, with an exemption limit of Rs. 5,000. This was equal to the annual material needs of a family. The CII, however, was of the view that the exemption limit should be fixed according to the value of 7.5 *tolâ*[30] of gold, as mentioned in the Koran.

6. The *sâhib-e nisâb*[31] was expected to pay Zakat only if he earned a certain minimum income. Ushr was compulsory only for those who produced crops above the level of subsistence. The CII consented to these proposals.

7. The "invisible goods" were not subject to compulsory Zakat. They pertained to the private sphere of the individual. Therefore, Zakat in this case would be voluntary. The CII agreed.

8. On "visible goods" Zakat had to be deducted. The CII stated that in the case of lotteries Zakat would have to be paid only on those lottery tickets which remain for more than one year in the possession of its owner.

9. Maritime produce, animals, forests and minerals were liable to an Ushr rate of 5 per cent. Agricultural produce was also liable to Ushr, if the peasant produced above his subsistence needs. As against this, the CII differentiated the rates of Ushr, varying between 5 per cent to 10 per cent, according to the condition of the land and the type of inputs.

10. To prevent evasion of Zakat, the Panel proposed to calculate the average of any account on which Zakat was to be deducted. The CII, on the other hand, insisted on a fixed rate of Zakat deduction.

11. All debts were to be deducted from the amount on which Zakat

was due. The CII added that only those debts could be deducted as had been incurred for an investment.

12. No Zakat was to be levied on luxury goods.

13. Part of the Zakat collected was to be distributed immediately to the needy, while the remaining was to be distributed to social institutions.

14. Zakat should primarily be spent where it had been collected from.

15. Existing institutions were to be integrated in order to save time and money while building up the Zakat administration. The future central Zakat administration was to be built in line with the existing administrative entities.

16. Preferably, Zakat should be spent on the poor, on institutions and on places of learning.

17. Finally, the Panel expressed the opinion that the introduction of Zakat would involve an alteration of the tax system.

The CII consented to items 12 to 17. However, it suggested, that the Zakat system be introduced in one go, and not step by step, as the Panel had proposed. Further, no income tax should be paid on the sum on which Zakat was to be deducted, and finally the payment of Zakat should be enforced according to the lunar calendar.[32]

Some members of the Panel estimated the likely proceeds from Zakat and Ushr if levied on existing financial assets, goods and products. Compared to the sums which have been collected since 1980, the amount thus calculated was very high. While receipts from Zakat were estimated to be Rs. 2.1 billion in the first year only one third of this, i.e. Rs. 855 million was collected. The calculations illustrated the inherent potential of Zakat, if the Zakat payer conformed to the rules. The items "financial assets" and "other assets" accounted for the bulk of Zakat since its introduction.

THE PROBLEMS OF THE MINISTRY OF FINANCE

The Ministry of Finance discussed the following items which were then commented upon by the CII:

- whether the rate of Zakat on products in irrigated and rainfed areas could be altered depending on the conditions of cultivation. The CII rejected this on the ground that if the Government meant to raise the receipts from agriculture, it could do so via other taxes.

- whether goods in stock and other goods of trade (industrial goods and agricultural products) could be exempted from Zakat. The CII's response was that while no Zakat was to be paid on machines and agricultural land, this was not the case with products and goods of trade; if the state was not able to enforce this in conformity with its duty, it should at least make it a "voluntary duty".

- whether it was possible to fix the exemption limit laid down by the Shari'a at 7.5 tolâ[33] of gold as an average amount for each family. The CII consented to this, as only a part of the population possessed gold;
- whether 25 per cent of Zakat could be considered the private affair of the Zakat payer (and thus could be deducted from the amount due) and up to which portion of his Zakat he could distribute to relatives and neighbours. According to the CII, the state would not have to consider this.
- whether only such official industries and institutions of trade would be liable to Zakat which were comparable to private institutions.[34] According to the CII these institutions would be liable to Zakat in case they earned a profit, just as they would be exempted in case they incurred losses.[35]

Under the chairmanship of Justice Muhammad Afdal Chimah the CII was apparently eager to cooperate with the Government to enforce governmental interests and to legitimize all this Islamically. Even the critical question of whether Zakat was due on goods in stock and on goods of trade—which would have raized the Zakat realization considerably—was circumvented by the classification of these possible sources of Zakat as "invisible goods".

This phase of discussion and exploration of the Zakat and Ushr Regulation was followed in February 1979 by the publication of the Zakat and Ushr Order 1979. It was prepared by the Planning Commission under the leadership of a functionary of the Jama'at-e Islami, Professor Khurshid Ahmad. Its proposals were again revized by the CII and altered in some essential respects. A criticism of some members of the CII was that according to this proposal the goods in stock would fall under the category of amwâl-e bâtinah (i.e. goods as in Schedule II of the Zakat Regulation), on which voluntary Zakat was to be paid. The "profit hungry" traders would continue to accumulate profits while poor peasants would have to pay Ushr.[36] The proposed Zakat regulation thus served to stabilize urban hegemony at the expense of rural areas by exempting large urban enterprises.

Public enterprises which had private entrepreneurs as shareholders were also supposed to pay Zakat. Twenty-five per cent of the Zakat due could be given to institutions, which were supervized by the Zakat administration. Zakat would only be deducted from savings certificates if they expired or became due for reimbursement. Finally, the CII opposed raizing the property tax as it had proposed a reduction of taxes in connection with the introduction of Zakat.[37]

The views of the Panel and the Planning Commission of the Ministry of Finance on Ushr were presented by a Working Group of the Planning Commission in November 1978 whose reports contained 16 items. The CII responded[38] saying that those liable to pay Zakat should be exempted from income tax and those liable to Ushr should be exempted from development cess and from taxes on landed property. Further, Ushr was to be levied on all agricultural produce. In rainfed areas the rate was to be 10 per cent, in irrigated areas only 5 per cent of the production was to be collected from landowners who had a minimum production of 948 kilograms of wheat. Subsistence holdings were to be exempted.[39] The proposal to allow a deduction of 25 per cent of the value of agricultural produce for inputs involved was not accepted as in that case the producer would be paying only 5 per cent Ushr on 75 per cent of his produce, which would be against Shari'a tenets.[40]

The chairman of the CII, Tanzil al-Rahman, supported this reasoning with the argument that land in which investments had been made in the form of fertilizers, etc., would turn out higher produce than rainfed land which had not received such inputs.[41]

The Government avoided dispute on this point by fixing Ushr generally at 5 per cent. Peasants in rainfed areas were encouraged to deduct another 5 per cent voluntarily. The socalled *Hamza Report*[42] which was expected to present proposals for the implementation of the Ushr system in the summer of 1982, advized against implementation of the Ushr system by force. The 25 per cent allowance for expenses of inputs, it was suggested, should be raized to 33 per cent, in case of tube-well irrigated production to 40 per cent and in case of irrigation by tube-wells driven by gas-oil even up to 50 per cent. If this does not prove feasible, the Government should provide support to the peasants otherwise.[43]

CII's CRITICISM

Inspite of the consessions made by the CII and the proposals made by the Panel, the Government introduced still another regulation in 1980. The CII under the chairmanship of Justice Tanzil al-Rahman and with a new membership did not agree with this and voiced bitter criticism. The main points of this criticism are summarized below.

The CII said that the largest part of the Zakat proceeds originated from savings accounts, and not from the wealth and property of large industrial entrepreneurs and owners of capital. This resulted in a *de facto* exemption of the well-to-do from Zakat, while it was a burden for the less affluent: only the middle class held savings accounts. Trading enterprises did their business mainly through current accounts from which Zakat was not deducted. The CII therefore suggested:

1. The integration of the following items into *Schedule I*:
   a. current invoices.
   b. goods of trade,
   c. raw materials and finished products of industrial enterprises,
   d. livestock,
   e. products of mines, forests and waters.
2. Obligatory Ushr for the Zamîndârs and tenant farmers.
3. Annual Zakat on the entire value of one's savings.
4. Special welfare tax for all those exempted from Zakat.
5. Spending of Zakat on the basis of "backwardness" of areas, and not numbers of population.
6. No Zakat on goods which had been inherited by orphans and the mentally disabled.[44]

It is evident that the Government was taking care that the economic *status quo* would remain untouched by the Zakat. Under the chairmanship of Justice Tanzil al-Rahman the CII, for the first time, took a critical stand.

STRUCTURE OF THE ZAKAT SYSTEM

After presenting the discussion between different institutions and the critique of the CII we shall now turn to the Zakat administration. To a considerable extent it was in position before the introduction of the Zakat system in 1980.

The Zakat administration was in place before the Zakat Regulation of 1980 had been drawn up, comprising the administrative units at the local level. For every 5,000 people a Local Zakat Committee (LZC) was established. When setting up these committees, no account was taken of the available infrastructure, as for example the Masjid Kamîtî or Mohallah Kamîtî.[45] The setting up of a new infrastructure made it quite evident that the Government was serious about implementing the Zakat Regulation.

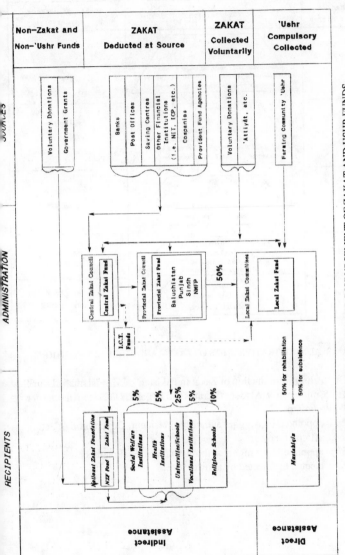

DIAGRAM 2: COLLECTION AND DISBURSEMENT OF ZAKAT AND USHR FUNDS

Sources: GoP, Ministry of Finance, *Central Zakat Administration Reports of Activity for the Year 1982/83*, Islamabad, 1984 (Urdu), and Chr. Gieraths and J. Malik, *Die Islamisierung der Wirtschaft in Pakistan*, p. 41.

Name and number of administrative bodies	Composition	Number of persons involved
Central Zakat Council 1 CZC	Chairman* 15 Members General Administrator Zakat*, Sec. Minister of Finance*, Sec. Minister of Religious Affairs*, 4 Provincial Chief Administrators Zakat*, 3 Ulamā'$, 1 other Member$	16
Provincial Zakat Council 4 PZCs	Chairman* 9 Members Provincial Chief Administrator*, Provincial Sec. Finance*, Provincial Sec. Social Welfare*, Provincial Sec. to the Government, 3 'Ulamā'$ and 2 other members$	Per PZC: 10 Total: 40
District Zakat Council 75 DZCs	Chairman* 6 Members District Deputy Commissioner*, at least 5 Members$, 1 of each Tehsil	Per DZC: 7 Total: 525
Tehsil-Zakat-Committee 297 TZCs	Chairman& 6 Members Tehsil-Assistent Commissioner*, 5 Local Zakat Committee Chairmen&	Per TZC: 7 Total: 2079
Local-Zakat-Committee 36555 LZCs	Chairman& 6 Members residents of the locality&	Per LZC: 7 Total: 255885

DIAGRAM 3: ADMINISTRATIVE UNITS OF ZAKAT AND THEIR COMPOSITION

Sources: Cf. "A brief Introduction of Zakat in Pakistan", CZA, Islamabad, June 1985, mimeo, p. 9. Also see Gieraths and J. Malik, *Die Islamisierung der Wirtschaft*, p. 37.

Remarks: * = appointed by a higher authority (President, Governor, PZC, etc.); official member.

$ = appointed by a higher authority; non-official member.

& = elected or selected by a lower level.

FLOW OF ZAKAT FUND

The institutional set-up of the Zakat system in Pakistan and the flow of Zakat funds from their sources via the administration to the target groups and institutions is given in diagram.[46]

On the first day of the fasting month of *Ramadân*,[47] the Zakat Deducting Agencies (banks, post-offices, etc.) by means of deduction at source withdraw 2.5 per cent from all savings accounts above a certain exemption limit (fixed at Rs. 1,000 in the first year of Zakat deduction, 1980). They transfer the Zakat thus collected to the Central Zakat Fund (CZF). This fund is fed also with proceeds from "voluntary Zakat" and "donations" and from funds of other institutions. Following certain criteria, the Zakat is then distributed among the Provincial Zakat Funds (PZFs)[48] and the National Zakat Foundation (NZF).[49] Following pre-scribed quota, the PZFs turn over funds to the Local Zakat Funds (LZFs), to other institutions, to the needy (*mustahiqîn*) and to the National Zakat Foundation.[50] Governmental funds also flow into the NZF. The funds serve to support either institutions or the *mustahiqîn* themselves directly. Proceeds of Ushr are distributed in the locality where they were collected.

Local authorities keep a record of how the funds are spent. These records are then presented to their superiors.[51] The Zakat system is thus characterized by a strong element of control. The CZF is the central organization for the distribution of funds.

PERSONNEL

Diagram 3 shows the composition of the personnel of the Zakat adminis-tration.

Even though the set-up of the Zakat system was meant to reflect a certain democratic composition of its members, the diagram shows how, in fact, the autonomy of its members is limited. The hierarchically structured system reveals a degree of local selection of members only at the level of tehsils and within the localities. Members of the remaining three tiers are appointed "from above". Even the seven members of the LZC are most likely to be appointed by other, traditional procedures.[52] This is far from unusual in a system in which functions, rights and duties are ruled by relationships, fraternities or other traditional organizational patterns.[53] The criteria set up for a candidate to a LZC (ability to read and write, knowledge about the Zakat system) are in line with the colonial tradition and are thus unfamiliar to a predominantly peasant society. Therefore, training programmes were instituted by the 'Ulamâ Akademî' in Lahore, taking into account the local conditions and needs of the future Zakat

Committee members.[54] Until July 1980, the members of the LZCs of all provinces had undergone training, although they had already been elected or appointed prior to this.[55] Consequently, there was criticism of the composition of the LZCs and complaints were filed with the Central Zakat Administration (CZA). A large number of these complaints seems to have been redressed. This points towards an effective and authoritarian Zakat administration.

Granting that the members and chairmen of the committees enjoy a certain degree of recognition and power and that they have a tendency to represent the interests of the state—after all it was the state that provided them with these influential positions—one may think of a huge, newly set up governmental bureaucracy. The monthly journal of the Zakat administration, Al-Zakât, in its first issue referred to over 250,000 persons engaged in the Zakat administration, almost as if an army had been mobilized.[56]

Al-Zakât from Islamabad is an important Government publication that influences public opinion. It has a circulation of more than 40,000, reaching down to the poorest sections of society. The Provincial Zakat Administrations (PZAs) issue a quarterly, Al-Zakât. All these publications not only report on the Zakat system in the most dazzling colours but also serve to present the latest reports of the success of Islamization. The propaganda of Zakat reached its peak first in July 1980 with a circulation of 50,000 pamphlets in Urdu, the Nizâm-e Zakât wa 'Ushr. Simultaneously, quarterly conferences on Zakat and Ushr were organized at different levels of the Zakat administration, often in collaboration with the Auqaf Department.

It appears that the Government has been successful in penetrating the traditional strata of society and is continuing with its policy of expanding its influence over these. At the same time the Government acquired access to and control over some rather remote areas. This normative interference of the state was legalized, among other ways, through the Tehsil/Taluka/Subdivisional and Local Committees (Removal of Chairman and Members) Rules at the end of 1981.[57] It authorized the removal of the chairman of a Zakat-Committee if he did not act according to the rules of the Zakat administration.[58] The influence of the bureaucracy was thus enhanced in Pakistan.

ZAKAT IN RELATION TO FEDERAL RECEIPTS AND EXPENDITURE

Receipts from Zakat are limited to deductions from savings accounts and term deposits and from other monetary deposits of the urban middle classes.[59] As the middle class is quite narrow in Pakistan, the receipts of Zakat are limited as well.

As an *'ibâdah* (religious duty) Zakat is not accounted for under the "yearly receipts of the state". The CII had labelled Zakat as a "direct tax"; however, to raise consumption it seemed to make sense to reduce the indirect taxes which, by any standards, were too high considering the poverty of the people. The shortfall in receipts was to be levelled out through Zakat.[60]

Table 3 illustrates the low proportion of Zakat–both with and without Ushr–in relation to the ordinary revenues of the state. It does not even reach 2 per cent, if only deductions at source are considered. The proportion in the total of direct taxes amounts only to about 12 per cent inculding Ushr.

Taking the governmental expenditure as a parameter, the amount of funds distributed by the CZF does not even reach 2 per cent, sometimes hardly surpassing 1 per cent. In contrast, the proportion of Zakat in the

TABLE 3: ZAKAT IN PROPORTION TO OTHER
FEDERAL RECEIPTS AND EXPENDITURE

Budget Figures	1980/81	1981/82	1982/83	1983/84	1984/85
					(in Rs. million)
1. Total revenue	46.349	51.166	59.080	72.309	77.777
2. Indirect taxes	29.325	31.883	37.267	41.808	43.062
3. Direct taxes	7.184	8.486	8.943	8.836	9.619
4. Expenditure	39.216	43.103	56.183	68.949	84.114
5. Social expend.	1.350	1.496	1.804	2.300	2.506
Zakat and Ushr in Rs. million					
6. Zakat and Ushr	0.844	0.799	1.031	1.263	1.417
7. Deducted at source	0.844	0.799	0.855	1.011	1.231
8. Ushr	—	—	0.176	0.252	0.186
8a. Land tax	0.241	0.230	0.189	0.169	0.219
9. Zakat distributed	0.750	0.500	0.750	0.750	1.000
Relative Figures					
10. 6 per cent of 1	1.84	1.56	1.75	1.75	1.82
11. 6 per cent of 3	11.70	9.41	11.53	14.29	14.73
12. 7 per cent of 1	1.84	1.56	1.45	1.40	1.58
13. 9 per cent of 4	1.91	1.16	1.33	1.09	1.19
14. 9 per cent of 5	55.56	33.42	41.58	32.61	39.90

Sources: Calculations on Zakat and Ushr based on GoP, Ministry of Finance, Central Zakat Administration, *Nizâm-e zakât wa 'ushr kê pehlê pânch sâl, aik jâ'izah,* Islamabad, 1986 (*Five-Year Report*), pp. 50 and 59f. Figures on the federal budget based on *Pakistan Statistical Yearbook 1986,* op.cit., pp. 255-260, 266.

funds distributed for social institutions (education, health, social welfare) of the federal budget amounted to about 40 per cent. It must be mentioned, however, that the federal expenditure for the social sector make up only a fraction of the amounts spent for this purpose by the provinces, as education is a provincial, not a federal subject.

The provincial social expenditures were as below:

1980: Rs. 3.5538 million,
1981: Rs. 4.1502 million,
1982: Rs. 5.2812 million,
1983: Rs. 6.5623 million, and
1984: Rs. 7.9473 million.[61]

The Zakat distributed thus made up for about 15 per cent of the social expenditure in the provinces in the five years in question. The total spending on Zakat in this period did not even amount to 10 per cent of social expenditure,[62] indicating its comparatively minor importance.

Proceeds from Ushr[63] were below those of the land tax (see line 8 of the table). Compared to the value of agricultural produce, it only reached 0.15 per cent in 1982/83, 0.29 per cent in 1983/84 and only 0.18 per cent in 1985/86,[64] instead of 5 per cent and 10 per cent for different kinds of land. For these shortfalls in the Ushr proceeds, the Government held the Zakat administration responsible.[65]

Ushr turned out to be a tax falling more heavily on small-sized farm-holdings than on large ones. This was due to the possibility of a reduction of 25 per cent to 33 per cent from the Ushr due to costs of production. The ratio of cost of production to net income falls as farm sizes increase, thus making Ushr a "regressive tax".[66]

The Shia were exempted from Zakat and Ushr. The Shiite landowners were, however, faced with a higher land tax above the corresponding value of Ushr.[67]

The low level of Ushr proceeds on the one hand and the preferential treatment of large farm holdings on the other make the effectiveness of the Ushr system questionable.

As spending of Zakat by the PZAs can be considered a social expenditure, it would seem appropriate to compare ordinary social expenditure wth the spending of Zakat in the provinces. Table 4 presents this comparison.

It shows that the amount spent by the provinces on the social sector

TABLE 4: PROPORTION OF ZAKAT AS COMPARED TO
THE SOCIAL EXPENDITURE OF THE PROVINCES

Province	Zakat Spent 1980-85 1	Social Expenditure 1980-85 2	1 as per cent of 2
Punjab	2,109	14,975	14.1 per cent
Sindh	659	5,454	12.1 per cent
NWFP	551	3,450	16.0 per cent
Baluch.	227	1,708	13.3 per cent

Sources: 1 = Calculations based on the CZA: *Five-Year Report*, op.cit. (Urdu), pp. 52-56.
2 = Calculations based on the *Pakistan Statistical Yearbook 1986*, op.cit., pp. 178-284.

(education, health, social welfare, etc.) and that spent out of Zakat is merely a fraction of the regular social expenditure.

The distribution of the central Zakat (by the CZF to the PZAs) is in the same proportions as for various categories of funds in the federal budget, which are distributed province-wise mainly on the basis of population shares. These distribution patterns support the criticism made by CII that the Zakat disbursements follow the population criterion instead of the relative requirements of the regions. The comparison of data reveals a slight preference for the province of Punjab and of the Islamabad Capital Territory at the expense of Sindh.

Zakat Receipts and Expenditure at Different Levels

There are strong fluctuations in the receipts and expenditure of Zakat as shown in Table 5.

TABLE 5: ZAKAT RECEIPTS AND EXPENDITURE AT DIFFERENT LEVELS

Year	Receipts in (in Rs. 1000)			Expenditure in (in Rs. 1000)		
	District	Province	Nation	District	Province	Nation
1980	417,857	744,220	844,000	317,573	530,309	750,000
1981	484,298	502,650	799,000	411,805	552,376	500,000
1982	387,570	746,510	855,000	367,343	372,408	750,000
1983	850,775	751,080	1011,000	525,033	980,964	750,000

Sources: GoP, Ministry of Finance, Central Zakat Administration: *Kârkardagî repôrt barâ-e sâl 1983/84*, Islamabad: 1984 (Yearly Report CZA, 1983/84, Urdu), pp. 42 and 46.
For the district levels: *Compiled Computerized Data*, as of May 1986 (mimeo).

The comparison of receipts (exclusively from deduction at source) and expenditure at the national level is surprizing due to the pronounced difference between the two figures. This difference is especially high in the second year of Zakat (Rs. 300 million) and in the third year (Rs. 250 million) with receipts exceeding expenditure.

At the provincial level, we witness a compensating development: the funds received by the CZF are disbursed, though with delay; the receipts and the expenditure are of about equal size (there is a difference of only Rs. 300 million in four years, compared to more than Rs. 760 million at the national level).

The fluctuation between receipts and expenditure is repeated at the district level. The disbursements effected by the LZCs are generally below their receipts. This is especially evident in the fourth year in which the difference amounts to more than Rs. 300 million. At this level the total accruing in the course of four years comes to Rs. 520 million.

According to these findings, each level spends less than the funds at its disposal. Thus, the Zakat payer may rightfully ask where the money in the Zakat funds is actually going to.

According to the Zakat Regulation, the administrative costs of the committees at the local level may be met from up to 10 per cent of the Zakat receipts of each locality.[68] This 10 per cent is, however, rarely reached, as this would hurt the self-respect of the members of the committee. At the local level the share of administrative costs is very modest when compared to the receipts of the LZCs from the PZFs. The proportion is still less when compared to the share of administrative costs in the total receipts of Zakat.

The expenditure for the administration at higher levels is met out of the budgets of the provinces and/or of the federal budget, even though one of the eight lawful ways of spending Zakat according to Shari'a is financing the Zakat administration: "The alms are . . . for those who collect them . . ." (sura 9/60). The state can thus be given credit for not financing this bureaucracy out of Zakat funds.

At the provincial as well as tehsil level, a different scenario prevails. Even though the Zakat administration proudly points to the low administrative costs—especially at the local level—there is a steep increase at higher levels. Adding up the expenditure at all levels, the amounts for the different years were:

1980/81:   Rs. 16.454 million (without Punjab from the tehsil level onwards);

1981/82:   Rs. 24.061 million;

1982/83:   Rs. 20.552 million (without Sindh from the tehsil level onwards); and

1983/84:   Rs. 68.432 million. This is equal to about three to four times the administrative costs at the local level. Here too one observes rizing costs.

In order to obtain an authentic estimate of the real costs, the working contribution of the following functionaries have to be added: One Secretary, Ministry of Finance, one Secretary, Ministry of Religious Affairs, four Provincial Secretaries, Finance, four Provincial Secretaries, Social Welfare, four Provincial Secretaries, to the Government and 75 District Deputy Commissioners as well as 297 Tehsil Assistant Commissioners and their corresponding personnel. All these are on the pay-roll of agencies other than the Zakat administration. Therefore, there are no exact figures available of the cost of these functionaries actually involved in the activities connected with Zakat. By just assuming an annual minimum expenditure of Rs. 20,000 for each functionary (this being a rather modest assumption when considering costs of transport, rents and other costs), the amount reaches about Rs. 8 million per annum. This would have to be added to the costs from the local up to the provincial level in order to present a realistic estimate of the recurring costs involved in the Zakat system. The proportion of administrative costs during the first four years would thus amount to:

1980/81:   Rs. 24 million = 2.8 per cent of the compulsory Zakat as compared to Rs. 5.3 million for the LZA

1981/82:   Rs. 32 million = 4.0 per cent of the compulsory Zakat as compared to Rs. 7.2 million for the LZA

1982/83:   Rs. 28 million = 3.8 per cent of the compulsory Zakat as compared to Rs. 6.2 million for the LZA

1983/84:   Rs. 76 million = 7.5 per cent of the compulsory Zakat as compared to Rs. 26 million for the LZA

totalling Rs. 160 million. This amounts to 4.6 per cent of the total receipts from compulsory Zakat.

The proportion of cost is evidently not extraordinarily high. At the same time, the actual costs involved are four times as high as those stated in the Zakat publications which account only for the costs at the local level.

Despite the rizing expenditure of the Zakat administration, it would be quite possible to finance it out of the regular Zakat receipts, instead of resorting to other budgets. The Koran authorizes this (sura 9/60).

Voluntary Zakat

Later, we shall examine in detail the "Islamic" or "un-Islamic" behaviour of Pakistani Muslims as far as the official Zakat system is concerned. At this point we deal with the voluntarily paid Zakat (*zakât radâkârânah*) as an indicator of the acceptance of the official Zakat system.[69]

The proportion of voluntary Zakat is extremely small. Even more significant is the constant decline in this source of Zakat, which has come down to less than 50 per cent after five years, as compared to the collection in the first year (Rs. 3.1 million as compared to Rs. 7.7 million).

The meager collection of voluntary Zakat— only Rs. 1.2 million up to 30.9.1980[70]–obviously disappointed the CZC. As a reaction, the Council suggested that the *imâms* and the <u>khatîbs</u> should try to encourage Zakat payers during the Friday sermons in the local language in order to raise contributions towards the Zakat fund. A main incentive was that the PZFs would contribute to the LZCs an amount equal to that collected by voluntary Zakat in a locality. Further, there was a proposal to issue receipts for voluntary Zakat paid by an individual which could be presented during income tax assessment. Later, it was decided to issue Zakat vouchers in amounts of Rs. 100, 500 and 1,000.[71]

As compared to the Zakat deducted at source, the percentage of voluntary Zakat in 1980 amounted to 1.2 per cent, in 1982 to 0.8 per cent, in 1983 to only 0.2 per cent and in 1984 to only 0.3 per cent. Faced with this development, the protagonists of the Zakat system were in an uncomfortable position as they had relied on voluntary Zakat as an indicator of the success of their policy. The incentives failed to raise the amounts of voluntary Zakat paid.

REFUNDING AND EVASION OF ZAKAT

The sudden, unannounced deduction of Zakat at source from the bank and post-office accounts, and other Zakat deducting agencies, such as deposits, shares, etc., led to grievances among the Pakistani urban population.[72] As Zakat was deducted indiscriminately from any account, including those of the Shia, non-Muslims and non-Pakistanis, these groups felt affronted by this governmental measure and demanded refund of the amounts deducted.

It had been well known to the CZC since its fourth session on 17 January 1980, i.e. well before the Zakat system was implemented, that the Shia would rebel against it.[73] The report of the Administrator, General Zakat reads:

Composite Law on Zakat and Ushr, practically ready for promulgation, except for the resolution of some Shia-Sunni differences expected to be solved soon.[74]

This problem was resolved only after its introduction in June 1980. In September, the Shia were able to push through their exemption from paying Zakat; the President issued an order on 15.9.1980 to refund the Zakat deducted from accounts pertaining to the Shia.[75]

It took the CZC until December 1980 to propose a Draft Rule,[76] which was presented only after the first deadline set by the Shia ran out, on 23.4.1981.[77]

The applications for refunding reveal interesting insights into "Islamic" versus "un-Islamic" behaviour. The refunding of the alms tax deducted by the CDAs can be analysed as shown in Table 6. While the amounts refunded decline over the years, the number of cases dealt with remain constant. One may suppose that those exempted from Zakat on the basis of the Zakat and Ushr Regulation on the ground of their affiliation to a particular school of thought, their religion or for being a foreigner would present their affidavits in due time (i.e. three months prior to the Zakat

TABLE 6: REASONS FOR REFUNDING, NUMBER OF CASES
AND AMOUNTS REFUNDED

Reason for Refunding	Number of Cases					Refunding (Rs. 10,000)				
	1980	1981	1982	1983	1984	1980	1981	1982	1983	1984
errors of calculation	n.d.	n.d.	n.d.	429	516	n.d.	n.d.	n.d.	392	625
non-Pakis. accounts	1814	n.d.	n.d.	740	548	170	n.d.	n.d.	349	284
minimum amount	n.d.	n.d.	n.d.	297	150	n.d.	n.d.	n.d.	316	101
school of thought	1590	n.d.	n.d.	1531	1165	660	n.d.	n.d.	454	592
other reasons	1612	n.d.	n.d.	63	1618	626	n.d.	n.d.	948	384
non-*sâhib-nisâb*	n.d.	n.d.	n.d.	60	n.d.	635	n.d.	n.d.	41	n.d.
Total	n.d.	n.d.	n.d.	3120	3988	1497	6567	2500	2499	1986

Sources: Cf. CZA, *Annual Report*, Islamabad, 1986 (Urdu), p. 9.
           CZA, *Annual Report*, 1980/81, op.cit. (Urdu), p. 54.
           CZA, *Annual Report*, 1982/83, op.cit. (Urdu), p. 18.
           CZA, *Annual Report*, 1983/84, op.cit. (Urdu), p. 40f.
           n.d. = no details given

deduction date). The more or less constant number of Shia cases makes it likely that a large part of these cases represent increases in the number of Shia claimants, as the "real" Shia would not hesitate to present their affidavits in time, while the new Shia needed more time. More Sunni seem to be converting to Shiism or at least claiming to be Shia, in order to circumvent the official Zakat system.[78]

One may assume that the urban middle class Zakat payers are somewhat inclined towards evasion of Zakat. This is examined later.

The Annual Reports of the CZA show that by far the largest portion of Zakat originates from savings accounts and deposits (68.6 per cent of the deduction at source, in five years amounting to Rs. 4,740.14 million),[79] while only 25 per cent of the Zakat deducted originates from term deposits and savings certificates.[80] The remaining 6.4 per cent from another seven categories of Zakat deduction.[81] Taking the figures of Table 7 as a basis, the following becomes evident: during the first two years of the levy of Zakat by "scheduled banks"[82] the difference between term deposits on which Zakat was levied and the total amount of term deposits in these banks almost equalled the amount of funds in accounts remaining below the exemption limit (*nisâb* = Rs. 1,000) (cf. columns 3, 4 and 5 in the Table 7). In the third year, the position changed; the difference between the total amounts in the banks and the "zakatable" amounts deposited increased and could only be explained through the presence of such categories as non-Pakistani, non-Muslim or Shia accounts.

The following years witnessed a dramatic increase of amounts in the accounts of non-Pakistanis, non-Muslims and Shia. This trend reached its peak in 1984/85 with Rs. 11,787 millions apparently not "zakatable". It is very likely that more and more ways of evading Zakat were found. The increase of amounts exempted from Zakat becomes especially evident when comparing the rates of increase of columns 2 and 7.

As it is quite difficult for a Muslim in Pakistan to present himself as a non-Muslim or as a non-Pakistani, one may suppose that the increase in column 7 is due to account holders affiliating themselves increasingly with the Shia school of thought in order to circumvent Zakat.

Another significant indicator of the evasion of Zakat is the fact that transactions by account bearers are extraordinarily high a few days prior to the Zakat deduction date.[83] Even though it is not possible to quantify the level of Zakat evasion, the following examination of transactions may give some idea of the dimensions of such evasion. Table 8 indicates an almost complementary relation between the movements in current accounts (on which no Zakat is levied) and the changes in amounts of savings accounts

TABLE 7: SAVINGS ACCOUNTS AND TERM DEPOSITS
EXEMPTED FROM ZAKAT

1	2+	3	4	5	6	7
Year	Zakat in million Rs.	x 40 in million Rs.	Amount of Funds in Scheduled Banks in million Rs.	Difference between 3 and 4 in million Rs.	Funds on Accounts below Nisâb in million Rs.	Residual Amount of Funds of Non-Pakistanis, Non-Muslims and Shia (Difference between 5 and 6)
1980	765,1	30,604	32,325	1,721	1,072	649
1981	708,8	28,352	33,513	5,161	4,910	251
1982	760,6	30,424	39,485	9,061	5,063	3,998
1983	882,7	35,308	52,931	17,623	8,824	8,799
1984	1.078,2	43,128	64,942	21,814	10,027	11,787

Sources: + = CZA, *Five-Year Report,* op.cit. (Urdu), p. 50 (i.e. Zakat from savings accounts and from term deposits).

Col. 3 = basis of calculation: column 3 multiplied by 2.5 per cent = column 2.

Col. 4 = actual amounts of funds in the *scheduled banks.* Data from *Bulletin of the State Bank of Pakistan (BSBP)*, Feb. 1982, p. 12. stated as of end 1980; *BSBP,* Feb. 1982, p. 12, stated as of May 1981; *BSBP,* Feb. 1983, p. 14, stated as of May 1982; *BSBP,* Feb. 1984, p.16, stated as of May 1983; *BSBP,* Feb. 1985, p.16, stated as of April 1984.

Col. 6 = *BSBP,* Sep. 1986, p. 35f, author's calculations on this basis.

Remarks: The *nisâb* in 1980 was Rs. 1,000, in 1981 and 1982 Rs. 2,000, in 1983 and in 1984 Rs. 3,000.

For the last two years I have added up the amounts of only those accounts with funds between Rs. 1,000 and Rs. 2,000.

and term deposits in "scheduled banks" coinciding exactly with the Zakat deduction date. While there is a decrease in the amounts in the savings accounts, the amounts in current accounts increase correspondingly. After the deduction date, the amounts in savings accounts increase again, while those in current accounts decrease.

When subjecting the data on deposits in current accounts and term deposits to a correlation test,[84] a linear relation is established between the two variables. A correlation coefficient (0) presents the 0-hypothesis that there is no correlation between the variables. In this case, however, a correlation coefficient of 0.94720 is found, meaning that there is a strong linear relation. This is found to be significant at 0.1 per cent far below the 2 per cent level. Thus, there is a highly significant association between the current accounts and the term deposits.

The analysis of regression shows[85] a normal distribution of the

TABLE 8: ZAKAT EVASION 1981-1985, CURRENT ACCOUNTS AND
SAVINGS ACCOUNTS IN RS. MILLION

Zakat Date/Year/Month	Current Acc. in Rs. million Increase/Decrease as compared to Previous Year	Term Deposits in Rs. million Increase/Decrease as compared to Previous Year
1.7.1981/1981/April	34.832,3	33.545,3
1.7.1981/1981/May	35.552,3 2.1%	33.512,5 -0.1%
1.7.1981/1981/*June*	38.379,3 8.0%	32.983,8 -1.6%
1.7.1981/1981/July	36.229,6 -5.6%	34.598,9 4.9%
1.7.1981/1981/Aug.	35.986,3 -0.7%	35.015,8 1.2%
21.6.1982/1982/April	38.483,4	39.972,4
21.6.1982/1982/May	39.509,2 2.7%	39.485,3 -1.2%
21.6.1982/1982/*June*	42.853,4 8.7%	38.895,2 -1.5%
21.6.1982/1982/July	41.880,3 -2.3%	41.624,7 7.0%
21.6.1982/1982/Aug.	42.341,2 1.1%	42.739,9 2.7%
11.6.1983/1983/April	46.661,6	51.271,4
11.6.1983/1983/May	47.777,0 2.4%	52.930,9 3.2%
11.6.1983/1983/*June*	50.703,8 6.1%	53.184,0 0.5%
11.6.1983/1983/July	48.949,8 -3.5%	54.868,9 3.2%
11.6.1983/1983/Aug.	49.897,6 1.9%	55.974,6 2.0%
31.5.1984/1984/March	49.252,3	64.396,2
31.5.1984/1984/April	48.593,7 -1.4%	64.961,5 0.9%
31.5.1984/1984/*May*	51.492,6 5.7%	60.843,3 -6.3%
31.5.1984/1984/June	51.183,8 -0.6%	64.402,7 5.7%
31.5.1984/1984/July	50.476,8 -1.4%	64.933,8 0.8%
21.5.1985/1985/Jan.	58.582,3	69.677,6
21.5.1985/1985/Feb.	58.351,0 -0.4%	70.849,3 1.7%
21.5.1985/1985/March	58.442,5 0.2%	70.974,8 0.2%
21.5.1985/1985/April	58.934,5 0.8%	70.418,6 -0.8%
21.5.1985/1985/*May*	60.000,4 1.8%	66.562,8 -5.5%
21.5.1985/1985/June	63.717,0 6.2%	71.120,7 6.8%
21.5.1985/1985/July	61.537,3 -3.5%	71.479,1 0.5%
21.5.1985/1985/Aug.	61.146,2 -0.6%	73.558,8 2.9%

Sources: Selected months from the *Bulletin of the State Bank of Pakistan (BSBP)*: for 1981 *BSBP*, Feb. 1982, p. 12, for 1982 *BSBP*, Feb. 1983, p. 14, for 1983 *BSBP*, Feb. 1983, p. 16, for 1984, *BSBP*, Feb. 1984, p. 16, for 1985 *BSBP*, Feb. 1985, p. 16.

Remarks: The months in italics mark the months of Zakat. Percentages were calculated by author. Only relevant months were taken into account.

residuals. Its deviations are not high in May, but very much so in June, the month of payment of Zakat.

The Zakat evasion becomes even more pronounced when examining the weekly movements in the accounts as seen in Table 9.[86]

TABLE 9: MOVEMENT OF AMOUNTS ON ACCOUNTS AT WEEKLY INTERVALS
(ZAKAT DATE 21ST MAY 1985)

Stated as of	Current Accounts in Rs. million	Term Deposits in Rs. million
2. 5.1985	22,949	55,222
9. 5.1985	23,120	53,975
16. 5.1985	26,257	51,152
23. 5.1985	30,055	47,464
30. 5.1985	27,278	49,946
6. 6.1985	24,987	52,192
13. 6.1985	24,910	53,122
18. 6.1985	24,123	53,913
27. 6.1985	24,546	55,453
26.12.1985	24,631	62,142
6. 3.1986	25,055	65,206

Sources: Data from the Pakistan Banking Council (mimeo).
Data from the Nationalized Banks; Deposits in Pakistan.

The target date for the calculation of Zakat was the first of *Ramadân*, i.e. 21.5.1985. Corresponding to the decrease of funds on savings accounts, the amounts with current accounts increase up to and including 23.5.1985. During the following weeks, the amounts in savings accounts catch up again. This reveals the association between the decrease and increase of term deposits and current accounts respectively, prior to and after the target date.[87] The data suggest that the evasion of Zakat is widespread in Pakistan. The state has so far not been able to curb this.

THE DISTRICT LEVEL

So far, the financial aspect of the Zakat system has been examined from different angles, focusing on the national level. An analysis of the district level based on the available data[88] on receipts and expenditure follows.

The question of the criteria according to which the PZAs distribute the Zakat funds received from the CZF to the LZCs in each district will be examined.

It may be recalled here that the governmental Zakat system postulates it to be a "social welfare system" contributing to the eradication of regional disparities. Receipts and expenditure per district are subdivided into the following sub-categories:

Receipts:
    Ushr
    Voluntary Zakat
    Transfers from the Provincial Zakat Fund
    Alms, *'attiyyât* and other receipts (Grants)

Expenditure:
    Direct support to individuals
    Support via Institutions
    Administrative expenditure
    Others

Mean Value Deviations

The analysis below concentrates on total receipts and expenditure. As shown earlier, the receipts at district level were above the expenditure -especially in 1984; the same was the case at the provincial and national level.[89]

The calculation of mean deviation and standard deviation of receipts and expenditure at district level for all four years shows that there is less deviation from the mean value under expenditure as compared to receipts. So while the expenditure remains more or less constant at district level over the years—with only small variations—that is not the case for receipts.[90]

Furthermore, it can be observed that the standard variation increases with the decline in the sums received by the districts. This is especially true in the districts of Baluchistan and the NWFP.[91] High fluctuation of receipts as well as of expenditure point to the very low stability of the Zakat system during its first four years.

When adding the expenditure and receipts of all 65 districts and calculating their correlation coefficient, the result shows significant relationships between receipts and expenditure in only 23 per cent of all districts.[92]

The statistical mean value of receipts of Rs. 8232.7 per district in the years 1980-1984 could only be achieved by very few districts. The figures for the Punjab are far above the mean value: no district comes anywhere near this. In contrast, all districts of Baluchistan have receipts far below the mean value. In Sindh only Hayderabad, Tharparkar, Larkana and Nawabshah districts are slightly above, in NWFP only Peshawar and Mardan[93] are above. The richest districts of the country[94] thus show Zakat receipts above average, while poorer districts and provinces (Baluchistan, NWFP and Sindh) fall behind, which is contrary to the postulate of redistribution. This means that only a small portion of the districts shows a significant correlation between expenditure and receipts, while most districts have no correlation at all or only a very minor one. Funds therefore do not seem to be distributed according to the amounts received from the PZCs. This again emphasises the weaknesses of the system.[95]

The irregularities revealed in connection with the receipts of Zakat and of its distribution pose questions as to the criteria according to which the Zakat funds are distributed by the PZAs to the LZCs.

Zakat Receipts and Level of Development

The relationship between the Zakat receipts of the provinces and their population has been indicated above. What follows is an analysis of the relationship between the receipts of Zakat and the level of development in different districts.

The postulated redistributive character of the Zakat system suggests that there might be a linear relation between the level of development of a district and its Zakat receipts through the PZFs. The amount of Zakat received should increase, for every 1,000 inhabitants, the more "backward" a district is.

In order to calculate these amounts, the first step is to divide the mean value of Zakat receipts of four years by the corresponding number of inhabitants (in 1,000). This mean value of Zakat is then arranged in order of magnitude. The highest Zakat value of the 66 districts is placed first, the second highest is at rank 2 and so on; the smallest value is at rank 66. This ranking is then correlated to rankings of districts arranged according to indicators of development elaborated in different sociological inquiries.[96]

The correlation test rejects the hypothesis of positive association between backwardness and Zakat receipts significantly. In each of the five cases (compare Table 10) the coefficient is below 0.23 when correlating the two rankings. The correlations between the Zakat ranking and the other rankings are as given in Table 10.

It appears that there is no relationship between the "low" level of development of a district and the "high" receipts of Zakat.

TABLE 10: CORRELATION-COEFFICIENTS OF THE RANKING OF
ZAKAT RECEIVED PER DISTRICT PER 1,000 INHABITANTS AND THE
RANKING ACCORDING TO STAGES OF DEVELOPMENT IN THE DISTRICT[97]

Rg A[1]	Rg B[2]	Rg C[3]	Rg D[4]	Rg E[5]
0.121717	0.18417	0.22014	0.06836	0.15766

Sources and remarks: [1] = Pasha/Tariqs first ranking with 27 indicators[98]

[2] = Pasha/Tariqs second ranking with 27 indicators[99]

[3] = Khan/Iqbals first ranking with 6 indicators[100]

[4] = Khan/Iqbals second ranking with 16 indicators[101]

[5] = Khan/Iqbals third ranking with 22 indicators[102]

An analysis now follows of the relation between the receipts of Zakat as dependent variable and the number of population as independent variable.

Correlations with Population

The hypothesis is that there is a correlation between the receipts of Zakat on the one hand and the numbers of people on the other. The method of testing is to calculate the Spearman rank correlation coefficient for the districts arranged respectively by amounts of Zakat collected and by number of people.

Receipts and Expenditure

The Punjab with its 21 districts does not reveal any association between the receipts of Ushr and the size of population.[103] There is also no significant relationship between the receipts of voluntary Zakat and the size of population.[104] The correlation coefficients between funds received from the PZFs (transfers from PZF) and the population of different districts are significantly higher than in other provinces. In two years, it even reached 0.81688 with a value of significance of 0.0001. The lowest correlation coefficient was 0.54416 with a value of significance of 0.0108. Similar is the situation as far as alms (grants, etc.) are concerned.

The correlation coefficient between the total receipts and the numbers of population is highest in the Punjab.[105] If not a strong correlation it is at least a significant one with a positive, linear increase over the years. Sindh has hardly any correlation at all between different categories of Zakat receipts and the number of population in its districts. Only in the first year, there is a correlation coefficient of 0.78820 between the total receipts and the number of population. The NWFP is the only province showing a strong association of voluntary Zakat with the number of population, even though this tendency is on the decline during the last two years.[106] The correlation between the transfers from the PZF and the population is equally strong and constant over the years.[107] This is true also when it comes to grants and population, the trend even increasing over the years.[108] The correlation between population and total receipts is accordingly high and reaches a high coefficient of 0.89510. In Baluchistan the correlation between the transfers from the PZF and the population as well as beween total receipts and number of inhabitants is remarkable. In the first case, the coefficient values remain between 0.89330 and 0.82561, in the second case they even reach a value of 0.91538.

The next point of analysis is the relationship between the separate categories of expenditure and the number of population.

A relatively high positive correlation is evident between the direct support to individuals in the 21 districts of the Punjab and their number of population, at least during the first two years of the Zakat system.[109] The following two years experience a fall of the correlation coefficient to 0.62987. In the same manner the amount of Zakat distributed to institutions through the LZCs declines in the 21 districts. During the first year, the correlation coefficient reached 0.75325, decreasing to 0.26753 in the fourth year. The correlation between the total expenditure and the population is correspondingly high over all years.[110] The relationship between administrative expenditure and number of population is not considered here.

In Sindh there is no relevant correlation, suggesting a dismal picture of the Zakat system in this province.[111]

In NWFP the association between the individual support and the number of population is very strong,[112] while it is weak between payments to institutions and number of population. Total expenditure, once again, shows a strong positive correlation with the number of population.[113]

In Baluchistan there is only a correlation between the number of population and the total expenditure.[114]

Thus, high values of correlation only seem to exist between the total receipts and expenditure of a district and its number of population, not between its stage of social and economic development and the difference in posts of Zakat. The result therefore is that the postulate about bringing about a social welfare system has not been fulfilled by the Zakat administration or by its principles of distribution.

CONCLUSION

The introduction and implementation of the Zakat system since 1980 is the visible form of colonization of traditional values and systems of order.[115] The latter are increasingly dissolved without putting adequate substitutes in their place. At the same time, the governmental Zakat system stands for the traditionalization of colonial institutions (taxes and bureaucracy) and reflects the integrationist character of Islamization.

With its administrative set-up, institutions of control and financial aid which create new dependencies, the Zakat system makes possible an integration of large areas and institutions hitherto partly beyond governmental scope into the colonial sector. In the nationalization of Islamic endowments also, the state tries to extend its influence into hitherto autonomous and autochthonous areas. The evaluation of the Zakat data shows that the Zakat system has little to offer by way of "social welfare". The instability of the system becomes evident in the evasion of Zakat, large deviations from mean values of some Zakat categories at the district level, lack of correlation between payment of Zakat and level of development, poverty in the Zakat-receiving areas as well as the strong tilt towards the Punjab. These elements can even be considered mechanisms inherent in the system. Doubts are strengthened further by the low amount of Zakat collection, the procedure of levy and the effects of distribution as to whether the system has any effect on alleviating poverty.

The role of the Government is of vital importance in bringing about an Islamic social welfare system. The Government's representatives within the new Zakat system are not likely to give up their role, as they are able to extend their own influence and also to create new jobs at the lower and middle levels of the bureaucracy.

The state is in a position to have its policy legitimized as Islamic through the representatives of the Islamic *avant-garde*. It can also increasingly mobilize the traditional clergy as authorities of legitimacy in the implementation of this "modern" social welfare system. Nevertheless, large parts of the population have been able to free themselves from the compulsory Zakat payments. Besides the Shia, those able to withdraw from participation in this governmental measure of Islamization were the representatives of the traditional sector and of the intermediary sectors.[116] Sections of the Pakistani clergy consistently reject the Zakat system and are even capable of preventing its implementation. When doing so, they refer to a judgement (*fatwâ*) of Mufti Mahmud who rejected the newly introduced Zakat system in a ten-point declaration.[117] The background for this rejection has been the fear of the supporters of autochthonous institutions of losing their autonomy as a result of governmental interference.[118] This rather isolationist position is so far limited to one province: Sindh and reflects a particular socio-economic and political situation.[119]

Basically it is possible to engage in social welfare politics with the help of the Zakat and Ushr system. The precondition for this, however, is actually to levy 2.5 per cent or 5 per cent on all those goods on which Zakat is due according to the Shari'a. A dynamization of the Ushr system could bring about higher receipts. This would mean an innovation in taxation, as the farmers do not have to pay any taxes on agricultural income so far.

NOTES

1. Tanzil al-Rahman, *Introduction to Zakat in Pakistan*, Islamabad, n.d., p. 5. Thus, Zakat is a kind of tax on wealth.

2. The *avant-garde* have a predilection for the English term *divine duty*, which is, however, misleading. It is not a duty of God but rather a duty of man towards God.

3. This rate is not fixed in the Koran but is derived from the tradition of the Prophet. Cf. A.I. Qureshi, *The Economic and Social System of Islam*, Lahore, 1979, pp. 107ff, esp. 112-122. For the Shia an additional rule says that a non-Sayyid (i.e. a non-descendant of the Prophet) may not give any Zakat to a Sayyid as a Sayyid does not need any alms. Instead, the Sayyid may receive *khums*, i.e. one fifth of the annual deposits of a non-Sayyid (cf. sura 8/41). Half of this *khums* again belongs to the *imâm* or his representative. The descendants of the Prophet may give Zakat among themselves as well as to needy non-Sayyids (cf. also Moojan Momen, *An Introduction to Shi'i Islam*, New Haven and London, 1985, pp. 180f and 206f). According to Shia rules, Sayyids (sadât) may give Zakat to each other as well as to non-Sayyids.

4. Sura 21/73, 19/31, 19/55, 7/156, 2/3, 2/43, 2/177, 2/83, 5/12, 5/55, 9/11, 9/18 et passim.

5. Also sura 2/177.

6. Among these are gold, silver, cash and jewellery, and, of late, Savings Certificates.

7. These, now include shares, accounts with banks and other financial institutions, Government Savings Certificates, National Investment Trust Units, Investment Corporation of Pakistan Accounts, Life Insurances, Provident Funds, other forms of financial assets, Governmental lotteries, etc.

8. "...this was a new source of revenue under the head of Zakat and its levy began in the reign of Omar" (cf. Shibli Numani, *Omar the Great*, vol. II, Lahore, 1981, p. 63). Others hold the opinion that "it is not exactly known when Zakat began to be collected by the Prophet or his agents in Medina. The

Muslim authorities place it between the second and the ninth year" (cf. Qureshi, *The Economic and Social System of Islam*, Lahore, 1979, p. 111).

9. Tanzil al-Rahman, *Introduction*, op.cit., p. 16.

10. Ibid., p. 21.

11. This committee consisted of four members of the clergy of different schools of thought and of seven seculars.

12. *Pakistan Gazette*, Extra., July 23rd, 1954, pp. 1481f.

13. Ibid., p. 1485.

14. Ibid., p. 1501.

15. Tanzil al-Rahman, *Introduction*, op.cit., pp. 8f. Details on the working method of this committee unfortunately were not available.

16. For the proceedings of the conference cf. "International Islamic Conference", Feb. 1968, in *Islamic Studies*, Islamabad, 1970.

17. Constitution of 1962, Part II, "Fundamental Rights and Principles of Policy", chapter 2, "Principles of Policy 1 A, Islamic Way of Life" reads: ". . . the proper organization of Zakat, Wakfs and mosques should be ensured. . . ."

18. *Kharâj* means land tax levied by a Muslim ruler in an area conquered by Muslims. Based on this argument by Shahab, the Ushr system was supposedly not introduced in Pakistan in 1980.

19. *Islâmî Riyâsat kâ mâliyâtî nizâm*, IRI, Islamabad, 1973.

20. GoP, Council of Islamic Ideology (CII), *Consolidated Recommendations on the Islamic Economic System*, Islamabad, 1983 (Urdu/English), p. 135.

21. This questionnaire, which appeared in the national media was sent to 33 '*ulamâ*', economic experts and financial institutions. Only about 19 of them replied. Cf. CII, *Recommendations*, p. 138.

22. This referred to the minimum value of wealth respectively of agricultural produce which would be liable to Zakat.

23. CII, *Recommendations*, op.cit., pp. 136f.

24. See also 8(4), Part II, in chapter 2 of the Constitution of 1962.

25. CII, *Recommendations*, op.cit., p. 139; on May 8, 1976.

26. See also chapter II.

27. Earlier, the CII had been in a position to submit to the Government a survey on the number of needy and destitutes (CII, *Recommendations*, op.cit., p. 140). The Panel comprized banking experts and economists and, after completing the report on Zakat, also elaborated the report on the "Islamization of the Economy". See C. Gieraths and J. Malik, *Die Islamisierung der Wirtschaft*.

28. CII, *Annual Report, 1977-78*, Islamabad, 1979 (Urdu), pp. 258-287.

29. This seems to refer to the means of production.

30. One *tolâ* is equal to 11.82 gram.

31. That is a person owning minimum wealth.

32. This would be favourable to the *Mustahiqîn* as the solar calendar has ten additional days. Cf. *Panel Report on Zakat 1978*, Islamabad (mimeo); CII, *Recommendations*, op.cit., pp. 141-145, 147-158; *CII, Annual Report,*

1977/78, op.cit. (Urdu), pp. 160-178, 258-286. The Panel often argued by analogy.

33. This is equal to 88.65 gram.

34. The Ministry of Finance seems to refer to the difference between institutions aiming at earning a profit and those which do not.

35. CII, *Recommendations*, op.cit., pp. 158-162; this statement was made by the CII on August 5, 1978. The session took place under the chairmanship of Ghulam Ishaq Khan, the then Minister of Finance.

36. Cf. CII, *Recommendations*, op.cit., pp. 168 ff, 197-202; according to the CII the reason for this was administrative.

37. CII, *Recommendations*, op.cit., pp.169-174.

38. The following statement was given by the CII at the end of January, and the beginning of February 1979.

39. CII, *Recommendations*, op.cit., pp. 167f.

40. Ibid., pp. 216f.

41. Ibid., pp. 219f; this was at the end of August 1982.

42. Its members were exclusively representatives of the *avant-garde* and landlords.

43. *Wafâqî konsil sekreteriat: Khusûsî kamîtî barâ-e 'ushr kî ripôrt*, Islamabad, n.d.

44. CII, *Recommendations*, op.cit., pp. 206-213.

45. Only the Ushr committees established later on collaborated with the Union Councils and the Land revenue offices.

46. Tehsil and the District Zakat Committees are not included here as both are only institutions of control.

47. Shari'a, in contrast, prescribes the month of *Rajab*.

48. On the distribution in detail cf. below.

49. This is an institution established under the Charitable Endowment Act 1890 in 1981/82. It was established with the help of governmental funds of Rs. 100 million in order to finance those expenses which according to the Shari'a could not be met out of Zakat. Examples of such expenses are the repair of buildings, rents, salaries, electricity, water, gas, etc. During three years, the NZF has spent more than Rs. 55 million on 111 enterprises [cf. GoP, Ministry of Finance, Central Zakat Administration, *nizâm-e zakât wâ 'Ushr ke pehle pânch sâl, aik jâ'izah*, Islamabad, 1986 (Urdu), pp. 43ff in the CZA, *Five-Year Report* (Urdu)]. This institution can thus be considered to be an auxiliary instrument to resolve the dilemma the state faces due to the religious character of Zakat. It is therefore a *hîlah*, a legal trick.

50. At the provincial level, the rates are 50 per cent to Local Zakat Committees, 25 per cent for scholarships (in formal schools), 10 per cent for the students of religious schools, 5 per cent for social institutions, 5 per cent for hospitals, 5 per cent for other purposes; these rates have been changed several times, cf. CZC, *Annual Report, 1983/84*, İslamabad, 1984 (Urdu), p. 5.

51. Nevertheless there is corruption which cannot be avoided in such a comprehensive system.

52. GoP, Ministry of Finance, Central Zakat Administration, *Central Zakat Council Proceedings*, vol. I, 1-7 meetings, Islamabad, 1983, p. 83, item 41, p. 101, 111, item 16; vol. II, 8-15 meetings, p. 16, item 35, p. 564, item 67, pp. 571f, item 97.

53. Such misconceptions about the traditional society is evidence of armchair planning by theorists.

54. *Zakat Proceedings*, vol. I, p. 79; Ibid., vol. II, p. 108.

55. Ibid., vol. I, p. 144.

56. *Al-Zakât*, vol. I, no. 1, Islamabad, 1981 (Urdu), p. 26; *Zakat Proceedings*, vol. II (Urdu), p. 407.

57. *Zakat Proceedings*, vol. II (Urdu), pp. 240, 295, 351-355.

58. Sometimes the higher authorities could act in a high-handed manner.

59. That was not the case for deposits in current accounts. The CII had already noticed this, as is explained in detail below (compare item 5).

60. CII, *Annual Report, 1977-78*, Islamabad, 1979 (Urdu), pp. 277f.

61. Data from the *Pakistan Statistical Yearbook*, 1986, op.cit., p. 276.

62. In 1980, this amounted to Rs. 4,903.8 million for social purposes (the Zakat distributed equals 15.3 per cent of this amount), for 1981 Rs. 5,646.2 million (the Zakat distributed amounts to 8.9 per cent), for 1982 Rs. 7,085.2 million (the Zakat distributed amounts to 10.6 per cent), for 1983 Rs. 8,862.3 million (8.5 per cent of the Zakat distributed) and for 1984 Rs. 10,453.3 million (the Zakat distributed comes up to 9.6 per cent).

63. A thorough analysis of Ushr in Pakistan may provide substantial insights into the problems of agricultural structure which are not dealt with here.

64. Calculated on the basis of the data of the "National Accounts" "16.2 net national product at current factor cost (Agriculture)", in *Pakistan Statistical Yearbook 1986*, Islamabad, 1986, p. 389 and *Ushr data*.

65. GoP, *Pakistan Economic Survey, 1984-1985*, Islamabad, n.d., p. 14.

66. N.S. Zahid, "Ushr, a Theoretical and Empirical Analysis", Discussion paper no. 39, Karachi, 1980, p. 14 (unpublished). A case study demonstrates that the levy of Ushr is relatively higher for a small farmer than for a big landowner. Cf. A. Mohammad Kashif, "A Sociological Study of the Response Patterns of the Enforcement of Ushr", M.Sc. Thesis, Faisalabad 1984, p. 61.

67. This was supposedly brought about by a circular stating that all landowners with more than 2.5 acres would be liable to land tax while the minimum size prescribed earlier was 12.5 acres. This is still valid for the Sunnis (cf. Al-Wafâq, *Wafâq-e 'ulamâ'-e shî'iyyah Pâkistân ke chothe sâlânah ijtimâ' kî tafsîlî ripôrt*, Lahore, 1985, pp. 54f, Urdu).

68. *Zakat Proceedings*, vol. II (Urdu), Session on 11.12.80, item 9.9, pp. 10f.

69. This is also valid for the payments effected on the basis of Ushr self-assessment.

70. *Zakat Proceedings*, vol. II, session on 11.12.80, p. 3.

71. Ibid., sessions on 9.4.81, p. 111, 2.7.81, pp. 244f, p. 436, 12.3.82, p. 494.

72. The target date is usually announced only on television, not in newspapers and radios (cf. Al-Wafâq: *Wafâq-e 'ulamâ'-e shî'iyyah Pâkistân ke chothe sâlânah ijtimâ' kî tafsîlî ripôrt*, op.cit., p. 54 Urdu). The Government only aims at certain stratas of the society.

73. On the reaction of the Shia community to the Zakat Regulation cf. also *Pakistan Commentary,* vol. 3, no. 8, Hamburg, August 1980, p. 1.

74. *Zakat Proceedings,* vol. I, p. 111.

75. Cf. CII, *Recommendations,* op.cit., item 77, p. 201.

76. Ibid., item 75, pp. 177f. The Shia in this case behaved in a "counter-integrationist" manner.

77. *Zakat Proceedings,* op. cit., vol. II (Urdu), pp. 48ff, 113, 229, 583 and "Deduct Refund Rules 1981", 2(c), 17(1), 26(i) and 27(i) as well as *Zakat Manual,* op. cit., pp. 45, 53, 56.

78. This was confirmed in numerous interviews. The Zakat Regulation forced the Shia to change their customary practice *taqiyyah* (the hiding of the personal affiliation to Shiism). Thus, the number of Shia for the first time can be calculated more precisely.

79. CZA, *Annual Report, 1983/84,* p. 37 and CZA, *Five-Year Report,* p. 50. The savings make up the largest portion of the total deposits in the "scheduled banks". These are banks registered with the State Bank of Pakistan. They comprise nationalized as well as private banks.

80. Whether a change in saving habits can be seen in the context of the introduction of the "Profit and Loss Sharing (PLS)"-accounts since 1982 cannot be explained in detail here. It is, however, absolutely certain that the state subsidized the new PLS-accounts heavily, as, for example by a tax relief on profits on PLS-accounts up to Rs. 15,000 and by the additionally introduced special tax on profits from interest-accounts since July 1st, 1984. This governmental support to "Islamic Banking" might be responsible for the increase of the term-deposits and savings accounts.

81. These are: NIT Units, ICP Mutual Fund Certificates, Government Securities, Securities including debentures and shares, annuities, Life Insurances and Provident Funds. Cf. CZA, *Annual Report, 1983/84,* p. 37 and CZA, *Five-Year Report,* p. 50.

82. We may suppose that the accounts where there is Zakat evasion are mainly accounts held in nationalized banks.

83. Personal observations, 1985 and 1986.

84. Current accounts are the dependent variable, term deposits the independent one.

85. Furthermore, the square of the correlation coefficient has a value of 0.8972, i.e. one may deduce the dependent variable (current accounts) from the independent variable (term-deposits) with a certainty of more than 89 per cent.

86. This is examined here for the nationalized banks with national deposits. I suppose that here there would be few "foreign exchange accounts" and that

fewer foreigners would deposit their money here than in foreign banks. The data given here therefore mostly refer to Pakistani citizens living in Pakistan.

87. Submitted to a correlation test, here too we obtain highly significant values of positive nature between the two variables.

88. These are aggregated data of the LZCs of all districts for four years (1980-1984) for the different categories.

89. See above receipts and expenditure of Zakat on different levels.

90. Strikingly lower are the deviations from the mean value as much in the expenditure as well as in the receipts in the district Sheikhupura, Rawalpindi, Sargodha, Faisalabad, Jhang, Peshawar, Kohat and Kohistan.

91. Especially high deviations from the mean values (over 50 per cent) can be witnessed in the following districts: Islamabad, Lahore, Kasur, Gujranwala, Sialkot, Rawalpindi, Attock, Mianwali, Multan, Vihari, Bahawalnagar, Rahim Yar Khan, Karachi Ost, Hayderabad, Badin, Thatta, Tharparkar, Sanghar, Nawabshah, Abbottabad, Mansehra, and all districts in Baluchistan except Quetta.

92. The 0-hypothesis (= correlation rejected significantly) gives a value of 0.93108, thus rejecting the 0-hypothesis with high significance. The coefficient of significance is 0.0001.

93. For a detailed analysis of the Zakat system in Mardan district see J. Malik, "Fallstudie zum System der sozialen Sicherung in den ländlichen Gebieten des Mardan Districts in der Islamischen Republik Pakistan", in B.N. Schubert, G. Balzer, Überlebenssicherung durch Kaufkrafttransfer. *Gesellschaft für Technische Zusammenarbeit (GTZ),* Berlin/Eschborn, 1990, pp. 133-146.

94. Especially in the Punjab but also in two districts of the NWFP and of Sindh with the exception of Tharparkar.

95. That might be understood as the downright "system" itself.

96. These rankings have been taken from the elaborations of Mahmood Hasan Khan and Mahmood Iqbal, "Socio-Economic Indicators in Rural Pakistan: Some Evidence", in Ijaz Nabi, ed., *The Quality of Life in Pakistan,* Lahore, 1986, pp. 93-108. And H.A. Pasha and Tariq Hasan, "Development Ranking of Districts of Pakistan", in Ijaz Nabi, op.cit., pp. 47-92. For an explanation of the indicators see below, chapter VIII on the labour market problems of the *'ulamâ'*. Both rankings developed by Pasha and Hasan (op.cit., pp. 66f) take into account 27 indicators of development. They reveal a significant positive correlation (a coefficient of 0.97336). This correlation of rankings is author's. A similar picture is revealed by a correlation of the six indicators selected by M. H. Khan and M. Iqbal (op.cit., pp. 100f) based on the availability of inputs and employment opportunities in the villages of each district, the 16 indicators based on the distance between the villages and work sites (with a correlation coefficient of 0.95744; correlation of these rankings is author's).

97. All correlation coefficients below have high values when tested for significance.

98. Pasha and Hasan, "Development Ranking of Districts of Pakistan", op.cit., pp. 66f.

99. Ibid.

100. M.H. Khan and M. Iqbal, "Socio-Economic Indicators in Rural Pakistan: Some Evidence", op.cit., pp. 100f.

101. Ibid.

102. Ibid.

103. The same is true for all other districts in other provinces.

104. The correlation coefficients are between 0.77273 and 0.37403.

105. With a correlation coefficient of 0.82468 and a coefficient of significance of 0.0001 in 1981.

106. The correlation coefficients here are between 0.76923 and 0.04196. Whether this relatively high portion of voluntary Zakat is a reflection of the pietist character of the Pakhtuns, cannot be dealt with here. Certainly, the majority of religious students originates from this province and there exist a large number of religious schools. This may be one reason for the association between voluntary Zakat and the number of population in this province.

107. With correlation values of 0.80420 and 0.89510 and values of significance of 0.0016 and 0.0001.

108. With correlation values of 0.31469 up to 0.87413.

109. With correlation values of 0.81039 and 0.86753 and the coefficient of significance of 0.0001 each.

110. The correlation values here are 0.82208; 0.86753; 0.67532; 0.62078.

111. This may also be seen in the context of the rejection of the Zakat system by some supporters of the traditional sectors of society; cf. chapters V and VI.

112. Up to 0.92308 in the second year.

113. With correlation values of 0.91608.

114. With correlation values of 0.54936 up to 0.84243.

115. This became evident in the preceding analysis. It is further backed up by the discussion on the Zakat system in the context of the religious schools (cf. chapter V).

116. In the sense of the theoretic model.

117. Cf. chapter VI.

118. This became evident in the process of book-keeping of the funds spent by religious schools and the governmental influence on the religio-political parties which went along with it. Cf. the chapter on the Islamic education system.

119. Cf. chapter V.

CHAPTER V

THE ISLAMIC SYSTEM OF EDUCATION

INTRODUCTION

The introduction of Islamicist principles was also sought in the area of traditional educational system, in the religious places of learning, the Dînî Madâris, henceforth referred to as DM. They are significant in several ways: First, they play an important role in Pakistani educational policy—as they had in the pre-Pakistan period. Second, they are an important factor in the Islamization drive of General Zia ul Haq. Third, the leading clergy is recruited from these schools. Fourth, they have an incalculable impact in times of social and political conflict.

Up to 1981, only a few DMs were integrated into the formal educational system[1] and therefore had hardly any impact on administrative and political processes. The schools with their teachers and students were outside the national processes of decision making and, from that point of view were marginalized.

This educational system was aligned to the traditional sector and trained those who were part of the traditional society. Increasingly, however, it adjusted to the needs of the colonial sector. As the traditional sector of society was able to mobilize large numbers, it was politically a most significant factor. An example of this is its role in the Pakistan National Alliance (PNA) movement in 1977.

During the last few years, there have been a number of publications on Islamization in general, but there has hardly been any academic assessment of the Islamic educational system since 1977. The literature on the subject is briefly examined below.

Since 1977, a number of studies on religious education have been published. There is, however, so far no comprehensive presentation on the current situation of the Pakistani educational system as far as Islamization is concerned; only isolated aspects have been dealt with on different occasions.

The most striking fact at first glance is that many contributions have been published for the first time in the sixties. They were published again, mostly unaltered, due to their alleged topicality, in view of the latest developments. Frequently, they are idealized presentations of the system of the Dînî Madâris and of the "Islamic educational system" they represent. This literature often limits itself to the era between the times of Prophet Muhammad and the arrival of the British on the Indian subcontinent. Some studies deal with the era of the British invasion, mostly depicting how the imperialist power subverted the traditional educational system and introduced a system aligned to the new colonial interest.[2] There has hardly been any academic study on the traditional educational system in Pakistan since 1947.[3]

This does not mean that there was no traditional education after Pakistan came into existence; it has continued since 1947. The likely explanation for such dearth of academic research on the subject lies in the low importance attached by the colonial sector to this form of education. The time-honoured system of education has, in fact, been superseded by the formal one since 1947.[4]

Only the integrationist Hafiz Nadhr Ahmad made an effort to examine the DM and presented four studies on this subject.[5] The official statistical survey of 1960 and the corresponding report, both calling for a reorganization,[6] were followed ten years later by a further comprehensive inquiry by Nadhr Ahmad.[7] Once again reformation of the religious schools was demanded.

A remodelling of the DM was also proposed by a nationwide survey on the Dînî Madâris undertaken in 1979 by the Ministry of Religious Affairs.[8] The most recent statistical survey on DM in 1982/83 had been undertaken by the Ministry of Education[9] which, for the time being, brought to an end governmental studies concerning the Islamic educational system and the clergy.[10] The governmental surveys are not general studies on the Islamic educational system, but are rather collections of materials, often more of an administrative nature than academic.[11]

There is a vast amount of Urdu literature originating from the clergy itself. They mostly reject the proposals for reform, without, however, presenting any constructive alternatives themselves.

BEFORE AND AFTER THE COLONIALIZATION

During the times of the Moghuls, the DM and other autochthonous institutions (e.g. the _khânqah_) were places of education and learning for both the Muslims and Hindus in the Indian subcontinent. The language of instruction was mostly Persian.[12]

Already under Muhammad Ibn Tughluq (1325-51), rational sciences ('ulûm-e 'aqliyyah or ma'qûlât) were widespread, as "Hindustan could not keep aloof from the rational sciences and arts ('aqlî 'ulûm o funûn)" which were common during this time.[13] Philosophy, Logic, Mathematics, Astronomy, Geometry, Medicine and Music were considered to be especially important.[14] It is generally recognized that the Islamic mystics (Sûfîs) played an outstanding role in the transmission of knowledge. They were the ones who taught the 'aqliyyat.[15]

Like many other authors inquiring into the Islamic educational system Gilani too idealized it and presented it as humane, free from elitist tendencies and not oriented in a functional way. The educational content and methods had, however, been greatly influenced by leading personalities of the time. Gilani himself stresses this fact: the students only learned the "teachings of the sun and of the books" and belonged to groups dealing with educational (ta'lîmî halqe).[16] They were thus integrated into a kind of guild: "together with the teacher, they (the students) formed a guild of the educated–ashab-e 'amamah".[17] Various changes in the curricula of the DM point towards a social adaptation of the institutions of learning,[18] thus revealing their functional character. The curriculum valid up to this day in the Indian subcontinent for the DM is the so called dars-e nizâmî[19] stressing ma'qulat, introduced in the 18th century by Mulla Nizam al-Din (died 1748)[20] near Lucknow and having absorbed a number of secular modernizations.[21]

With the arrival of the colonial rulers, traditional educational was more and more marginalized. The British substituted with a new formal system, tailored to the British needs.[22] Since then, the formal educational system was heavily promoted by the Governments, while the religious schools enjoyed little official backing. They eked out a precarious existence by partly financing themselves through private donations. The educational system was representative of traditional society, socially coherent, hierarchical and stable.

The policy of modernization was continued by the supporters of the new nation state of Pakistan; the modern system of education was promoted, and the traditional way increasingly neglected. Such a policy of giving a modern orientation to educational nevertheless could not ignore completely the clergy and other traditional forces. This led to a number of concessions towards the 'ulamâ partly to meet their demands for the realization of a state based on Islamic principles, and partly to guard and guarantee at least formally the national ideology of Pakistan.

The state also had to make an effort to integrate the heterogenous Muslim community of Pakistan with its variety of ethnic, linguistic and sectarian orientations, and to try and win over the elite of the clergy. The politicians however were careful not to grant too many rights and priviliges to the clergy.

Mainly for political reasons, the *'ulamâ* and their schools were neglected to a considerable degree. The reason for such neglect was the presumed ignorance in worldly affairs and their supposed incompetence, which was again and again stressed by representatives of the state and of the formal system. A closer look reveals, however, that this ignorance and incompetence were brought about by the state itself.

UNDER AYUB KHAN

Under Ayub Khan (1958-69), the disputes between governmental authorities and the clergy increased. This is reflected in various measures which Ayub Khan took regarding the upholders of Islamic tradition— such as the establishment of the CII and of the IRI.[23]

THE ORGANIZATIONS OF DÎNÎ MADÂRIS

The Government's attempts to modernize traditional Islamic activities may be seen in the nationalization of the system of Awqâf [24] and the move to attach the DM to the formal system of education so as to serve the national interest.

The polemics of Ayub Khan against the clergy are well known. The Government's evaluation of the entire system of DM is indicated by the fact that only those persons were considered to be literate who had enjoyed a formal education, while even a student who had reached the highest degree of a madrasah was considered an illiterate.[25] This concept, widespread among representatives of the colonial sector to this day, is reminiscent of the eurocentric outlook of Macaulay.

In order to control the *'ulamâ'* in Pakistan and to put the DM in their place, the state attempted to attach the schools to governmental departments. The administrative restructuring of the mosques and madâris achieved this goal only in a limited way. A number of these institutions were, in fact, nationalized. Administrative control, and with it the exercise of economic and political influence on the clergy, were now meant to be achieved in a more effective way by means of curricular reform.[26]

The emergence of umbrella organizations of the DM in Pakistan was a reaction to these governmental measures. Up to this point, the DM had financed themselves exclusively out of endowments that were attached to them and out of private donations. As has been shown before, the Government meant to take hold of the waqf endowments in order to channel their profits to the exchequer and to weaken their position as autonomous institutions. All this was meant to advance the politics of modernization and to integrate the clergy as modern *mullas*.[27] In order to protect themselves better against this kind of attack, traditionalists, especially the Muslim dignitaries, organized themselves in associations, just prior to the proclamation of the West Pakistan Waqf Property Ordinance 1961 and the transfer of private endowments to the state which was connected with it. As the *'ulamâ'*, however, were not a monolithic group they organized themselves, their adherents and their centres according to different schools of thought. These schools of thought established mainly in British India in the nineteenth century. They were the following:

> *The Deobandis.* Originally from the seminary in Deoband and consisting mostly of *ashrâf* and state employees, the Deobandis continued after the creation of Pakistan. They were able to establish a DM organization in the course of the nationalization of the Islamic endowments. In 1959, they founded the Wafâq al-Madâris al-'Arabiyyah in Multan.

> *The Brelwis.* This group emerged as a reaction to the anti-colonial Deobandis, and mainly addressed the peasants and the poorer strata of the rural society. In 1959, they established the Tanzîm al-Madâris al-'Arabiyyah in Dera Ghazi Khan.

> *The Ahl-e Hadith.* With a high degree of organization, members belonging to this school of thought mostly comprised well-to-do merchants. As a reaction to the Brelwis as well as the Deobandis they took a "fundamentalist" stand, i.e. they rejected any intermediation between man and God like the canonical law or the cult of saints. In 1955 they established the Markaz-e Jam'iyyat Ahl-e Hadith in Lyalpur (today's Faisalabad).

> *The Shias.* Their long history on the Indian subcontinent enabled them to assemble their DM in 1959 in Lahore under the Majlis-e Nazârât-e shî'ah Madâris-e 'Arabiyyah.

The main tasks of these umbrella organizations were to organize the DM, to reform the curricula and enrich them with modern subjects as well as standardize the system of examinations. None of the umbrella organizations were, however, able to achieve their goals till the late seventies, when a new "attack" was launced by the state with the rise to power of Zia ul Haq which mobilized them and initiated a new phase of reform.

The readiness of the '*ulamâ*' to reform the schools as well as the DM umbrella organizations, reveals both their desire for political participation[28] and their view that their system was backward and therefore in need of reform. This distorted view was a result of the colonial penetration and was cultivated by the Islamic intelligentsia and the religious elite. The acceptance of their own backwardness and their failure in putting through the goals of their umbrella organizations, nevertheless, illustrated the incapacity of the traditionalists to meet the "requirements of modernity" as understood by the *avant-garde*. This failure seems to have been sufficient ground for considering the clergy as "backward".

CURRICULAR AFFILIATION

In 1961, a committee for the revision of the curricula of the DM was formed to bring about the affiliation of the DM.[29] The clergy was under-represented in this body.[30] This tilt towards the state was also reflected in the committee's proposals for the reform of curricula.

The report of the committee covered around 700 of the better known, larger DM in which *dars-e nizâmî* was taught. The necessary investigation was financed largely by the Asia Foundation,[31] indicating an American interest in the religious schools.

Already in the fifties, Hafiz Nadhr Ahmad had researched the subject and had made certain modernising and reformist proposals. The committee which worked entirely in the interest of the state pursued the same goal. This was evident in its proposals, suggesting general education besides the religious educational in the DM. The reforms were justified by stating that the current needs of the nation and the "challenges of the time" had to be met. While translating the proposals into action, the clergy was to play their "full part as citizens".[32] This was only possible, according to the committee, if "unnecessary non-religious subjects from the existing syllabus" were limited and substituted by "religious subjects based upon undisputed sources of knowledge".[33] The committee furthermore aimed "to widen the outlook of Darul Uloom students and to increase their mental horizon". This, they said, was only possible, if new disciplines were introduced, enabling the students to also enter puplic professions.[34]

This view was shared by the authors of the Report of the Commission on National Education 1959.[35]

Very much on the lines of the report of 1959, the committee stressed the importance of religious education and instruction and applauded the contribution of the DM in this context.[36] An extension of the syllabus through the introduction of secular subjects was, however, unavoidable. In contrast, the report of 1959 had suggested the enrichment of the formal educational system with Islamic rites and verses from the Koran: as a subject, religion was to be made compulsory up to the eighth grade and optional in secondary education. In tertiary education opportunities for Islamic Sciences were to be created.[37]

Research was to be conducted to establish the compatibility of Islam with the modern world.[38] Alongside the modernization of the system of education and of Islam, the maktabs and madâris were to be reformed.[39] Against this background, the Committee for the Improvement of Syllabus proposed: "The whole of the primary education as approved by the Department of Education shall be compulsory for all students of Darul Uloom under the scheme now prescribed by *us*".[40]

It was only following this that the ordinary courses of *Dâr al-'Ulûm* were to be taught. The formal schools, in contrast, were to integrate the religious subjects at the primary level,[41] as their students did not have sufficient religious instruction at this level.[42]

The change of syllabi aimed at the reform of the system geared more towards an "effective and realistic" education, which would limit the *dars-e nizâmî*, fade out non-religious subjects, and to extend the courses to ten years, preceded by five years of primary education.[43]

The new school system had five stages. The innovations at each stage are presented in Table 11.

Following the stage of *al-'la*–the highest stage–the committees designated five examinations on "Hadith", "Astronomy" and "Euclidic Mathematics". Traditional components of the syllabus of the DM were not taken into consideration in the committee's proposals.[44]

The neglect of some traditional subjects and the proposal to give more space to new subjects point towards an intention of bringing about a basic change in religious education. Other changes concern the language of instruction. Urdu was to remain compulsory only at the primary level; at the secondary level English and/or Arabic would be the medium of instruction.[45]

The reasoning for the curricular changes were many: learning English was considered very important for the handling of modern life and for the mission of Islam; the introduction of Mathematics was explained by saying that people now lived in the age of mathematical physics. Urdu, in contrast, was "recommended... as medium of instruction". The singling out of the subject logic, was explained by saying that it was "not essential in achieving the objective of religious education".[46]

These reforms of the content of education reflect the integrationist outlook of the Ayub Khan regime.

TABLE 11 : PROPOSALS AND CHANGES OF THE COMMITTEE OF 1960/61

Arabic	Primary Level	Lower Secondary	Middle Secondary	Upper Secondary	Highest Level
	ibteddiyah	*thanâwi tahtâni*	*thanâwi wustâni*	*thanâwi fawqâni*	*al'la* (sic)
Duration	5 Years	3 Years	2 Years	2 Years	3 Years
Class	1-5	6-8	9-10	11-12	13-15
Suggestions and modifications by the Committee	According to directions of the Ministry of Eductaion	1. More Koran and Hadith 2. Prophet's tradition Islamic law 3. Modern Arabic lit. 4. English 5. Mathematics 6. Social Sciences 7. Sports 8. Urdu	1. Islamic History 2. Alternative books 3. English 4. Sports 5. Optional subject (preferably Urdu)	1. Principles of tafsir 2. More Hadith 3. Modern Arabic lit. 4. English 5. Less Philosophy 6. Less Logic	1. History of Hadith compilation 2. *Fatâwâ* 3. Modern Philosophy
Summary		All but 2 are new subjects; Arabic and English preferred	All subjects are new and obligatory	All Subjects are new or modified; four subjects are obligatory one is optional	English and subsidiary subjects are additional; in the final year only the study of Hadith

Sources : Based on the "Report of the Committee set up by the Governor of West Pakistan for recommending improved syllabus for the various Darul Ulooms and Arabic Madrasas in West Pakistan", Lahore, Appendix I.

In order to supervise the working of the DM a Directorate of Religious Education was proposed to be established within the Auqaf Department. It was to monitor and evaluate the standards of work of the students and teachers.[47]

Future teachers of the DM were to attend six months' re-orientation courses at Teachers' Training Centres, to be established, in order to adequately learn the new subjects. Educational sciences, school organization and clarification of national goals made up their programme.[48]

These proposals for the reform of the religious educational system were translated into action only in a limited way. They illustrate, however, the attitude of the Government towards the clergy: they were to participate at least formally in the affairs of the Government[49] and were not to confine themselves merely "to the teaching of Islamic knowledge", but were to help in modernizing the nation "by selling fertilizers, opening poultry farms, distributing high-yield seeds to farmers. . . ."[50] This policy reflected the then strategy of the Green Revolution. It aimed at reaching at least 45,000 students and teachers in more then 400 DM. These modernization measures were to reach as many areas of society as possibe in order to be profitable to the state. However, such endeavours failed, at least in so far as the traditional sector was concerned.

The official strategy of optimization (i.e. reaching the maximum number of people at minimum cost) has not been altered. It is still of current importance within the Islamization drive.

Basically this approach was an attack on the understanding of the purpose of education of the students and teachers of the DM, and was opposed by many of them. It was, however, backed up by representatives of the *avant-garde*, like Mawdudi.[51]

The proposals of the committee thus adopted a different interpretation of religious education from that prevailing within the DM. According to the committee, religious education not only included instruction in Koran, Hadith and other traditional subjects but was also concerned with issues of national importance and the propagation of an Islamic nation or even of an Islamic community (*ummah*). This meant the transformation of Islam from a theological concept to an ideological one.

ISLAM AND DÎNÎ MADÂRIS UNDER BHUTTO

The Ayub Khan administration's attempts to integrate the '*ulamâ*' via their schools, was not at first pursued under the Bhutto regime (1971-77). The overwhelming victory of the Pakistan People's Party (PPP) gave rise to the idea that the clergy in Pakistan had vanished once and for all from the political and social scene[52]—an idea which was to prove a fallacy a few years later.

Bhutto's ideas were dominated by the wish to modernize the country. Under his policies, the society experienced an increased centralization, from which the clergy suffered as well. One has to mention awqâf and education in this context. As in many other areas in politics, economy and administration, the educational system as well was nationalized[53] and thus placed under the control of governmental authorities. This led to a reorganization of the Tanzîm al-Madâris al-'Arabiyyah, in 1974. The aim was to unite, in order to counteract the menace of nationalization.

It has frequently been maintained that Bhutto rejected the clergy and did little to translate Islamic principles into reality. Therefore, his measures of Islamization are viewed as having been confined to his last year in office, when he made a number of concessions to the '*ulamâ*'; this view ignores the fact that the 1973 constitution gave more importance to Islam and its institutions–however modernized, like, the CII and the IRI, than ever before.[54]

There was a drive to ideologise the formal educational system under Bhutto, reflected in a reorganization of the curricula and the introduction of religious subjects.[55] By order of the Government, the CII in 1975/76 prepared a comprehensive report on a future Islamic system of education.[56]

It is remarkable that towards the end of the Bhutto era there was an attempt to improve the economic and social status of the DM students and teachers, who were, in fact, not affected by the politics of nationalization. Thus, the higher diplomas of the DM were recognized by the UGC. The official recognition was justified by saying that the graduates of the DM should have more socio-economic mobility. The National Assembly put the Certificate (*sanad*) of the Wafâq al-Madâris al-'Arabiyyah on the same level as an M.A. degree in Islamiyat, provided the students could qualify for a B.A. in English. The leaders of the DM, however, rejected recognition subject to this kind of a condition, so the proposal petered out.[57]

In order to discuss the equivalence of certificates, an equivalence committee of the UGC was established. The demands of the Tanzîm al-Madâris were presented to this committee in the National Assembly in 1973,[58] but adopted by the Assembly only in 1975. In 1976, the Ministry of Education finally recognized the certificates, so that the graduates of the religious schools could play "an effective role in the field of Education". The recognition was, however, limited only to B.A. degrees. Besides, not all universities agreed to this regulation. Thus the graduates of religious schools met with difficulties in admission to formal institutions of education. The issue was not taken up again until 1978.

SINCE ZIA UL HAQ

Under Zia ul Haq the activities concerning the DM increased in their effectiveness, reflecting the importance of religious schools in society and the role they were to play for the Zia Government. One may recall here that the movement of 1977 derived its momentum from the DM and the mosques,[59] even if it grew out of long term social and economic developments.

General Zia, taking advantage of the discord between the PPP and the PNA—led by certain sectors of the '*ulamâ*'—had to bear in mind the clergy and the DM as well, while he propagated Islam. During his visit to Sargodha in the middle of 1978, he lent an ear to the delegation of '*ulamâ*' asking him for greater autonomy for the DM. If Zia's campaign of Islamization was to have any credibility, he had to give in to the demands of the '*ulamâ*' at least partially.

THE *SARGODHA REPORT*

On 2 September 1978, Zia ul Haq informed the Ministry of Religious Affairs about his plans to prepare a survey of the DM:

... a Team or Sub-Committee should proceed to Sargodha and prepare a report, in the next three weeks, on Deeni Madrassahs currently established there. This report will be a prototype of the principal one which is to be compiled on a nation-wide basis.[60]

The issue was passed on to the Auqaf Wing of the Ministry of Religious Affairs whose Joint Secretary requested data on the subject from the CII.[61] After the expiry of the three weeks set by Zia, the so-called *Sargodha Report* was submitted to him in the English language.

It gives a short historical introduction which is followed by a description of the DM system in Sargodha. The DM education is reported to be spread over 9-10 years, subdivided into the following three phases:

Preparatory stage	3 years
Intermediate stage	2-3 years
Final stage	4 years

It is stated that after passing the examination of the formal primary stage, the students are sent to a madrasah, where they learn to read Arabic and Persian, without, however, learning how to write.[62]

There were 223 DM in the Sargodha Division where

...the owner is responsible for collecting donations.... The staff is ill paid with no
security of service or other benefits.... The students mostly hail from the rural areas
and belong to humble families.[63]

Education was free of charge and the prospects of securing jobs made
the DM attractive centres for socialization.[64] Through their different
curricula, knowledge in a number of areas was transmitted to the students.
The income of the DM came from the following sources:

- alms;
- collections during Muslim festivities, such as *'îd*;
- income from properties (shops, houses, agriculture land, endowments); and
- small incomes from adjacent shrines.[65]

This listing is followed by a number of proposals about how to improve the
finances of the DM, and their curricula.
The Team held that the Government should not deprive the DM of
their autonomous status. The Government did not have the means to
improve the situation of the DM nor was the curriculum sufficiently
flexible to allow the Government to intervene in a supportive manner.

What is to be done is to extend the recognition and patronage to the Deeni
Madrasahs.... Most of the difficulties of these institutions relate to proprietary
rights over lands on which they are situated, grant of scholarships to the students
and teachers for higher education and recognition of their *sanads* for the purpose
of obtaining jobs in the army and civil services.[66]

In order to overcome the shortcomings of the DM, changes of
curriculum should be undertaken, more precisely by introducing technology and science. Thus, an integration of the DM students into the formal
system of education could be ensured. The first step would be to establish
an All Pakistan Education Advisory Board in order to report on the DM.[67]
For higher education (M.A. and M.Phil.) a Federal *'ulamâ'* Academy or
university was to be established and the system of examination
standardized.[68]
The report served as a model for the survey of 1979. It is necessary to
discuss it here, as it reveals which areas were of special interest to the
Central Government. It is preceded by the chronological presentation of
the developments within the Ministry of Religious Affairs concerning the
DM in order to give an insight into the administration and the events
concerning the projected survey.

ITTIHÂD AL-MADÂRIS

Before establishing a committee which was to lead the investigations on the DM, Zia ul Haq asked the Ministry of Religious Affairs on December 6, 1978 to report on the Ittihâd al-Madâris.

The answer in Urdu stated that after Pakistan was established the *'ulamâ'* had tried to put the different schools of thought of the madâris under a unified umbrella organization. The Ittihâd al-Madâris, however, had not achieved any influence and in fact had now ceased to exist.[69] The Wafâq al-Madâris al-'Arabiyyah was said to have argued against a policy of unification.

From this it appears that some religious leaders were against the prevailing *status quo* in the madâris and expressed their dissatisfaction with merely religious education and made suggestions for its improvement. On the other hand, at least one school of thought—that of the Deobandis—was opposed to these proposals. The mutual polemics among the schools of thought might eventually have brought down the movement of the Ittihâd al-Madâris.

It was this awareness of the need for reform within the DM, which made it easy for Zia ul Haq to demand an alternative programme following the National Survey of 1979.

A NATIONAL SURVEY

The National Committee for Dînî Madâris·,[70] established in Islamabad on January 17, 1979, was to draw up proposals with reference to the *Sargodha Report* with the purpose of "extending their (the DM) scope with a view to transforming them into an integral part of our educational system".[71] The *Halepota Report* is named after the chairman Dr. A.W.J. Halepota, then director of the IRI, and former member of the CII,[72] who was largely responsible for the report of 1961 under Ayub Khan. According to this report, the DM were not only worse in their quality of education than the formal educational system but also their curricula were not meeting the needs of the nation. For making the DM "better institutions of learning and training in the comprehensive sense",[73] the report recommended

... concrete and feasible measures for improving and developing Deeni-Madrassahs along sound lines, in terms of physical facilities, curricula and syllabi, staff and equipment ... so as to bring education and training at such Madrassahs *in consonance with the requirements of modern age and the basic tenets of Islam* ... to expand higher education and employment opportunities for students of the Madrassahs ... integrating them with the overall educational system in the country....[74]

This concept of Islam stood in sharp contrast to the concepts of the traditional *'ulamâs'*.

A National Committee for Dînî Madâris

Sixteen of the 27 members of the committee had been nominated by the Ministry of Religious Affairs.[75] Of them, eleven were theologians or scholars of religious affairs, with eight of them bearing the title of *mawlânâ* and being chairmen of Madâris in urban centres of the Punjab.[76] Other members were vice-chancellors of the universities of Peshawar, Quetta, Bahawalpur and Sindh; two were from the Ministry of Religious Affairs and one from the Ministry of Education.[77] Even though eleven members of the committee originally were to be coopted,[78] the Government nominated six more: four religious scholars,[79] one educational scientist and one natural scientist. The remaining five, nominated by the committee itself, included three religious scholars,[80] a bureaucrat and an educational scientist, Hafiz Nadhr Ahmad,[81] who had proved his competence through numerous publications on the DM.

The committee thus had strong representation from the Government and the *'ulamâ'* (15 *mawlânâs*) and therefore was considered a legitimate body whose proposals would be acceptable both to the clergy and the Government. The Government obviously had gone through a process of learning and had taken the *'ulamâ'* more into confidence than in 1960. Yet, the relatively high proportion of religious scholars could be misleading: the dignitaries in question were all representatives of a religious elite the majority of whom were concerned with protecting the interests of the state. They often served as a means of legitimation of governmental policies.

The *Halepota Report*

In order to tackle its task the committee established five sub-committees.

The report at first provides a short historical overview of the genesis and dispersion of the DM and the influence of the colonial rulers on the Muslim system of education. It states that the financial situation of the DM was as lamentable as the state of their curricula, which did not help students gain access to the civil service.[82]

A further problem according to the report was the lack of uniformity of the curricula and the systems of examination. It stressed, however, that the DM were the transmitters of the cultural heritage of the society and that the students could boast of a motivation for learning not known within the formal system, while formal schools suffered from corruption. The committee was of the view that the DM should only receive aid through governmental institutions which they themselves deemed proper. This meant that the Government should not force the DM in any way to adopt new concepts and directions.[83]

For the integration of the two systems of education, the committee proposed to insert modern subjects into the *dars-e nizâmî*. While the report of the committee for the modern subjects only referred to the curricula of the Ministry of Education, the religious subjects were dealt with in a detailed manner.[84]

At the primary school stage, i.e. up to grade five, Urdu, Arithmetic, Social Rules and General Science were to be introduced. On the secondary stage up to grade ten General Mathematics, General Science, Pakistan Studies and English were proposed. At the graduation stage, leading up to B.A. and M.A., two out of three optional subjects—Political Economy, Political Sciences and English—were to be taken.

According to the report, at the secondary stage, the newly introduced subjects were to form at least one-third of the instruction.[85] At the M.A. level Comparative Religious Sciences were to be offered as an optional subject, while Islamic History, Islam and Economy, and Islam and Politics would be compulsory. Institutions of *qirâ'at,* the artistic recitation of the Koran, were expected to offer similar combinations and to integrate modern subjects. The representatives of the four large schools of thought were basically agreed on the changes in the curricula.[86]

A further proposal of the committee concerned the establishment of an autonomous National Institute for Dînî Madâris. It was to consist of 18 members, i.e. three representatives of each of the four schools of thought, one representative each from the Ministry of Education, the Ministry of Religious Affairs and the UGC and the Inter Board Commission, the chairman and a secretary. This institute was to have the task of conducting the examination of the madâris up to M.A., to publish the results, to award the certificates and to compile the curricula as well as to revise them.

In order to make the system of examination an effective one, the committee proposed to hold final examinations. This governmental examination was to be supervised by a responsible institute. Such governmental recognition of the examination system would enable the students to compete for better jobs.

The hope of achieving a better integration was based on the fact that there were written examinations in the added subjects under a newly established commission of examinations. In order to put the certificates of the commission at par with certificates of formal schools, the final certificates of the diffferent stages of the DM were furnished with an Arabic attribute.[87]

In order to improve the economic situation of students, teachers and of the DM, which were reported to have little financial resources as compared to the schools of the formal educational system, the Government was to provide them with landed property or Awqâf. The Government was also asked to ensure supplies to DM of water, gas and electricity.[88] Future housing programmes were to include the construction of DM. They were to be provided with furniture, books, teaching and writing equipment and, similar to colleges and universities, book banks would be established with the help of the National Book Foundation. Libraries of the DM were to enjoy Governmental support.[89] The DM under the umbrella of the National Institute for DM would not have to pay income tax. Financial aid would be granted without any condition. These projects were to be financed by Zakat funds.[90]

The teachers were to be supported economically and socially and in their further education; students should be enabled to attend school through granting of scholarships and they should be supported to continue their studies at other institutions of further education.[91]

The discrimination against teachers and students of the DM in the public employment was to be reduced and they were to be helped to establish themselves economically. At the same time students from formal institutions of education were to be given opportunities to enter the religious field, e.g. the Auqaf Department or the Ministry of Religious Affairs.[92] The actual prospects of integration in the field of employment were, however, not probed. How and where the officially examined army of *mawlânâs* would be absorbed into the labour market was not considered. This sort of short-sighted planning may soon result in problems, as discussed below.

The committee asked the DM to indicate their needs. The satisfaction of these needs later became feasible through the flow of Zakat funds.[93] The foundation was thus laid for a change in the structure of consumption within the DM.

The proposals of the committee were based apparently on a perception that the DM were inferior to the formal educational system. These ideas may be considered as attempts of the representatives of the Islamic *avant-garde* and the religious elite to raise the level of the DM and demonstrate the Governmental strategy of integrating the DM into political system and encouraging their participation in the political process. This also coincided with the interest of the religious elite.

The report of the committee was submitted six months behind schedule, on December 17, 1979. During the discussion within the committee, the non-interference of the Government in the affairs of the DM was frequently emphasized. On August 4, 1980 the sub-committee also suggested that the DM themselves should decide on the acceptance or refusal of the reformed curriculum. They stressed, however, that only the graduates from the DM were to be considered eligible for jobs who had English as a compulsory subject up to grade 10.[94]

REACTION OF THE DÎNÎ MADÂRIS

At first, the DM reacted to the activities of the committee in a positive manner. The representatives of the Islamic *avant-garde* especially welcomed the attempts at reform. The Urdu daily *Hurriyat* stated that a reform aiming at the unification of the different theological schools of the DM was important and necessary. According to the daily, it was difficult to adequately judge the achievements of the students due to the variety of procedures in examination and admission and due to the different standards. The committee for DM was considered an important step in the direction of uniformity.[95]

By this time some disagreements had, however, emerged within the different schools of thought and also between these schools and the committee. More and more Islamic dignitaries of the traditional sector considered the committee to be a representative of state power. Serious objections were raised, especially by the Deobandis who, like the representatives of other schools of thought, would see their predominance in the traditional sector affected. In his call for boycott (*radd-e 'aml*) in February 1981, an important representative of the Deobandis, Muhammad Yusuf Ludhianwi, sharply criticized the committee and expressed his concern about the Government control inherent in the measures of reform, which he labelled as irreligious (*lâ dînî*).[96] Once the DM was brought under a legislative framework they would be important only as official institutions and would become the toy (*khêlônâ*) of state power; they would thus lose their autonomy.[97] He pointed out to the Government three dangers in any intervention into the affairs of the DM:

(1) It could lead to a countrywide uproar (*hijân*) as the Deobandis rejected the plans of the Government and were preparing for resistance.

(2) The Government would have to provide a considerable amount of money for the implementation of the DM project; the cost in

the first six years were estimated to be Rs. 67.19 million. This expenditure would have to be met out of tax income which would burden the tax payer.

(3) There would be strikes and demonstrations which until now had not been part of the tradition of the DM; therefore, all other madâris would be called upon to resist the implementation of the proposals according to their duties to God and Islam.[98]

One year earlier, Ludhianwi had made polemical statement against the DM committee,[99] saying that the committee was continuing the policies of the British and was willing to subordinate the traditional content of education to the current sciences. He did not consider the formal system of education worth striving for. He pointed to the arrogance of the representatives of the state who intended to make the illiterate students of the DM literate. This reflected, he said, the tradition of Macaulay (1800-1859). As the teachers and students of the DM were discriminated against by society, he endorsed some of the proposals made by the DM committee. The problem was, however, that the proposed improvements were linked to conditions. Thus, the affiliation with the national institute for DM or with a *muqtadirah* (authority) was presupposed.[100] Furthermore, the proposal to improve the economic situation of the DM went against the eight basic rules of Muhammad Qasim Nanotawi (1832-1879)[101] who had stated:

As long as the *madrasah* does not receive a regular income it will exist with the help of God. In case a regular income is found, as landed property, factories, trade or the promise of a rich gentleman, the grace of God will vanish so that the invisible help will stop and there will be dispute among the workers. An uncertain source of income is helpful, while the participation of the Government and of rich personalities is damaging. It is true that those who do not seek reputation by giving alms will receive higher blessings and prosper. Thanks be to God; the alms of righteous people is a permanent source of income.[102]

The representatives of the DM, according to Ludhianwi would fall under state control, following stupid people (*malghûbah*) and finally be eductated to become loyal bureaucrats (*wafâdâr sarkârî mulâzamîn*) who would neither be proper scholars nor proper theologians. Mawlana Muhammad Yusuf Lùdhianwi held a radical point of view: The '*ulamâ*' were to insist on their own curricula till all non-religious content of education was eradicated from formal institutions of education.[103] This implied, in the first place, a change of the formal educational system.

Finally he called upon the DM to reject the proposals of the committee entirely, in order not to make the gaining of certificates and titles the aim of the *'ulamâ'*.[104] Moreover, he considered the proposed curriculum overloaded and that the implementation of the proposals would destroy the proper character of the DM.[105]

This call for boycott was followed by a campaign against the proposals which now had an official character. The DM committee received 39 telegrams addressed to Zia ul Haq. All of them rejected the proposals of the committee. Among the reasons given were:

> ... as these (proposals) are against the sanctity of religious institutions;[106]

or

> Government should not interfere in the affairs of religious institutions;[107]

or

> ... it is against the spirit of Dini Madaris to be run privately and if promulgated it would be against national interest and harm religious education.[108]

Even the central organization of the Wafâq al-Madâris expressed its disappointment with the proposals of the committee in a letter dated 25.3.81 to Dr. Halepota and refused to cooperate with its chairman.[109] A campaign of this kind was easy to organize as the four largest DM of Pakistan belonged to an interconnected, very influential family, close to the thinking of the Deobandis.[110]

Besides the four DM under the control of these families the influence of religious schools in the NWFP is important. In this context one should mention the non-conformism of Mufti Mahmud, the former leader of the Pakistan National Alliance (PNA) manifested against Bhutto.[111] As a politicised member of the clergy he advocated the introduction of Islam as a norm for the state even before the movement of 1977 became public.[112] He opposed any state interference in the curricula of the DM (*dînî madâris kê nisâb meñ kissî tabdîlî kî darûrat nahîñ*);[113] considered the syllabus of the DM "perfect and comprehensive", but agreed that it should be extended to modern sciences and that the standard of living of the students and their teachers should be raised.[114]

Statements of this nature demonstrated the affinity of Mufti Mahmud to the colonial sector of society and his realization that the religious dignitaries were backward. He could well be considered as belonging to one of the intermediary groups. As is now clear, representatives of this sector also had access to other more traditionally inclined intermediary groups and the traditional sector. In rejecting the colonial sector, the

representatives of these intermediary sectors tried to provide themselves
with a mass base via traditional institutions. As they had access to such
institutions they were able to do so and were in a position to organize mass
movements.

In spite of the campaign of the 'ulamâ', the Ministry of Education on
March 15, 1981 insisted "in the interest of the nation" to arrange a meeting
with the 'ulamâ'.[115] Dr. Halepota confirmed that the DM were not to be
nationalized and that they were only to obtain financial support and that
their graduates would receive equal treatment.[116]

On April 19, 1981, the Ministry of Religious Affairs and the Ministry
for Minorities (Auqaf Section) which had borne the costs for the DM
committee wrote to the Islamic Research Institute, whose director was the
chairman of the committee:

Since the 'ulamâ' themselves do not want that the Government should take any
initiative in this behalf and since the Government's intentions have been suspected
quite unjustifiably, no further action will be taken in this behalf, at least for the time
being.

According to Dr. Halepota, Zia ul Haq had expressed his regret to the
committee members later on and had mentioned his weariness with the
'ulamâ'.

In December 1980, the Centre of the Deobandis in Multan had written
to Zia and had asked him not to implement the proposals of the committee.
On that occasion, they pointed out to him some mistakes in the report.[117]
The integration of the DM by the state was, however, implemented despite
all the criticism of the clergy.

THE DÎNÎ MADÂRIS REGULATION

Due to the resistance of the DM, Zia ul Haq was forced to postpone for the
time being the reform of the DM as proposed by Dr. Halepota. It projected
an assimilation of the two systems while conserving the autonomy of the
DM.[118] A National Institute for Dînî Madâris Pakistan (NIDMP) was to be
established with two chambers.

The Syndicate was to consist of 'ulamâ', representatives of the
Ministries and institutions of education as well as of the provincial
Governments. Out of 22 members, 12 were 'ulamâ', pertaining to different
schools of thought. The tasks of the syndicate included the supervision of
the DM attached to the NIDMP. Furthermore, it was to be responsible for
improving the qualifications of the teachers, conduct examinations at the
higher and intermediate stages, lay down conditions for affiliation to the
NIDMP, conduct admission tests, issue certificates, levy and collect

contributions, administer the funds of the institute (NIDMP), present the annual budget and take care of any other administrative matters.

The second chamber was the Academic Council comprising 32 members with 20 '*ulamâ*' and 12 administrative experts and academicians. Its tasks were to advise the syndicate in all matters of scientific and pedagogical nature, with special emphasis on matters of curricula and examinations.

The chairman of the NIDMP had quite a unique position; he was chairman of both chambers, the Syndicate and the Academic Council. Only the President could substitute for him. In exceptional cases the chairman could take over the absolute leadership of the NIDMP and was then responsible only to the President. He was not subject to state jurisdiction. The President of Pakistan was the ultimate authority.

The working languages of the institute were to be Urdu and Arabic. The institute was to be financed from different sources: contributions of the DM, grants-in-aid by the state and by different institutions, scholarships, awqâf funds and other sources.[119]

This outline obviously is merely a modified version of the "secular" statutes of the Islamic University of 1980. Its secular character is said to have frightened off the '*ulamâ*'; strategicallly, it would have been better for the Government to have the clergy chalk out a regulation for the DM themselves.[120] The outline reflected the proposals on the religious educational system submitted by the CII in 1978.[121]

As the DM were at first able successfully to escape the "control" of the Government and to prevent the introduction of the proposals of the National Committee for Dînî Madâris (NCDM) the regulation with its inbuilt poor drafting[122] was once more ineffective. It had been the most important part of the crucial report.[123] The proposals in fact at first could not be implemented due to the resistance of large sections of the clergy. The critical questions concerned the absolute authority of the proposed umbrella organization (NIDMP) and the economic autonomy of the DM.[124] In spite of the regulation being cancelled in its totality, the proposals of the *Halepota Report* and of the DM were implemented.

FORMAL RECOGNITION OF RELIGIOUS SCHOOLS

The Government continued through its policy of reform, its attempt to control the DM, in order to deprive them of any political influence. Doing so through the proposals of the NCDM had proved infructuous. As the political clout of the organized Pakistani clergy could not be underestimated, the Government tried to associate them at least formally with the making of state policy. For this purpose, a few '*ulamâ*' and *mashâ'ikh* conventions were organized between 1980 and 1984.[125] These conventions were meant to convey to the clergy that not only were they important for bringing about the Islamization but were indispensable for the national politics of Pakistan, which could not function without their cooperation. In reality, however, these conferences merely served to pacify the clergy, which, according to Yusuf Talal Ali[126] was easy to achieve due to their comparatively modest status.

A further important attempt to integrate the clergy was to recognize the final examination certificates of the DM. Already in June 1980 the sub-committee on equivalence of the degree of Tanzeem-e Madaris al Arabiyyah with B.A. /M.A. Islamiyat had limited the criteria for their recognition to the field of examination. As the madâris had a satisfactory procedure of examination which was free of any irregularities, their certificates were to be put on par with those of the formal educational system provided English and some other modern subjects were integrated into the religious curriculum. In principle, the certificates of a madrasah would be equal to a B.A. or M.A. in Islamiyat or in Arabic. Such equality in status for DM certificates had in the past been rejected by the universities (except the Peshawar University).[127] One may suppose that the universities were afraid of the competition from the new *mawlânâs* as teachers, especially in such subjects as Arabic and Islamic Sciences. Following the discussion on the recognition of the DM certificates between the CII, the UGC, the Establishment Division and the President since the end of 1980[128] the next attempt at integration was the establishment of the UGC Committee for the equal status of the DM certificates. Its proposals were finally implemented on April 16, 1981.[129] The *fawqâniyyah* certificate of Islamiyat and Arabic was to be recognized by colleges and universities on condition that the graduates of the DM would have successfully passed two more subjects which were compulsory for a B.A. examination.[130] This meant the revival of the proposals made in 1976.[131] Half-a-year later,[132] it was decided that for teachers of Arabic and Islamic Studies, parity of status with M.A. in these subjects should be given to the *Shahadatul-Fazila Sanad* of the Wafâq al-Madâris (Deoband), the *Shahadatul-Faragh* of the Tanzim al-Madâris (Brelwi) as well as to the final certificates of the two other schools of thought, the Shia and Ahl-e Hadith.[133] For all other professions the DM graduates would have to take examinations in two more subjects (excluding Arabic, Islamic Studies, Persian and Urdu).[134]

For the sake of uniformity, the certificate should bear the title of *Shahadah-ul Alamiya min uloom il islamia* for which in fact a 16-year DM education was necessary.[135] With this, the institutions of education of the '*ulamâ*' seemed to be integrated, and the *Pakistan Times* on 25.10.1982 solemnly announced: "Deeni Madaris degrees' equivalence decided".

THEIR ECONOMIC SITUATION

Besides the formal recognition of their graduates, there were changes in
the financial position of the DM. Table 12 gives a picture of rising deficits
in the annual budgets of the DM over the years. Thus for the country as a
whole, the income of the DM exceeded their expenditure by 2 per cent in
1960. Ten years later, the ratio of income to expenditure was 97:100. In
1979 the expenditure was 8.3 per cent higher than the income, with large
differences between the provinces.

The ever increasing deficit of the DM budgets threatened to grow even
more. The DM and their teachers and students did not seem to be capable
of checking this trend or taking any corrective action. They had little or no
access to any resources as they were mostly people of modest origins. This
is the context in which the Committee for DM demanded Government
support for them.

By eliminating the deficit, the Government could prove the sincerity
of its intentions towards the DM. Financial support was at first given
through Zakat.[139] As will be demonstrated later the official Zakat system
served as a political means to neutralize the clergy and its organizations.

TABLE 12: INCOME (I) AND EXPENDITURE (E) OF THE DÎNÎ MADÂRIS

	1960		1970	
	I in Rs	*E* in Rs	*I* in Rs	*E* in Rs
W.-Pakistan	3173258[136]	3098724	7883003	8157406
Punjab	2438245	n.d.	5400183	5672294
Sindh	n.d.	n.d.	1380808	1346060
NWFP	n.d.	n.d.	803174	812254
Baluchistan	n.d.	n.d.	159051	156759
Kashmir (Pak)	n.d.	n.d.	142078	130027
North. Areas	n.d.	n.d.	n.d.	n.d.
Islamabad	n.d.	n.d.	n.d.	n.d.
	1979		1983	
W.-Pakistan	39291850	42860844	n.a.	n.a.
Punjab	23657193	27943777	n.a.	n.a.
Sindh	9209988	8740197	n.a.	n.a.
NWFP	4833752	4492088[137]	38289997[138]	n.a.
Baluchistan	1590917	1684782	n.a.	n.a.
Kashmir (Pak)	n.a.	n.a.	n.a.	n.a.
North. Areas	n.a.	n.a.	n.a.	n.a.
Islamabad	n.a.	n.a.	n.a.	n.a.

Source: *Ahmad I*, pp. 730ff; *Ahmad II*, pp. 701ff; *Halepota Report*, p. 62 and pp. 214-217.
n.a.= not available, n.d. = no details given

ZAKAT FOR DÎNÎ MADÂRIS

The Zakat and Ushr Regulation of June 1980 did not in fact provide for the DM institutions to receive Zakat, as, according to the Shari'a, this was not permissible. The Koran reads:

The alms are only for the poor and the needy, and those who collect them, and those whose hearts are to be reconciled, and to free the captives and the debtors, and for the cause of Allah, and (for) the wayfarers....[140]

The needy among the DM nevertheless received Zakat through these institutions.[141] A precondition for receiving support through Zakat was a scrutiny of the DM according to the proposals of the *Halepota Report:*

This report should be examined and analysed, and recommendations formulated in respect of financial assistance to be provided to the present Deeni Madrassahs and their students, and there should be no discrimination whatsoever on sectarian basis.[142]

Even though Section 8 of the Zakat Regulation made clear that DM students were eligible to receive Zakat, a committee on the eligibility of Religious Institutions and their students for Zakat was convened.[143] The CII supported the receipt of Zakat by DM students.[144] It explained that the chairman of a madrasah (i.e. a *muhtamim*) could function as an "agent of the Zakat recipients",[145] but, at the same time pointed out that the institution of DM as such was not "eligible to receive Zakat under Shariah or under the Zakat Ordinance", but only the poor and needy students:

In order to fulfill the requirements of the principles of '*tamleek*' the recipient students will have to be made the exclusive owners of the Zakat received by them individually.[146]

According to the Ministry of Religious Affairs there were about 100 DM who "could be considered for financial assistance on priority basis" and proposed to the Provincial Zakat Councils (PZCs) 100 "prominent" DM.[147]

The total number of DM was 99 of whom 42 were Deobandi, 35 Brelwis, 17 Ahl-e Hadith and 5 Shia (Punjab), demonstrate a clear predominance. The distribution of schools of thought is approximately in proportion to their distribution in the country.[148] It is remarkable that the Shia DM are granted Zakat as well, even though its members have been exempted from the compulsory collection of Zakat.[149]

The Central Zakat Council (CZC) distributed the Zakat funds to the Provincial Zakat Councils (PZCs),[150] and prescribed the distribution on the following lines:

50 per cent to Local Zakat Committees
25 per cent for scholarships (of the formal educational systems)
10 per cent for DM students
 5 per cent for social institutions
 5 per cent for hospitals
 5 per cent for other purposes.[151]

According to the Zakat Regulation, Zakat funds distributed to the DM were not to be used for purchase of land, buildings, renovations, etc. but exclusively for current expenses such as subsistence of the students, remuneration of the teachers[152] and thus should serve to keep the DM functioning. The option for the DM to receive Zakat funds from the PZCs might have had a positive impact on their financial situation. Income from the traditional sources however declined due to the compulsory deduction of Zakat. It was alleged that "since the introduction of the Zakat system, the Deeni Madaris have voiced complaints that their source of private donations has dried".[153]

Next, one has to examine the impact of Zakat on the DM. To be eligible to receive Zakat, it was necessary to fulfil two conditions: the DM had to be registered as a society and had to have an account showing the correct use of the funds. Despite these rules, cases of corruption, both among the '*ulamâ*' as well as within the Zakat Administration were not unknown. Therefore, an 'Ulamâ' Committee with 12 members representing the different schools of thought was nominated by the Provincial Zakat Administration (PZA) in order to lay down the rules for the distribution and employment of Zakat funds. The '*ulamâ*' in question belonged exclusively to the religions elite, and were already integrated into the governmental establishments, either as members of the CII, the Auqaf Department or the *Halepota Report*. It is doubtful whether such a committee represented adequately either the interests of the traditional society or its capacity to effectively combat corruption.

CRITERIA FOR ZAKAT DISTRIBUTION

The 'Ulamâ' Committee at first had classified the DM into three groups:

(1) DM with more than 100 boarding students or with 200 and more students not living on the premises.
(2) DM with 50 to 100 boarding students or with 100 and more students not living on the premises.

(3) DM with 20 to 50 boarding students or with 50 and more students not living on the premises.

During the first year of the functioning of the Zakat system, Zakat funds were distributed according to the following lines:

Category 1: Rs. 20,000 per DM
Category 2: Rs. 15,000 per DM
Category 3: Rs. 10,000 per DM[154]

In order to increase the distribution of Zakat to the DM, additional criteria were introduced from 1981/82 onwards and a revised classification into five grades was laid down.[155]

Special Grade: Rs. 75,000 per year for a madrasah, in which *dars-e nizâmî* plus *dawrah-e hadîth* was taught, whose maintenance costs exceeded Rs. 300,000 per year and which had more than 200 students living on the premises.

First Grade: Rs. 50,000 per year for a madrasah, in which *dars-e nizâmî* and *dawrah-e hadîth* was taught with more than 100 students living on the premises.

Second Grade: Rs. 30,000 per year for a madrasah with 51 to 100 boarding students in which *dars-e nizâmî* up to *mawqûf 'aliyyah* was taught.

Third Grade: Rs. 20,000 per year for a madrasah with 20 to 50 boarding students in which *dars-e nizâmî* was taught.

Fourth Grade: Those madâris, where less than 20 students were living on the premises and with more than 100 students living outside were to be scrutinized by the 'Ulamâ' Committee and receive Zakat if the occasion arose. According to the *Pakistan Times,* dated 1.8.82, these DM were to receive Rs. 10,000 per year, while a fifth category (10 to 20 students) was to receive Rs. 7,000.[156]

Table 13 gives a summary of all the criteria for the receipt of Zakat by DM, the amount of Zakat funds spent and their rates of increase from 1981 to 1984.

Some trends in the distribution of Zakat may be pointed out. The first classification, differentiating only three grades, may be considered to be only a preliminary subdivision of the DM. The amounts allocated between Rs. 10,000 and 20,000 were too modest to cause any changes within the

TABLE 13: CATEGORIZATION OF THE DÎNÎ MADÂRIS ACCORDING TO RECEIPT OF ZAKAT

Grade of Education	No. of Boarders	Category 1980-81*	Category 1981-84	PZC Zakat 1981-82 1982-83 in 1000 Rs.	Inc. %	Rs per Student	PZC Zakat 1983-84 in 1000 Rs.	Inc. %	Rs. per Student	Inc. %	Inc. of Zakat 1981-84 in %
D.N.;D.H. <300000 Rs.	<200	special		75 100	33	42	300	200	125	198	300
Yearly expenditure for building											
D.N.;D.H.	<150	first	first	50 75	50	42	225	200	125	198	350
D.N.;D.H.	<75	second	second	50 75	50	58	150	100	125	116	200
D.N. up to mawqūf	<75		third	30 50	67	56	110	120	122	118	267
D.N. up to mawqūf	<50	second	fourth	30 50	67	83	75	50	125	51	150
D.N. with hifz and nāzirah	<20	third	fifth	20 30	50	125	30	0	125	0	50
D.N. hifz and nāzirah	<10		sixth	10 15	50	125	15	0	125	0	50
hifz and nāzirah	<20		seventh	10 15	50	63	20	33	38	-40	33
hifz and nāzirah	<10		eighth	7 10	43	83	10	0	83	0	43
hifz and nāzirah >10 boarder & <100 locals			ninth	>7 >10	—	—	>9.5				

Sourc:s: Calculations on the basis of al-Zakāt, vol. 1, no. 1, July 1981, p. 22. Punjab Provincial Zakat Administration (PPZA): Subā'i zakāt fund se dīnī madāris ko sālānah imdād ki fihrist, Lahore, 1985 (memeo); PPZA: Fihrist dīnī madāris jin ko sāl 1984/85 ke li' e subā'i zakāt fund se mālī imdad farāham ki gai, Lahore, 1986 (mimeo).

Explanations: D.N. = dars-e nizami: D.H. = dawrah-e hadith (nowadays equal to M.A.) mawqūf = secondary level (nowadays equal to B.A.);
hifz = Koran learning by heart; nāzirah = Reading and recitaiton of the Koran.
* = The first level includes schools having < 100 boarders or < 200 local students; they received a yearly amount Rs. 20,000 from the PZC.
The second level includes schools having 50-100 boarders or <100 locals; they received a yearly amount of Rs. 15,000 from the PZC.
The third level includes schools having 20-50 boarders or < 50 locals; they received the amount of Rs. 10,000 from the PZC.

DM. Later on, this rather rough classification was differentiated by splitting the first grade into three and the second grade into two further sub-groups. This classification was further extended by the '*ulamâ*' of the PZC Punjab by another five sub-groups, so that finally 10 grades for the receipt of Zakat emerged. This, in fact, implemented a proposal of the CZC of December 1980 aiming at the improvement of the Zakat distribution.[157]

The first two grades (special and first) had the highest increases in the Zakat funds allocated to them. Between 1981 and 1984, rates of 300 per cent up to 350 per cent were reached.[158] A similar, even though not as pronounced an increase took place in the next two grades with rates ranging between 200 per cent and 267 per cent for the same period. The fifth grade in the same period still registered a rate of increase of 150 per cent. The increase of the next two grades, in contrast, only came up to 50 per cent each. The second to last grade increased only by 33 per cent, the last one increased by 43 per cent.

As to the rates of increase of Zakat for students, those of the large DM enjoyed much larger increases than those of small DM. Thus, the rate of increase of funds for students of large DM reached 198 per cent while the rate for students belonging to small DM remained constant (0 per cent) and even decreased (-40 per cent). Also, the disbursement of Zakat decreased proportionally to the decrease of the size of the DM. This is especially true for the seventh grade. The steady increase of the number of small DM is certainly one reason for the stagnation and even decrease of Zakat received by their students.[159]

The Zakat administration followed a consistent policy of distribution from the very beginning. The Ministry of Religious Affairs had proposed 100 large DM for the disbursement of Zakat. These were well established schools with surplus budgets. This policy was also followed by the PZC and its '*ulamâ*': the large DM profited more from the Zakat system than the small ones. Most of the large DM were located in big cities or within the urban hinterland. This indicates a policy of directing most of the Zakat funds to the urban and away from the rural areas, as had frequently been demanded. These are areas where the bulk of the small fifth and sixth grade DM are located. The preference for urban centres can be seen in many political measures, not limited to those initiated by Zia ul Haq.[160]

The new categorization by the PZC Punjab results in a clear preference for the district of Lahore from 1981 to 1984, a tendency demonstrating the urban preference of the PZC.[161]

In the years 1981/82, 1982/83 and 1983/84 the proportion of Zakat for the Lahore DM out of the funds for the Punjabi DM amounted to 13.1 per cent, 12 per cent and 4 per cent respectively.[162] Equally pronounced is the increase in the absolute amounts of Zakat disbursed to the Lahore DM. This again is a reflection of the policy followed by the PZC since 1983/84 to give marked support to the urban DM at the cost of those in rural areas.

Zakat funds were disbursed to the DM according to the grades as shown in Table 13. Table 14 concerns the disbursement of Zakat to the DM in Punjab.

In 1982/83 the *dawrah-e hadîth* level of education received more support than it did two years later, in 1984/85. In 1982/83, the intermediate level (*mawqûf*) was the main recipient of the Zakat disbursements (Rs. 45,750,000 i.e. 66 per cent); in 1984/85 the contribution to this level was reduced to Rs. 11,695,000 (21 per cent) of the Zakat disbursement. In 1982/83 and 1984/85, the percentages for the *dawrah-e hadîth* were 25.9 and 18.6 respectively, those for the *mawqûf* 65.9 and 21. The *tahtânî* level

TABLE 14: DISBURSEMENT OF ZAKAT TO THE
DÎNÎ MADÂRIS IN THE PUNJAB, 1982-1983

Category	Numbers of DM	Amount of Zakat in 1000 Rs.	Zakat Disbursement According to Level of Education in 1000 Rs.	
Special	21	2100		
First	39	2925	*dawrah-e hadîth*	18000
Second	173	12975	(25.9 per cent)	
Third	484	24200	*mawqûf*	45750
Fourth	431	21550	(65.9 per cent)	
Fifth	174	5220	*tahtânî*	5640
Sixth	42	420	(8.1 per cent)	
Total	1364	69390	(100 per cent)	
		1984-1985		
Special	20	6000		
First	8	1800	*dawrah-e hadîth*	10350
Second	17	2550	(18.6 per cent)	
Third	47	5170	*mawqûf*	11695
Fourth	87	6525	(21.0 per cent)	
Fifth	515	15450	*tahtânî*	16575
Sixth	75	1125	(29.8 per cent)	
Seventh	601	12020		
Eighth	396	3960	*hifz, nâzirah*	17082
Ninth	116	1102	(30.7 per cent)	
Total	1882	55702	(100 per cent)	

Source: *fihrist dînî madâris jin kô sâl 1984/85 kê lîê sûbâ'î zakât fund sê mâlî imdâd frâham kî gâî*, PZC Punjab, Lahore, 1986 (mimeo, Urdu) and author's calculations. Cf. also Table 13.

at first received 8.1 per cent, reaching 29.8 per cent in 1984/85. In this year, the small DM were supported as well and received the largest proportion of Zakat funds (30.7 per cent).

This shows that the early disproportionate support to large DM (*dawrah* and *mawqûf*) had been shifted two years later in favour of the small DM, *tahtânî* and those of the lower grades. This shift in favour of small DM is contrary to what emerges in Table 13, which showed a preference for the large DM on the part of Zakat. Such a contradiction is all the more remarkable, as the number of small DM eligible for Zakat funds was extended considerably. Parallel to this, the flow of Zakat funds of the PZC to the small DM increased. The decrease of Zakat funds to large DM may have been due to the fact that many of the large schools rejected Zakat or that Zakat was withdrawn from them for political reasons.

Despite this clear redistribution from the large DM to the small, one should bear in mind that the rate of increase of Zakat funds to the large DM was much higher than to the small ones. The overall reduction of Zakat funds for the small DM may have been due to the increase in their number. Although the small schools received less support each time, the total amount received by them in 1984/85 was the highest in absolute figures.

DISBURSEMENT AT PROVINCIAL LEVEL

Table 15 showing Zakat disbursement from the provincial Zakat funds to religious schools demonstrates that the number of small DM receiving Zakat increased only slowly in the beginning. Ten per cent of the Zakat funds disbursed to the provinces by the CZC were to go to the DM. Instead, during the first year, only 1.9 per cent reached the DM. The subsequent years saw only a nominal increase. Up to 1984, only 3.5 per cent (Rs. 2,752 million) of the Zakat funds went to the DM and 9.4 per cent in 1984/85. This equals an average of about 5.2 per cent for the first five years. Only 50 per cent of the amount earmarked for the DM actually reached them.

In 1983/84, the proportion of Zakat funds reaching the DM went down from 5.2 per cent to 3.1 per cent. This reduction was the result of the Government move to curb the ever-increasing number of religious schools eligible to receive Zakat.

The reduction of Zakat disbursements in 1983/84 may be demonstrated not only by the payments effected but also by the decreased number of DM supported, which fell from 1,433 to 1,125 DM, a decrease of more than 20 per cent DM "worthy of Zakat". However, in 1984/85, the number of DM increased rapidly, reaching a peak of 2,525 DM. The reason for this may have been the special support to DM in Sindh.

TABLE 15: ZAKAT DISBURSEMENTS FROM THE PROVINCIAL ZAKAT FUND TO THE DÎNÎ MADÂRIS

(A) Zakat funds disbursed in 1,000 Rs.

Year	Punjab	Sindh	NWFP	Baluchi.	Islamabad	Total
1980-81	9400	10	2755	1811	—	13977
1981-82	17230	59	4122	317	—	21759
1982-83	28190	1308	5741	3807	—	39109
1983-84	8890	4735	8463	1290	78	23457
1984-85	64590	7475	12098	9369	418	95950
Total	128300	13588	33181	16595	486	193161

(B) Number of Dînî Madâris

Year	Punjab	Sindh	NWFP	Baluchi.	Islamabad	Total
1980-81	634	2	189	210	—	825
1981-82	939	3	261	190	—	1203
1982-83	1033	40	300	60	—	1373
1983-84	362	123	328	310	2	815
1984-85	1749	135	357	253	31	2272
Total	4717	303	1435	1023	33	7511

(C) Number of students

Year	Punjab	Sindh	NWFP	Baluchi.	Islamabad	Total
1980-81	35000	269	7785	24147	—	67201
1981-82	45000	364	10068	2133	—	57565
1982-83	46000	1354	13720	25802	—	86876
1983-84	13813	8115	14596	2151	65	38740
1984-85	69677	9700	15361	15615	697	111050
Total	209490	19802	61530	69828	762	361432

(D) Average annual amount per student in Rs.

Year	Punjab	Sindh	NWFP	Baluchi.	Islamabad
1980-81	269	40	354	75	—
1981-82	283	164	410	150	—
1982-83	613	966	418	150	—
1983-84	644	583	580	600	1200
1984-85	927	771	788	600	600

(E) Proportion of funds disbursed to Dînî Madâris out of Zakat funds passed on to the provinces by the CZC, 1980-1985

Year	Punjab in %	Sindh in %	NWFP in %	Baluchi. in %	Islamabad in %	Total in %
1980-81	2.1	0.01	2.6	4.0	—	1.9
1981-82	5.8	0.06	5.9	1.1	—	4.4
1982-83	6.4	0.9	5.5	8.5	—	5.2
1983-84	2.0	3.0	8.1	2.9	1.0	3.1
1984-85	10.9	3.7	8.6	15.6	4.2	9.4
Total	5.8	1.6	6.3	7.4	1.3	5.2

Sources: Data by the CZC, Islamabad, 1985 (mimeo) and author's calculations.

At the provincial level, different trends are discernible. In 1983/84, the Zakat funds for Punjab and in Baluchistan decreased, while those for Sindh and the NWFP increased. This was either due to the absence of the *'mushrooming* of DM'[163] in these two provinces or to a different internal policy of the Zakat administration. It may be presumed that the increase of DM in the Punjab and in Baluchistan is more widespread than in the other provinces.[164] It would appear that the Zakat administration in Sindh is highly interested in supporting its DM. This is also true of the NWFP and of Baluchistan. The Punjabi DM are strongly supported in any case.

Aspects of the DM in NWFP, in Baluchistan and in Sindh, traced here, are of special interest. The DM in the NWFP and in Baluchistan are largely under the umbrella of the Deobandi Wafâq al-Madâris, and are in contact with Afghanistan and are engaged to a certain extent in the holy war (*Jihâd*) there. The same is true of the DM of the Jama'at-e Islami even if their numbers are insignificant as compared to the Deobandi DM. Some of the DM of the Jama'at-e Islami have been established exclusively for the *Jihâd* and need financial and other support, granted among other sources out of Zakat. Thus, it was important to strengthen the DM of this province, binding it more closely to the state. Secondly, this province was to be mobilized for the fight against socialism. The amount of Zakat for the DM in the NWFP does not seem to have been significantly reduced, as the Central Government was obviously aware of the problems for the Punjab if these DM would join with the socialist regime of Afghanistan. The DM were used as a bulwark of the ideology of the state and therefore received support from different sides.[165]

A similar problem arose in Sindh. Here, the dominant DM of the Deobandis[166] had formed a national movement against Punjabi chauvinism. This is also evident from the Movement for the Restoration of Democracy (MRD) in Sindh. The refusal of Zakat by the DM in this area did not result in the decrease of disbursement of Zakat funds to the DM as expected. On the contrary, over the years the amount of Zakat funds has substantially increased especially in this region. While disbursement of Zakat faced certain problem, during the first two years, the third year marked the victory of the Zakat system. The reason was that majority of DM accepting Zakat in Sindh pertain to the Brelwis, the Jama'at-e Islami and the Ahl-e Hadith while schools of the Deobandis usually did not accept Zakat. It is easy to understand that the Government, facing the opposition of the Deobandis in Sindh against Zia ul Haq's regime,[167] tried and succeeded in enforcing its interests by supporting other forces, like the Brelwis. The official policy of discrimination leads, however, to increasing sectarian clashes in the country.

The increase of funds for the DM corresponds to the heavy increase of payments per student. This is true of every province, especially of Sindh. The high annual contribution of Rs. 966 per student can be considered an incentive to motivate the Sindh DM to accept Zakat.

Students in Islamabad receive an amount of Rs. 1,200 per year, which is well above the average. This policy led to an increase in the number of students in Islamabad. The amount was then cut down by 50 per cent in order to curb the flood of *mullas* into the capital.

Inspite of the obvious increase of payments per student of a DM, the expenditure on this is substantially less than the costs involved in scholarships for students of the higher formal education system which are also partly met out of the Zakat funds. A student in the field of medicine, engineering, agriculture or trade costs the Zakat administration an annual amount of Rs. 3,500 to Rs. 5,600.[168] Thus, for the Government, the heavy increase of disbursements to students of DM might be considered a low-cost investment for its policy.

CONTRIBUTION OF PZC-ZAKAT TO THE ANNUAL BUDGET OF DÎNÎ MADÂRIS

The significance of Zakat as a political means of influencing the religious schools becomes clear only if its role within the budget of the DM is clearly understood.

The proportion of Zakat from the PZC in the budgets of the DM is considerable. It accounts for one-fifth to one-third (18 per cent-32 per cent). The receipts of Zakat of madrasahs amount to almost 50 per cent of Zakat disbursed by the PZC.[169] These funds are to be passed on from the headmaster of the school, the *mohtamim*, to the students. However, the students do not receive any cash. Instead the PZC Zakat is sometimes spent on behalf of the students on teaching materials and other needs. But even this is done in rare cases.[170] The Zakat funds usually stay at the disposal of the headmaster and are spent on costly construction activities. As a school usually belongs to a family and as such is heritable, these families profit considerably from this policy.

POLITICAL IMPACT VIA THE ZAKAT SYSTEM

The religio-political parties recruit their leading members from the well established, mostly urban DM with a large number of students, schools which are institutions for the education of *muftîs,* i.e. a *dâr al-iftâ'*. The

Government may use the Zakat disbursement as a means to exert influence on the schools, its students and teachers—clergy in a wide sense—and thus indirectly on the membership of the political parties to which they belong. Concrete examples of Zakat being used as a political instrument are the cases of the Jâmi'ah Madaniyyah and the Hizb al-Ahnâf in Lahore, two large DM of the "special grade" category. Referring not to political activities but to "illegal, sectarian activities", the Zakat administration justified its cut-back on Zakat disbursement to them. Thus, in 1984/85, Zakat worth Rs. 300,000 was withheld from the Jâmi'ah Madaniyyah, Karimpark, Lahore,[171] accused of spreading sectarian unrest. The school was, in fact, one of the centres of the opposition Fadl al-Rahman wing of the Jam'iyyat-e 'Ulamâ'-e Islam (JUI). The leader of this madrasah, Hamid Miyan, is the son of the famous anti-Pakistan Deobandi Sayyid Muhammad Miyan (1903-1975)[172] who was also *Amîr* of the JUI. In the case of the Hizb al-Ahnâf,[173] one of the oldest Brelwi schools in Pakistan, the sharp criticism by Mawlana Ridwi (member of the CII and of the Zakat 'Ulamâ' Committee) of the activities of the Auqaf Department, resulted in a cut of Zakat funds due to "sectarian activities", a cut effected for the first time in 1984/85.

The schools concerned suffer greatly under these sanctions and are often forced to abstain from political—or sectarian—activities. New necessities have surfaced which cannot be met anymore from their traditional income alone. The Zakat administration—mostly quite successfully—tries to force opposition groups into conformity with it.

The state is thus able to impose sanctions on politicized religious schools, and to control the establishment of new, small DM. Its integration policy has thus succeeded, at least partially, in subordinating parts of the clergy and their centres to its own interests.

NOTES

1. Only the certificates of some large DM, especially in the NWFP, had been recognized by the Ministry of Education in the sixties.
2. G.W. Leitner, *History of Indigenous Education in the Punjab since Annexation and in 1882*, New Delhi, 1971 (first published in 1883). S.M.A. Gilani, *Hindustân men Musalmânoñ kâ nizâm-e ta'lim o tarbiyyat*, vols. I and II, Delhi, 1966. Sayyid Sulaiman Nadwi, *Maqâlât-e Shiblî*, vol. 3, n.p., 1955.
3. See however, Zia ul Haq, "Muslim religious education in Indo-Pakistan", in *IS*, vol. 14, no. 1, 1975, pp. 271-292; Sayyid Muhammad Salim, *Hind o Pâkistân men musalmânon kâ nizâm-e ta'lun o trabiyyat*, Lahore, 1980; Abual Ala Mawdudi, *Ta'limât*, Lahore, 1982.

4. The academic black-out of the traditional educational system is the result of scientific discussion being restricted to the formal sector of education. It also reflects the dominant secular tendency of the scientific sector, confined to the urban areas.

5. Hafiz Nadhr Ahmad, *Hamârî Darsgâhon meñ dînî ta'lîm,* presented at the conference "Kull Pâkistân Mu'tamar 'arabî wâ 'ulûm islâmiyyah" in Peshawar, 1955 (mimeo, Urdu); same author: *A preliminary survey of madaris-i-deeniyyah in East & West Pakistan,* presented at the first Pakistan Oriental Conference, December 1956 (mimeo, Urdu); same author: *Jâ'izah-e Madâris-e 'arabiyyah Islâmiyyah maghribî Pâkistân,* Lyalpur, 1960, Urdu (*Ahmad I*); same author: *Jâ'izah-e madâris-e 'arabiyyah maghribî Pâkistân* (Overview on the Arabic madâris in West-Pakistan), Lahore, 1972, Urdu (*Ahmad II*).

6. *Ahmad I.*

7. *Ahmad II.*

8. GoP, Ministry of Religious Affairs (*Halepota Report*); Islamic Research Institute, *Pâkistân meñ Dînî Madâris kâ (sic!) fihrist,* Islamabad, 1982 (Urdu).

9. GoP, Ministry of Education, Islamic Education Research Cell, *Pâkistân ke dînî madâris kî fihrist 1984,* Islamabad, 1984, Urdu.

10. Besides these reports the manuscript by Arbab Khan Afridi on the *dînî madâris* in NWFP, Institute of Education and Research (IER), Peshawar University, 1984 (unpublished, Urdu), is worth mentioning. He limits his study to the DM of the NWFP. Smaller studies on the Islamic system of education have been presented as M.A. dissertations at different universities. They are also characterized by a strong trend towards reform. For example Mohammad Afzal, *Integration of Madrasah Education with the formal System of Education at Secondary Level,* M.A. Thesis, Islamabad, 1985 (unpublished); Bibi Sakina, *Dâr al-'Ulûm Haqqâniyyah, Akorâ Khattak, Peshawar,* M.A. Thesis, Peshawar, 1985, Urdu (mimeo).

11. Worth mentioning is a comprehensive bibliography on the topic of Islamic educational system by S.M. Khalid, *Islamic system of education and annotated bibliography with special emphasis on Pakistan,* IPS, Islamabad, 1984 (Urdu). The IPS, a branch of the Jama'at-e Islami, is especially active in publications on the topic of Islamic education. The Jama'at itself aims at combining religious and secular educational systems.

12. Gilani, *Hindustân meñ Musalmânoñ kâ nizâm-i ta'lîm o tarbiyyat,* op.cit., vol. I, p. 186.

13. Ibid., p. 213.

14. Ibid., pp. 206ff. Cf. also chapter V.

15. Ibid., pp. 232f.

16. Ibid., pp. 273f.

17. M.A. Quraishi, *Some Aspects of Muslim Education,* Lahore, 1983, p. 75.

18. For the development of the curriculum in the religious schools up to the foundation of the state in 1947 cf. Haque, op.cit. and G.M.D. Sufi, *Al-*

Minhaj, Evolution of curricula in the Muslim educational institutions, Lahore, 1981 (first published 1941).

19. Akhtar Rahi, *Tadhkirah-e musannifîn dars-e nizâmî,* Lahore, 1978.

20. Mulla Nizam al-Din from Sehala in the Bara Banki District, U.P.; cf. also *EI* vol. I, p. 936b and vol. II, p. 132a.

21. F. Robinson, "The 'Ulamâ' of Farangî Mahall and their Adâb", in B.D. Metcalf, ed., *Moral Conduct and Authority,* op.cit., pp. 152-183, esp. 154f.

22. Leitner, *Indigenous,* op.cit. He was one of the few Europeans to have a high regard for the traditional educational system in India and considered the changes brought about by the British as unsuitable.

23. Both institutions had been established to "modernize" Islam and to thus make it compatible with Western ideologies.

24. Chapter on the system of endowments.

25. Muhammad Y. Ludhianwi, *lamhah-e fikariyyah,* ed. by Wafâq al-Madâris al-Arabiyyah Pâkistân, n.d. (Urdu), pp. 25f.

26. Cf. the criticism of the governmental policy of integration by Muhammad Y. Ludhianwi, *radd-e 'amal,* ed. by Wafâq al-Madâris al-'Arabiyyah Pâkistân, 1981 (Urdu), esp. p. 20.

27. Cf. chapter V on the curricular discussion since 1979/80.

28. Even if their function is reduced to that of providing legitimation.

29. Report of the Committee set up by the Governor of West Pakistan for Recommending improved Syllabus for the various Darul Ulooms and Arabic Madrasah in West Pakistan, Lahore, 1962 (*Report*).

30. It consisted of a total of eleven members, of whom three were active chairmen of madâris, six were from the universities and two were from the Government.

31. *Ahmad I,* p. 6.

32. *Report,* op.cit., p. 1.

33. Ibid., p. 9.

34. Ibid.

35. The secular strategy of education had also been drawn up with the scientific cooperation and financial support of the USA.

36. *Report,* op.cit., p. 11.

37. GoP, Ministry of Education, *Report of the Commission on National Education,* Karachi, 1959, pp. 21ff, cf. also *PT,* 8.3.60: "Future of Religious Education in Pakistan", praising this proposal; cf. op.cit., 25.4.60: "Diniyat Compulsory Subject in Schools" from Kindergarten up to eighth grade. On the discussion in the media cf. *MCG,* 20.10.55: "Confusion and Moral Irresponsibility", *MN,* 3.1.62: "Defective Islamic Educational System" and *D,* 9.10.67.

38. *Report of the Commission,* pp. 209ff. This demand resulted in the establishment of the CII and the IRI.

39. Ibid., pp. 277f.

40. Ibid., p. 12.

41. Ibid., Appendix II, p. XXIX.

42. Ibid., p. 12.
43. Ibid., p. 14.
44. Ibid., pp. 18-21.
45. Ibid., p. 24; cf. also *MCG*, 29.12.61: "Study period extended to 15 years" with Urdu, and, at higher levels Arabic as medium of instruction.
46. *Report*, op.cit., pp. 22f.
47. Ibid., pp. 14, 34.
48. Ibid., pp. 36f; *MCG*, 14.12.61: "Report on Syllabi for Dar ul Uloom". The committee is said to have been pressed for time and had presented a delayed report. Therefore, "The Government is not likely to appoint any special committee to scrutinize the Syllabi reports". The programme was to be introduced in 12 Dâr al-'Ulûms. To make this feasible, financial promises were made: cf. *PT*, 6.1.62: "Aid for institutions adopting new Syllabi". The Karachi-based *Dawn* praised the activities of the committee (*D*, 25.4.62). Earlier, on 28.1.60, *The Statesman* had pointed to the fact that India had established a "Committee on religious and moral instruction" with the purpose of "promoting spiritual values".
49. *D*, 12.11.62: "Ulama urged to help solve problems (of industrial era)"; also *Daily Ittehad* (Dacca), 12.11.62.
50. *Pakistan Observer* (Dacca), 13.3.68.
51. In a modified form, however; cf. *Tasneem*, 23.3.59; *Shahbaz*, 26-29.3.59 and 12.4.59 as well as *MCG*, 10.4.59.
52. Manzooruddin Ahmed, "The Political role of the 'Ulama' in the Indo-Pakistan Sub-Continent", op.cit., pp. 327-354.
53. The DM system was, however, exempted.
54. Cf. chapter on the CII.
55. Thus, e.g. the curricula of 1975.
56. GoP, CII, *Consolidated Recommendations of the CII relating to Education system in Pakistan, 1962 to 1982,* Islamabad, 1982 (Urdu/English), pp. 20-28.
57. *Qurtâs 'amlî/pi<u>sh</u>nâmah bârâ-e kâmîtî ma'âdalah isnâd dînî wa jamî'î,* August 25, 1982, UGC, Islamabad (Urdu); cf. UGC, *A Guide to the Equivalences of Degrees and Diplomas in Pakistan,* Islamabad, 1978, p. 84. This is primarily true for the Deobandi Madrasah al-Islâmiyyah, Tando Allah Yar; its *mohtamim*, Ihtisam al-Haq Thanwi, is a passionate PPP activist to this day. The final certificate entitled one to teach Islamiyat, Islamic Studies and Islamic Ideology in the colleges and in Karachi University (cf. UGC, *A Guide*, p. 88). The certificate of the Wafâq al-Madâris and of the Tanzîm al-Madâris was put at par with the M.A.-Islamiyat. Other jobs required a B.A. in English; this Regulation was to be valid for all universities and colleges with the exception of the universities for engineering, technology, agrarian sciences and other technical disciplines.
58. By Abd al-Mustafa and Sayyid Muhammad Ridwi. The Wafâq presented its resolution by Abd al-Haqi.

59. Cf. above, chapter I.
60. File no. S 1/I/CMLA of September 28, 1978.
61. File M/RA u. o. no. /JS-Auqaf, October 1, 1978.
62. *Sargodha Report* of September 28, 1978, Islamabad (unpublished), p. 11. This means that students of the DM have at least basic knowledge in reading, writing and arithmetics.
63. Ibid., pp. 12f; these statements are not based on empirical investigation.
64. Ibid., pp. 13f; the report did not specify the kind of job.
65. Ibid., pp. 14f.
66. Ibid., p. 17. This hint to the creation of jobs was, however, neither picked up in this report nor in any of the following official reports on the DM system.
67. Ibid., op.cit., pp. 18f.
68. Ibid., op.cit., pp. 27ff. In these items, only the proposals made by the CII on the religious educational system are copied; cf. *Report of the CII on the educational system,* op.cit.
69. Ministry of Religious Affairs, *Madâris-e 'arabiyyah kî mutahhidah tanzîm; aik sarsarâ jâ'izah,* December 19, 1978, unpublished. See also the analysis of Afridi op.cit.; personally, I did not find any evidence of a common platform with the DM.
70. The committee comprised representatives of the religious elite, intellectuals as well as representatives of the state.
71. Ministry of Religious Affairs on 8.10.78 Dyno 1586/38 Din.
72. Cf. chapter on the CII and Appendix A; since 1986 he was chairman of this body.
73. *Halepota Report*, p. 119.
74. Ibid., pp. 115f and pp. 8f; Italics mine.
75. M/O Religious Affairs, O.O. No. 370/Scey/78, dt. 26.12.78.
76. Four are Brelwis, two Deobandis, one Shia and one is Ahl-e Hadith. The DM selected are well-established schools, some of them dating from before the foundation of the state in 1947 (on identifying these schools cf. *Ahmad II,* pp. 18ff, 27f, 31, 105f, 123f, 164, 219ff and 253ff as well as *Halepota Report,* p. 210).
77. *Halepota Report*, pp. 3ff, 113-115.
78. Ibid., pp. 115f.
79. One Deobandi and three Ahl-e Hadith listed according to *Ahmad II*, pp. 126f, 171, 309ff, they were representatives of institutions established in the sixties (ibid.) and originated from the Punjab; only one pedagogic scientist came from Baluchistan.
80. Among the three there were two Deobandis and one Shia. The latter came from Lahore, while the other two were from Karachi and Peshawar (according to *Ahmad II,* pp. 407ff, 479ff and 32ff).
81. Cf. *Halepota Report,* op.cit., pp. 6f.
82. *Halepota Report*, pp. 41ff, 47ff.
83. Ibid., pp. 50ff.

84. Ibid., pp. 147ff. On the curricular discussion cf. also the summary on the different curricula, chapter VI.

85. *Halepota Report*, p. 72.

86. Ibid., pp. 77ff, 138ff, 147ff.

87. Ibid., pp. 89ff.

88. As many of the small DM are located in inaccessible rural areas these basic necessities can rarely be met.

89. *Halepota Report*, pp. 102f.

90. Ibid., p. 104.

91. Ibid., pp. 105ff.

92. Ibid., p. 109; none of these institutes asks for a theological education as a precondition for entry into employment. All this is quite close to the proposals made by the CII.

93. Cf. below Zakat and DM, chapter V.

94. Proposals of the "Main and Sub-Committee on Deeni Madaris", August 4, 1980, p. 2 (mimeo). There were a number of disagreements between the different committees as well. "The National Committee on Deeni Madaris and the high-powered Sub-Committee grappling with the subject have yet to reconcile their divergent views and put forward agreed recommendations before three main bodies of Ulama in the country" (*TM*, 16.7.80, p. 4). The cabinet had in fact received the DM report despite the disagreements between the different committees. The proper procedure would have been to find out an agreement, present it to the three 'Ulamâ' Boards and then, finally, publish it "for eliciting public comments on it". Also, a delegation was to visit other Muslim countries and investigate the situation of the DM there. (cf. *PT*, 14.7.80 and *D*, 14.7.80). The points of disagreement were, however, not recorded and the report was never presented to the public.

95. Karachi, 11.2.1979, *Dînî Madâris kî islâh*. This newspaper is owned by the Jama'at-e Islami. The state owned *Nawâ'-e Waqt*, Karachi, November 11, 1980 (Urdu), also reported positively on the activities of the committee.

96. Y. Ludhianwi, *radd-e 'aml*, op.cit., pp. 17f.

97. Ibid., pp. 21f.

98. Ibid., pp. 23f; cf. also *al-Haq*, vol. 16/6/1981, pp. 2-5, 63.

99. M.Y. Ludhianwi, *lamhah-e fikriyyah*, op.cit., approximately end of 1980.

100. Ibid., pp. 23f; cf. the rejection of the proposals of the *Halepota Report* by the Deobandi Muhammad Idris Mehrti, in *Halepota Report*, op.cit., appendix.

101. Qasim Nanotawi was the founder of the Dâr al-'Ulûm Deoband; cf. Hafiz Muhammad Akbar Shah Bukhari, *Akâbir-e 'Ulamâ'-e Deoband*, Lahore, n.d., pp. 13-18 (*AUD*); Metcalf, *Revival*, op.cit., and Faruqi, *Deoband* passim.

102. M.Y. Ludhianwi, *radd-e 'aml*, pp. 27f.; cf. *Ahmad I*, pp. 732-734 and *Ahmad II*, pp. 684ff.

103. Ibid., M.Y. Ludhianwi, p. 17, 27f.

104. Similar criticism was levelled by influential representatives of the Brelwis

in spring 1986. They stated that now, after the recognition of the DM certificates the students no more studied for the sake of god (*fi sabîl allâh*) but only for their own sake (*fi sabîl al-nafs*).

105. Resolution of the Wafâq al-Madâris, in, M.Y. Ludhianwi, *radd-e 'aml*, op.cit., pp. 31f.

106. Telegram of 11.3.81 from M. Khadim Muh., *muhtamim* of D.I. Khan.

107. Telegram dated 29.2.81 from Mr. Muh. Umar of Muzaffargarh.

108. Telegram dated 19.2.81 from Mr. Umar Daraz, *muhtamim* Madrasah Daruloom Qoran Qurashivabad Dehatar Tandomohdkhan. It was interesting that all the telegrams were in English. This points towards the high degree of integration of the clergy into the colonial sector.

109. According to statements by Dr. Halepota all the telegrams were the handiwork of Deobandis suggesting an "organized conspiracy" against the committee.

110. Personal interview with Dr. Halepota on 15.12.84 and on 12.10.85 in Islamabad. These four DM are located in Sukkur, Lahore, Multan and Tando Allah Yar and are connected with the families Faruqi and Uthmani, descendents—not neccessarily referring to genealogy but spiritual descendence—of Ashraf Ali Thanwi (1860-1943); for Thanwi cf. Bukhari, *AUD*, pp. 33-45. The four schools are (1) Jâmi'ah Ashrafiyyah, Lahore, founded by Mufti Muhammad Husain Amratsari; (2) Qâsim al-'Ulûm, Multan, founded by Khair Muhammad Jallundari (cf. Bukhari, *AUD*, p. 43 and *Ahmad II*, pp. 18ff, 300ff, 530); (3) Dâr al-'Ulûm al-Islâmiyyah, Ashrafabad, Tando Allah Yar founded by Shabbir Ahmad Uthmani (cf. *Ahmad I*, pp. 147ff); (4) Jâmi'ah Ashrafiyyah, Sukkur, founded by Muhammad Ahmad Thanwi (cf. *Ahmad I*, pp. 251f). The founders of all four DM received the title of *khalîfah*, and/or *ijaza* from Ashraf Ali Thanwi and by this considered his spiritual descendants.

The Faruqis, together with the Shuyyukh, Uthmani, Siddiqi and Ansari families, are considered to be those *muhajirîn* from India who are the transmitters of Islamic culture. They were known for their knowledge on religious matters and established centres in Nanotah, Kandhlah, Deoband, Gangoha and Thana Bhawan—to mention the outstanding ones – being the cities where the families had settled (cf. Bukhari, *AUD*, p. 13). Following partition between India and Pakistan, these families moved to Pakistan.

The teachings of Ashraf Ali Thanwi were very much in the tradition of Nanotawi. In addition, Thanwi was of the opinion that the Muslims were in a weak economic and social position; they should therefore look to his former students for guidance. They were either bureaucrats of the state, "'Ulamâ', Sûfîs and teachers... doctors, businessmen, judges, engineers who have received my *ijâzah* (permission to teach), beggars (*Faqîr*), aristocrats (*Nawwâbs*), who are my *khulafâ'* (spiritual descendents) ..." All are "submerged in their tasks" and simultaneously Muslims and busy at earning a living by economic means (*tahsîl-e ma'âsh meñ masrûf hain*). In this aspect, Islam was in fact easy to live by (cited according to Bukhari, *AUD,* op.cit., pp. 39f).

111. Mufti Sahib was born in 1909 in D. I. Khan and enjoyed both a formal and a traditional education. As *khalîfah* in all of the four large *Sûfî* orders and as Deobandi he was in a position to mobilize the masses on a large scale, especially in NWFP. His career was that of a political activist; he was Chief Minister of the NWFP in 1976, besides being president of the Wafâq al-Madâris and director of the Qâsim al-'Ulûm in Multan (cf. among others Bukhari, *AUD,* pp. 355ff and also Hashmi, op.cit.). In 1956 Mufti Mahmud convened an 'Ulamâ' Convention, in order to unify the *'ulamâ'* and to make them more mobile in matters of politics. The Jam'iyyat-e 'Ulamâ'-e Islam (JUI) was supposedly founded on this occasion. He had established a JUI-Committee in order to examine the Constitution of 1956 in the light of Islamic tenets and in order to submit a report (the members of the committee were Mufti Mahmud, Shams al-Haq Afghani, Prof. Khalid Mahmud, Shaikh Hisam al-Din), bearing the title of *Tanqîdât wa Tarmîmât* (Critique and Change; Urdu) (cf. Hashmi, op.cit., p. 10). During the military regime of Ayub he convened an 'Ulamâ' Convention in Multan and founded the Nizâm-e 'Ulamâ' party, demanding from the Government adherence to the tenets of Islam. It had, however, little political impact. Under the Government of Bhutto, Mufti Sahib had a weak standing. Thus in PID file a white paper charaterizes him as a "tyrant and a greedy ruler" who had only agreed to the alliance with the National Awami Party in order to hold the post of minister. On his rejection of the Zakat system introduced in 1980 see chapter VI.

112. In February 1976; cf. *The Sun,* 26.3.76; *NW,* 13 and 23.3.76; *D,* 2.4.76; *J,* 5.4.76.

113. *J,* 16.5.78, stated that supporting the Wafâq was specially necessary in Lahore.

114. *D,* 16.5.78 and *Imroze,* 16.5.78.

115. Letter to Dr. Halepota, no. F.2-4/81-IES-II.

116. M. of R/A to Dr. Halepota on March 25th, 1981 cites "President's minutes No. 587, 1980, 14.3.81" in Baluchistan Governor's House.

117. Thus, for Sahiwal only one Deobandi madrasah was reported, in Karachi only one Shia madrasah, etc.; the report supposedly discriminated against the Deobandis due to the composition of the committee (cf. below).

118. *Qâwmî idârah bârâ-e dînî madâris Pâkistân ordinens 1401 hijrah*; Proposal for President Zia ul Haq, presented by Dr. Abdul Wahid Halepota, November 9th, 1980 (Urdu, unpublished).

119. Op.cit., p. 110; this was in conformity with the "Report of the Sub-Committee of the Council on Islamic System of Education" of 1976; cf. CII, *Recommendations on the System of Education,* op.cit., p. 24.

120. This supposition was confirmed by a leading technocrat of the Islamic Education Research Cell. The committee and its report is said to have been rejected by the cabinet as "unsatisfactory". A sub-committee with seven

secretaries of state (3 of the federal level and 4 of provincial level) were to scrutinize the report (*D*, 23.7.80).

121. Chapter II on the CII.

122. Especially no. 12 (1), p.7 of the Ordinance.

123. Members of the IRI stressed the "weak and uncoordinated" character of the *Halepota Report*, a polemical rather than a factual criticism.

124. This had also been stated by the only Sindh representative, the Deobandi Muhammad Idris Mehrti (Mehrti was nâzim-e 'alâ of the Wafâq al-Madâris al-'Arabiyyah Pâkistân and *muhtamim* of the Jâmi'ah Islâmiyyah 'Arabiyyah, Karachi), in his contrasting opinion, pp. 7, 218f and annexure).

125. Proceedings of the 'Ulamâ' Convention 1980 and, the Mashâ'ikh Convention 1980, 'Ulamâ' Convention 1984 and Nifâz-e Islâm Conference 1984.

126. Personal conversation on 2.5.85 in Islamabad; Talal is an American Muslim and was temporarily advisor to the Ministry of Education on Islamic education.

127. Cf. Equivalence of Deeni Sanads, Ministry of Religious Affairs, n.d. (mimeo).

128. CII, *Recommendations on System of Education,* op.cit., pp. 44f.

129. This is only a new interpretation of the proposals by the UGC-Committee of 1975. The final recognition of the certificates in 1981 became possible only after a personal inervention of Zia ul Haq, bypassing the bureaucracy and thus clearing the ground for an official recognition of the certificates of the *mawlânâs* (cf. CII, *Recommendations on System of Education*, op.cit., pp. 44f).

130. *Qurtâs 'amlî*, p. 2 (Urdu).

131. Cf. UGC, *A Guide to the Equivalences of Degrees and Diplomas in Pakistan*, Islamabad, 1978, p. 84, cf. above: "Islam and Dînî Madâris under Bhutto".

132. On 12.9.1982.

133. The certificates of the *Râbitah al-Madâris al-Islâmiyyah* of the Jama'at-e Islami were not recognized right away. Up to 1986 they continued to present their theological qualifications of their DM to the Ministry of Education. This supports the hypothesis that representatives of the Islamic *avant-garde* (Jama'at) participated only marginally in theological discussion. They were more interested in their political programmes.

134. Appendix B: Notification.

135. Cf. UGC, *Higher Education News*, vol. II, no. 10, October 1982, pp. 1 and 8.

136. Income not only in cash but also in kind.

137. *Halepota Report*, p. 216. The amount mentioned there is Rs. 449,288 instead of Rs. 4,492,088.

138. GoP, Ministry of Education, *Important Statistics of the Dini Madaris of NWFP*, Islamabad, 1983 (mimeo).

139. See chapter on Zakat.

140. Sura 9/60. Trans. by M. Marmaduke Pickthall. Other references in the Koran on the distribution of Zakat are suras 2/177, 2/215, 2/273.

141. The same is true for the needy in vocational institutions, public hospitals and clinics, etc., cf. Tanzil al-Rahman, *Zakat and Ushr Ordinance 1980: Introduction of Zakat in Pakistan*, CII, Islamabad, n.d., especially section 8 a., p. 39.

142. Report of the Committee on the Eligibility of Religious Institutions and their Students for Zakat, annexure I (mimeo), Zia ul Haq on July 24, 1980.

143. This committee consisted of the Secretary of Finance, the Director of the IRI and the Additional Secretary Religious Affairs.

144. Cf. UO no. 6 (3)/ 80-R.CII of 29.7.80, annexure II.

145. Report of the Committee on the Eligibility of Religious Institutions and their Students for Zakat, op.cit., p. 3.

146. Ibid.

147. Ibid., pp. 4f. The Government seemed to have been pressed for time.

148. See Table 34 in chapter VI. The Jama'at-e Islami at this time did not exist as an autonomous DM organization.

149. See chapter IV on Zakat.

150. On the influence of Zakat on the different levels cf. chapter IV.

151. Central Zakat Council (CZC), *Annual Report, 1983/84*, Islamabad, 1984 (Urdu), p. 5; these rates had already changed several times in the course of events.

152. Report of the Committee on the Eligibility of Religious Institutions, op.cit., p. 6.

153. *MN*, 27.2.82.

154. *Al-Zakât*, vol. 1, no. 1, July 1981 (Urdu), p. 22.

155. Ibid., vol. 1, no. 5, November 1981 (Urdu), pp. 19f.

156. All this would only be possible when the DM would have presented their corresponding book-keeping for the year 1980/81 to the PZC.

157. The CZC had already proposed improvements in December 1980. Cf. CZC, *Zakat Proceedings,* vol. II, Islamabad (Urdu), pp. 8ff.

158. This does not take into account the inflation rate.

159. On this topic cf. chapter VI. This phenomenon is certainly due to the rapid increase of the number of DM following the formal recognition of their certificates and also due to the disbursement of Zakat.

160. On the problem of urban hegemony before the Zia era cf. Burki, *Pakistan under Bhutto*, op.cit.

161. See *List of Zakat-receiving DM from the Provincial Zakat Fund,* mimeo., as well as Table 13 and *Al-Zakât*, vol. 4., no. 10, April 1984 (Urdu), p. 19.

162. See Table 15. The calculations were made on the basis of the total disbursement of Zakat funds to Punjab DM, divided by the total Zakat allocated to Lahore DM, multiplied by 100 for the corresponding years.

163. Cf. chapter VI, as well as chapter VII on the increase of DM.

164. This is supported by the files of the different PZCs.

165. Cf. discussion on *Jihâd*, chapter VI.
166. Table 34c.
167. This refers to the so-called Fadl al-Rahman Wing. The loyalists among the Deobandis rather belonged to the *Darkhâstî* Group. It included Mawlana Abd al-Haq, the chairman of the large school in Akora Khattak (cf. chapter VI).
168. Calculated according to CZC Proceedings, vol. II, 12th session on 1.10.1981 (Urdu), pp. 392f and CZC, *Annual Report*, 1982/83 (Urdu), pp. 36ff. Figures refer to 1981.
169. These statements are primarily valid only for the large DM.
170. This becomes clear in the interviews with students of the Hizb al-Ahnaf, Lahore and the Jâmi'ah Salafiyyah, Faisalabad (spring 1986). The students complained that despite the Zakat funds the *muhtamim* "does not serve any better food and puts the whole money into construction and renovation of the school".
171. On the information of this school cf. *Ahmad I*, pp. 473ff and *Ahmad II*, pp. 24ff.
172. Author of the *'Ulamâ'-e Hind kâ Shândâr Mâdî*, vols. I-IV, Delhi, 1957 (Urdu). On *Miyân* cf. also Peter Hardy, *Partners in Freedom and True Muslims*, Lund, 1971, pp. 31-37; cf. also Yohanan Friedmann, "The attitude of the Jam'iyyat al-'Ulama'-i Hind" and "The Jam'iyyat al-'Ulama'-i Hind in the Wake of Partition".
173. Cf. *Ahmad I*, pp. 447ff and *Ahmad II*, pp. 27f.

CHAPTER VI

REACTION OF RELIGIOUS SCHOLARS AND DÎNÎ MADÂRIS TO THE OFFICIAL POLICIES

THE CURRICULA AND INTEGRATIONISM

A first positive reaction to the proposals of the DM Committee of 1979 came from the largest umbrella organization, the Deobandi Wafâq al-Madâris in 1983. It presented an extended curriculum. In 1979/80 the same organization had turned against the proposals of the committee and had successfully campaigned against the Government. The Tanzîm al-Madâris of the Brelwis also was soon able to produce a new, modified curriculum.

The new curricula drawn up by the DM organizations comprised 16 instead of the usual 8 years of instruction[1] in accordance with the proposals of the National Committee for Dînî Madâris. While the Curriculum Committee of the *Halepota Report* had proposed a subdivision in four levels similar to the formal education system (primary, matric, B.A. and M.A. levels—middle and F.A. having been dropped), the Wafâq and the Tanzîm preferred a stricter subdivision into six levels (cf. Table 16). The religious scholars thus wanted to adapt their system of education primarily to the colonial system of education. The English denominations of certificates received an Arabic nomenclature in the DM system, thus opening the possibility of putting the formal secular aspects of the DM curricula on a religious, traditional level.

In the course of instruction of the Wafâq al-Madâris some innovations were added to the *dars-e nizâmî*. The curriculum nevertheless was still essentially different from the one proposed by the DM Committee of 1979. It had been the aim of the National Committee for Dînî Madâris to integrate new disciplines into the traditional system of education of the madâris (especially by introducing subjects like Social Sciences and General Science). The classical, traditional curriculum would thus be simultaneously modernized and legitimized in an Islamic-fundamentalist manner.

The enthusiasm for integration of the members of the *Halepota*

TABLE 16: SUBDIVISION AND CATEGORIZATION OF
DIFFERENT LEVELS OF EDUCATION

Grade	Level acc. to the Halepota Report	Years	Qualification in the Ed. System of D.M. acc. to the Wafâq	Years	Corresponding Level in the Formal Ed. Sys.
(1- 5) X	darjah-e ibtedâ'iyyah	5	shahâdah al-ibtedâ'iyyah	5	primary
(6-10) X	darjah-e mutawassatah	5	shahâdah al-mutawassatah	3	middel
	darjah-e thâniyyah 'âmah		shahâdah al-thâniyyah 'âmah	2	matric
(11-14) X	darjah-e thâniyyah khâssah	4	shahâdah al-thâniyyah khâssah	2	F.A.
	darjah-e 'aliyyah		shahâdah al-'aliyyah	2	B.A.
(15-16) X	darjah-e âlamiyyah	2	shahâdah al-'âlamiyyah	2	M.A.
		16			

Sources: *Halepota Report*, p. 66; *solah sâlah nisâb-e ta'lîm; Wafâq al-madâris al-'arabiyyah Pâkistân*, passed in Quetta 1983, ed. by Wafâq al-madâris, etc. (Urdu) (mimeo) (*manzûrkardah I*), p. 4; additionally, a special course is offered, in which so-called "modern subjects" may be taught; cf. *solah sâlah nisâb-e ta'lîm; Wafâq al-madâris al-'arabiyyah Pâkistân*, passed in Multan, 1984, ed. by Wafâq al-madâris etc. (Urdu) (mimeo) (*manzûrkardah II*), pp. 21ff.

Explanations: X = levels proposed by the *Halepota Report*
Ed. Sys. = Education System
darjah = level
shahâdah = certificate

Report and of the Islamic *avant-garde* was based on the concept of knowledge which had been presented by Islamic intellectuals in 1977 in Mecca at the first World Conference on Islamic Education. Here, the perception by the Islamic *avant-garde* of cultural inferiority, and an unquestioning belief in technology were obvious.[2] The intellectuals took for granted the dichotomy between tradition and modernity. It was the result of their orientation towards the colonial system as well as towards fundamentalist Islam. The integrationist approach leads to an alienation from traditional Islam, finally resulting in a corroboration of the colonial *status quo* at the cost of Islamic tradition. An estranged and alienated Islam is introduced into the hitherto "untouched" institutions of Islamic tradition, placing them within the parameters of the colonial system and norms. In this way, the necessary preconditions for the integration of the autochthonous culture into the expanding colonial sector are sought to be achieved. The architects of such an education policy are mostly members of the colonial sector and of the *intermediary sector* II. None of the representatives at the national and international conferences on Muslim education thus belonged to the *intermediary sector* I, not to speak of the traditional sector. The reformers may be found among the Jama'at-e Islami, among representatives of the religious elite as well as among the group of modernists.

The integrationist education policy advocated a curriculum which came quite close to the course of instruction proposed by A.A. Mawdudi, one of the most prominent representatives of fundamentalist Islam.[3]

Some parts of religious elite of different schools of thought were rather inclined towards the policy of reform of the Government and reacted in a positive way. As representatives of the *avant-garde* they were clearly in favour of modernization.[4] The task was to integrate the traditionalism into the given (colonial) structures thus strengthening the *status quo*.

The curriculum can be divided into two main sections: the Shari'a-oriented sciences which always existed (*'ulûm naqliyyah*), and the rational sciences acquired by man in the course of time and which differ according to time and place (*'ulûm 'aqliyyah*). This categorization corresponds to the one devized by the well-known sociologist Ibn Khaldun, whose views are referred to here. He had subdivided knowledge into two main areas:[5]

A. Sciences handed down (based on the revelation):
1. Interpretation and recitation of Koran
2. Hadith and its sciences
3. Islamic Law and jurisprudence
4. Theology
5. Mysticism
6. Linguistics (Grammar, Lexicography, Literature)

B. Rational sciences (based on empirical experience):
1. Logic
2. Natural sciences or Physics (medicine, agriculture)
3. Metaphysics (magic, sciences of the hidden and the occult, alchemy)
4. Science of quantity (Geometry, Arithmetics, Music, Astronomy)

Inspite of the strong support of modernism by the Islamic *avant-garde* the traditional sciences were regarded as "the basis and essential foundation of the second kind, for knowledge of the latter one (i.e. rational sciences) alone, without the guiding spirit of the former (i.e traditional sciences), cannot truly lead man in his life, but only confuses and confounds and enmeshes him in the labyrinth of endless and purposeless seeking".[6]

The two pillars of the new Islamic policy of education, ideology and pragmatism, were to be reflected in the Pakistani education policy[7] without doing away with a "purely indigenous education policy" and without plunging the next generation into "chaos and nihilism".[8] In order to safeguard education and to form "good Pakistanis and good Muslims" the private sector would have to be mobilized. The Government, it was said, was in fact not able "to shoulder the entire responsibility . . . there is a requirement of encouraging private individuals, private parties, private institutions to come forward and either get hold of the educational institutions and run them or even raise new private educational institutions".[9] This—as will be dealt with at length later—eventually led to a commercialization of the education system by private schools and further widened the gap between the social classes.[10]

Pragmatism and ideology were especially evident in the mobilization of the mosque schools;[11] DM illiteracy (up to 85 per cent) was to be reduced and the dichotomy within the education system was to be resolved.

Traditionalization of the Reform

Demands for integrationist curricula were ignored by the Wafâq and Tanzîm in their new religious course of instruction at least at the primary level (compare Table 17). Only some books of the formal education system were included in the courses (Arithmetic and Urdu) in order to enable the primary level student to attain a formal standard.

During the first five years, one-third of the school hours of instruction were allotted to the modern subjects, while Koran, Prayer and Ablutions and Islamic Rites continued to form the major part of the instruction.

In Table 18, the subjects proposed by the NCDM of 1979 are listed. The main subjects of the formal education system such as, Mathematics, General Science, Pakistan Studies, English, Natural Sciences and Social Sciences were to be taught with formal books, recognized by the Ministry of Education. Up to this point, these subjects had neither been part of the DM curriculum nor did the DM have the required books or teachers.

Between grade six and grade ten the new subjects were considered of primary importance, unlike classical subjects such as Morphology, Exegesis of Koran and Hadith which were neglected. Furthermore, little importance was attached to "Rhetorics", "Philosophy", "Methods of Exegesis of Koran", "Hadith" and "Arabic". "Methods of Jurisprudence" (*usûl-e fiqh*),

TABLE 17: SUBJECTS SUGGESTED BY THE DÎNÎ MADÂRIS COMMITTEE,
BY THE WAFÂQ AND THE TANZÎM AT THE PRIMARY LEVEL

Grades/ Subject	1	2	3	4	5
Reading Koran	x,y,z	x,y,z	x,y,z	x,y,z	x,y,z
Prayer and basic Islam	x,y,z	x,y,z ,	x,y,z	x,y,z	x,y,z
Intro. to Persian	x	x	x	x	x
Urdu/Writing	x,y,z	x,y,z	x,y,z	x,y,z	x,y,z
Arithmetics	x,y	x,y,z	x,y,z	x,y,z	x,y,z
Social Sciences	x	x	x	x	x
General Science	x	x	x	x	x
Multiplication	z	z	z	z	z

Sources: *Halepota Report*, pp. 66f, 147 as well as *solah sâlah nisâb manzûrkardah I*,
op.cit., p. 6 and *manzûrkardah II* etc. for the wafâq. For the tanzîm cf. *La'hah-
e 'aml*, etc. pp. 9f.

Explanations: x = Proposal of the D.M. Committee
               y = Proposal of the Wafâq al-madâris
               z = Proposal of the Tanzîm al-madâris
               The books for Urdu and Arithmetics were to be taken from the formal
               education system.

in contrast, was integrated into the matriculation level.

At the level of *fawqânî* (grade 11 to 14) it is remarkable that "English"
as well as other modern subjects were introduced as against Philosophy,
Scholastics, Islamic Law and Arabic.

At the highest level, according to the traditional course reserved
exclusively for studies in Jurisprudence and Hadith, the student could now
choose between Islamic Law, Exegesis of Koran and Hadith subject
to passing four examinations and submitting a written final paper.
Simultaneously, he was expected to follow compulsory courses in three
modern subjects and to pass a total of three examinations. The combination
of the subjects of examination raized doubts on whether an religious
scholar after 16 years of an integrated, secularized curriculum would still
retain the exclusive qualification of a theologian or specialist in Islamic
Law.

The reform of the DM system brings back memories of Ayub Khan,
who had followed an integrationist policy in the sixties especially aimed
at the clergy.[12] One may ask whether any thought was given to the
employment potential of the students. The *Halepota Report* did not deal
with such considerations and mentioned in passing that the graduates of the
DM should be integrated into secular institutions.

Not all religious scholars were ready to accept such a secular reform of the curriculum and there were protests against it from the '*ulamâ*', for the traditional orders and their monopoly, particularly in matters of law and daily disputes, were in danger of being questioned. Besides this, up to this point there had been no internal opposition or any other negative reaction within the existing traditional, hierarchical set-up of the DM. The teacher had a central and an almost unvulnerable position, due to his role as a teacher and by virtue of his holy office.

Divergence among Deobandis

In response to NCDM's proposal, the Wafâq al-madâris and the Tanzîm al-madâris drafted their own curricula, as they had been promized equal recognition for their degree. At least formally this was to open the door to the graduates of the DM to all those professions requiring an officially recognized final degree, including the civil services.

While the clergy by and large paid no heed to the proposals of the *Halepota Report* for the curricula at the primary level (cf. Table 18), the proposal for a curriculum of the Wafâq at the middle level (grades 6 to 10) actually included new subjects. The classical subjects of the *dars-e nizâmî* were part of it only towards the end of this level. The studies of Islamic Law were, nevertheless, still at the core of the curriculum, in contrast to the proposal of the NCDM, in which modern as well as classical subjects were compulsory. Still, subjects such as English, Pakistan Studies and General Science were not taken into consideration in the proposal of the Wafâq, while Economics, Comparative Religious Sciences as well as Communism and Capitalism, Social Sciences and other new subjects were merely offered as optional subjects.

The proposals of the Wafâq were examined by a committee of five, whose members had a modern orientation and an enthusiasm for reform.[13] These religious scholars may have belonged to the *salafî* wing of the Deobandis. Their proposal for the introduction of "modern" subjects was, however, strongly criticized by the older, traditionalist '*ulamâ*' and finally led to a split within the camp of the Wafâq. Two groups evolved, the "*jayyid 'ulamâ*'" (the modern forces) and the representatives of the old establishment who rejected at first any innovation whatsoever. In order to settle the dispute, the Wafâq in Multan (official seat of the Wafâq) decided to raise the number of members in the Curriculum Committee from five to twenty.[14] Most of the members of this expanded body for the reconstruction of the curriculum were students of famous '*ulamâ*' of the *ancient regime*.[15]

At the sessions in Multan on March 11 and 12, 1984, the proposals of

TABLE 18: THE CURRICULUM PROPOSED BY THE DÎNÎ MADÂRIS COMMITTEE FOR THE INTERMEDIATE AND HIGHER STAGE

Subject	darjah-e wustânî Grade					darjah-e fawqânîyyah Grade				darjah-e takhassus Grade	
	6	7	8	9	10	11	12	13	14	15	16
Koran	x	x	x	x							
Morphology	x	x									
Syntax	x	x	x	x	x						
Arabic	x	x	x	x							
Sîrat	x	x	x	x	x						
Mathematics	**x**	**x**	**x**	**x**	**x**						
Gen. Science	**x**		**x**	**x**	**x**						
Pak. Studies	**x**			**x**	**x**						
English	**x**	**x**	**x**	**x**	**x**	-	-	+	+		
Fiqh/Hadith		x									
Natural Sc.		x									
Social Sc.		x	x								
Fiqh			x	x	x	x	x			*	*
Methods of Fiqh		x	x	x	x	x	x				
Logic			x	x							
Arab. Literature				x	x	x					
Hadith or Literature				x							
Rhetorics				x							
Exegesis of Koran					x	x	x	x		*	*
Hadith						x	x	x	x	*	*
Methods of Hadith Sc.						x	x				
Scholastics						x	x				
Philosophy						x					
Islam. History					x	x	x	x	x	x	
Economics						-	-	+	+	x	x
Political Sc.						-	-	+	+	x	x
Cultural Sc.						-	-	+	+	x	x
Methods of Exegesis						x					
Fiqh al-Hadith							x				
Comparative Sc. of religions, esp. Islam										x	x

Source: *Halepota Report*, pp. 68-77, 147-155.
Explanations:
x = compulsory subjects
x = Subjects taught exclusively with media of the formal education system
- = two of four subjects have to be chosen
+ = one of four subjects has to be chosen
* = one of three subjects has to be chosen, with four examinations to be passed in this subject

The five subjects in bold letters carry with them three examinations to be passed. For the modern subject from grade 11 onwards, the books are not specified anymore.

the five-member committee for the primary and intermediate level were retained, while those for the highest level were altered. The new subjects now were to be offered only additionally as compared to the old curriculum, in a special course—*darjah-e takmîl* (level of perfection). This course was to last for two years and was to follow the *darjah-e takhassus*, i.e. equal to the M.A. It included Logic, Philosophy, Euclidic Mathematics, Basics of Jurisprudence, Refutation of other Religions and of Apostasy as well as Economics, and Communism and Capitalism.[16]

With subjects such as Reading of Koran, Prayer, Arithmetic, Persian, Urdu, Social Sciences and General Science at the primary level and the expansion of the instruction in these subjects up to grade eight the Wafâq was able to enlarge their curriculum from eight to nine years to a total of sixteen years. Thus, the five years of primary instruction (whose contents of instruction was, in any case, a precondition for the studies of religious sciences together with three years at the intermediate level) were integrated into a sixteen-year curriculum. Grades one to eight and nine to sixteen were thus taken from totally separate systems of education: the first one was secular, completed by Koran and Basics of Islam, just as it is offered at present in the formal school system. The second one continues as before: the *dars-e nizâmî*.

In the preface of the second and final version of the curriculum of the Wafâq al-madâris it was pointed out that the '*ulamâ*', as always, had adjusted the curriculum to the new conditions and circumstances. The teaching of the new subjects was said to have caused some problems (*thaqîl*) to many of the DM. Some '*ulamâ*' had even rejected (*matrûk karnâ*) to teach the new subjects. However some of the "*jayyid 'ulamâ*'" stressed the importance of the new subjects and their integration into the course of instruction.

The alterations effected by the second committee mainly aimed at the proforma support to the modern subjects while actually cutting down on them. Due to the pressure from the "*jayyid 'ulamâ*'" as well as from the Government, the proposals made by the first committee could not be ignored completely. A factor in this was also the fear of losing teachers otherwise—the previous years had witnessed a brain-drain away from the madâris to the formal institutions and to foreign countries. The decision in favour of the new curriculum was further facilitated by the prospect of official recognition and financial support by the Government. The Government accepted the sixteen-year curriculum as it apparently fulfilled the conditions for a formal recognition.

•

There was, however, no essential alteration of the classical DM course of instruction. The '*ulamâ*' had been able to profit by these "alterations", gaining official recognition. This showed the ability of the '*ulamâ*' to meet the demands of innovation and pragmatism without acting against their own interests. With the new curriculum, they gained rather than lost influence. They finally achieved formal recognition via these curricula, and on this basis were now able to influence the secular sector. Moreover, the number of students in religious schools is at present on the rise, as a formal primary level education is now offered. The poor parents prefer the DM which are free of charge instead of the official, fee-paying schools. The DM can thus evolve into an alternative to the secular, official or commercial system of education.

To evaluate the situation correctly it is important to grasp that Zia ul Haq, the bureaucracy and the '*ulamâ*' had different objectives. The President sought the acceptance of his leadership by the '*ulamâ*' and thus an "Islamic" legitimation of his rule. For the bureaucracy and the colonial sector, formalization of the DM served as a means to bring them under control and thus to neutralize them politically. The '*ulamâ*', in contrast, aimed at finally escaping their "backwardness" and achieving social recognition without giving up their tradition.

The fact that Zia in his bill put the degrees of the *mawlânâs* at par with those of universities and colleges may thus be judged as an extremely pragmatic move, even if he did so against the advice of the bureaucracy. What remains to be discussed is what kind of problems may arise from this group of officially recognized religious scholars, a potential of conflict on the one hand, and an army moving onto the labour market on the other.

The Brelwi Tanzîm

The Tanzîm of the Brelwis also did not hesitate for long when confronted with the prospect of having their certificates recognized, and soon presented an integrated curriculum. Details of their proposal for a curriculum can be taken from Table 19. The Tanzîm responded more readily to the official proposals for reform than the Wafâq: at the intermediate level Social Sciences, English and Regional Languages were offered. Also there seemingly were no divergences of interest among the members of the Tanzîm (cf. Table 19).

TABLE 19: CURRICULUM OF THE TANZÎM AL-MADÂRIS FOR GRADES 1-8

Subject	Primary darjah-e ibtedâ'iyyah					Middle darjah-e mutawassatah		
	1	2	3	4	5	6	7	8
Koran, Recitation, Reading								
Memorization	x	x	x	x	x	x	x	x
Basics of Islam	x	x	x	x	x	x	x	
Urdu	x	x	x	x	x	x	x	x
Writing	x	x	x	x	x	x	x	
Multiplication	x	x	x					
Arithmetics		x	x	x	x	x	x	x
Arabic						x	x	x
Social Sciences						x˙	x	x
English/Persian							x	
Regional Languages³						x	x	
Biography of the Prophet								x
Scholastics								x

Source: *La'hah-e 'aml*, Tanzîm al-madâris, Lahore, 1983 (Urdu), pp. 9-12.
Explanations: ³= Languages offered include Sindhi, Kashmiri, Sara'iki, Punjabi, Balochi, Pashto.
Books in the subjects Arithmetics, Urdu, Arabic, Social Sciences and regional languages were to be furnished by the Ministry of Education.

While Brelwis and Deobandis use identical books from the primary level up to the final graduation (except in Scholastics and Jurisprudence)[17] they still differ in many ways. First, there are differences in the manner of the transmission of knowledge: the Brelwis place more stress on discussions as an element of instruction; the Deobandis, in contrast, put imitation of the contents transmitted by the teacher at the centre of their instruction. Secondly, the Brelwis differ from the Deobandis in the importance they accord to the transmission and practice of rites. Thirdly, the solution of conflict is left to the hereafter as far as the Brelwis are concerned and the mastering of problems is put in the hands of their renowned saints. They have a tendency to accept the *status quo* and seem to be more obedient to worldly authorities.[18] The Deobandis, in contrast, are more oriented towards the here-and-now and are rather quick in turning to opposition against the Government.

The new curriculum of the Brelwis is also characterized by the additional eight-year-phase put in front of the old curriculum. The innovations to the old curriculum are of no particular value; Mathematics, History and Geography (⁺) are listed but not specified as to their contents. The new subjects are said to cover only the classes up to grade 10.[19]

TABLE 20: THE CURRICULUM PROPOSED BY THE TANZÎM FOR GRADES 9-16

Subject	Classes (Number of Books)							
	9	10	11	12	13	14	15	16
Morphology	x (3)	x (2)						
Scholastics	x (1)				x (1)	x (1)	x (2)	
Literature	x (1)	x (3)	x (3)	x (3)	x (3)	x (2)		
Syntax	x (1)	x (2)	x (1)	x (1)				
Koran recitation	x (1)	x (3)						
Islam. law		x (1)	x (1)	x (1)	x (1)		x (1)	
Logic		x (1)	x (3)	x (2)	x (1)			
Principles of Law		x (1)	x (1)	x (1)		x (1)		
Philosophy			x (1)	x (1)	x (1)		x (1)	
Biography of the Prophet and Moral			x (1)				x (2)	
Principles of the Exegesis of Koran		x (1)			x (1)	x (2)		
History and Geography+				x (?)	x (?)	x (?)	x (?)	
Principles of Traditional Sciences					x (2)	x (2)		
Mathematics+								
Art of Discussion				x (1)				
Exegesis of Koran					x (1)	x (2)		
Tradition (Hadîth)					x (2)	x (2)	x (6)	
Laws of Inheritance						x (1)		
Rhetorics				x (2)				
Astronomy					x (1)	x (1)		

Source: Compiled according to La'hah-e 'aml, Lahore, 1983, pp. 17-22.

Pakistan Studies in Religious Schools

Special mention must be made of the subject Pakistan Studies in the alterations of curricula. In the formal education system this subject served to present the history of the evolution of Pakistan and of its idelogical basis–Islam–in order to form new conscious patriots. Among the goals set by the curriculum of Pakistan studies are:

"2. To understand Islam as a complete code of life which constitutes the basis of the ideology of Pakistan. . ."
"4. To show that great national objectives can be achieved by cooperation, discipline, proper ordering of loyalties and rooting out selfishness".

The text further states:

> "6. To make the students realize that the bonds that unite the people of Pakistan are far more real than the superficial differences that seem to divide them. The Pakistan culture . . . is essentially made of those fundamental beliefs and values for the preservation of which Pakistan came into existence.
> "To promote understanding and appreciation of the fundamentals of Islam and the basic ideology of Pakistan . . ."[20]

According to the Government, however, the ideology of Pakistan is Islam. As the DM primarily teach Islam, a large part of all the teaching materials in "Pakistan Studies" would consequently be redundant, especially in terms of ideology. The DM however, pay little attention to the question of national progress. The refusal of the DM to teach "Pakistan Studies" may be explained by the fact that the clergy obviously reached the limit of their willingness to integrate. They had demonstrated goodwill by including Arithmetic, Social Sciences, Economics and Political Sciences, even if only in a limited way. A large section of the '*ulamâ*' put up a strong resistance against the attempt to turn the DM into instruments of nationalism.

Overview on Different Curricula

Table 21 gives an overview on the alteration of curricula enacted by different umbrella organizations.[21]

TABLE 21: DIFFERENT CURRICULA AT A GLANCE

Subject	1a	1b	1c	2	3	4	5
Koran, Reading, Memorization		x	x	x	x	x	x
Morphology	x	x	x	x	x	x	x
Syntax	x	x	x	x	x	x	x
Arabic		x	x	x	x	x	x
Biography of the Prophet (*Sîrat*)		x	x	x	x	x	x
Arithmetic	x	x	x	x	x	x	x
Pakistan Studies			x				x
General Sciences			x				x
English			x			x	x
Islamic Law and *Hadîth*			x				
Natural Sciences			x				x
Social Sciences			x	x	x	x	
Islamic Law	x	x	x	x	x	x	x
Methods of Islamic Law	x	x	x	x	x	x	x
Logic	x	x	x	x	x	x	
Arabic Literature	x	x	x			x	x

Subject	1a	1b	1c	2	3	4	5
Tradition or Literature			X				
Rhetorics	X		X	X	X	X	
Interpretation of Koran	X	X	X	X	X	X	
Tradition	X	X	X	X	X	X	X
Methods of Tradition	X	X	X	X	X	X	
Principles of Belief, Scholastics	X	X	X	X	X	X	X
Philosophy	X	X	X	X	X	X	X
Islamic History		X	X	X	0	X	X
Economics			X	X	0		
Political Sciences			X	X	0		
Cultural Sciences			X	X	0		
Methods of Interpretation of Koran	X		X			X	
Law of Tradition			X				
Comparative Sciences of Religion			X	X	0		
Discussions (Munâzara)	X					X	
Prosody	X						
Religious Studies (Dîniyât)				X	X	X	X
Urdu			X	X	X	X	
Persian			X	X	X	x[1]	
Gymnastics (Tamrîn)				X	X		
Moral (Ikhlâqiyyât)		X		X	X	X	
Law of Inheritance (Farâ'id)		X		X	X	X	
Dictation		X				X	

Sources:

1a = *Dars-e nizâmî*; cf. *Halepota Report*, pp. 122, 135, 147-155.

1b = Curriculum of eight years of the Wafâq al-madâris al-'arabiyyah; cf. *Halepota Report*, ibid.

1c = Proposal of the National Committee on Dînî Madâris, 1979; cf. *Halepota Report*, ibid.

2 = Wafâq-proposal, partly enacted in 1983; cf. *solah sâlah nisâb-e ta'lîm (tajwîz)*, Multan, 1983, Wafâq al-madâris (*manzûrkardah I*).

3 = Wafâq-proposal as enacted in 1984, cf. *solah sâlah nisâb-e ta'lîm*, Multan, 1984, Wafâq al-madâris (*manzûrkardah II*).

4 = Tanzîm-proposal, enacted in 1983; cf. *solah sâlah nisâb-e ta'lîm (manzûr)*, Lahore, 1984, Tanzîm al-madâris.

5 = Jama'at-e Islami: *Cheh sâlah nisâb-e fâdil 'âlim-e islâmî*, 'Ulamâ' Akademî, Mansurah, Lahore, n.d.; exams are to be passed in "English", "Pakistan Studies", "Mathematics", "General Science", "Islamic History" and "Diniyat".

Explanations: 0 = These subjects are to be taught after graduation (*farâghat*) in a special two year course (*darjah-e takhassus*); cf. *solah sâlah nisâb-e ta'lîm*, Wafâq al-madâris al-'arabiyyah, Multan, 1984 (*manzûrkardah II*), pp. 7ff, pp. 21, 39.

[1] = Persian is a precondition for the course of the Tanzîm.

There were almost no alterations to the classical DM course of instruction. This is evident from a sentence contained in the curriculum of the Tanzîm in 1983:

"The curriculum of the Tanzîm al-madâris comprises eight years."[22]

INCREASE OF STUDENTS, TEACHERS AND MADÂRIS

In response to the alterations in the curricula, the number of students and teachers in the DM has increased over the last few years. It is apparent from Table 22.

Though Table 22 indicates large increases in numbers, the actual figures have to be looked at with caution:

1. The survey undertaken by the Ministry of Education in 1982 was not complete. Only the figures referring to the NWFP may claim to be so.
2. Figures for students and teachers were only available for the NWFP. Figures for other provinces in 1982 are based only on incomplete data. Figures on students and teachers given in the Table have been calculated on the basis of figures for the NWFP (number of students per madrasah).
3. The Zakat administration works with different figures of students. Thus, according to the PZC Punjab there were 206,454 DM students in 1984/85 alone.[23] This would raise the number of students in Pakistan to at least 341,611.
4. As there are both unregistered students and DM,[24] the figures of the PZCs covering exclusively the registered DM do not agree either with figures of different DM surveys or with author's extrapolations. The number of students and teachers in the DM is likely to be much higher. The projections are indicative of the possible distribution and trends.

According to Table 22, in 1982 there were 35.1 students per teacher, with an average of 137 students to each madrasah and 3.9 per cent teachers per madrasah,[25] the last figure having tripled since 1979: according to the *Halepota Report* the number of students per madrasah came up to 35.5 students with 3.1 teachers per madrasah. At the national level, the report accounted for 56.8 students per madrasah and 2.9 teachers per madrasah thus resulting in 19.8 students per teacher.

The reason for the increase in the student-teacher ratio in the last DM census may be found in the carefully and patiently conducted survey in NWFP.[26] In the course of the survey, schools had been categorized as "new" although they existed earlier but had not been registered, as in the tribal areas. The number of students in these schools is above average. As the official influence in these areas is weak, there is very little of formal education offered. Secondly, the effects of integration measures have to be taken into account. The increase in the number of students has been due to the Zakat funds as well as the prospect of formal degrees. On the basis of

TABLE 22: NUMBER OF STUDENTS AND TEACHERS OF
DÎNÎ MADÂRIS IN DIFFERENT YEARS

| | 1960 | | 1971 | | 1979+ | | 1983 | |
Provinces	S	T	S	T	S	T	S	T
W.-Pakistan	44407	1846	45238	3186	99041	5005	259827[1]	7394[1]
Punjab	24842	1053	29096	2063	80879*	2992	124670[1]	3549[1]
Sindh	6218	401	5431	453	8344	1245	37949[1]	1080[1]
NWFP	7897	312	8423	515	7749	673	78439[2]	2217[2]
Baluchistan	519	46	1207	95	1814	95	8083[1]	280[1]
Kashmir (Pak)							1644[1]	41[1]
N. Areas	763	23	1083	60	n.d.	n.d.	4384[1]	125[1]
Islamabad	n.d.	n.d.	n.d.	n.d.	n.d.	n.d.	4638[1]	133[1]

Sources: *Ahmad I*, pp. 692ff, 705ff; *Ahmad II*, pp. 693-696; *Halepota Report*, pp. 198-201.

Explanations: S = Students; T = Teachers
+ = erroneously in the *Halepota Report*, 839 D.M. instead of 1745 (cf. op.cit., pp. 56ff and Annexure).
* = cf. *Halepota Report*, pp. 58, 198; erroneously 81834 instead of 80879.
[1] = calculated on the basis of figures of the Ministry of Education: GoP, "Important statistics of the Dini Madaris of NWFP", Islamabad, 1983 (mimeo).
[2] = ibid.

the NWFP figures, from 1979 up to 1983, the national increase of students was 162.3 per cent while that of the teachers was 47.7 per cent.[27]

The increase of students and teachers has advantages as well as disadvantages from a Government point of view: The large number of formally recognized religious institutions, supported financially by Zakat funds, with a neutralizing effect on the religious scholars and students, produced for Zia ul Haq an army of loyalists. This army was consolidated by the network of the Zakat administration and of the Auqaf Department. On the other hand, the increasing number of registered DM, and their students and teachers mean an increase in the demand for jobs by graduates. The regime will hardly be able to absorb hundreds of thousands of DM graduates. Even if a few hundreds are employed as teachers for Arabic and/or Islamiyat or if they even find jobs in the army,[28] this would only temporarily stem the demand for jobs among the DM graduates. One may wonder whether the integrationist policy will be capable of absorbing the traditional potential in a profitable and productive way. It is quite possible that the scholars supported by the regime of Zia ul Haq may become a problem which the military bureaucratic alliance might have great difficulty in dealing with in the future.

Along with the increase in students in religious schools, the number of DM increased as well. This aspect is examined in Table 23.

The following points emerge from this: between 1950 and 1979, there was a rate of increase of 803 per cent. The number of DM is related to the number of population in the same period in each province respectively.

The total increase of DM between 1979 and 1982 is surprisingly low (8.6 per cent). It is equally surprising that the number of DM seems to decrease in all provinces except in NWFP. The increase is due exclusively to the disproportionate growth in NWFP. This unusual development is explained by a more detailed examination of the 1982 survey: The strong increase of DM in NWFP between the last two surveys is partly due to the fact that the functionaries conducting the survey originated from this province and tended to neglect the other provinces.[29] Another reason may lie in the special interest of the Central Government in the DM of the NWFP due to the possibility of mobilizing them as centres from which *Jihâd* could be launched in Afghanistan.[30] While the figures are relatively complete for the NWFP, the data in the 1982 survey for the other provinces is incomplete and can only serve as indicative figures with some reservations.

"Mushroom-Growth"

The introduction of the Zakat system in 1980 and the official recognition of the DM degrees in 1981 led to a swelling of the number of religious schools and to certain worries within the Zakat administration. They rightly assumed that there was a direct connection between the availability of Zakat funds for the DM and the increase in their numbers. Recently, the increase has been countered by the Zakat administration through its selective policy.[31] According to the new policy of distribution, Zakat may only be given to those madrasah which are registered under the Societies Act 1860. The progress in the registration of DM indicates their response and that of the clergy receiving Government aid. Furthermore, it gives information on the increase of private schools and thus about the degree of privatization of the system of education. Both variables together shed light on the respective stage of development and social structure of a given area, with one or the other institution dominating.

As Table 24 demonstrates, the eighties witnessed a significant increase in DM registration under the Societies Act 1860. This Act had been passed in order to bring about the registration of religious institutions and institutions of education as well as of endowments. Section 20 of the Act reads: "The following societies may be registered under this Act: Charitable societies, societies for the promotion of science, literature or the fine arts, for instruction, the diffusion of useful knowledge".

TABLE 23: QUANTITATIVE DEVELOPMENT OF DÎNÎ MADÂRIS IN PAKISTAN (FORMERLY WEST PAKISTAN)

Province	Pre-Pak	1950	1956	1960	1971	1979	1982	Increase (%)	
								1950-79	1979-82
W. Pakistan	137	210	244	401	893	1745	1896	803	8.6
Punjab	87	137	159	264	580	1012	910⁺	639	-10.1
Sindh	19	25	25	44	120	380	277	1008	-27.1
NWFP	20	31	43	66	127	218	572	1784	168.0
Baluch.	7	11	12	20	44	135	59	1127	-56.3
Kashmir (Pak)	4	6	10	11	22	—	12		
N. Areas	—	—	—	—	—	—	32		
Islamabad	—	—	—	—	—	—	34		

Sources: Nadhr Ahmad: *A Preliminary Survey of Madaris-i-deeniyyah in East & West Pakistan*, December 1956, pp. 12ff.

Ahmad I, pp. 705-708.

Ahmad II, pp. 691 ff.

GoP, Ministry of Religious Affairs: *Riport qâwmî kamitî bârâ-e dînî madâris Pâkistân*, Islamabad, 1979 (Urdu), pp. 194-197.

GoP, Ministry of Education: *Pâkistân kê dînî madâris kî fihrist 1984*, Islamabad, 1984 (Urdu), p. 100.

Explanation: ⁺= According to data by the Punjab Provinical Zakat Council in Punjab in 1984/85, 1856 DM already existed .

TABLE 24: REGISTERED DÎNÎ MADÂRIS AND PRIVATE SCHOOLS
IN PUNJAB, 1974-85

Year of Registration	Total number of Registered Institutions %		Dînî Madâris in %		Private Schools in %	
1974	117	(100)	21	(17.9)	-	
1975	444	(100)	38	(8.6)	-	
1978	815	(100)	175	(21.5)	17	(2.1)
1983	966	(100)	389	(40.3)	199	(20.6)
1984	2864	(100)	715	(25.0)	443	(15.5)
1985	2296	(100)	624	(27.2)	141	(6.1)

Source: Investigation in the Punjab Stock Company, Punchhouse, Lahore, in February 1986 and August 1987.

While in 1974, the DM made up 18 per cent of the total institutions registered (they were only 8.6 per cent in 1975, reflecting the secular policy under the Bhutto regime), their proportion in 1978, i.e. one year after Zia ul Haq came to power and shortly before the official proclamation of the "Nizâm-e mustafâ" in 1979, rose to 21.5 per cent. In 1983, their proportion reached 40.3 per cent, numbering 389 DM and, in the following year culminated with 715 DM,[32] equal to 25 per cent of the total entries of registration.

The increase of registered institutions must be discussed keeping in mind the campaign for privatization of 1979. It is also reflected in the number of private schools shooting up like mushrooms, reaching their peak in 1984.

The drop in the registration of DM to 624 in 1985 is astonishing at first glance. It reflects, in fact, the policy of the Zakat administration, which tried to stop the "mushroom-growth" by any means. One way was to cut off funds for small DM.[33] The most effective measure introduced in 1984 was the limitation of disbursement of Zakat to those DM which had already been registered for at least four years. These measures have been able to stem the flood of DM for the time being. The drop in the registration of private schools seems to be a reaction to the saturation of the market.

The situation described above is reflected in Graph 1; while there is a constant increase of entries, even a steep rise one from 1983 to 1984, their number visibly recedes after 1984. The decrease of private schools results in an especially steep fall of the graph.

Similar tendencies of "mushroom-growth" are seen in the NWFP (Table 25).

TABLE 25: "MUSHROOM-GROWTH" IN THE NWFP

District	1962-81		1983-86	
	Total Entries	D.M.	Total Entries	D.M.
Peshawar	192	42	n.d.	n.d.
Mardan	30	19	n.d.	n.d.
Kohat	10	6	n.d.	n.d.
Bannu	52	49	n.d.	n.d.
D.I.Khan	38	31	n.d.	n.d.
Dir	3	3	n.d.	n.d.
Hazara	78	21	n.d.	n.d.
Swat	6	6	n.d.	n.d.
Total	319	177	255	176

Source: Investigation in the Peshawar Registration Branch, Directorate Commerce, Industries and Mineral Development, Peshawar Cantonment, March 1986 and author's calculations.

While the percentage of DM in the total entries in the NWFP reached 55.5 per cent between 1962 and 1981, this percentage rose to 69[34] between 1983 and February 1986. Here too the Zakat Regulation and the formal recognition of DM degrees had a direct effect on the number of religious schools.

At the local level, particular districts have relatively high numbers of DM; this is the case in Bannu,[35] a district from where many graduated from religious schools and one with a traditional social structure.[36]

Similar tendencies of "mushroom-growth" may be expected in the provinces of Baluchistan and Sindh (excluding Karachi).[37] The figures for the Karachi metropolis are indicated in Table 26.

TABLE 26: "MUSHROOM-GROWTH" IN KARACHI

Year	DM	P.S.	Total Entries
1974	5	2	134
1979	10	65	1401
1980	14	110	380
1981	19	176	496
1982	26	181	495
1983	11	220	528
1984	22	220	551
1985	23	183	447
Total	130	1157	4432

Source: Investitgation at the Sindh Department of Industries, Karachi, for the region of Karachi, June 1986.

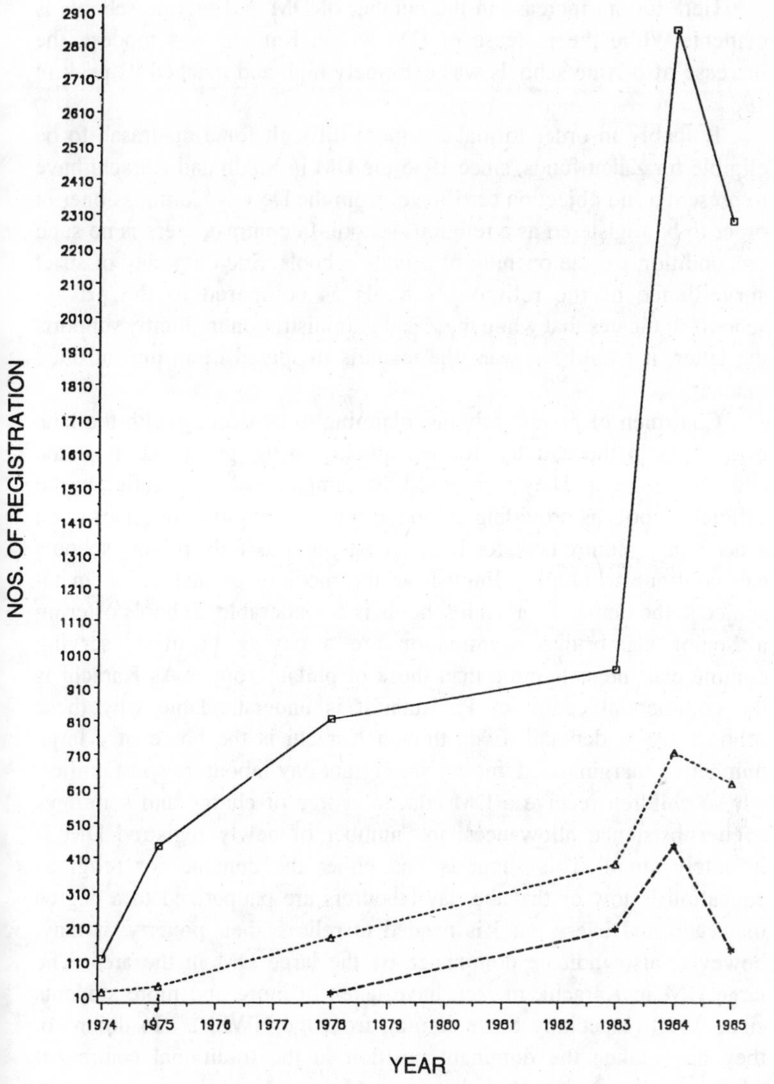

GRAPH 1: REGISTRATIONS ACCORDING TO THE SOCIETIES ACT 1860
FOR PARTICULAR YEARS IN THE PROVINCE OF PUNJAB

Source: Punjab Stock Company, Punchhouse Lahore, Feb.1986/Aug.1987

□ = Total Registrations

▲ = Dînî Madâris

* = Private Schools

Here too an increase in the number of DM and private schools is evident. While the increase of DM within Karachi was modest, the increase of private schools was extremely high and reached its peak in 1983.

Probably in order to make it more difficult for a madrasah to be eligible for Zakat funds, since 1985 the DM in Sindh and Karachi have to present a 'no objection certificate' from the Deputy Commissioner in order to be registered as a religious school. In contrast, there is no such precondition for the opening of private schools. Such a policy of strict surveillance of the religious schools as compared to the private schools indicates that while the Zakat administration implicitly supports the latter, it would not want the madâris to spread in an uncontrolled manner.

Chairmen of private schools, claiming to be dealing with the lack of schools in the country, reacted quickly to the privatization of the education system. They recognized the campaign of Urduization in the official schools as providing an opportunity: as English continues to be a necessary requirement for higher posts, and as only private schools can continue to employ English as the medium of instruction in all subjects, the demand for such schools is considerable. Schools offering a Senior Cambridge examination are a paying business, serving commercial interests more than those of philanthropy.[38] As Karachi is the commercial centre of Pakistan, it is understandable why these schools are in demand. Even though Karachi is the home of a large number of marginalized, mostly immigrant day-labourers and families, whose children receive a DM education free of charge and somtimes even subsistence allowances, the number of newly registred DM is infinitely small. This suggests that either the demand for religious education is low or that the day-labourers are pauperized to a degree that each and every hand is needed to relieve their poverty; it may, however, also indicate dominance by the large DM in the area. The large DM in Karachi, in fact, have taken in more and more students since 1980 (especially those coming from the NWFP).[39] In doing so, they have taken the dominant position in the traditional centres of education like Peshawar, Lahore and Multan. At the same time, they have added to the potential of conflict in the metropolis.[40]

The examination of the registers of Joint Stock Companies offers another possibility, of identifying the location of DM in Punjab at the level of Divisions.[41] Table 27 illustrates some interesting trends.

TABLE 27: REGISTERED INSTITUTIONS IN PUNJAB
ACCORDING TO DIVISIONS: 1984 AND 1985

Divisions	Total Number of Regist. Institutions (%)		Dînî Madâris %				Private Schools %			
	1984	1985	1984		1985		1984		1985	
Rawalpindi	343 (100)	163 (100)	58	(17)	49	(30)	84	(25)	22	(14)
Faisalabad	345 (100)	327 (100)	65	(19)	76	(23)	38	(11)	21	(6)
Lahore	830 (100)	678 (100)	140	(17)	81	(12)	188	(23)	53	(8)
Gujranwala	370 (100)	318 (100)	74	(20)	73	(23)	64	(17)	17	(5)
Sargodha	272 (100)	186 (100)	53	(19)	70	(38)	25	(9)	14	(8)
Multan	335 (100)	315 (100)	106	(32)	102	(32)	28	(8)	10	(3)
D.G. Khan	146 (100)	101 (100)	85	(58)	82	(81)	3	(2)	3	(3)
Bahawalpur	223 (100)	209 (100)	134	(60)	91	(44)	13	(6)	1	(0)
Total	2864 (100)	2296 (100)	715	(25)	624	(27)	445	(16)	141	(6)

Source: Investigation in Punjab Joint Stock Company, Punchhouse, Lahore, February 1986 and August 1987 and author's calculations.

The table shows that the "mushroom-growth" of the DM in Divisions like Multan, D.G. Khan and Bahawalpur is especially pronounced. They differ from the four Divisions–Rawalpindi, Lahore, Faisalabad and Gujranwala. As their infrastructure is poor, there are few important industries and thus less urbanization; in short, they do not have a high level of development.[42] They are, however, more integrated in their traditional systems of social order and social security and thus are possibly more cohesive than "modern areas". These Divisions are marked by large landed properties and a high number of small farmers or landless peasants.[43] It is therefore understandable that there is little or no demand for private schools in these areas. The picture is different when it comes to the Divisions with a better infrastructure. Here, the level of urbanization is higher, there are industries in some areas and one may expect a higher level of income. As such, Lahore, Faisalabad, Gujranwala and Rawalpindi are among the most important interior market towns in Pakistan. As the tendency in these areas is probably to be more "modern" than in other (more traditionalist) Divisions, the number of private schools is more than religious schools. At the subordinate district level, there is an analogous development.[44]

Even though Rawalpindi is a relatively urbanized Division, here too traditional districts can be distinguished from the more modern districts.

The Jhelum district has few DM. The reason for this may go back to the British policy which in the nineteenth and twentieth centuries had its military centres in this area to recruit its army. This remains true to this day.[45] The social structure in Jhelum district with its basic population of soldiers and officers and the corresponding service sector seems to foster little interest in DM. The degree of modernization and social conditions thus seem to play pivotal role for the establishment of DM and private schools. Both proportion of DM and their absolute numbers in Jhelum district are thus lower than in Rawalpindi district.

This had not always been the case. Prior to the colonial penetration in Punjab, the districts of Jhelum and Rawalpindi as well as some districts further north in the Punjab had far more DM than in 1979. In 1850 Lahore alone had 152 religious schools.[46] In 1880, W.G. Leitner had counted 660 DM in the district of Rawalpindi, 455 in Sialkot, 295 in Lahore, 275 in Gujrat and 200 in Jhelum.[47] In 1979 these numbers had been reduced to 33, 29, 61, 17 and 11 respectively. The colonial policy towards the DM was obviously followed by the Pakistani state. The fact that during the past few years more DM were set up even in "modern" districts like Jhelum points to a broad marginalization of large parts of the population, a marginalization which is inevitable in the context of an unequal development within a colonial market economy. Whenever necessary, these masses can be employed as cheap and profitable labour. The necessary social support is offered by the families[48] or, at best, by the DM.

Just as the number of religious schools is low in Jhelum, there are very few graduates of DM in this district.[49] The small "developed" district of Attock, in 1984/85 in contrast, had a higher number of DM with an equal population (1981 census).

The rural character of DM—mainly the small DM—is especially revealing in districts like Bahawalnagar, Rahim Yar Khan (in the Bahawalpur Division) and in the districts of the Dera Ghazi Khan Division. Here private schools are found rarely as there is no demand for them in largely agricultural areas. The people of this area cannot afford high fees of the private schools. The DM therefore have a large influx of students, and there is an increase in the number of DM

In 1983-84, the proportion of DM in "traditional" districts was 47 per cent (656 DM). The number of private schools was correspondingly small, 10 per cent, or 102 schools. Out of 141 private schools 72 were located in Rawalpindi district, more precisely in the urbanized areas of this district.

Between 1984 and 1985 similar trends can be seen. Table 28 clearly shows that the DM have their domain within the traditional areas. This is especially evident in the districts of Bahawalpur and Muzaffargarh Divisions. The districts of Gujranwala, Sialkot and Sargodha also have increasing number of DM. The demand for DM in these relatively less developed areas may be due to the increasing marginalization of large parts of the population.[50] On the other hand, one may notice that it was predominantly the Ahl-e Hadith who put up DM in such areas as Sialkot, Gujranwala, Gujrat and Lahore, i.e. in centres of trade. There thus seems to be two factors at work: one is the correlation between high number of DM and low levels of development of the relevant area; the other is the correlation between high number of DM and developed areas with marked trends of marginalization of large parts of the population.

DIFFERENT LEVELS

As can be seen from tables 29 and 30 most of the DM offered education at the lower levels.[51] Every second DM which had been accounted for in the two surveys was a *makâtab*.

TABLE 28: REGISTERED INSTITUTIONS IN SELECTED DISTRICTS
OF THE PUNJAB 1984-85

Districts	1984		1985	
	DM	P.S.	DM	P.S.
Rawalpindi	29	67	19	20
Attock	16	4	18	2
Jhelum	14	10	7	1
Gujranwala	32	9	35	6
Sialkot	25	37	23	5
Gujrat	17	18	15	6
Sargodha	21	18	35	22
Khushab	12	—	15	1
Mianwali	5	—	7	—
Bhakkar	15	1	13	1
D.G.Khan	20	1	25	1
Muzaffargarh	45	1	34	—
Rajanpur	3	—	10	—
Leiah	14	1	15	1
Bahawalpur	72	1	53	—
Bahawalnagar	19	—	33	—
Rahim Yar Khan	43	12	53	1

Source: Investigation in the Punjab Stock Company, Punchhouse, Lahore, February 1986
          and August 1987 and author's own calculations.

It is evident from the tables as well as from examination of the "mushroom-growth" phenomenon of DM that between 1979 and 1983 the small DM increased more than the large ones. The number of institutions offering *nâzirah*, *hifz*, *tajwîd* and *qirâ'at* and that of the *tahtânî*-DM in 1983 came to 1218. As against this, there were only 717 DM of the *ulâ* (primary level) in 1979. This shows a growth of almost 70 per cent in four years, a typical tendency of the flood of DM under the regime of Zia ul Haq.

At the higher levels the number of institutions declined from one survey to the next. This is especially true for schools teaching up to the *mawqûf* stage. In contrast to the official data, the data of the Deobandi Wafâq al-Madâris and of the Brelwi Tanzîm al-Madâris on the DM under their organizational umbrella show an increase of the institutions teaching *mawqûf*. Thus, the Deobandi Wafâq in 1982 alone counted 352 *wustânî* DM (middle size DM offering the level of *mawqûf*) in its registers.[52] This number by itself is as high as the total number given in the 1982 census. It remains to add those DM affiliated to the Tanzîm al-Madâris as well as those of other Wafâqs.[53] The data in the census thus appear to be unreliable approximations.

With the help of the membership lists of the Wafâqs and Tanzîms an assessment can be made of the development at the higher levels. In this area–*dawrah-e hadîth* or *fawqânî*–the Deobandi Wafâq counted 101 DM in 1982 alone, the Tanzîm 33 in 1983, and the Wafâq al-Madâris al-salafiyyah more than 70 DM. The Shia DM on which no data is available, have to be added. The total number of all these Dâr al-'Ulûms is, nevertheless, below that reported in the 1982 survey. This may be due to

TABLE 29: EDUCATION IN DÎNÎ MADÂRIS
ACCORDING TO LEVELS OFFERED, 1979

Province	Primary L. ulâ Proportions in %		Intermediate L. mawqûf Proportions in %		Upper L. hadîth Proportions in %		Proportions without Specification in %		Total Proportions in %	
Pakistan	717	(41.1)	540	(30.9)	265	(15.2)	614	(35.2)	1745	(100)
Punjab	594	(58.7)	352	(34.8)	129	(12.7)	206	(20.4)	1012	(100)
Sindh	77	(20.3)	62	(16.3)	40	(10.5)	208	(54.7)	380	(100)
NWFP	103	(47.2)	89	(40.8)	60	(27.5)	105	(27.5)	218	(100)
Baluch.	32	(28.7)	37	(27.4)	27	(20.0)	98	(75.6)	135	(100)

Source: *Halepota Report*, pp. 57, 194-197.

Explanation: A madrasah may offer different levels at the same time; therefore, over-
               lapping is possible.

TABLE 30: EDUCATION IN DÎNÎ MADÂRIS
ACCORDING TO LEVELS OFFERED, 1982

Province Region	nâzirah Proportion in %		tahtânî Proportion in %		mawqûf Proportion in %		hadîth Proportion in %		Total Proportion in %	
Pakistan	742	(39.1)	476	(25.1)	352	(18.6)	326	(17.2)	1896	(100)
Punjab	447	(49.0)	187	(20.5)	134	(14.7)	141	(15.6)	910	(100)
Sindh	120	(49.0)	68	(24.5)	47	(27.0)	42	(15.4)	277	(100)
NWFP	135	(26.3)	190	(32.2)	136	(23.8)	111	(18.4)	572	(100)
Baluch.	6	(10.2)	13	(22.0)	22	(37.0)	18	(30.5)	59	(100)
Kashmir (Pak)	—	—	3	(25.0)	3	(25.0)	6	(50.0)	12	(100)
N. Areas	13	(40.6)	6	(18.8)	7	(18.9)	6	(18.8)	32	(100)
ICT	21	(61.8)	9	(26.5)	3	(8.8)	1	(2.9)	34	(100)

Source: GoP, Ministry of Education; Islamic Education Research Cell: *Pâkistân kê dînî madâris kî fihrist 1984*, Islamabad, 1984 (Urdu), p. 100; own calculations,

Explanations: Here only the main levels offered are accounted for, so there is no overlapping.
Baluch. = Baluchistan, N. Areas = Northern Areas, ICT = Islamabad Capital Territory.

the fact that not all DM are affiliated to one of the umbrella organizations and thus some are neither registered as members of the Wafâq nor as members of the Tanzîm. At the provincial level the NWFP, being a traditional area of origin of religious scholars, has the largest proportion of the higher level religious institutions in relation to population.

TABLE 31: COMPARISON OF LEVELS OF EDUCATION IN
FORMAL SCHOOLS AND IN DÎNÎ MADÂRIS

Levels of Education	Number of Inst.	Formal Schools	Dînî Madâris Schools
Primary level	69058	86.4%	64.2%
Intermediate level	10016	12.5%	18.6%
Higher level[54]	885	1.1%	17.2%

Sources: Calculations on the basis of *Pakistan Economic Survey 1983-1984*, GoP, Islamabad, n.d., pp. 222f as well as Tables 29 and 30.

To conclude, the different levels of DM increased their numbers in varying degrees. The increase was especially pronounced at the lower levels. Table 31 gives a comparison of primary, intermediate and upper levels of the formal educational system.

The proportions of the different levels of education show considerable differences. This is especially true in the area of higher education. Higher religious education is offered in many more institutions than higher secular education: arts, technical or medical. Perhaps financial reasons are the most important in explaining this. It appears that modernization of the Pakistani society has only been partial.

THE BUDGET OF DÎNÎ MADÂRIS

Islamization not only altered the curriculum of the DM and increased the number of students and the number of the DM, it also changed the income situation and therefore the consumption patterns of the traditional institutions.

To give an example of the characteristics and the development of DM budgets, the budget of one particular madrasah is examined in more detail. As the data of the Dâr al-'Ulûm Jâm'iyyah Nizâmiyyah Ridwiyyah in Lahore is fairly complete, this madrasah has been selected. The school is also the administrative centre of the Brelwi Tanzîm al-madâris.

The growth in income of this school between 1959 and 1984/85, is given in Table 32.

TABLE 32: GROWTH RATES OF THE RECEIPTS AND EXPENDITURE OF THE JÂM'IAH NIZÂMIYYAH RIDWIYYAH, LAHORE

Year	Receipts		Expenditure	
	Growth as Compared to Previous Year in %	In Period in %	Growth as Compared to Previous Year in %	In Period in %
1958/59	—		—	
1969/70	304.8 %		95.5 %	—
1971/72	-5.3 %	283.4 %	71.7 %	236.4 %
1981/82	1289.8 %		1402.9 %	—
1983	13.3 %	16.8 %		—
1984	46.5 %	65.9 %	48.3 %	31.1 %

Sources: Calculated according to different budgets of the Jâm'iah Nizâmiyyah, Lahore (Urdu).

The size of the total budget increased steadily since the establishment of the school. The main reason for the especially pronounced increase in 1982/83 was the additional income from official Zakat funds. The budget lists 12 categories of income. The largest share of income usually comes from (private) Zakat, monthly alms (*chandah*), the irregular receipts (*'attiyyât*) and, lately, official Zakat by the PZC. The remaining income comes from credits, students or their parents, *sadaqah fitrânah* and *sadaqah wa khairât*, both alms tied to special occasions, income from publications and rents and from skins (collected after slaughtering for festivities and then sold), and from the Auqaf Department. These account for only a fraction of the total receipts.

The figures show that the proportion of the PZC Zakat in the total income increased over time. In contrast, the amount of private Zakat at first stagnated but picked up again from 1981/82 to 1983. There was a strong increase as well in *'attiyyât* and in the monthly alms. The only source of income declining was the *sadaqah fitrânah wa qurbânî*. These are alms given at certain festivities, such as the reading of Koran, circumcision, birth, etc. It was customary to invite students of DM to these festivities and to give presents to them. The decline of these alms indicates a change in the social status of those receiving and those giving alms and also indicates a reaction against the Zakat policy. The report to the president accordingly reads:

Indeed the occasion of a child's beginning the recitation of the Holy Quran with the "Bismillah" became an occasion for a family gathering and distribution of sweets among relatives and acquaintances. Unfortunately, however, all of this is rapidly becoming a thing of the past. The responsibility for teaching Nazira Quran (reading of Koran) has passed to the (formal) schools, particularly among the rural populace and the urban poor.[55]

The expansion of the colonial sector seems to have led to a change of the social structure. This affected the DM too. The alms by students and parents declined as well. The reduction of the traditional sources of income made the DM increasingly dependent on official support. Therefore, the criticism that the introduction of the Zakat system resulted in lessening the traditional sources of income is partially justified. The receipts of the DM have, however, risen if all sources are taken into account.

Given that most students are considered needy recipients, it should not be surprising that there would be only a meagre income from traditional sources; a recipient of Zakat does not have a surplus from which he could give alms to the DM. Those who have already paid Zakat to the state consider their duty done and will seldom give additional alms to religious schools (Table 33).

The expenses for food show a different trend. Its proportion rose between 1971/72 and 1981/82. Salaries of teachers reached their peak in

1981/82 to 1984. This may be due to the altered consumption pattern of the teachers,[56] contrary to their obligation to have a modest life-style.

Another major item of expenditure is the cost of alteration and additions to the madrasah as well as the purchase of land for the construction of another school or for an annexure to the existing one. Other expenses such as those for freezers, fans, matting, typewriters and photocopying machines point at a certain modernization of the equipment.

Expenses for books, paper, writing materials, telephones, mail, electricity and the entertainment during 1981/82 indicate a higher level of activity and propagation of the madrasah as well as of the Tanzîm al-madâris.

To conclude, one may state that the receipts have risen more than the expenditure. Further the PZC Zakat makes up for an essential part of the yearly income. The acquisition of so-called modern goods—unthinkable before 1980 and not essential as there was no conscious need for these goods—was quite an innovation. The same is true of the extension of construction of the DM. All this indicates towards new needs and a new way of meeting those needs through additional Zakat funds for the religious scholars and for their schools. In order to finance these new needs, the loyalty of the schools toward the state was indispensable.

THE PROVINCIAL AND DISTRICT DISTRIBUTION

As mentioned above, the schools of thought are spread out in different areas and clearly illustrate the regionalization of Islam in Pakistan. Whether the statements on the distribution of the 'ulamâ'-to-be[57] in relation to their districts of origin and their districts of graduation are consistent with the distribution of DM in different provinces can be examined here. Perhaps the concentration of the graduates would correspond to the concentration of the DM of a certain school of thought.

Tables 34(A) to (F) confirm this pattern. The Deobandi school of thought is the most prominent.[58] It is followed by the Brelwis, the Shia, the Jama'at-e Islami and the Ahl-e Hadith. This ranking corresponds approximately to the number of candidates for graduation of the different schools.

The affiliation of madrasahs to one or other of the umbrella organizations had been quite deliberate until 1979. The situation changed by 1983/84.

The DM and the clergy were formalized and integrated under Zia ul Haq. The number of DM affiliated to umbrella organizations increased as

TABLE 33: BUDGETS OF THE JĀMIʿAH NIZĀMIYYAH, LAHORE

Receipts from	1	2	3	4	5	6	7	8
Balance of previous year			1635	38217	16820	6018		57285
Receipts from credits						2000		
Montly alms			7298	54247	35567	6738	70895	98320
Alms from students			2322	11910	5155	1145	10164	
Irregular receipts ('attiyyāt)			–					
Zakat (private)			18778	56219	41563	4003	96497	111090
Sadaqah fitrānah			8123	292762	143152	14215	219605	323093
wa qurbānī								
Publications			2401	12771	11533	2000	15934	10395
Skins #				473	15797		16405	24927
Sadaqah wa khairāt				14915	2241	70	5522	
Rents				6553	300	50	6300	16290
Auqaf Dept.				600	1300		1300	3000
Total of alms				488688	273429	36302	438573	635402
Zakat from PZC				75000*	50000*		200000*	300000*
Total receipts	10579	42820	40558	563668	323429	36302	638573	935402

Sources: 1: (1958-59) *Ahmad I*, p. 477.
2: (1969-70) *Ahmad II*, p. 37.
3: (1971-72) *Sālānah goshwāra, Dar ul-Ulum Nizamiyyah*, published by Dar ul-Ulum Nizamiyyah, Lahore, 1972 (Urdu), p. 3.
4: (July 1981-June 1982) *Sālānah goshwāra*, op.cit., Lahore, 1982, p. 13.

5: (July 1982-Dec. 1982) *Sālānah goshwāra*, op.cit., Lahore, 1982, p. 13.
6: (Feb. 1983) *Sālānah goshwāraa*. op.cit., Lahore, 1983, p. 11.
7: (Jan. 1983-Dec. 1983) *Sālānah goshwāra*, op.cit., Lahore, 1983, p. 13.
8: (Jan. 1984-Dec. 1984) *Sālānah goshwāra*, op.cit., Lahore, 1984, p. 3.

* These include private Zakat as well as Zakat from the PZC. They have not been recorded separately. In order to distinguish between these two Zakat items in the budget, the PZC amount was split into half-yearly amounts. For example: Jan. 1983-Dec. 1983 (cf. column 7): 50 per cent of the PZC Zakat 1982/83 = Rs. 50,000.

\# Refers to skins of sacrificed slaughtered animals on occasion of the main festivities of slaughtering.

Expenditure for	1	2	3	4	5	6	7	8
Nutrition and health of students			9732	140016	60742	12355	182822	196305
Library			210	37085	7548	62	10059	17379
Salaries of teachers			19053	158030	96809	16540	212101	261972
Writing utensils and similar items			565	5132	3422	43	3903	11998
Mail			108	2106	3540	2	348	831
Telephone			1269	10476	4177	344	2569	5306
Law affairs			1090	1051	665	772	4918	7183
Water				2281	533	1012	1372	1239
Electricity			567	9552	5652	195	2675	4191
Travelling and transport			1141	5729	3164	318	8029	9291
Functions			610	5923	4422	206	5176	6704
Newspapers and magazines			115			122	519	323
Repairs (buildings)			131	122210	192199		35599	13508
Property tax on Waqf houses							451	1866
Fees to Tanzīm ul Madāris				400		400	400	400

Expenditure for	1	2	3	4	5	6	7	8
Alms							2200	2600
Ceremonies				13427	2919		9030	16098
Bookkeeping			200	100	1000		600	1250
Miscellaneous			1295	3518	3766	376	3196	4294
Purchase of land								169764
Firewood			276	15887	7783	1848		7875
Deep Freezer					4800			
Photostat								2450
Fans							7124	
Typewriters								1010
Shelves							83992	
Repayment of debts								
Carpets etc.				1789	3657			10123
Furniture				9795	580			1400
Scholarships				1470		550		
Total expend.	10815	21185	36386	546848	407422	35745	638573	755364

Sources: Cf. Table on receipts of the Dâr ul-ʿUlûm Nizâmiyyah.

a result from 430 in 1979 to 1,781 in 1983/84. This might be due to the fact that only a madrasah affiliated to umbrella organization could offer an officially recognized degree.[59] From the available data, one may expect a further swelling of the number of DM affiliated to umbrella organizations. At the provincial level, there is a clear hegemony of the Deobandis in Sindh, NWFP and Baluchistan.[60] In Punjab, however, the Deobandis had to concede their dominance to the Brelwis who were strongly organized in this area since their reorganization in 1974, while other areas were neglected.[61] A concentration of DM similar to the one in Punjab exists for the Ahl-e Hadith, who had established 77 per cent of their schools in 1983/84. The Ahl-e Hadith apparently had no ambition to expand into other areas. There are gaps in the network of DM in NWFP, Sindh, and especially in Baluchistan.

The Shia DM are maximum in Punjab and in the Northern Areas, such as Gilgit and Baltistan. Over 46.4 per cent of their DM are located in Punjab and 36.2 per cent in the Northern Areas. In 1983/84 Sindh, NWFP and Baluchistan as well as Kashmir (Pak) had very few, if any Shia DM.[62]

The Jama'at-e Islami started organizing their DM under its own umbrella organization Râbitah al-Madâris al-Islâmiyyah only a few years ago, like the Shia and the Ahl-e Hadith. Out of 107 affiliated DM in 1983/84 only 37 were located in Punjab, while 41 pertained to NWFP and to the Tribal Areas where most of the schools were situated close to the Afghan border.

The distribution of DM also demonstrates that each school of thought has its own "reserved" area: Punjab is the domain of the Brelwis,[63] Sindh, NWFP and Baluchistan of the Deobandis and the Northern Areas of the Shia. As the Tables 34(A) to (F) further illustrate, the umbrella organizations have experienced different growth rates over the last few years. The highest growth is that of the Deobandi and the Shia DM (from 1979 to 1983/84 almost 500 per cent and 625 per cent respectively). Growth rate of the Brelwis, the Ahl-e Hadith and the Jama'at-e Islami in the same period are 195 per cent, 16.4 per cent[64] and 107 per cent. The Deobandi Wafâq thus was most efficient at the national level in affiliating its DM. In Punjab, the domain of the Brelwi Tanzîm, the increase of the Deobandi Wafâq even surpasses that of the Brelwis (214.9 per cent). Even more remarkable is the strong growth of the affiliated Deobandi DM in Sindh (an increase by a factor of 19!), in the NWFP (39.1 per cent) and in Baluchistan (an increase by a factor of 11 per cent). Kashmir (Pak), in contrast, does not seem to be an area of activity of the Deobandi Wafâq.

The high rates of increase of Deobandi DM in the different provinces needs further examination. In Sindh, the rise may be connected with the problem of regional nationalism.[65] One may exclude the connection between the official payments of Zakat and the increase of DM,[66] as the number of DM in Sindh increased even though the majority of the Deobandi DM did not accept any official Zakat funds. This shows that there are other motives for the expansion than the official financial support via the Zakat system. The stronghold of Deobandis in Sindh is partially explained by the fact that some of the leading 'ulamâ' put up their centre, the Dâr al-'Ulûm Ashrafabad, in Sindh soon after the partition of India. This theological seminary was to be the "Pakistani Deoband". In fact, many leading 'ulamâ' of Deoband met here and this Dâr al-'Ulûm produced many of the leading religious scholars of Pakistan.

The pronounced dissemination of the Deobandis in NWFP is historically explained by the connection between the Indian Deoband and the city of Kabul in Afghanistan since the late nineteenth century. There is, however, no explanation for the acceptance the Deobandis received in. Baluchistan.

The forces of opposition, for example some of the Deobandis and the Shia, have consolidated and expanded their sphere of influence during the last few years through indigenous institutions, especially in provinces where there is a latent potential for conflict. Among these are Sindh and Baluchistan as well as the Northern Areas. The latter are considered sensitive areas in the context of Pakistani foreign policy.[67] They are under the influence of the Shia. Referring to our theoretical outline, one may state that the Deobandis hold an isolationist position[68] in Sindh, in Baluchistan, and also in parts of NWFP. They seem to receive some support from the Shia,[69] and are also present in Sindh.[70]

Punjab with its role as guarantor or *Thekedar* of Pakistan is characterized by a strong influence of the Brelwis. This suited the policy of the Zia administration, which supported the Punjab and thus assured its political neutrality. Thus, the Punjabis may be considered to have adopted a position of conformity towards the system and become the mainstay of the regime.[71] The DM of the Brelwis and Ahl-e Hadith located in this province may be looked upon as integrationist groups. The Jama'at-e Islami, a prototype of the integrationist *avant-garde,* even assists the state in its strategic-military affairs; their DM are concentrated in locations close to the border.

TABLE 34 (A): DÎNÎ MADÂRIS ACCORDING TO THEIR SCHOOL OF THOUGHT AND THEIR AFFILIATION TO AN UMBRELLA ORGANIZATION IN PAKISTAN

School of Thought	1960	1971	1979	1983/84		Up to Jan. 1984
Deobandi	233	292	354	(158)	(945)[1]	(1097)[6]
Brelwi	98	123	267	(189)	(557)[2]	
Ahl-e Hadith	55	47	126	(67)	(56)[3]	(76)[7]
Shia	18	15	41	(16)	(116)[4]	
Jama'at-e Islami	13[5]	41[5]	57[5]	(107)[5]		
No data	55	390	900			

Sources and explanation: cf. Table 34(F).

TABLE 34 (B): DÎNÎ MADÂRIS ACCORDING TO THEIR SCHOOL OF THOUGHT AND THEIR AFFILIATION TO AN UMBRELLA ORGANIZATION IN PUNJAB

School of Thought	1960	1971	1979		1983/84
Deobandi		173	198	(106)	(353)[1]
Brelwi		93	197	(148)	(466)[2]
Ahl-e Hadith		42	122	(66)	(43)[3]
Shia		13	38	(16)	(54)[4]
Jama'at-e Islami	6[5]	14[5]	20[5]		(37)[5]
No data		244	437		

Sources and explanation: cf. Table 34(F).

TABLE 34 (C): DÎNÎ MADÂRIS ACCORDING TO THEIR SCHOOL OF THOUGHT AND THEIR AFFILIATION TO AN UMBRELLA ORGANIZATION IN SINDH

School of Thought	1960	1971	1979		1983/84
Deobandi		68	67	(16)	(319)[1]
Brelwi		11	40	(20)	(38)[2]
Ahl-e Hadith		2			
Ahl-e Hadith		5	1		(5)[3]
Shia		1	3		(14)[4]
Jama'at-e Islami	3[5]	7[5]	10[5]		(15)[5]
No data		57	259		

Sources and explanation: cf. Table 34(F).

TABLE 34 (D): DÎNÎ MADÂRIS ACCORDING TO THEIR SCHOOL OF THOUGHT AND
THEIR AFFILIATION TO AN UMBRELLA ORGANIZATION IN NWFP

School of Thought	1960	1971	1979		1983/84
Deobandi		62	69	(22)	(108)[1]
Brelwi		9	16	(9)	(24)[2]
Ahl-e Hadith		2	3	(1)	(3)[3]
Shia		1			(5)[4]
Jama'at-e Islami	2[5]	15[5]	21[5]		(41)[5+]
No data		38	109		

Sources and explanation: cf. Table 34(F).

TABLE 34 (E): DÎNÎ MADÂRIS ACCORDING TO THEIR SCHOOL OF THOUGHT AND
THEIR AFFILIATION TO AN UMBRELLA ORGANIZATION IN BALUCHISTAN

School of Thought	1960	1971	1979		1983/84
Deobandi		15	20	(14)	(163)[1]
Brelwi	1	14	(12)		(23)[2]
Ahl-e Hadith					
Shia					(1)[4]
Jama'at-e Islami	2[5]	5[5]	6[5]		(13)[5]
No data		12	95		

Sources and explanation: cf. Table 34(F).

TABLE 34 (F): DÎNÎ MADÂRIS ACCORDING TO THEIR SCHOOLS OF THOUGHT
AND TO THEIR AFFILIATION TO AN UMBRELLA ORGANIZATION IN
KASHMIR (PAK) AND IN THE NORTHERN AREAS

School of Thought	1960	1971	1979	1983/84
Deobandi		6		(1)[1]
Brelwi		2		(6)[2]
Ahl-e Hadith		3		(1)[3]
Shia				(42)[4]
Jama'at-e Islami		1[5]	1[5]	(1)[5]

Sources: For figures without footnotes: *Ahmad I*, pp. 705-708; *Ahmad II*, p. 691; *Halepota Report*, pp. 194-197.
For figures with footnotes:

[1]*Fihrist al-Jâm'iât wa-l madâris al-mulhiqah bi wafâq al-madâris al-'arabiyyah Bâkistân*, ed. by Maktab Wafâq al-Madâris al-'Arabiyyah Bâkistân, Multan, 1403/1982 (Arabic).

[2]*Fihrist madâris-e mulhiqah tanzîm al-madâris Pâkistân*, ed. by Tanzîm al-Madâris al-'Arabiyyah, Lahore, 1984 (Urdu).

[3]*Amad wa Kharch, Jâmi'ah salafiyyah 1984*, Lahore, 1984, pp. 12ff (large DM only) (Urdu).

[4]*Repôrt bârâ-e sâl 1984*, ed. by Markaz-e 'ilm wa dânish, Jâmi'ah al-muntazar, Lahore, 1984 (Urdu).

[5]*Ta'âruf; Râbitah al-madâris al-islâmiyyah Pâkistân*, Lahore, 1984 (Urdu).

[6]Personal conversation with the Nâzim-e Ta'lîm of the Wafâq al-Madâris al-'Arabiyyah in Multan on 2.2.86.

[7]Personal conversation with the Nâzim-e Imtihân in Lahore in Jan. 1986.

Figures in brackets indicate those DM which are affiliated to an umbrella organization.

+ = All the new DM (20) have been established after the Soviet intervention in Afghanistan.

Statements on the regional distribution of DM of different schools of thought can now be extended to the district level. At this level the results correspond to those in the statements on the origin of graduates.[72]

As data on the distribution of Dînî Madâris in the provinces according to their schools of thought demonstrate, the majority of Deobandi DM in Punjab are located in districts of Faisalabad, Multan, Muzaffargarh, Rahim Yar Khan, and Rawalpindi. This is generally true for the years 1960 to 1983.

The Brelwis, in contrast, have their DM in the districts of Mianwali, Lahore, Gujranwala, Gujrat, Multan and Bahawalnagar. It is, however, significant that Mianwali, Gujranwala, Multan, Bahawalpur and Bahawalnagar, which had been centres of the Deobandis in the sixties, came increasingly under the influence of the Brelwis during the last decade, possibly due to the strong support from the Government. The southern and central part of Punjab is characterized by the predominance of agriculture and the pronounced cult of saints, while the northern districts are more urban and industrially developed. The Shia have been able to strengthen their position in the Sargodha Division, in the districts of Jhang, Multan and Muzaffargarh. These districts are also of rural character and strongly under the influence of saints.

The DM of the Ahl-e Hadith are concentrated in Faisalabad, Multan, Lahore and Qasur. These areas are characterized by their pronounced commercial character. They are important interior markets of the Punjab.

The Jama'at-e Islami is found in urban centres as Lahore and Islamabad. This corresponds to the social origin of its followers from the intermediary sectors.

The Deobandis dominate in the province of Sindh[73] in rural districts. Even in Hayderabad and Sukkur,[74] the strongholds of the Jam'iyyat-e 'Ulamâ'-e Pakistan (Brelwi), only very few Brelwi DM can be found. The access of the Brelwis to Sindh is possible due to their connection to Pîr Pagaro. The approximately 40 DM linked to Pagaro are administered by the Tanzîm al-Madâris.

The Ahl-e Hadith in Sindh are concentrated only in Karachi, corresponding to the merchant character of the followers of this school of thought.

NWFP and Baluchistan are under the influence of the Deobandis as well. Only in Mansehra in the NWFP the Brelwis seem to be present to a more pronounced degree. All these are rural areas where tribal societies predominate. Only the provincial capitals, Peshawar and Quetta are to some extent modernized.[75]

The Northern Areas are dominated by the Shia. The Jama'at-e Islami can be met in areas close to the border such as Dir and the Agencies, Bajor and Mohmand, especially since 1979.

Thus, each school of thought has its own area of influence, be it rural, urban, trade-oriented or strategic.

The explanation of the distributive pattern lies in the social basis of the different schools of thought or organizations. The candidates for graduation of the Deobandis, Brelwis and Shia are, above all, representatives of the traditional sector. Accordingly, they are found primarily in areas having traditional social structures. As they have some representatives in the intermediary sectors as well, they are also settled in areas such as urban Sindh or in other modern districts, as in northern Punjab. As typical representatives of the intermediary sector II, members of the Ahl-e Hadith and of the Jama'at-e Islami are located in modern, trade-oriented regions or in politically sensitive areas. Certain groups of the Ahl-e Hadith are able to act on a broad basis due to their strong integration into traditional systems of order. The representatives of the Jama'at-e Islami, in contrast, rely on occupying political positions in order to exert any influence.

Map 1 is based on the data of Table 34 and gives a rough overview of the distribution of the different schools of thought in Pakistan.

At first sight there seems to be an overwhelming predominance of the Deobandi school. There is in fact a tendency among the Deobandi Wafâq to systematically position its offshoots in different regions of the country and to build them up. This apparently is not the case—or only under special conditions—with the other schools of thought. The map should, however, not obscure the fact that schools of the Brelwis, the Ahl-e Hadith and the Shia are predominantly located in areas of high population density. Thus, they may be found mainly in Punjab, where 56 per cent of the Pakistani population lives. It is also here that the conurbations of the country are located. In Sindh, in the NWFP and in Baluchistan—areas considered to be exclusively under the influence of the Deobandis—their percentages, in contrast, reach only 22.6 per cent, 15 per cent and 5.1 per cent of the Pakistani population respectively. The large extension of Baluchistan (43.6 per cent of Pakistan's area) and its low density of population (12.5 inhabitants per square kilometre in contrast to Punjab with 230.3 inhabitants per square kilometre) has to be kept in mind. The spatial distribution of schools of thought in Map 1 therefore should not give the impression that the Brelwis and the other small schools of thought have only a small following.

It is possible that the distribution of religious schools of thought does not correspond to their relative political importance, as is the case with the Jama'at-e Islami who are sometimes also present in other areas and where some representatives of the Deobandis have joined them.

THE POLITICAL DIMENSIONS OF RELIGIOUS SCHOOLS

The DM are not to be considered merely as pure institutions of learning for the socially weak but also as institutions of political importance. This is evident as much from the 1977 movement as from the regional movement of the province of Sindh especially since 1980.[76] Besides investigating the role of the DM in the internal politics of the country, their part in the external policy must be examined as well. Their role in the *Jihâd* for Afghanistan is dealt here. It had implications on the jobs front: many Afghan students in Pakistan took advantage of the "holy war". On the other hand the thesis of Olivier Roy of the *mujâhidîn* and their leaders being mainly religious scholars is not unfounded. In the following pages we limit ourselves to examining one large school.

Dâr al-'Ulûm Haqqâniyyah and Jihâd

One of the most important and largest DM in Pakistan is the Dâr al-'ulûm Haqqâniyyah in Akora Khattak in the district of Peshawar,[77] established in 1947. This Dâr al-'Ulûm is important for the fact that about one third of all the Deobandi 'ulamâ' or *fudalâ*' of Pakistan originate from here. It is an important school within the Islamization drive and represents the *salafî* wing of the Deobandis.

The school was founded by Abd al-Haq Akorwi,[78] who had graduated from the Dâr al-'Ulûm Deoband in India. It soon developed into one of the main institutions absorbing religious scholars in the north of Pakistan and achieved a reputation beyond the borders of Pakistan and India within a short time.

The remote but nevertheless well connected location of this Dâr al-'ulûm[79] made it possible even for students from far away regions to enjoy their religious education here.

Nowadays, the geographic position of a madrasah is of special importance, a factor pointed out by representatives of the Jama'at-e Islami as well. They in fact like to put up their schools in locations which are remote enough to guarantee a good education, while being close to important points of intersection. Similar indicators can account for the location of the Dâr al-'Ulûm Haqqâniyyah.

TABLE 35: CANDIDATES FOR GRADUATION OF THE WAFÂQ OVER THE YEARS
AND THE PROPORTION OF THE DÂR AL-'ULÛM HAQQÂNIYYAH

Year of Examination H. Chr.	Number of Candidates of Graduation	Examination Passed	Number of Candidates of the Dâr al-'Ulûm Haqqâniyyah
1380/1960	231	183	
1381/1961	216	176	
1382/1962	282	199	
1383/1963	214	214	
1384/1964	218	145	
1385/1965	194	121	
1386/1966	—	—	90
1387/1967	267	176	77
1388/1968	282	239	105
1389/1969	340	270	94
1390/1970	—	—	114
1391/1971	307	232	118
1392/1972	401	260	140
1393/1973	366	260	139
1394/1974	396	212	128
1395/1975	297	219	106
1396/1976	360	273	128
1397/1977	—	—	119
1398/1978	412	315	141
1399/1979	410	286	115
1400/1980	387	242	88
1401/1981	396	299	93
1402/1982	725	412	103
1403/1983	814	431	109
1404/1984	997	679	106
1405/1985	1,333	866	118
Total	9,845	6,709	2,231

Sources: Manuscript of the Nâzim-e Ta'lîm of the Wafâq (mimeo) (Urdu) and register of the graduates of the Dâr al-'Ulûm Haqqâniyyah, Akora Khattak, Peshawar (mimeo) (Urdu) as well as author's calculations.

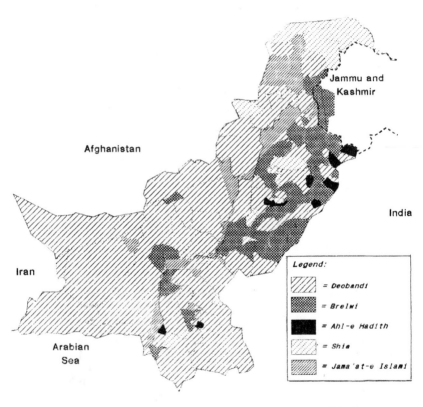

The external boundaries of India depicted in this map are neither correct nor authentic (Editor).

MAP 1: SPATIAL DISTRIBUTION OF SCHOOLS OF THOUGHT IN PAKISTAN,
ACCORDING TO THE NUMBER OF THEIR RESPECTIVE INSTITUTIONS, AS OF 1983
(SOURCES AS IN TABLE 34)

From 1947 up to 1985, the Deobandi Dâr al-'Ulûm produced about 3,000 candidates for graduation.[80] In 1960, it affiliated itself to the Wafâq al-Madâris al-'Arabiyyah; this organization having a record of 6,709 graduates between 1960 and 1985,[81] representing 68.1 per cent of all the candidates for examination of the Wafâq. Out of 9,845 candidates, 2,231 (22.7 per cent) pertained to the Dâr al-'Ulûm Haqqâniyyah since 1966 (compare table below). As the last years witnessed a shift of the production of graduates of the Wafâq to Karachi, the relative dominance of this seminary was reduced. Its proportion of graduates between 1967 and 1980 reached 41.3 per cent. Up to 1980 the Dâr al-'Ulûm Haqqâniyyah therefore has to be considered as the main institution for the production of graduates of the Deobandis. Furthermore, we may state that it consciously kept the number of students low and even encouraged the migration of its students.[82]

In order to give an overview of the budget of this large school it is useful to consider the receipts and expenditure over the years. Up to 1980 the receipts and expenditure increased very modestly the increase in receipts started only after 1982. The data shows that the expenditure shows an increase at a much higher rate than in earlier years or in the years between 1980 and 1981. In order to put the rates of increase in relation to inflation rates Table 36 has been compiled:

TABLE 36: BUDGETS OF THE DÂR AL-'ULÛM HAQQÂNIYYAH
IN SELECTED YEARS

Year	Receipts in Rs.	Incr. in %	Real[1,2] Receipts	Incr. in %	Expend. in Rs.	Incr. in %	Real[1,2] Expenditure	Incr.[1,2] in %
1970	196666		196666		195020		195020	
1975	304026	55	143884	-27	362716	86	171659	-12
1975			304026				362716	
1981	1216930	300	743390	145	1231141	240	752071	107
1984	1755569	45	834000	12	1309577	6	622127	-17
				INCREASE				
1970-84		793				572		
1975-84		477		174		261		72

Sources: 1 = 1970: 100 per cent (Index); 1975: 211.3 per cent (this is the official rate of inflation; cf. Pakistan Economic Survey 1982-83).

       2 = 1975: 100 per cent (Index); 1981: 163.7 per cent and 1984: 210.5 per cent (cf. Pakistan Economic Survey 1984-85).

       The budgets have been calculated on the basis of the information asked for in my questionnaire in December and January, 1983/84.

It is not clear why such high rates of increase occurred in the periods stated. It is, however, confirmed that the Dâr al-'Ulûm received Zakat from the PZC since 1980 (see Table 37 for the amounts of Zakat for the last five years).

TABLE 37: AMOUNT OF ZAKAT FOR THE DÂR AL-'ULÛM HAQQÂNIYYAH

Year	Zakat in Rs.	Per cent of Total Receipts
1980	50,000	5.2 per cent
1981	100,000	8.2 per cent
1982	120,000	10.6 per cent
1983	175,000	10.7 per cent
1984	330,000	18.8 per cent

Source: "NWFP: Statement of Deeni Madaris granted Zakat assistance", CZA, Islamabad, 1985 (mimeo) and author's calculations.

Like in other DM it is not only that the Zakat from the PZC increased but also the proportion of this Zakat to the ordinary receipts.

Besides the heavy financial support to the seminary via official Zakat funds, there was a clear increase in the Islamization policy in this school on the ideological level. This may be a result of the integration of its leading functionaries into Pakistani politics. The founder, Abd al-Haq Akorwi has been a member of parliament; his son, Sami al-Haq is already a member of the senate.

Also, a report written by Abd al-Haq[83] in Arabic for the Saudi-Arab Consulate in Islamabad points towards a strong interest of the Saudis in the *salafi* policy of this school. The report highlighted the traditional connection to Arab states, especially to the Al-Azhar University and to the Islamic University in Medina.

Furthermore, the participation of the students of this school in the "Holy War" of Afghanistan points towards the strong interest of the state. As the *Jihâd* is supported materially, spiritually and strategically,[84] such support was available to those DM actively participating in the *Jihâd*.

It is important that in NWFP in 1982 about 9 per cent of the DM students came from Afghanistan. As Olivier Roy points out in *Islam and Resistance in Afghanistan*, the clergy to a considerable degree spearheaded the guerilla war in Afghanistan. The "resistance parties" not only have Islamic denominations,[85] their members also are largely recruited from religious schools and/or belong to mystical orders.[86] As the religious scholars are often not part of the tribal culture, they are capable of overcoming the tribal feuds and have a uniting effect.[87] That is why they can become the leading agents of mobilization in the Holy War.[88]

The Dâr al-'Ulûm Haqqâniyyah is one of the numerous religious schools taking in the *mujâhidîn* (holy warriors), providing for them, educating them and preparing them for the *Jihâd*. An increase of 67.8 per cent of the receipts between 1979 and 1984 as well as the 68.5 per cent increase in expenditure in the same period unmistakably point in this direction. The proportion of Afghan students and scholars in this seminary is high. In 1959-60 out of 397 boarding students 15.1 per cent were from Afghanistan, in 1970 the numbers are 204 out of 550 (37.1 per cent), and in 1985 about 400 out of 680 (about 60 per cent).[89]

While there is no direct linking of this school to any form of military training and education of the students, according to the statements made by representatives of the Dâr al-'ulûm many of its Afghan students have gone to the *Jihâd* and there are many more to go. This "does not disturb the instruction during the years at all".[90] The monthly magazine of this seminary, *Al-Haq*, publishes many articles on the subject of *Jihâd*. *Al-Haq* indeed developed into a war reporting magazine.[91] In fact, this religious school describes itself as the leading centre for training the *mujâhidîn* and its leaders: "Thanks be to God that the Afghan *'ulamâ'* and students who have been studying in the Dâr al-'Ulûm Haqqâniyyah are fighting in the first line of the *Jihâd*".[92]

In his latest book Sami al-Haq pointed out that the leading heads of the *Jihâd* had studied with his father and still consult him, and that Abd al-Haq Akorwi and his students had actually laid the "foundation stone for the *Jihâd*".[93] "Since the beginning of the *Jihâd* the Dâr al-'Ulûm Haqqâniyyah has lifted any rule concerning attendance, coming and going for the Afghan students and for those who . . . participate in the *Jihâd*. Groups of students leave to participate in the Holy War for a month or two or more and when they come back, others leave". Afghan and non-Afghan students take part in the *Jihâd* along with Pakistani students on a rotation principle. Furthermore, this school is not the only one participating in the *Jihâd*. That is why the PZC in NWFP has raized its disbursements tenfold in five years to this school, with its large number of *'ulamâ'*, students and educated religious scholars from Afghanistan.

A closer look at the areas of origin of the students would substantiate claims made by *Al-Haq*. This is done on the basis of registers of the candidates of graduation of this school.

Origin of the Graduates

The data of 799 graduates in the years 1397/h. (1977) to 1404/h. (1984) show the following distribution according to their area of origin:[94]

We may deduce that the second largest group of the graduates originate from Afghanistan. Most of them come from the provinces of Kandahar, Nu'man, Ghazni, Parwan, Jalalabad and Paktia, i.e. from areas bordering Pakistan where the heaviest fighting has taken place.[95] Most Afghan students also have a religious family background.

The connection of the Dâr al-'Ulûm Haqqâniyyah to Afghanistan may be traced back to the time when the school was established. A connection between the original institution of the Indian Deoband and Afghanistan already existed in the last century, reinforced by other strongholds of the Deobandi movement as far away as Kabul and even further than that. The schools of Lahore and Peshawar were also two of these strongholds. There had always been a large number of Afghan students in the Dâr al-'Ulûm Deoband itself and it received alms from the Amir of Afghanistan.[96] With the passage of time, the Dâr al-'Ulûm Haqqâniyyah crystallized into an important offshoot of the Dâr al-'Ulûm Deoband, even though there is little collaboration between the two schools.[97]

There existed an ethnic, linguistic and a cultural affinity among the students, due to the close contact of the Dâr al-'Ulûm Haqqâniyyah and Afghanistan and the relatively numerous graduates from the tribal areas of the NWFP—especially from the districts of Bannu/North Waziristan, Dir and the Bajor Agency in the border areas to Afghanistan as well as the district of Mardan and Baluchistan. The social structure of the students is thus likely to be quite homogeneous.[98] Based on this contact between the tribes in Pakistan and Afghanistan it is plausible to suppose that Pakistani students were mobilized for the holy war fought in Afghanistan.

Jihâd and Jamâ'at-e Islâmî

Next to the Jihâd, activities of the salafî wing of the Deobandis one should mention the activities of the salafî Jama'at-e Islami. As suggested above they established their DM in sensitive areas. As the data show, out of 107 of the DM affiliated to the Râbitah al-Madâris al-Islâmiyyah in 1983/84, 41 were located in the North West Frontier Province and in the tribal areas (more than 38 per cent). More schools are actually located here than in Punjab, the administrative centre of the Jama'at-e Islami. Nineteen schools were established after the Soviet intervention, six in the district of Dir and seven in the Bajor Agency. Both areas are located directly on the Afghan

TABLE 38: AREAS OF ORIGIN OF THE GRADUATES OF THE DÂR AL-'ULÛM

District/Region of Origin	Number of Graduation Candidates	%	Thereof with a Traditionally Religious Family Background in %
Afghanistan	129	16.2	(34.9)
Bannu/North Waziristan	133	16.7	(9.0)
Mardan	103	13.0	(20.4)
Peshawar	75	9.4	(18.7)
D. I. Khan	71	9.0	(14.1)
Dir	39	4.9	(10.3)
Swat	38	4.8	(31.6)
Kohat	35	4.4	(28.9)
Hazara Division	25	3.1	(20.0)
Chitral	6	0.8	(16.7)
Bajor Agency	21	2.6	(14.3)
Other Agencies	18	2.3	(5.6)
Quetta	12	1.5	(16.7)
Pishin	28	3.5	(25.0)
Zhob	24	3.0	(29.2)
Lorelai	20	2.5	(30.0)
Sibi	9	1.1	(11.1)
Kashmir	1	0.0	(0.0)
Attock	12	1.5	(8.3)
Total	799	100.0	

Source: Register of the graduates of the Dâr al-'Ulûm Haqqâniyyah (1397-1404) (mimeo) and author's calculation.

border. According to the Jama'at-e Islami, it only indirectly involved in the Holy War. In fact, many DM were established especially for the *muhâjirîn* (refugees from Afghanistan).[99]

The support by the integrationist Jama'at-e Islami was invaluable to the Government, resulting in further official support to Jama'at-e Islami projects, whether DM or hospitals. The establishment of DM was to serve as a bulwark of Islam against the communists. This traumatic fear of the Soviet system led to a book *The Islamic Threat to the Soviet State* by Bennigsen and Broxup becoming a bestseller in Pakistan. It deals with the agonies of Islam in USSR.[100]

Islam and the DM are thus mobilized for different purposes. They are not only meant to reduce the rate of illiteracy but also to keep away "communism". It is therefore in the interest of the Government to put up DM along the border with Afghanistan.[101]

REGIONAL NATIONALISM

The investigation undertaken here has demonstrated that the majority of 'ulamâ' and representatives of religious schools did not agree with the integrationist policy of Islamization of the Zia Government. Critics of the official policy came primarily from the MRD (Movement for the Restoration of Democracy), a movement which also united the religio-political parties under a secular leadership.[102] Parts of the traditional sector also put up a resistance against the official measures though temporarily. Unifying Islamization could not be enforced in Pakistan due to the dispersal of Islam into different schools of thought, dominant in different areas. This was partly due to the fact that there existed forces within the different schools of thought fearlessly resisting the offical policy of expansion, causing quite a headache to the regime even years after the proclamation of the Islamic system. These reactions, sometimes expressed in isolationist activities, are noted below. Two sectors, interlinked with each other, are analysed here: the resistance against the Zakat system and the internal political situation in the province of Sindh.

The Boycott of the Zakat System

A truly spectacular reaction of the 'ulamâ' and of the DM against the official measures of Islamization is the boycott of the Zakat system.

The most important point of controversy between the state and the clergy was the regulation that institutions receiving Zakat were to maintain an account on the Zakat funds received and that this book-keeping was to be audited by the Zakat administration. The bureaucracy would thus have information on the budgets of the DM, the 'ulamâ' and ultimately of the religio-political parties. The auditing personnel was to be nominated by the Chief Administrator Zakat. The official entrusted with this task would be senior even to the chairman of the respective PZC.[103] The Central Zakat Administration (CZA) was actually demanding from the mohtamims proof that the funds had been spent according to the rules of the Shari'a–as understood by the CZA.

The Zakat 'Ulamâ' Committee[104] of the PZC had proposed the compulsory book-keeping while members of the PZC foresaw problems of implementation as most DM leaders were against it. Lifting the compulsory book-keeping from the DM would, however, create a precedent for other institutions which might demand similar exemptions from auditing. The CZA therefore suggested to the 'ulamâ' and to the leaders of the DM to evaluate the demand for book-keeping and the auditing connected with it in the light of the Shari'a. If they arrived at the conclusion that book-keeping of the Zakat funds received (by the PZC) and spent was superfluous they should put this down in writing in the form of a *fatwâ*.[105]

In the same session of the Central Zakat Council (CZC) the Urdu daily *Jasârat* on June 16, 1981 from Karachi was quoted as saying that those DM affiliated to the Wafâq al-Madâris al-'Arabiyyah would not accept any Zakat (from the PZC) as long as the *muftîs* did not agree on the compatibility of the new regulation with the Shari'a.[106] Three months later, the Punjab PZC announced that the 'Ulamâ' Committee (of the PZC) had established a sub-committee to draft a *fatwâ* and present it to the CZC. According to a report of the PZC, the reason for the boycott of Zakat by the Wafâq was not unequivocal; the Wafâq al-Madâris did not agree to some parts of the Zakat Regulation, this being the reason why they presently (*fi'l hâl*) rejected to accept Zakat.[107] The Wafâq in fact had called upon all the DM affiliated to it not to accept any Zakat funds from the Zakat Administration and even to return the amounts already received.[108] With this call the Deobandi 'Ulamâ' paid heed to a *fatwâ* of the late Muftî Mahmûd.[109]

Mufti Sahib had taken up a position against the Zakat and Ushr regulation of 1980. His comment reflected the attitude of the Deobandi clergy who had been part of the opposition against Z. A. Bhutto and who later, in 1980, had collaborated with the MRD, known as Fadl al-Rahman Group of the JUI. Mufti Mahmud listed ten shortcomings, which according to him were to be removed by the Government in order to bring the system in line with the Shari'a. As explained below, this could hardly be achieved by the Government.

1. The exemption limit on the payment of Zakat had been fixed at Rs. 1,000,[110] even when the Shari'a had put the limit for the payment of Zakat at 7.5 *tolâ* of gold or 12.5 *tolâ* of silver or the equivalent thereof. Currently the money value for gold would be equivalent to Rs. 13,000, for silver to Rs. 5,000 (this being more than the official *nisâb*). Thus the exemption limit fixed by the Government was not in accordance with Shari'a.

2. An Islamic Government was allowed to levy Zakat on the *amwâl-e zâhirah*, not however on the *amwâl-e bâtinah*. According to the Shari'a it was the responsibility of the individual to pay Zakat of the latter kind.

3. The *niyyat* (intention) was part of Zakat and therefore also indispensable with the payment of Zakat.[111] By making the system of Zakat an official affair, it became an anonymous payment and a direct connection between the giver of Zakat and its recipient no longer existed.

4. The money was deducted from savings accounts and from term deposits. The money in the bank was, however, money deposited for the purpose of safety (*amânat*) which the bank was not to employ in its undertakings. Zakat was payable in case the money was deposited as a special credit (*qard*) with the depositer receiving a certain return. The return is given to him because the bank may employ the money in its undertakings. According to Shari'a the person receiving a return on a credit would have to pay Zakat on it. The deduction of Zakat as executed by the nationalized banks under the new Zakat system was not permissible.

5. Zakat was not to be paid on *harâm* (objectionable) funds[112] on which interest was paid, which is prohibited by the Koran. Furthermore, the interest was above the rate of Zakat of 2.5 per cent, with the result that the *harâm* funds were not purified by Zakat.

6. If the whole economic system was un-Islamic, the state also could not and should not levy Zakat.

7. Zakat should neither be levied on credits taken up by a person nor on debts of a person as this was not in accordance with Shari'a. The current regulation did not check on whether a client with an account might have debts.

8. Children and insane persons would not have to pay Zakat but were condemned to do so under the new system.

9. Zakat would be welcome as a national system if the citizens would agree on the rightful spending of the Zakat funds. The citizens, however, did not trust the Government; just as the Government appropriated Auqaf funds it would similarly misuse the Zakat funds.

10. The fixing of the date for the levy of Zakat by the Government was not in accordance with Shari'a and therefore it would have to be changed.[113]

This *fatwâ* presented by Mufti Mahmud on July 26, 1980[114] served as a point of reference for the DM of the Wafâq. They were able to renew their demand for autonomy and for more rights of participation by boycotting the Zakat system.

The call to boycott by the Wafâq in June 1981 was, however, far from unanimous; there were large and influential DM which accepted Zakat.[115] These were mostly conformist forces like the Jâmi'ah Ashrafiyyah in Lahore.[116]

Among the large DM returning the Zakat were the Qâsim al-'Ulûm in Multan, the Jâmi'ah Islâmiyyah and the Jâmi'ah Fârûqiyyah in Karachi, Makhzan al-'Ulûm in Rahim Yar Khan and Matlâ' al-'Ulûm in Hayderabad.[117]

The boycott by the Wafâq at first prompted the CZA to continue with the disbursement of Zakat to the DM. It was, however, not in a position to abandon the demand for book-keeping and finally made book-keeping a precondition for the receipt of Zakat.[118]

The CZA was able to insist on this point as most of the DM received the Zakat gratefully. The Tanzîm al-Madâris of the Brelwis, unlike the Deobandis, even explicitly asked the Government to disburse Zakat to the DM,[119] presenting this demand in October 1980, i.e. a few months after the introduction of the Zakat system. They reasoned that the Zakat which earlier reached the DM directly was now flowing into the Zakat fund. In March 1985 the Tanzîm still held the opinion that the Zakat to DM should be raized and that its flow should be eased.[120] The Brelwis were, in fact, the main beneficiaries of the Zakat system. The Wafâq of the Deobandis in contrast still claimed to reject Zakat from the Central Zakat Fund:

1378 Dini Madaris to refuse Zakat. All the 1378 Dini Madaris nasims will refuse Zakat-funds in future if they are collected in the wrong way. Special meeting of Wafaq ul Madaris-e Arabia.[121]

The Wafâq continued to complain about Zakat being deducted from accounts earning interest. In their opinion, the Zakat was thus turned *harâm*. It therefore appealed to the *ashâb-e nisâb* (those obliged to pay Zakat due to their economic status) to directly deliver their Zakat to the DM instead of doing so via the Zakat fund.[122]

Some Deobandi DM thus refused to accept official Zakat. Its receipt can be proved in almost all provinces except in the province of Sindh. There, Zakat was rejected almost completely, due more to political reasons than for religious considerations.

It is predominantly the Brelwis, the Ahl-e Hadith and the Jama'at-e Islami who profit from this financial support. Even if the Shia refuse to cooperate with the Pakistani Government due to ideological and political reasons, some of its DM do receive Zakat as well.[123]

The religious schools played a central role in the movement of 1977. They were at the centre of political agitation,[124] thus pointing to their potential impact which could be mobilized at any time either from outside by the colonial sector or by internal impulses of the traditional sector.

Even after 1977 the DM were important institutions and could not be left out in the Islamization process. This became evident in the disputes of Sindh with the Central Government.[125]

Sindh is dominated by a few feudal landowners and a large army of serfs, the *Hârîs*. The unequal distribution of land in this province has already frequently led to conflicts between the landlords and the peasants,[126] most recently in 1984. Furthermore, many non-Sindhis came to settle in Sindh, especially the *muhâjîrûn*, Indian refugees flowing into Pakistan after the partition of India and the Pakhtuns, who had migrated to the south in the course of the last twenty years.[127] Thus, the Sindhis themselves have almost become an ethnic-linguistic minority; of all households in Sindh, in 52.4 per cent Sindhi was the language predominantly spoken.[128] Under the "One Unit" policy of Ayub Khan Sindhi was abolished as a language of administration and of instruction; this happened, however, to all other regional languages as well. The Punjabis and lately the Pakhtuns also predominantly occupy elevated positions in the public services of Sindh.[129] These circumstances, among others, eventually caused Sindhi nationalism to bloom. The Sindhis in turn accused the Punjabis and also the *muhâjîrûn* of exploitation.[130]

The fathers of Sindh had always claimed more rights for their province than was granted to it by the federation. Even though they were linked to the MRD by its opposition to Zia ul Haq they did not recognize the MRD which aimed at restoring democratic rights in the country. The movement had been established in 1981 with the cooperation of several parties. G.M. Syed, the "Prophet of Sindh", accused the MRD of pursuing goals of "Bhuttoism" and carrying on the Punjabi chauvinism.[131] In spite of this rejection the MRD was very heavily represented in Sindh,[132] especially in those districts in which the popularity of the PPP was high.[133] The MRD also had supporters in cities where there were few Sindhis. Even the peasants who did not identify themselves with the MRD were able to express their grievances with the help of the movement.[134] The main factor which explains the take-off of the MRD in Sindh is probably the high degree of deprivation of the population by their own landlords, as well as by non-Sindhi landlords, and the exploitation it faced by the Punjab.[135] According to *Baghâwat*, many non-Sindhis have received Government owned lands in Sindh, while about 150,000 Sindhi peasants continue to own less than 5 acres.[136] "The 'revolution of the rising expectations' among *Hârîs* in Sind, has resulted in an experience of rising frustration for landless tenants and their absentee landlords".[137]

The conflict escalated in 1983 in Sindh, culminating in bloody disputes between Sindhi nationalists and the Central Government.[138] According to Ziring

... it was in Sindh where the chief opposition developed to Zia's vision of an Islamic State. Sindh contains the largest concentration of Shia Muslims and Zia's Sunni orthodoxy distressed this group. Riots resulting in the loss of life and property were allegedly provoked by Shia resistance to rules and directives that were anathema to their own Islamic teachings.[139]

Based on the available literature there is, however, no proof of the Shia playing a role in the disturbances.[140]

Sindh continues to be a smouldering focus of crisis. The official media reduces the national struggle of the Sindhis to the level of banditry. However, the resistance in Sindh is politically motivated, stemming from the unequal distribution of economic and political power.[141] In Sindh, Pîr Pagaro, who collaborated with Zia, guaranteed the law and order situation with the help of his private army, the Hûrs.

The Sindhi nationalists articulated their uneasiness exclusively through the MRD as expressed in its (isolationist) "bandit" conduct. Their special regional interests were opposed by the Central Government in the name of Pakistani nationalism.

The DM may be considered a vehicle for regional nationalism. A note of dissent to the proposals of the National Committee for Dînî Madâris 1979 (NCDM) had been presented by the only Sindhi representative in this body, Muhammad Idrîs Mehrti.[142] This note reflected the situation prevailing in Sindh. It was the Sindhi Deobandi DM which brought to an almost complete halt the official Zakat system in the province. Within the first two years the boycott by the Deobandi DM seems to have spread to the entire province.[143] During the first three years, the PZC could disburse only a meager 1.84 per cent of the total amount at its disposition[144] among the Sindhi DM. Only 45 DM received Zakat during this period, and only 1,987 students profited from the disbursements.[145] However, after 1983/84, in contrast, the number of DM supported and their students increased considerably. This increase was due to the enhanced support to DM of other schools of thought than that of the Deobandis, such as the Brelwis. In this context it is revealing that the Brelwis affiliated about 40 DM to their Tanzîm with the permission of Pîr Pagaro.

The analysis of the distribution of Zakat in Sindh revealed that the majority of the DM receiving Zakat belonged to the Brelwis, the Ahl-e Hadith and the Jama'at-e Islami. The 24 Deobandi DM in the districts of Sukkur and Hayderabad, which were enlisted among the DM in the *Halepota Report* in contrast, did not accept Zakat.[146]

As the Deobandi Mufti Anwar Shah[147] explained, the Sindhi DM did not accept Zakat as Sindh was in a "special political situation", suggesting that the DM demonstrated solidarity with the local population. Zakat, he stated, served the purpose of political bribery (*siyâsî rishwat*).

The Deobandis are quite strongly represented in Sindh. The decisive factor seems to have been the Dâr al-'Ulûm Ashrafabad, an institution established in 1949 in Ashrafabad by those *'Uthmânîs* and *Thânwîs* who had studied in Deoband.[148] Leading Deobandi religious scholars lived and taught there.[149] With the increasing importance of Karachi this school was neglected and today is in total decay.[150]

The Deobandi DM followed the call of boycott of their umbrella organization and simultaneously increased heavily in numbers during the last years.[151] This meant that the connection of "mushroom-growth" of DM and the receipt of official Zakat is not valid for the DM of the Deobandis in Sindh. These schools seem to have been established without any official incentives.[152]

Thus while the DM of the Deobandis turned out to be supporters of Sindhi nationalism and isolated themselves from the Central Government, the DM of other schools of thought could be used by the Government to counter the Sindhi nationalism and to a certain extent keep the situation under control.

As it turned out, the representatives of the DM included strong forces of isolationist as well as of integrationist elements. Depending on their degree of integration into one sector or another, they could execute official interests or stand up against them.

NOTES

1. Cf. *Solah sâlah nisâb-e ta'lîm;* Wafâq al-Madâris al-'Arabiyyah Pâkistân, passed in Quetta 1983, published by the Wafâq al-madâris (Urdu) (Mimeo); *manzûrkardah I*; cf. also *Halepota Report*, pp. 122f.

2. On the dilemma between tradition and modernity cf. K.H. Osterloh, "Traditionelle Lernweise und europäischer Bildungstransfer. Zur Begründung einer adaptierten Pädagogik in den Entwicklungsländern", in, T. Schöfthaler and D. Goldschmidt, eds., *Soziale Struktur und Vernunft*, Frankfurt a.M., 1984, pp. 440-460.

3. A.A. Mawdudi, *Ta'lîmât*, Lahore, 1982, esp. pp. 123-164. Mawdudi's concept of education has not been completed satisfactorily to this day. The International Institute for Islamic Education in Mansurah, Lahore, are institutions trying to integrate modern and traditional subjects into one curriculum. The representatives of the Jama'at-e Islami were, however, not able to conduct the course of *dawrah-e hadîth* in their DM until 1986; thus, the *Shaikh al-Hadîth* of the Jama'at, Abd al-Malik, had to ask a representative of the Deobandis, Hamid Miyan in Lahore, to offer the *dawrah*-course in the central madrasah of the Jamaat. Miyan refused, however, on ideological grounds (talks of the two religious scholars in the Jâm'iah Madaniyyah, Karimpark, Lahore, on 13.2.1986). A degree of *dawrah* is not offered, the final certificates of the religious schools of the Jama'at were not recognized as equal to an M.A. degree of a university by the UGC. The representatives

of the Ahl-e Hadith could not present a comprehensive 16-year curriculum until 1986. This, however, did not prevent the Government from recognizing their final certificate as equal to an M.A. degree (possible owing to other pressures). The Shia could not present an integrated 16-year curriculum either, but its final certificates were, nevertheless, recognized as equal. The reason may be that the Government wished to avoid further disputes.

4. For an even more modernist interpretation, see Fazlur Rahman, *Islam and Modernity: Transformation of an Intellectual Tradition,* Chicago, 1982, esp. pp. 130-162.

5. Cited according to Seyyed Hossein Nasr, *Science and Civilization in Islam,* Lahore, 1983, pp. 63f.

6. S.N. Attas, ed., *Aims and Objectives of Islamic Education,* Jeddah, 1979, pp. 31f.; for further debates on Islam, education and science from an *integrationist* point of view cf. Wasiullah M. Khan, *Education and Society in the Muslim World,* Jeddah, 1981; S.S. Hussain and S.A. Ashraf, *Crisis in Muslim Education,* Hodder and Stoughton, 1979; Muhammad Muslehuddin, *Islamic Education, its Form and Features,* IRI, Islamabad, n.d.; *Muslim Education*: Quarterly, ed. by the King Abdul Aziz University, Jeddah. Furthermore cf. A.W.J. Halepota, "Islamic Conception of Knowledge", in *Islamic Studies,* vol. 14, no. 1, 1975, pp. 1-8; Amanullah Khan, "The Scientific Methodology in Islam", in *Journal of Research (Humanities),* Lahore, vol. X, no. 2 and vol. XI, no. 1, July 1975 and January 1976, pp. 67-80; Qamaruddin Khan, *The Methodology of Islamic Research,* Institute of Islamic Research, Karachi, 1973 (first published 1967); Azmatullah Khan and Abdul Qadeer Salim, *Ideological Basis of the Teaching of Social Sciences,* Islamabad, 1983 (Urdu); J.D. Kraan, *Religious Education in Islam with Special Reference to Pakistan,* Rawalpindi, 1984; Hakim Muhammad Said (comp.), *Theory and Philosophy of the System of Education in Islam* (4. *Hamdard Sîrat Konferenz*), vol. I, Karachi, 1984 (Urdu); Muslim Sajjad, *Instruction for the Making of an Islamic System of Education in Pakistan,* Islamabad, 1982 (Urdu); by the same author, *Ideological basis of Zoological Teaching,* Islamabad, 1982 (Urdu); Abd al-Sami, *Ideologial Basis for the Teaching of Chemistry,* Islamabad, 1982 (Urdu); Mohammad Abdus Sami and Muslim Sajjad, *Planning Curricula for Natural Sciences: The Islamic Perspective,* Islamabad, 1983; Ghulam Nabi Saqib, *Modernization of Muslim Education,* Lahore, 1983; *Science and Technology in the Islamic World,* a Quarterly Journal, Islamabad; *Seminar on Islamization of Knowledge,* January 4-9, 1982. Papers contributed, vol. 1, Islamabad, 1982.

7. National Education Conference 1977, Islamabad, 1978, pp. 6 et passim.

8. Op.cit., pp. 1f.

9. Op.cit., p. 8.

10. The "responsibility" seemed too big for the Government. Among other factors, 60-80 per cent of the budget went into the armed forces. For an analysis of the Pakistani army cf. "Dragon Seed", in H. Gardezi and R. Jamil,

eds., *Pakistan: Roots of Dictatorship*, op.cit., pp. 148-172; R.W. Jones, "The Military and Security in Pakistan", in C. Baxter, ed., *Zia's Pakistan: Politics and Stability in a Frontline State*, Lahore, 1985, pp. 63-91 and Stephen P. Cohen, *The Pakistan Army,* Berkeley, 1984.

11. National Education Conference 1977, Islamabad, 1978, p. 8 et passim.

12. Cf. above: Curricular integration under Ayub, chapter V.

13. Thus, Dr. Razzaq had studied in the Jamiah Islamiyyah, Madina in Saudi Arabia. This institution has several modern subjects in its curriculum. Justice Muhammad Taqi Uthmani, the son of Mufti Muhammad Shafi (cf. chapter on the CII and Appendix A), had enjoyed a madrasah education besides a formal education and had already offered an integrated curriculum in his Dâr al-'ulûm, Karachi. Mufti Ghulam Qadir had adjusted the curriculum of his school Khair al-Madâris to that of the Jamiah Islamiyyah, Bahawalpur, which had been under the supervision of the Auqaf Department since the sixties (cf. chapter III). The schools of Salim Allah Khan, the chairman of this committee also offered an "integrated" curriculum, just as in the schools of Muhammad Asad Thanwi.

14. This results from the lists of the members of the Wafâq Curriculum Committee (members with names in italic have been members also of the previous committee), (1) Salim Allah Khan (Karachi), (2) *Mufti Wali Hasan* (Karachi), (3) Dr. Abd al-Razzaq (Karachi), (4) Muhammad Taqi Uthmani (Karachi), (5) Muhammad Musa (Lahore), (6) *Muhammad Malik Kandhalwi* (Lahore) (cf. Bukhari, *AUD*, pp. 306ff), (7) Muhammad Asad Thanwi (Sukkur), (8) *Mufti Ahmad Said* (Sargodha), (9) *Mufti Zain al-Abidin* (Faisalabad), (10) *Sarfaraz Khan Safdar* (Gujranwala) (cf. Bukhari, *AUD*, pp. 348 ff), (11) Mufti Ghulam Qadir (Bahawalpur), (12) *'Abd al-Ghafur* (Quetta), (13) *Qadi Abd al-Karim* (Karachi), (14) *Sadr al-Shahid* (Bannu), (15) *Faid Ahmad* (Multan), (16) *Muhammad Sadiq* (Multan), (17) *Samial-Haq* (Akora Khattak), (18) *Muhammad Amin* (Kohat), (19) *Mufti Muhammad Anwar Shah* (Multan), (20) *Ghulam Muhammad* (Shams al Huda Club Jail).

15. The *ancient regime* was represented here by Muhammad Malik Kandhalwi, Sarfaraz Khan Safdar, Mufti Wali Hasan and Mufti Muhammad Anwar Shah. They were mostly successors of Yusuf Binori from Karachi, who had always taken a critical stand towards the policy of the Pakistani Government (cf. Appendix A).

16. Cf. *manzûrkardah II*, op.cit., pp. 21ff.

17. On the books for instruction cf. *La'hah-e 'aml, Tanzîm al-madâris*, op.cit., pp. 17f and *manzûrkardah I*, op.cit., pp. 8-13.

18. B.D. Metcalf, *Revival,* op.cit. As has been shown recently, the Brelwis do have a potential of political mobilization. Cf. S. Jamal Malik, "The Luminous Nurani", in *Social Analysis*, no. 28, 1990.

19. *La'hah-e 'aml 1974*, op.cit., p. 18, paras 15 and 19.

20. Pakistan Studies Curriculum for Secondary Classes IX-X, GoP, MoE, National Curriculum Committee, Islamabad, 1976, pp. 2f, *Specific Objectives*.

21. Curricular innovations of the umbrella organization of the Shia, Ahl-e Hadith and Jama'at-e Islami had not yet been presented.
22. Cf. *La'hah-e 'aml 1983*, op.cit., p. 28, para B; questioned as to how many years the curriculum had been in place (1986), representatives of the large DM still stated that it comprized eight years.
23. *Fihrist dînî madâris jin kô sâl 1984/85 kê lîê sûbâ'î zakât fund sê mâlî imdâd farâham kî gâ'î*, Lahore, 1986, PZC, Punjab (Urdu), mimeo. Out of the 206,454 students, 43,743 were boarding school students studying *hifz* and *nâzirah* (in contrast to 122,715 students living in the localities) and 24,731 boarders were studying *tajwîd* up to *dawrah-e hadîth*.
24. Out of 553 DM in the NWFP in 1982, 392 had not been registered.
25. This includes all the DM irrespective of their stages of the instruction they offer.
26. As accurate figures are available only for the NWFP, we have made it the basis of the following projected calculation.
27. The rates of increase vary from province to province and are not discussed here.
28. Cf. below, chapter VIII.
29. Information of a leading functionary of the Ministry for Education, who asked not to be identified.
30. See below on *Jihâd*.
31. Cf. above "Zakat for Dînî Madâris", chapter V.
32. These are mostly small religious institutions of instruction, located in a mosque or attached directly to it. They may be referred to as maktabs, i.e. institutions in which a basic religious education is offered including reading of Koran, Islamic basics, reading and writing. Simultaneously there is a significant number of registred DM which do not exist in reality but have been created only to guarantee a constant source of income to some religious scholars. In the area of formal education Punjab alone has 1350 so called ghost-schools. Unfortunately there are no details on DM-ghost-schools.
33. Cf. chapter V.
34. One has to state here that the Zakat administration of the NWFP is more lenient in the distribution of Zakat than in Punjab.
35. For a discussion on the ethnic and social composition of the DM students in the different districts see chapter VII, on areas of origin of the graduates.
36. On the discussion of the economic situation and the problems of the labour market cf. chapter VIII.
37. There were no more detailed data available on Baluchistan and Sindh.
38. *Dawn*, 26.4.85, "Want to be rich? Open a 'Cambridge' school", or *The Muslims*, 7.5.85, "Private schools are commercial centres". My own observations support these views.
39. Cf. chapter VII, on the origin of the graduates.
40. On this demographic change and migration via DM, cf. later on the centres of graduation, chapter VII.

41. A Division comprises several districts.
42. When referring to a standard of development, I do so on the basis of the parameters laid down by Zingel and Pasha and Tariq as well as Khan and Hasan (for bibliographical references cf. chapter VIII on problems of the labour market). I am, however, critical of the approach based on the modernization theory. For a discussion of the socio-economic situation in some of the districts see also chapter VIII.
43. On the distribution of land cf. Mahmood Hasan Khan, *Underdevelopment and Agrarian Structure in Pakistan*, Lahore, 1981.
44. In order to verify the rural dominance of the DM the data on the registration of religious schools at the district level give many clues; cf. chapter VIII on the problems of the labour market.
45. Thus, Stephen P. Cohen states that up to this day three-fourths of the army are recruited from traditionally military districts like Jhelum, Attock, Kohat and Mardan (Cohen, *The Pakistan Army*, Berkeley, 1984, pp. 42-45).
46. Muhammad Tufail, *Nuqûsh Lâhôr nambar*, Lahore, 1962 (Urdu), p. 442.
47. W.G. Leitner, *History of Indigenous Education in the Punjab since Annexation and in 1882*, New Delhi, 1971 (first ed. 1883).
48. Cf. the contributions by Ray Bromley, "The Urban Informal Sector: A critical perspective", in *World Development* 9/1978, no. 9-10; Stephen Guisinger and Muhammad Irfan, "Pakistan's Informal Sector" in *The Journal of Development Studies*, vol. 16, no. 4, July 1980, pp. 412-426; Anibal Quijano, "Marginaler Pol der Wirtschaft und marginalisierte Arbeitskraft", in D. Senghaas, ed., *Peripherer Kapitalismus*, Frankfurt a.M., 1981, pp. 298-341; Barbara Stuckey and Margaret Fay, "Produktion, Reproduktion and Zerstörung billiger Arbeitskräfte, Ländliche Subsistenz, Migration und Urbanisierung", in *Starnberger Studien* 4, Frankfurt a.M., 1980, pp. 126-168; Kh. Mahmood Siddiqui, "Some Aspects of Unemployment in Pakistan", in *Economic Quarterly*, East Berlin, 16/1981, 3, pp. 20-36.
49. Chapter VII on the identification of the districts of the graduates.
50. In the sense of D. Senghaas and B. Stuckey and Margaret Fay.
51. The following stages are referred to, *ulâ* and *tahtânî* = primary stage; *nâzirah*= reading of Koran; *mawqûf* = B.A.; *hadîth* = M.A.
52. *Fihris al-Jâmi'ât wa'l madâris*, etc.; author's calculations.
53. Unfortuantely there are no accurate figures available on this.
54. This refers to primary schools, middle and high schools, and secondary vocational institutions, arts colleges, professional colleges and universities.
55. This was stated by the American Muslim Yusuf Talal Ali in his Task Force Report, chapter on Islamic Education for inclusion in the *Report of the President's Task Force on Education*, Ministry of Education, Islamabad, 1982 (mimeo), p. 2.
56. In fact, more religious scholars have transport facilities than ever before.
57. Districts of origin, chapter VII.

58. The statements below are made on the basis of the quantitative dispersion of DM, i.e. the school of thought with the most DM is considered to be the one most widespread.

59. The affiliation to one of the four umbrella organizations is a precondition for the _shahâdah al-'âlamiyyah_ certificate. In 1986, the UGC had not yet recognized the _Râbitah_ of the Jama'at-e Islami as an authority for issuing officially recognized certificates.

60. On the problems in Sindh cf. below.

61. 83.7 per cent of the Brelwi DM in 1983/84 were located in Punjab while 7 per cent were located in Sindh and only 4 per cent each in the NWFP and in Baluchistan as well as 1 per cent in Kashmir (Pak). This tendency is also revealed in the analysis of the graduates.

62. Similar relations are valid for the other years.

63. Some urban centres in Sindh are, however, strongholds of the Jam'iyyat-e 'Ulamâ'-e Pakistan, led by the Brelwis, as in Hayderabad and Sukkur.

64. One should not suppose that the number of DM affiliated to the Ahl-e Hadith has declined. Much to the contrary, the large number of candidates for graduation over the last years suggests that the number of their DM has also increased. The numbers for 1983-84, in fact, reflect only the mayor DM. As a leading functionary of the Ahl-e Hadith put it, the Ahl-e Hadith "did not have any necessity to account for each and every small maktab as the other makâtib-e fikr might do" (bureau of the Wafâq al-Mandâris al-Salafiyyah in Lahore, spring of 1986).

65. Cf. below, regional nationalism.

66. Cf. below, mushroom-growth.

67. Christoph Müller-Hofstede, _China und Pakistan, Modellnachbarn in Asien oder Kooperation unter geostrategischen Vorzeichen (1963-1987),_ Berlin (FU), August 1987.

68. Not always, however, in its radicalized form.

69. Sometimes appearing also in its radicalized form.

70. Lawrence Ziring, _Pakistan: The Enigma of Political Development,_ Dawson Westview, 1980, p. 147.

71. Cf. the contribution "Punjab, The Silent Majority?", in _Herald,_ vol. 18, no. 4, Karachi, May 1987, pp. 57-80.

72. Cf. chapter VII et passim.

73. Especially the Sukkur Division seems to have caught the interest of the Deobandis in the last few years.

74. These are districts of urban culture, where autochthonous institutions from the traditional sector have few possibilities to develop.

75. As in Sindh and in the NWFP, other organizations of DM are not able to counter the monopoly of the Deobandis here.

76. Cf. below, regional nationalism.

77. For the output of graduates of this school cf. Table 35.

78. For biographical data cf. H. Muh. A. Sh. Bukhari, _Akâbir-e 'ulamâ'-e Deoband,_ Lahore, n.d., Urdu, pp. 323ff.

79. The school is located at the Great Trunk Road (GTR), between Rawalpindi and Peshawar. One may find it at about 50 km east of Peshawar and at 5 km east of Nowshera, a garrison town. Parallel to the much frequented GTR runs the Pakistan Railway, thus providing easy access to the school.

80. Calculated according to data supplied by the Dâr al-'Ulûm.

81. Cf. chapter VII.

82. Cf. chapter VII.

83. *Dalîl Dâr al-'Ulûm al-Haqqâniyyah Akorâ Khattak Madîna Bishâwar, Bâkistân, Taqaddamah Idârah al-Ta'lîm,* Peshawar, n.d. (Arabic). This report has been attested on 21.8.1984 by the Pakistani foreign office in Islamabad.

84. Olivier Roy, *Islam and Resistance in Afghanistan,* Cambridge, 1986, pp. 76, 209ff, et passim.

85. *Hizb-e Islâmî* or *Jam'iyyat-e Islâmî,* etc.

86. Olivier Roy, op.cit., pp. 110-117 and 219 et passim. "Most of the Pashtun-speaking 'ulamas carried out their studies at Peshawar and then returned to the tribal zones" (p. 113). For a pro-Soviet interpretation of the activities of the *mawlânâs* cf. Abdullah Malik, *Yeh muftî, yeh mashâ'ikh awr inqilâb-e Afghânistân,* Lahore, 1985.

87. Cf. chapter VII.

88. Olivier Roy, *Islam and Resistance in Afghanistan,* op.cit., pp. 25f. et passim.

89. Calculated according to information received in December 1985 in the *Dâr al-'Ulûm Haqqâniyyah.* Similar data may be found in *Sami al-Haq, Aqâ'id wa Sunnan,* Peshawar, 1985, p. 14.

90. Information received in December 1985 in the Dâr al-'Ulûm.

91. *Al-Haq,* vol. 16/6 (1981, Urdu), pp. 6-10 and 55, where a number of battles between *mujâhidîn* and Afghan troups are described, based on reports of graduates of the Dâr al-'Ulûm. Cf. *Al-Haq,* vol. 16/11 (August 1981, Urdu), pp. 17ff; vol. 17/1 (Oct. 1981), pp. 22-27 (Urdu); vol. 17/3 (Jan. 1982), pp. 13-15 (Urdu). Many *mujâhidîn* came from Afghanistan to the Dâr al-'Ulûm, in order to discuss strategic issues with Abd al-Haq and to receive his blessings, vol. 19/2 (Nov. 1983), pp. 43-46 (Urdu); vol. 19/3 (Dec. 1983), pp. 6-9 (Urdu); vol. 19/4 (Jan. 1984), pp. 37-41 (Urdu); also vol. 19/5 (Feb. 1984), pp. 43-45, describing a delegation of *mujâhidîn* coming to Abd al-Haq who encouraged them and asked them to continue in their fight; cf. furthermore vol. 19/7 (April 1984), pp. 15-17 (Urdu); vol. 20/12 (Sep. 1985), pp. 9-20 (Urdu); vol. 21/1 (Oct. 1985), pp. 5-13 (Urdu). *Al-Haq* is said to have a monthly circulation of about 10,000 issues. The magazine displays a standard much above the usual publications of other DM. The relatively high standard of this magazine makes it possible to circulate it abroad as well, including in Europe.

92. *Al-Haq,* vol. 16/6 (Nov. 1981), p. 6 (Urdu); the names of eight *mujâhidîn* students are given here. The article states that an especially high number of students from the Afghan province of Paktia (where the fiercest battles took place; cf. Olivier Roy, op.cit., p. 193) had graduated in the Dâr al-'Ulûm;

among them, Muhammad Yunus Khalis and Jalal al-Din Haqqani, (*Al-Haq*, vol. 16/7 (April 1981), pp. 26f (Urdu)); on Khalis and Haqqani cf. O. Roy, op.cit., p. 128).

93. *Aqâ'id wa Sunnan,* Peshawar, 1985, p. 14.

94. For the statistical evaluation of the data below I am grateful to my father, N.A. Malik. Originally, there were 874 graduates, but photocopies of 35 entries were missing. Another 48 entries were illegible and could not be deciphered.

95. Cf. monthly issues of the *Afghanistan Report,* edited by the Institute of Strategic Studies, Islamabad.

96. Cf. Metcalf, *Revival,* op.cit., pp. 102, 112, 134, 135. Cf. also S. Mahbub Ridwi, *Tarîkh Dâr al-'Ulûm Deoband,* vol. I, Delhi, 1978 (Urdu), pp. 295ff, 326f et passim.

97. There might be political reasons for this. They cannot be discussed in depth here due to lack of source material.

98. This may well be the reason why access to this school was made so easy for Afghan students.

99. Worth mentioning are the Dâr al-'Ulûm Idârah-e Ta'lîmât-e Islâmî which established a "special section for 'Muhajirin'" and the Madrasah Ta'lîm al-Islâm, CCI Muhâjirîn Camp, Bajor Agentur; cf.*Ta'âruf Râbita al-Madâris al-Islâmî,* Lahore, 1982 (Urdu), pp. 46f.

100. The book has been republished in Pakistan by Pap-Board Printers Ltd., Rawalpindi under the name of Ferozsons, Lahore. The price for the new book is still quite high, but surprisingly it can be found in the second-hand book stores for a third of the original price. It would seem as if the sale of this book has been subsidized.

101. Interview with Ataullah Mengal, in *Herald,* Karachi, July 1986, p. 56.

102. With the exception of the Jama'at-e Islami which displayed conformity with the Government.

103. GoP, Ministry of Finance, CZA, *Council Proceedings,* vol. I, 1-7 meetings, Islamabad, 1983, pp. 8ff.

104. This comprises a religious elite with strong ambitions to participate in the power structure of the colonial urban sector.

105. GoP, Ministry of Finance, CZA, *Council Proceedings,* vol. II, 8-15 meetings, Islamabad, 1983, p. 249f; session on 2.7.81.

106. This press item was counter-checked by the Chief Administrator Zakat, Sind; cf. *Zakat Proceedings,* vol. II, op.cit., p. 254.

107. Op.cit., vol. II, pp. 302f.

108. *Karwâ'î ijlâs Wafâq al-Madâris,* Wafâq al-Madâris al-'Arabiyyah, Multan, 1981, p. 17.

109. It is interesting that this *fatwâ* could not be located in the leading non-conformist DM as the Jâmi'ah Madaniyyah, Lahore and in the central bureau of the Wafâq al-Madâris in Multan. It turned out that non-conformist DM accepted Zakat as well, as the Jâmi'ah Madaniyyah, Lahore.

110. Later on Rs. 2,000 and 3,000 respectively.
111. This is due to the fact that the Zakat payer no longer delivers his Zakat himself, as this is now done directly by the financial institutions after deduction at source.
112. For example income from interest or usury.
113. Al-Rahman, *Muftî Mahmûd nambar*, Lahore, n.d. (Urdu), pp. 43-46.
114. The criticisms are in many ways similar to the ones made by the CII, whose members had also voiced their dissatisfaction with the Zakat system. Cf. chapter IV on Zakat.
115. Not to mention the small DM.
116. In 1981, the *mohtamim* of this school had been a member of the CII, cf. Appendix A, Members 1981-84, no. 10. The leader of this Dâr al-'Ulûm had married into the family of Zia ul Haq. The daughter of Zia was married to the brother of Fadl-e Rahim, *mohtamim* of the Jâmi'ah Ashrafiyyah, Nila Gunbat, Lahore (information on 15.3.86 in the Dâr al-'Ulûm Ashrafâbâd in Ashrafabad, Tando Allah Yar). Accordingly, the policy of this school conforms to the Government.
117. Here only a few of them are listed; information by the *Nâzim-e Imtihân* of the Wafâq in Multan. This information is endorsed by the documents of the PZA. Boycotting of the DM is frequent in Sindh.
118. *Zakat Proceedings*, vol. II, p. 451.
119. *Annual report of the Tanzîm al-Madâris al-'Arabiyyah*, Lahore, October 1980 (Urdu), pp. 28f.
120. *Annual report of the Tanzîm al-Madâris al-'Arabiyyah*, Lahore, March 1985, p. 21.
121. Cf. *The Muslim*, 23.3.84.
122. Ibid.
123. This results from the documents of the PZAs.
124. Some DM have written down their role in the 1977 movement; cf. Muhammad M.T. Qasuri, *Tahrîk-e nizâm-e mustafâ awr Jâmi'ah Nizâmiyyah Ridwiyyah Lâhôre*, Lahore, 1978.
125. On the problematic issues of Sindh there are little academic investigations of a comprehensive nature. One may mention here S.S. Harrison, "Ethnicity and the Political Stalemate in Pakistan", Paper delivered at the Conference, *Islam, Ethnicity and the State in Afghanistan, Iran and Pakistan* held in Nov. 1982 in Tuxedo, N.Y., 1986, pp. 267-298; Hamida Khuro, ed., *Sind through the Centuries*, Oxford, 1982, as well as Lawrence Ziring, *Pakistan: The Enigma of Political Development*, Dawson Westview, 1980, pp. 142-148. Cf. the issues of *Herald*, Karachi from 1986 onwards.
126. Cf. Mahmood Hasan Khan, *Agrarian Structure and Underdevelopment in Pakistan*, op.cit., pp. 74, 133 et passim.
127. Today, Karachi is the largest Pakhtun settlement.
128. Urdu in 22.6 per cent and Punjabi in 7.7 per cent. Pushto, Baluchi, Siraiki and others together make up for approximately 14 per cent (data from the

1981 Census Report of Sind Province, Population Census Organization, Statistics Division, GoP, Islamabad 1984). For the problematic issue of Urdu and the *muhâjirîn* in Sindh cf. Mohammad Arif Ghayur and J. Henry Korson, "The Effects of Population and Urbanization Growth Rates on the Ethnic Tensions in Pakistan", in Manzooruddin Ahmed, *Contemporary Pakistan*, op.cit., pp. 204-227, esp. 212ff.

129. Rural Sindh is accordingly under-represented (excluding Karachi, Sukkur and Hayderabad) among the officers of the Federal bureaucracy (cf. tables 8.1 to 8.3 in Charles H. Kennedy, *Bureaucracy in Pakistan*, Oxford, 1987, pp. 194ff).

130. G.M. Syed, *Sindhu Desh, A Nation in Chains*, n.p., 1974, especially chapters IV and V.

131. Cf. Ilyas Shakir, *MRD, Kâmiyâbîâñ, Nâkâmîâñ*, Karachi, 1985, pp. 115f and 185 as well as Ghulam Nabi Mughal, *Sindh kîâ so<u>ch</u> rahâ hai,* Karachi, 1986, pp. 27ff.

132. Cf. *Asian Post,* August 27, 1983, cited in Shakir, *MRD*, op.cit., pp. 296- 300.

133. These districts were Larkana, Dadu, Nawabshah, Khairpur and Hayderabad; cf. Charles H. Kennedy, "Rural Groups and the Stability of the Zia Regime", in Craig Baxter, ed., *Zia's Pakistan, Politics and Stability in a Frontline State*, Lahore, 1985, p. 39.

134. Hamida Khuro in Ghulam Nabi Mughal, *Sindh kîâ so<u>ch</u> rahâ hai*, op.cit., pp. 128, 134.

135. Ibid.

136. Cited in *Pakistan Commentary*, vol. 3, No. 9, September 1980, pp. 4f.

137. Khan, *Agrarian Structure and Underdevelopment in Pakistan*, op.cit., p. 240.

138. *Pakistan Commentary*, vol. 6, nos. 9-12, September-December 1983, pp. 1-4.

139. Ziring, *Pakistan*, 1980, p. 147.

140. This possibly refers to the Shia of the area around Khairpur who came to Pakistan during the partition in 1947.

141. *Herald,* August-October 1986.

142. Nâzim-e 'alâ of the Wafâq al-Madâris al-'Arabiyyah Pâkistân, and *muhtamim* of the Jâmi'ah Islâmiyyah 'Arabiyyah, Karachi (cf. *Halepota Report,* p. 7 and Annexure).

143. For the statements below cf. Table 15.

144. Instead of the 10 per cent prescribed.

145. That is equal to 1.3 per cent of the DM receiving Zakat in Pakistan and to 9.2 per cent of all DM students up to this date.

146. According to an analysis of the files of the CZA on the DM with the handbook of the religious schools in Pakistan edited by the Idârah-e Tahqîqât-e Islâmî, *Pâkistân mêñ dînî madâris kî fihrist*, Islamabad, 1982 (Urdu), pp. 1-32 et passim. Other Deobandi DM who did not receive Zakat were the Dâr al-'Ulûm A<u>sh</u>rafâbâd, Tando Allah Yar, Hyderabad; the

Madrasah Madina al-'Ulûm, Bhinda Sharif, Hayderabad; Madrasah Dâr al-Fûyyûd, Sajjawal, Thatta; Madrasah Sirâj al-'Ulûm, Ber Sharif, Larkana; Madrasah Shams al-Hudâ, Khairpur Miras; Madrasah Mazhar al-'Ulûm, Jâmi'ah Hammâdiyyah, Manzilgah, Sukkur; Madrasah Miftah al-'Ulûm, Hyderabad (Information as given in the Dâr al-'ulûm Ashrafâbâd in March 1986).

147. Commissioner for examinations of the Wafâq al-Madâris al-'Arabiyyah.

148. *Ahmad I*, pp. 147-152. There had been contacts between Deoband and Sindh at an earlier stage; cf. S.F.D. Ansari, "Sufi Saints, Society and State Power", pp. 172-182.

149. The first *mohtamim* was Ihtiram al-Haq Thanwi. Teachers here had included Yusuf Binori, Badr-e Alam, Abd al-Rahman Kamalpuri, Mufti Ishfaq al-Rahman, Salim Allah Khan as well as Shabbir Ahmad Uthmani. Some are said to have left the school because they felt neglected by the *mohtamim*.

150. The *mohtamim* in the eighties was the PPP activist Ihtiram al-Haq Thanwi, settled in Karachi.

151. See Table 34(C). The Brelwis with their tendency towards conformism have increased their numbers in this province as well, but at a lower rate than the Deobandis.

152. It is not clear how close a contact exists between Sindh and Deoband. An investigation into this aspect would be worthwhile.

CHAPTER VII

TRADITIONALISTS ON THE ADVANCE?

THE BOOM IN EXAMINATIONS IN RELIGIOUS SCHOOLS

The number of DM and their students has risen in the wake of the Islamization policy. The number of graduates[1] affiliated to an umbrella organization has, however, risen in a truly spectacular manner.

In Table 35 (candidates for graduation of the Wafâq and the proportion of the Dâr al-'Ulûm Haqqâniyyah) a total of 9,845 Deobandi students presented themselves for examinations called *shahâdat al-'âlamiyyah*, of whom 32 per cent could not pass the examinations. From 1981 to 1985, 4,265 candidates appeared at the examinations. Thus 43.3 per cent of the Deobandi candidates were examined during these five years, while only 56.7 per cent were examined in the preceding 20 years (from 1960 to 1980).

As Diagram 4 (number of candidates for graduation of different schools of thought) reveals, the Wafâq of the Deobandis in eight years between 1978 and 1985 has produced 3,530 (52.6 per cent) candidates (Ulama-to-be), i.e. 441 *mawlânâs* per year. By comparisons, in the eighteen years from 1960 to 1977, only 3,179 candidates were examined, that is 177 *mawlânâs* per year. During the last two years the "annual production" of the Wafâq rose to 776 *'ulamâ'*. If this trend continues, one may expect a larger number of Deobandi *'ulamâ'* in the coming years as well.

Similar trends may be noticed for the Tanzîm al-Madâris of the Brelwis. Their number remained constant from 1974 to 1980/81. After the "revitalization" of the Tanzîm in 1974, the number of examinees was 145, decreasing to 85 only in 1977 (a decrease of more than 40 per cent). The numbers rose with the coming to power of Zia ul Haq, from 140 in 1978, to 174 in 1979 and to 460 in 1980. In the years 1981 and 1982 there were 477 and 487 graduates respectively, decreasing from 1983 to 1986 to an average of 366. Between 1974 and 1979 (six years) the Tanzîm thus produced 1,048 graduates (i.e. 175 graduates per year) and from 1980 to 1986 (seven years) a total of 2,890 (413 graduates per year). Here as well only about 66 per cent passed the exams; the total number of graduates in

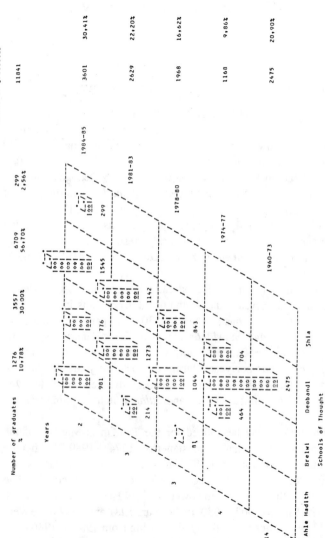

DIAGRAM 4: NUMBER OF CANDIDATES FOR GRADUATION OF THE DIFFERENT SCHOOLS OF THOUGHT

Sources: Different registers on the candidates for graduation.

1985 being 2,348.[2] Thus the Tanzîm too showed a large increase in the number of graduates.

A similar phenomenon is seen with the Wafâq al-Madâris Shia, which only started to hold formal examinations in 1984. According to the functionary in charge of the Jâmi'ah al-Muntazar, the centre of the Shia Wafâq, the system of examinations did not exist before 1984.[3] An increase in the number of graduates between 1984 and 1985 is evident here as well, reaching an increase of 16.7 per cent, from 138 to 161. Due to the stronger affiliation of the northern areas, especially of Baltistan and of Gilgit (of late more easily accessible via the Karakorum highway to the centre in Lahore)[4] a constant increase is also probable in the years to come. A number of graduates are absorbed by the religious centres at Qom and Najaf; the studies there are directed to the motivation and aims of Shia religious scholars.

There is a similar tendency among the Wafâq al-Madâris al-Salafiyyah of the Ahl-e Hadith. It introduced a uniform system of examination for its affiliated DM only in 1978. Even though this institution has been in existence since the late fifties–similar to the Shia umbrella organization – it only became significant with the rise to power of Zia ul Haq. During the first few years of its development from 1978 to 1982 only 135 students presented themselves for examinations. In the following three years (up to 1985) it accepted 1,141 students for examinations for graduation, an increase by a factor of 7.5 within three years! The reason for this is the financial aid received from the Governments of Saudi Arabia and of Pakistan. In his manuscript on DM of the NWFP, Afridi notes that the schools of the Ahl-e Hadith even employed Saudi teachers who received a monthly salary of Rs. 4,000, while their Pakistani colleagues received only Rs. 1,200 per month.[5]

Thus up to 1977 only 3,643 (30 per cent) candidates presented themselves for examination and between 1978 and 1985, 8,198 (70 per cent), leading to a degree in Islamic Sciences or in Theology. While this meant an average number of 202 candidates for graduation per year, the numbers in the second period (1978 to 1985) rose to 1,171 per year, an especially pronounced increase between 1981 and 1983. The peak in the number of candidates for graduation was reached during the last two years, when 3,601 or 30 per cent of all the 11,841 registered and officially recognized *mawlânâs* passed a formal examination.

Moreover, the diagram indicates that there is a difference in the attitude of the various schools of thought towards the official policies. The Brelwis and the Ahl-e Hadith reacted in a positive way as compared to the

Shia and the Deobandis; while there was a pronounced increase of the first two schools of thought from 1978 onwards—the Shia and Deobandis only followed in 1984. The belated positive reaction of the latter two schools of thought may be due to their critical stand towards the Government. Factions of the Shia (followers of Arif Husaini) as well as of the Deobandis (Fadl al-Rahman wing) rejected any collaboration with the Government and demonstrated their isolationist position by joining the Movement for the Restoration of Democracy and by boycotting the referendum in 1984 and the elections in 1985.

Ahl-e Hadith and Brelwis, in contrast, were ready to cooperate. While the Ahl-e Hadith received massive financial aid from Saudi Arabia and followed the ideological line of Saudi Arabia[6] and of Pakistani fundamentalism, the Brelwis profited from the Zakat system. It did not seem to disturb the pragmatic Zia-regime that the two schools of thought basically oppose each other. The number of candidates for graduation of different schools of thought is shown in Graph 2. It reveals especially the predominant numbers of the Deobandi school.[7]

The fact is that the "rule of equivalence" of the Government from 1981/82 in connection with the Zakat regulation of 1980 resulted in a steep increase of the number of graduates. This may appear as a banal statement at first glance. Keeping in mind, however, that these graduates are now M.A.-*Islamiyat* or M.A.-*Arabic*, eligible for equal status with other graduates in the job market, the potential for conflict is clear. In view of the slim chances in the labour market, especially for religious scholars, it seems almost impossible for the Government to provide "equivalent" jobs for thousands of 'Ulamâ'.

The swelling of the numbers of *fudalâ'* is however not to be viewed primarily in the context of employment opportunities. As Graph 3 on the development of the graduates in Pakistan shows, there is no change in the increasing trend of the *mawlânâs*. On the contrary, one may expect a further increase. According to a projection,[8] the number of those presenting themselves for examinations in 1990 will reach approximately 2300! The production of *mawlânâs* is of special significance as their numbers increase not in a linear but in an exponential manner. The aggregated number of potential '*ulamâ*' clearly appears in Graph 4 on the development of the *mawlânâs* in Pakistan in 1960-1995. Given the same trend, there will be about 14,500 officially recognized *mawlânâs* in Pakistan in 1990 and more than 20,000 in 1995, not counting 40,000 or so local religious scholars.[9] These projected numbers of *mawlânâs* indicate the potential of social and political conflict set in motion under the Zia regime. There is a

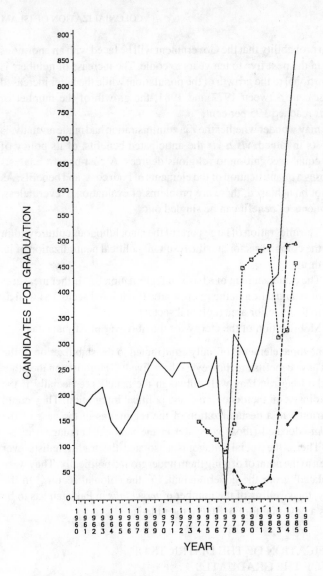

GRAPH 2: NUMBER OF CANDIDATES FOR GRADUATION OF DIFFERENT SCHOOLS OF THOUGHT

Source: Register of candidates for graduation of Wafâqs and Tanzîms.
           without marking = Deobandi
           □ = Brelwi
           △ = Ahl-e Hadith
           * = Shia

very high probability that the Government will be faced with an enormous problem in the next five to ten years to come. The increase of numbers is not proportional to the growth of the population: while the latter increased by 29 per cent between 1972 and 1981, the growth of the number of *mawlânâs* reached 195 per cent.

One may wonder whether the Zia administration had made an analysis of the costs involved, *vis-a-vis* the anticipated benefits, of its policy of granting equal recognition to religious degrees. A cost-benefit analysis presupposes a quantification of the elements of both costs and benefits. As this cannot be achieved, there are problems of evaluation. Nevertheless, three elements of benefit can be singled out:

1.   The integration of large parts of the autochthonous culture within the colonial sector and the resultant political neutralization of its thrust.
2.   The establishment of a basis of legitimation for further measures of Islamization in the interior area (traditional sector) as well as in the exterior area (colonial sector).
3.   Mobilization of the clergy for the holy war in Afghanistan.

All the three elements initially contributed to the stabilization of the regime. These benefits are, however, short-lived.[10] The costs on the other hand in the long run may well outweigh the benefits, especially if the *mawlânâs* insist on their economic and political integration. They could thus contribute to a destabilization of the regime, as in the case of the *swabhasha*-educated (those educated in the national languages) in Sri Lanka.[11] There, the social antagonism isolated the traditionalists ever more, even to the point of driving them underground politically. They were thus "isolated" from the governmental, i.e. the colonial sector.[12] In the same way, the swelling of the number of *mawlânâs* in Pakistan has to be judged as a potential for conflict in the nineties.

IDENTIFICATION OF THE DISTRICTS OF ORIGIN OF THE GRADUATES

The object of specifying the districts of origin of the candidates for graduation of religious schools,[13] having earlier identified the areas of concentration of different schools of thought, is to present an analysis of the social and economic background of the Pakistani clergy and to illustrate the fragmentation of Islam in Pakistan. This regionalization is of special significance in the context of the policy of Islamization of

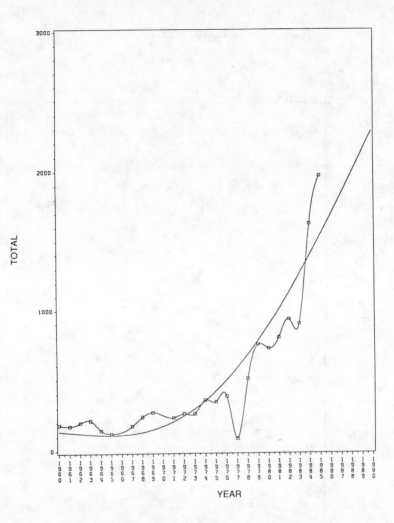

GRAPH 3: DEVELOPMENT OF GRADUATES IN PAKISTAN

Explanation: The line marked by the squares shows the actual number of candidates in the respective years; the line without squares marks the line of regression with the projected values for 1985 to 1990. The analysis is based on a polynomial regression, calculating the square values of the independent variable, with the SAS Procedure General Linear Model. This makes it possible to increase the significant value. The regression matrix therefore reflects a high value of probability of the significant value (F-value = 0,0001). The value given for the R square = 0,860480 means that 86 per cent of all candidates for graduation can be related to the respective year.

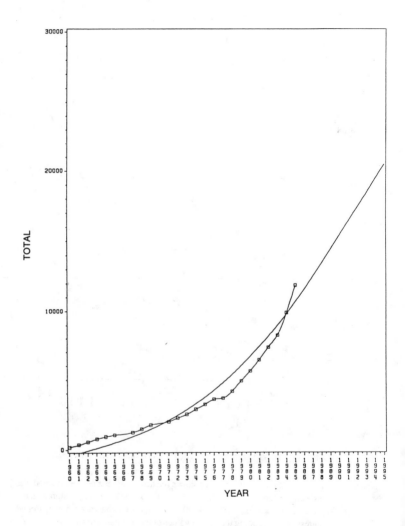

GRAPH 4: DEVELOPMENT OF THE *MAWLÂNÂS* IN PAKISTAN, 1960-1995

Source: Different registers of the Wafâqs and Tanzîms

Zia ul Haq. As has been stated before, the ever stronger effort to spread the "official culture" is based on the central interest in imposing uniformity in the different cultural forms of articulation and incorporating them. The results of the analysis of origin may be compared with other variables such as the stage of development of different regions and the problem of labour markets in different areas. This may not only throw light upon the existing regional disparities but also furnish an insight into the question of which areas are particularly "threatened" and might therefore become problem areas for a uniform policy of Islamization.

THE DEOBANDIS

The analysis of origin of the Deobandi candidates for graduation is based on data from the registers of the Wafâq al-Madâris for five years, i.e. 1963, 1965, 1974, 1975 and 1984.[14] The 2,077 candidates of these years are considered to be a representative sample of Deobandi candidates.[15] The majority of Deobandi candidates for graduation originate from the district of Bannu (8.9 per cent; including North Waziristan), Peshawar (7.2 per cent), Mardan (5.7 per cent), Mansehra (5.2 per cent), Multan (4.6 per cent), Swat (4 per cent), Dir (3.7 per cent), Dera Ismail Khan (3.2 per cent) and Karachi (3.2 per cent) and from Afghanistan (8.6 per cent). Only few of them originate from northern Punjab, Sindh and Baluchistan. This shows a concentration of candidates for graduation of the Deobandis in the NWFP. The only district in Pakistan outside the NWFP with a larger number of candidates is Multan.

The data illustrates that the number of candidates increased and reached their peak in 1984. The number in that year was equal to the total number of the four years of 1963, 1965, 1974 and 1975.[16] The analysis for the districts of origin in the years shows a constant proportion of candidates for graduation (14-28 per cent) originating from the districts Bannu, D.I. Khan, Mardan and Dir, from the agencies Khaibar, Bajor, Mohmand and from North-Waziristan. Only about 7 per cent originate from Baluchistan.

Punjab has just below 25 per cent of the candidates for graduation, especially from rural districts with agrarian relations of a feudal character, viz., Multan, Vihari and Sahiwal. It is striking that Karachi presents candidates for graduation—local and migrant—only in the last year of analysis (1984, 5.6 per cent).

There are few examinees from Sindh (excluding Karachi). By 1984, the origin of candidates for graduation has changed, particularly the numbers from Karachi. This development is connected with the problem of migration.[17]

In Punjab as well, the number of candidates for graduation rises rapidly in 1984. There are almost as many candidates coming from this province as from the traditional areas of origin such as Peshawar, Mardan, Kohat, Bannu, D.I. Khan and the agencies. The main areas of recruitment in Punjab are the Bahawalpur division, and the districts of Muzaffargarh and D.G. Khan. There is also an increasing number originating from the Divisions of Rawalpindi and Gujranwala (cf. Map 2 at the end of the chapter).

The number of Afghan examinees has also strongly increased over the last few years.[18]

From the detailed data compiled, the areas of origin can even be traced down to the level of the tehsil. In the NWFP, the areas of origin are predominantly the tehsils of the district of Bannu, as well as those of the district of Mardan, especially from Swabi, and Peshawar with Charsadda; furthermore, there is Mansehra with Batgaram as well as Mansehra, D.I. Khan with the centre of Tank as well as Karak. In Punjab the tehsils in Multan, Milsi and Lodhran stand out for their large numbers.

This clearly means that the examinees of the Deobandi school of thought originate primarily from rural areas, i.e from villages with less than 10,000 inhabitants.

So far we have based our evaluation only on the absolute and relative figures of the candidates for graduation, without relating them to other variables. The numbers of population of districts will now be considered for comparisons.[19] A comparison of the candidates for graduation per 10,000 inhabitants substantiates the premise that the majority of Deobandis originate from the NWFP (see Table 39). Chitral is another centre of recruitment; Bannu, Bajor and Zhob also stand out, while members from Mansehra and Peshawar stagnate and Dir and Multan show a decline. Karachi, in contrast, moves up from about 1,000,000 inhabitants per candidate for graduation to almost 100,000 inhabitants per candidate for graduation at the beginning of the eighties.

When comparing the number of inhabitants per candidate for graduation of the DM system with those of the formal education system, it is evident that the number of mawlânâs per 10,000 inhabitants is sometimes above that of the M.A. candidates. This is the case in predominantly traditional areas where the clergy presumably occupy a position of influence.

The analysis permits us to identify the districts from which an increasing number of mawlânâs come and those which show a decline. A ranking list of Deobandi candidates for graduation per 10,000 inhabitants gives the picture for three different census surveys on the population as shown in Table 40.

TABLE 39: INHABITANTS PER DEOBANDI CANDIDATE FOR GRADUATION AND
PER M.A. CANDIDATE FOR GRADUATION (FORMAL SYSTEM OF EDUCATION)

District	1961/63	1972/74	1982/84	M.A.-Grad.(1982)
Bannu	31,420	10,700	10,160	16,154
Bajor Agen.	93,330	52,000	11,115	12,050
Mansehra	15,420	49,390	17,210	35,553
Chitral	28,250	12,230	20,900	29,794
Dir	32,080	29,390	63,917	59,031
Mardan	30,220	57,330	48,610	60,260
D.I. Khan	36,200	23,700	24,423	12,710
Peshawar	58,700	64,110	40,035	7,313
Zhob	91,000	28,670	27,846	90,412
Multan	15,164	22,379	131,613	24,284
Karachi	1,024,500	601,500	104,577	4,270

Sources: Register of the Wafâq al-Madâris al-'Arabiyyah.
Hand Book of Population Census Data, Population Census Organisation; Statistics Division, GoP, Islamabad, Dec. 1985, pp. 2f, Table 2; *1981 Census Report of Federally Administrated Tribal Areas (FATA)*, Population Census Organisation; Statistics Division, GoP, Islamabad, August 1984.
Calculations on the M.A.-Graduates are based on Table 10, "Population of students (5 years and above) by educational attainment, sex and age group" of the districtwise Census reports.

TABLE 40: ORDER OF RANKING OF THE CANDIDATES FOR
GRADUATION PER 10,000 INHABITANTS PER DISTRICT

1964		1974		1984	
1	CTRL	1	BN	1	BN
2	MR	2	CTRL	2	BAJOR
3	BN	3	DIK	3	MN
4	DIR	4	ZHOB	4	MOHMAND
5	ST	5	DIR	5	CTRL
6	PR	6	MN	6	KT
7	ZHOB	7	BAJOR	7	DIK
8	BAJOR	8	MR	8	ZHOB
9	TH	9	PR	9	KHAR
10	BP	10	KT	10	QLT
11	LL	11	ST	11	CAGHI
12	KHAR	12	DGK	12	PR
13	ML	13	QT	13	KZDR
14	MN	14	MW	14	SIBI
15	MG	15	PSHN	15	ST
16	KT	16	AD	16	AK
17	AD	17	QLT	17	MR
18	DIK	18	TURB	18	MD

Contd.

1964		1974		1984	
19	MW	19	LL	19	QT
20	BR	20	V	20	MG
21	JD	21	ML	21	DIR
22	SG	22	MG	22	BR
23	V	23	DGK	23	DGK
24	SL	24	SG	24	LL
25	KI	25	BP	25	BP
26	J	26	SK	26	RK
27	RP	27	SL	27	KI
28	FD	28	AK	28	AD
29	SKT	29	HD	29	KOHISTAN
		30	KI	30	PSH
		31	FD	31	BADN
		32	TH	32	ML
		33	RK	33	MW
		34	J	34	KCHI
		35	RP	35	PANJGUR
		36	JM	36	LSBL
		37	BR	37	NSRBD
		38	QSR	38	HD
		39	LR	39	SR
				40	V
				41	TH
				42	SKT
				43	SK
				44	GT
				45	J
				46	KHAIBAR
				47	FD
				48	SL
				49	SG
				50	IS
				51	GW
				52	LR

Sources: Register of the Wafâq al-Madâris al-'Arabiyyah.

Hand Book of Population Census Data, Population Census Organisation; Statistics Division, GoP, Islamabad, Dec. 1985, pp. 2f, Table 2 and *1981 Census Report of Federally Administrated Tribal Areas (FATA)*, Population Census Organisation; Statistics Division, GoP, Islamabad, August 1984 as well as author's own calculations based on data of 1984.

BN = Bannu; MN = Mansehra; CTRL = Chitral; KT = Kohat; DIK = Dera Ismail Khan; KHAR = Kharan; QLT = Qalat; PR = Peshawar; KZDR = Khuzdar; ST = Swat; AK = Attock; MR = Mardan; MD = Muzaffarabad; QT = Quetta; MG = Muzaffargarh; BR = Bahawalnagar; RK = Rahim Yar Khan; LL = Lorelai; KI = Karachi; AD = Abbottabad; PSHN = Pishin; ML = Multan; MW = Mianwali; KCHI = Kachhi; LSBL = Lasbela; NSRBD = Nasirabad; HD = Hayderabad; SR = Sargodha; V = Vihari; TH = Thatta; SKT = Sialkot; SK = Sukkur; GT = Gujrat; J = Jhang; FD = Faisalabad; SL = Sahiwal; SG = Sanghar; IS = Islamabad; GW = Gujranwala; LR = Lahore; JD = Jacobabad .

The rank orderings reveal a continuing concentration of *mawlânâs* in the district of Bannu, and a rising trend in the districts or agencies of Bajor, Mansehra and Kohat. Dir, Mardan, D.I. Khan and Chitral, as well as Peshawar, Swat and especially Multan in contrast have not been able to maintain their ranks.

REGIONAL CENTRES FOR GRADUATION

The 1,950[20] entries reveal that most DM students graduated in Peshawar (34.3 per cent), followed by Karachi (19.4 per cent), Multan (7.1 per cent), Lahore (7 per cent) and Bannu (6.5 per cent).[21] This means that the districts of origin differ from the districts of graduation, indicating migration between the locality of origin and the locality of schooling. The reason for the movement into the districts of Peshawar, where the central schools of the Deobandis are located,[22] is the role these schools play as a catchment area for the Afghans and the candidates for graduation from the NWFP. These schools were able to extend their area of recruitment up to 1980. This had made Peshawar a cultural centre already in the beginning of the nineteenth century. "Peshawar seems to be the most learned city in these countries. . . famous for its Moolahs. . .[23] (who were) particularly powerful about Peshawar". Nowadays, the important schools of Peshawar[24] follow a conservative policy with regard to the number of students. The Dâr al-'Ulûm Haqqâniyyah even seems to promote the migration of students to Karachi by advertizing in its monthly magazine, *al-Haq*.[25]

One must of course stress the role of Karachi as a recent centre for DM education, whose schools are now much sought after. Peshawar and Karachi are currently competing for the predominance as centres of religious education, with the schools of Karachi increasingly catching up as Table 41 reveals.

TABLE 41: NUMBER OF CANDIDATES OF GRADUATION OF SCHOOLS
IN PESHAWAR AND KARACHI

Year	Number of Students/DM in Karachi	Number of Students/DM in Peshawar
1963	30/3	133/7
1965	18/1	99/3
1974	53/2	157/2
1975	56/2	139/4
1984	224/6	204/9

In the eighties, the position held by Peshawar for decades was taken by Karachi. In 1984, six schools there examined a total of 224 candidates for graduation, while in Peshawar nine DM examined only 204. The graduates in Karachi came mostly from abroad (especially Bangladesh, Sri Lanka and Iran) or from the rural areas of other provinces, especially the district of Mansehra (NWFP). There were, in contrast, no candidates for graduation from Peshawar, Lahore, Multan and Rawalpindi, and only three of a total of 41 Afghan students were examined here in 1984.

There is increasing migration into centres of religious education, all from north to south. This corresponds to the prevailing pattern of migration from the rural areas to the metropolis.

The rates of migration make it clear that Karachi (i.e. urban Sindh) is especially affected by it: between 1972 and 1981 Karachi had a rate of increase of 51 per cent (an annual addition of 5 per cent) and the number of immigrants was 1,728,213 or 32 per cent of its total population! Among them the immigrants from the NWFP represent the largest proportion.[26] This influx, especially of Pakhtuns into Karachi, is not without its problems, as the latest upheavals between the different ethnic groups have demonstrated.

The larger expansion of Deobandi DM in Karachi compared to those in Peshawar, however, cannot be explained solely by the migration of students to the metropolis. Karachi also recieved a strong influx from the rural areas of Sindh, Baluchistan and Punjab as well as from abroad.

The only exception is the migration of the religious students from Baluchistan to the NWFP. This movement may be of ethnic origin as many of the Deobandi students originate from the area surrounding Zhob in Baluchistan. There, the tribes of the *Mando Khel* branch of the *Ghurghusht* family and of the Pakhtuns dominate.[27]

Connected to this growing urbanization and centralization of the DM system one notices a detachment from traditional institutions of learning, as from the predominantly rural Dâr al-'Ulûm Haqqâniyyah in favour of Karachi.

Several areas turned out to be strongholds of the Deobandis as time went by. In these centres there are a number of schools which deserve a closer look because of their importance. Besides their political relevance, it is possible to show that the numbers of candidates for graduation in these schools have undergone changes.

Out of 1,987 candidates 423 (20.4 per cent) passed their examinations in the Dâr al-'ulûm Haqqâniyyah, Akora Khattak, Peshawar. This school may be considered the leading centre of Deobandi scholarship. In Multan the second largest madrasah was the Khair al-Madâris with 164 (7.9 per cent) candidates for graduation, followed by the Madrasah Arabiyyah Islâmiyyah in Karachi with 98 (4.7 per cent) students.[28]

The candidates for graduation of certain areas frequently attend certain DM.[29] The Peshawari schools of Dâr al-'ulûm Haqqâniyyah, Dâr al-'Ulûm Sarhad and Jâmi'ah Imdâd al-'Ulûm may be considered traditional catchment areas for Afghan students.[30] In contrast to this, not a single candidate for graduation of the DM in Peshawar originated from the Punjab and only 14 Punjabis were examined in schools located in Karachi. These schools also examined only three Afghans.

There has thus been a tendency in the last few years for candidates of the Deobandis originating from outside the NWFP to migrate from north to south, more precisely away from the traditional institutions of education in the NWFP towards those located in the metropolis.

Family Background

After the geographic categorization of the Deobandi '*ulamâ*' it is important to analyse the extent to which the Pakistani clergy is based on a family tradition with a clergical background. As mentioned in the chapter on the problem of dropouts, the majority of DM students originate from the economically weaker strata of society.

An analysis of the titles borne by the fathers of candidates for graduation can show how many among the graduated *mawlânâs* have a religious background, in that the father of the student had also been a student of a madrasah and had a religious title. As many as 757 out of 2,077 fathers of candidates for graduation possessed such a title. Among the 24 different titles present in this group,[31] 18 had a religious connotation, while six titles permitted statements in the registers on the social and economic status of the father.[32] In contrast, there were no statements on the usually very important affiliation to particular tribes, thus showing compliance with the egalitarian principles of Islam, which do not permit differentiation by origins.[33]

Only 63 out of the 757 titles were of a secular nature[34] (8.3 per cent of all titles and 3 per cent of all fathers of candidates). They are not considered here for the time being. Among the 757 titles, the most common one is that of *mawlânâ/maulwî/mullâ*, designating a religious teacher (342 or 45.2 per cent of all titles).[35] Next are the titles of *hâjî* (pilgrim to Mecca; 78 or 10.3 per cent), *al-hâj* (several pilgrimages to Mecca; 46 or 6.1 per cent), *shâh* (descendant of the Prophet; 67 or 8.9 per cent), *sayyid* (descendant of the Prophet; 53 or 7.0 per cent) and *hâfiz* (a person knowing the Koran by heart; 41 or 5.4 per cent). The compilation of the fathers' titles[36] shows that the number of "pilgrims" increased enormously in 1984. This may be due to the *Hajj* policy of the Zia regime.[37] A similar increase may be observed in the titles of *hâfiz, qârî, imâm, khalîfa, pîr, ghâzî* and *hakîm* (they are combined into one single group).

The highest increase was among the *mawlânâs*. While their number totalled 172 over the years 1962, 1965, 1974 and 1975, in 1984 alone it reached 173. With the exception of 1974 (25 per cent) the title of *mawlânâ* makes up for a constant proportion of 40 per cent of all titles. Almost half the candidates for graduation with fathers in the possession of a title can thus claim a religious family tradition.

The absolute increase of the title of *mawlânâ* could either point to the fact that more and more *mawlânâs* were sending their children to a religious school or that more and more fathers falsely adopted the title of *mawlânâ*. This is, however, not very likely, as there is a good network of information among the clergy.

The formal upgrading of the DM since Zia ul Haq seems to have added to the status of *mawlânâ*—a status it had lost over the past three decades.

The question is, which are the areas of origin of the traditional religious scholars–the *mawlânâs*, the *hâjjîs (hujjâj)*, the *al-hâjs*, the *hâfizs (huffâz)*, and especially the descendants of the Prophet (*sayyids* and *shâhs*)–and whether there has been a change over the years.[38] The data available reveals that most pilgrims originate from the Punjab. Out of 120 *hujjâj*, 47 came from this province, 22 from the NWFP; only 5 from Sindh, and 12 came from Afghanistan. An analysis of their distribution at the district level shows that the pilgrims rarely originate from the traditional centres of recruitment of the Deobandis but are rather from areas with high density of population.[39]

The *mawlânâs* were predominantly from the NWFP (122 or 47 per cent of all *mawlânâs*), Sindh had only 8 and Baluchistan 23. Twenty-nine (i.e. 8.7 per cent of all *mawlânâs*) were of Afghan origin.[40]

It is remarkable that the number of *mawlânâs* is relatively high in the division of Peshawar as well as in the districts of Bannu and Mansehra and especially in Zhob. This points to the fact that the profession of *mawlânâ* is more widespread in remote and "backward" regions than in "developed" ones. The profession still seems to be in demand there. In some areas of the NWFP (outside of the tribal areas) the title of *mawlânâ, maulwî* or *mullâ* is an honoured one,[41] as against the Punjab where these titles carry a negative connotation.

Almost every second descendant of the Prophet (*sayyid* and *shâh*)[42] is from the NWFP: 59 *sayyids* and *shâhs* represent about 10 per cent of the titles in this province; 11 _shâhs_ originate in Chitral. There is no descendant of the Prophet from Sindh; Baluchistan has only 2, Punjab 12 and Afghanistan 11. At the districts level, we observe a pronounced advantage of Bannu, Peshawar and Mansehra.[43]

The _hâfizs_ mostly originate from the districts of Multan, Muzaffargarh and Bahawalpur (30, or 73.2 per cent of all _huffâz_),[44] while there are almost no _hâfizs_ in the centres of the Deobandis (only 7 or 17.1 per cent of all _huffâz_).

In the NWFP we find the titles of _mawlânâ, hâjî_ and _sayyid/shâh_, whereas in Punjab it is _hâfiz_. However, the title of _mawlânâ_ is not necessarily tied to a theological education here. A _maulwî/mullâ_ may also be a religious scholar of a lower ranking, assisting the local population in every day questions with religious advice, whose activities are limited to the maintenance of local religious institutions. The titles of _sayyid/shâh_ and _hâjjî/al-hâj_ are hereditary or dependent on pilgrimage, not on theological studies or even a study of four years of the Koran, as for a _hâfiz_. From this, one should, however, not deduce that there is less religious authority in the NWFP than in the Punjab, where the title of _hâfiz_ dominates, as a _hâfiz_ enjoys little prestige among the religious scholars. Especially in Punjab he does not enjoy much respect.[45] In NWFP, in contrast, the religious scholars are respected, not least for their leading role in the freedom fight against the foreign expansionism. As they stand outside of the tribal society they are able to transcend the latent tribal feuds and often act as charismatic leaders. This is also a frequently quoted reason why the leading personalities in the _Jihâd_ for Afghanistan are often religious scholars.[46]

The type and number of titles indicate the degree of religious belief of an area. They also provide information about areas in which the profession of a religious teacher–_mawlânâ, maulwî, mullâ_–is most widespread. In NWFP, not only is the number of persons holding a relgious title higher than in Punjab, they also boast a higher level of theological education.

The above observations lead to the supposition that fathers with a religious title have a tendency to send their sons to the strongholds of Deobandi education and thus contribute to the reinforcement of Islamic scholarship of the Deobandi school in Peshawar.[47]

The available data also shows that there has been a marked increase not only in the number of persons holding a title but also in the types of title held. This points to an increased diversification of the titles.[48] The titles are supplemented with designations pointing to social status rather than the religious qualifications, such as _ghâzî_ (victorious fighter for Islam), _sâhib_ (title of honour), _khalîfah_ (descendant of a saint), _hadrat_ (title of honour), _mîrzâdah_ (descendant of a landlord or a saint) and _beg_ (honorific title;

landlord). This means that some members of the upper strata of society now send their children to religious schools. This has been the result of the formal recognition of the DM by the Government and the integration of these institutions into the official sector.

Until very recently it was considered impossible for holders of social (non-religious) titles in the NWFP to send their sons to religious institutions of education:

The son of a Khan would never engage in religious studies (at least in the twentieth century, for the situation seems to have been different in earlier times). To be a Pashtun is to be integrated into a tribal structure. Priests are outside the tribal system, (they are) either below it, or above it.[49]

This is due to the fact that the *Khâns*—the local landlord and head of village—were intellectually oriented to the local legal system, the secular *Pakhtûnwalî*.[50] The results of our analysis of titles, however, seem to demonstrate the opposite. Apparently, there is a connection between *Pakhtûnwalî* and the Shari'a, especially during the last few years. This is supported by the large proportion of "*Khâns*" among the titles held by the fathers (11.3 per cent).[51] On these results the thesis presented by Olivier Roy may be questioned. A *Khân* may well send his descendants to a religious school, to be sure not the first and second born sons, but those who due to the rules of inheritance do not have the prospect of receiving an income sufficient to ensure their living.

THE BRELWI GRADUATES

The analysis of the districts of origin of the candidates for graduation within the Tanzîm al-Madâris is based on the registers from 1974 to 1979/80.

TABLE 42: DISTRIBUTION OF THE CANDIDATES FOR GRADUATION WITHIN THE TANZÎM AL-MADÂRIS ACCORDING TO PROVINCES AND YEARS

Originating from	1974	1975	1976	1977	1978	1979/80	Total	%
Punjab	110	89	82	61	107	316	765	73.0
Sindh	10	7	4	10	13	37	81	7.7
NWFP	14	17	9	6	4	38	88	8.4
Baluchistan	1	1	4	2	2	10	20	1.9
Kashmir	10	11	10	5	14	36	86	8.2
Others	—	—	—	1	—	7	8	0.8
Total	145	125	109	85	140	444	1048	100.0

Sources: Register of the graduates of the Tanzîm al-Madâris al-'Arabiyyah for the years 1974 to 1979/80, Lahore (mimeo), and author's calculations.[52]

During the six years under consideration here, the Brelwis in 73 per cent of all cases originated from the Punjab. At the district level the following conclusions may be drawn.

The largest group comes from Sahiwal (143 or 13.6 per cent), the second largest from the district of Multan (86 or 8.2 per cent); the districts of D.G. Khan and Muzaffargarh are next (with a total of 91 students or 8.7 per cent).

Only 66 students come from urban districts such as Lahore, Rawalpindi and Faisalabad (6.3 per cent). The largest number come from the rural areas such as Sahiwal or Multan. Of the total of 1,048 fathers, 36 per cent have a religious title.[53]

The candidates for graduation are mostly sons of small landowners or landless peasants, who are numerous in the districts characterized by large landholdings such as Sahiwal and Multan, D.G. Khan and Muzaffargarh.[54] Like the Deobandis, Brelwis also mostly originate from villages with less than 10,000 inhabitants.[55]

The local landlord of a large holding and the local saint generally are the same person and this person often serves both functions, that of the *pîr* and of the landlord. The *pîrî murîdî* (veneration of saints) is accordingly widespread in the districts of Multan and Sahiwal.[56] Regions where Brelwis predominate often display Hindu elements of belief.

The small number of Brelwis in the NWFP and in Baluchistan may be partly explained by Hindu elements: the ideological orientation of the Pakhtuns and the Baluchis is hardly compatible with the Hindu influences which have been absorbed by the Brelwis.[57] The northern frontier province and Baluchistan have a social structure which differs from the social structure in the Punjab which is heavily influencd by Hindu elements. Ostensibly a tribal society without castes and with basically democratic features (as manifested in the institution of the *Jirga*)[58] is in sharp contrast to the society in the Punjab which has a pronounced and socially accepted system of castes.[59]

The traditional Deobandi connection between Deoband and Kabul via Lahore and Peshawar may have hindered or discouraged the Brelwis from coming to these areas. Furthermore, even before the Deobandis took charge of the area, the northern frontier province had a puritan orientation as became evident in the movement against the Sikhs and against the British under the descendants of Shah Wali Allah.[60] The Deobandi school of thought and the Brelwi syncretism are hardly compatible with one another.

The leading religious scholars of the Brelwis originating from a region now in India, are referred to as *muhâjirîn* (refugees) who during the migration following 1947 flowed into districts of Pakistan bordering India. No research has, however, been conducted on why hardly any Brelwis are settled in rural Sindh, a province which is also characterized by large landholdings and a cult of saints. There are, however, supporters of the Brelwis in urban Sindh as in Hayderabad and its surroundings, an area with a large proportion of refugees from India. Hyderabad is the stronghold of the Jam'iyyat-e 'Ulama'-e Pakistan.[61]

The distribution of landholdings, the roles of feudal landlords and of the *pîr*, and the Hindu influence make the seemingly syncretist Brelwi school of thought a rather conformist group. They contribute to the perpetuation of the *status quo* in Punjab, including its numerous saints. Due to their adaptability they are able to give new identities to a large proportion of rural and urban groups.[62]

REGIONAL CENTRES OF GRADUATION

Following the analysis of the districts of origin of the Brelwi candidates for graduation we will now identify the centres of education of the Tanzîm. As Table 43 shows, at least 840 graduates were examined in Punjab (80.2 per cent), most of them in the districts of Multan and Sahiwal.

TABLE 43: DISTRICTS AND TOWNS OF GRADUATION OF THE BRELWIS
FROM THE PUNJAB, 1974 TO 1979/80

District	Number of Candidates
Multan	183
Sahiwal/Okara	169
Lahore	162
Faisalabad	158
Rawalpindi	64
Others	104
Total	840

Sources: Registers of the garduates of the Tanzîm al-Madâris al-'Arabiyyah 1974 to 1979/
80, Lahore (mimeo), and author's calculations.

Districts of origin and districts of graduation are not always identical. The districts like Rawalpindi, Lahore and Faisalabad have many more candidates than one might suppose from the number of students originating from these districts. Out of 384 examinees only 66 came from the corresponding districts. This points towards a migration from rural to urban districts within the Punjab province. If the location of the large and well-established DM in Lahore, Faisalabad and Rawalpindi is taken into consideration, this migration of theologians is not so surprising. Interviews with students have shown that "the city is more profitable, as there is more money in the city and thus there are more opportunities to earn a living".[63] Religious scholars too are attracted to urban centres through the economic incentives which are provided.

In Sindh, 17.1 per cent of all students of the Tanzîm were graduates. Half of them came from Sindh with only 34 from Karachi. In contrast to this, 144 students (6 per cent above the total number of students from Sindh) graduated in DM which were located in Karachi. The role of Karachi in terms of graduate students underlines the readiness among the Brelwis to migrate to Karachi, just like the Deobandis. The metropolis is, thus, increasingly becoming the centre of the Tanzîm as well.[64] The smaller centres in Hayderabad and Sukkur produced a total of 34 candidates for graduation.

Only 20 students (1.9 per cent) graduated in the NWFP, more precisely in the DM of Peshawar, Mardan and Bannu. In contrast to this, however, 8.4 per cent of all candidates of the Tanzîm came from the NWFP. Here the students seem to have a tendency of leaving their province of origin. The same phenomenon may be observed in Baluchistan: out of 20 students originating in this province only 8 (0.8 per cent) graduated there, more precisely in Sibi. The candidates from Kashmir (Pak) were not examined there but mostly in the DM of Faisalabad, Rawalpindi, Lahore and Karachi. Thus, there is also a migration from Kashmir (Pak) towards the urbanized centres of the Punjab.

There is thus a migration from north to south within Sindh among the potential Brelwi 'ulamâ' as well. Furthermore, one may observe a movement from the NWFP towards Punjab. It is noteworthy that agricultural areas with large landholdings are increasingly avoided by the candidates for graduation. This may be connected to the employment situation.[65]

THE SHIA

Based on the system of records introduced during the formalization of the DM in 1981/82, it is possible to form an understanding of the areas of origin of the Shia candidates for graduation.[66]

As Table 44 reveals, most examinees come from the districts of Sargodha, Bhakkar, Jhang and Attock. They make up for 36.1 per cent of a total of 299 students. Besides these districts, Gilgit and Baltistan stand out as centres of recruitment of the Shia with a total of 14 per cent of the 299 candidates for graduation. The remaining students come from such areas in the Punjab as Lahore, Multan and D.G. Khan, to name just a few. Even though the Shia are influential in the northern areas,[67] only 13 candidates for graduation came from the NWFP.[68] The low figure of Shia in Sindh (five examinees only) is also reflected in Table 34(C).[69] Similarly, very few candidates originate from the urbanized districts, such as Lahore, Faisalabad, Gujranwala and Sialkot, a tendency which was pointed out in

TABLE 44: DISTRIBUTION OF CANDIDATES FOR GRADUATION OF THE WAFÂQ AL-MADÂRIS SHIA ACCORDING TO DISTRICTS OF ORIGIN, 1984 AND 1985

Districts of Origin	1984	1985	Total	%
Rawalpindi	1	8	9	3.0
Attock	9	11	20	6.7
Jhelum	7	3	10	3.3
Sargodha	10	23	33	11.0
Khushab	8	2	10	3.3
Mianwali	—	3	3	1.0
Bhakkar	9	20	29	9.7
Faisalabad	1	—	1	0.3
Jhang	12	14	26	8.7
Lahore	8	4	12	4.0
Shaikhupura	1	3	4	1.3
Okara	2	2	4	1.3
Gujranwala	2	4	6	2.0
Sialkot	1	3	4	1.3
Gujrat	3	5	8	2.7
Multan	6	8	14	4.7
Vihari	2	1	3	1.0
Sahiwal	4	—	4	1.3
D.G. Khan	5	8	13	4.3
Muzaffargarh	5	6	11	3.7
Leiah	3	—	3	1.0
Bahawalpur	3	—	3	1.0
R.Y. Khan	2	4	6	2.0
Kohat	1	1	2	0.7
D.I.Khan	4	7	11	3.7
Khairpur	1	2	3	1.0
Nawabshah	—	1	1	0.3
Hayderabad	1	—	1	0.3
Karachi	1	1	2	0.7
Gilgit	13	5	18	6.0
Baltistan	13	11	24	8.0
Parachinar	—	1	1	0.3
Total	138	161	299	100.0

Source: Register of the candidates for graduation of the Wafâq al-Madâris Shia with the collaboration of Ajmal Shah, Jâmi'ah al-Muntazar, Lahore, June 6, 1986.

relation to the students of the Deobandis and the Brelwis.

The distribution indicates that the potential *mujtahids* are concentrated in the Punjab, primarily in the Sargodha Division with approximately 25 per cent of all candidates. In this Division, which is largely rural, there are numerous Shia places of pilgrimage. The localities chosen by Shia DM in such regions is reminiscent of similar locations of the DM of the Brelwis.

The number of Shia '*ulamâ*' will increase in the coming years, especially in the northern areas,[70] and it is hoped they will probably graduate increasingly in the large DM of Lahore, and in Karachi.

THE AHL-E HADITH

The areas of origin of the Ahl-e Hadith may be analysed on the basis of the registers from 1978 to 1985. This school of thought has a rather strict "fundamentalist" orientation in contrast to the Brelwis, the Shia and even the Deobandis; they reject any veneration of saints and popular rituals,[71] and claim support from among the merchants and intellectuals. These claims are valid even today (Table 45).[72] The majority of the candidates for

TABLE 45: DISTRIBUTION OF THE CANDIDATES FOR GRADUATION OF THE WAFÂQ AL-MADÂRIS AL-SALAFIYYAH ACCORDING TO NUMBERS, DISTRICTS OF ORIGIN AND THE RELIGIOUS TRADITION, 1978-85

Year	Number	Most Frequent District of Origin	Father's Title Mawlânâ or Hâfiz
1978	49	Okara, Kasur, Faisalabad	1
1979	17	*too few data in the register*	4
1980	15	Sahiwal, Qasur, Faisalabad	2
1981	20	Faisalabad, Kasur, Gujranwala	1
1982	34	*too few data in the register*	
Total	135		8
1983	160	Okara, Sahiwal, Faisalabad, Kasur	27
1984	489	Okara, Qasur, Sahiwal, Multan	27
1985	492	Kasur, Okara, Faisalabad, Gujranwala	21
Total	1276		83

Source: Register of the graduates of the Wafâq al-Madâris al-Salafiyyah, Lahore, 1978-1985, Research on April 3rd, 1986 in the central office in Lahore.

Due to "reasons of security" it was not possible to obtain the complete data. Furthermore, the register was not kept in good condition. Only the number of examinees was recorded.

graduation come from districts such as Faisalabad, Okara, Qaur, Sahiwal and Gujranwala. With the exception of Sahiwal the districts referred to above may be considered commercial centres of the country. Consequently, this is where numerous DM of the Ahl-e Hadith are located.

Given the relatively urban character of the Ahl-e Hadith, a mere 5.7 per cent of the examinees come from _Chaks_, i.e. from villages established by the British in the middle of the last century for the perennial irrigation of monocultures.[73] At least a small proportion of the graduates originate from economically backward areas, while only 7.1 per cent have a traditionally religious family background.[74]

The urban character of this school of thought and their '_ulamâ_' are quite evident; the leader of this school,[75] the president of the Institute for Shariah in Lahore's Model Town, or the recently deceased chief functionary of the Ahl-e Hadith Zuhur Illahi; and other leading personalities are, or were, important industrialists or landlords based in Karachi.

The original characteristics of the Ahl-e Hadith were maintained, at least socially. After an initial political setback, this school of thought has gained tremendously in stature during the recent Islamization, a development reflected in the large number of candidates for graduation. It is currently competing with the Jama'at-e Islami for Saudi financial support.[76]

SUMMARY

It is possible thus to make the following statements on the candidates for graduation and for the clergy in Pakistan.

The examinees of the different schools of thought–basically four–are concentrated in different areas of origin. Even if there are inter-regional movements from time to time, we may nevertheless state that each school of thought has its own geographic centre. The geographic classification also throws light on the social and economic position of the representatives of different schools of thought, even if they sometimes belong to different strata of society. Most candidates for graduation have in common a pronounced rural background; more precisely, they come from villages with less than 10,000 inhabitants.

The geographic and socio-economic characteristics of each school of thought reflect its ideology. Thus, the populist syncretist school of thought of the Brelwis primarily turns to small farmers and the poor from the so-called canal colonies, i.e from regions which stand out because of their large landholdings and the numerous landless peasants. They are also present in regions where there is a high degree of veneration of saints due to the prevailing landownership.[77] After partition these regions were opened up for the newly migrated Muslims from India.[78] It was during the period following independence that there was an influx of Brelwis, especially in Pakistani Punjab.[79] About one-third originated from traditionally religious families.

The Deobandis are frequently found in Punjab as well but they have their centres in the NWFP, especially in the districts of Peshawar and Bannu as well as in the area of Hazara and in Afghanistan. We may infer a relation between the social structure and ideology of the Deobandis from the geographic dispersal of this school. Here too, the potential '*ulamâ*' originate from low-income families with a rural background and from landless peasants. Only one-third originate from religious families.

The Ahl-e Hadith candidates for graduation are recruited from districts which are centres of trade with a high degree of urbanization. Like the Shia, the Ahl-e Hadith remain limited to small areas in the country, outside of which there are hardly any representatives of these schools of thought. In Baluchistan and in the NWFP there are only few DM of these schools. No candidates for graduation originate from these areas.

The main areas where the Shia DM are located in two regions, from where most of the candidates for graduation originate are: the northern areas, especially Baltistan and Gilgit (Nagir) and the Sargodha Division in Punjab. Their examinees also originate from families with peasant background and little ownership of land.[80] This is especially true of the candidates from the northern areas. Thus, the different schools of thought "divide" Pakistan among themselves.

The number of members or affiliates differ with the different schools of thought. The Deobandi school of thought is by far the largest; it is also the most evenly spread across the provinces of the country. Since the completion of the Karakorum Highway they are able to extend their sphere of influence further into the northern areas,[81] not infrequently causing serious conflicts with the Brelwis, Ahl-e Hadith and Shia. The second largest school of thought is that of the Brelwis who are limited to the Punjab though slowly gaining ground in Sindh over the last few years. Third in importance are the Shia. Estimates of Shia affiliation vary between 5 per cent and 25 per cent of the total Pakistani population, depending on the source of information.[82]

The Ahl-e Hadith has been least subject to external un-Islamic influences. It attracted few affiliates within the cultural melting pot of Pakistan, as it was predominantly the urban strata of the society who had a tendency to follow the "fundamentalist" approach of the Ahl-e Hadith.

The low number is due not least to the elitist character of the Ahl-e Hadith, alienating the masses rather than attracting them. Furthermore, this school of thought leaves little room for the rites and rituals which are so important in Pakistan in representing the ways of Islam. They have, however, gained in influence in the course of the Islamization process.

Basically, the candidates for graduation originate from the so called "backward" areas, hardly touched by modernization, and marked by the expropriation of small peasants. The resulting migration to urbanized centres, such as Karachi, reflects an unbalanced policy of Islamabad.

Lastly, it is necessary to point out the phenomenon of the drop-outs. As the analysis of the areas of origin and of the social background of the candidates for graduation illustrates, they predominantly belong to the traditionalist part of the society. From the point of view of the colonial sector, they represent a "negative elite" dependent on the autochthonous system of education due to the lack of opportunities for schooling and professional training. Frequently, the candidates for graduation are former students of the formal system of education, in which they went through primary school.[83] Many of them may therefore be considered to be drop-outs. This aspect is examined in more detail below.

In scholarly inquiries poverty is listed as the main cause for the phenomenon of drop-out. At the primary level of education, this is seen as a lack of cooperation between parents and teachers and frequently in the poor treatment of the children by teachers. The economic incapacity of the parents to finance the attendance of the child in school and at the same time to sacrifice the potential labour contribution by the child leads to an early breaking off of the child's schooling. This is true of about 50 per cent of such cases.

At the secondary level of education, the main reasons given for dropping out are similar: lack of interest by the parents due to their own illiteracy, poverty, work in the fields, problems within the family, lack of cooperation between the teachers and the students as well as the parents' wish that their children should only acquire certain culturally recognized values. Other reasons may be the students' fear of teachers, the fear of failing, the incompetence and absenteeism of teachers, overcrowded classes, lack of financial support for poor children, corporal punishment, lack of a pedagogical concept in schools, an irrelevant curriculum, migration to the Middle East, political instability and poor health due to malnutrition as well as the dissolutuion of the traditional systems of order.[84]

The English language, being an alien element in the traditional rural society, is the largest obstacle, which makes it difficult for children to continue in a formal school at the secondary level.

The statistical survey by Khan *et al.* arrives at the following results: 12.3 per cent to 26 per cent of the students are not promoted to the second grade, with a drop-out rate in the primary stage (grades I to V) of more than 50 per cent.[85]

As the drop-outs constitute a substantial part of the Pakistani society[86] the question is what are the other options of further education open for them and in which sectors are they likely to find a job. They continue their education mostly in the religious schools and the DM serve as a catchment area for drop-outs.

The economic poverty, cultural constrains and the dissolution of traditional patterns of order were often decisive for the phenomenon of dropping out. The DM, in contrast, are places of education which accept students without any fees (for the school, books, uniforms, tuition, etc.).

They not only guarantee board and lodging but even sometimes a small monthly allowance. At the same time, the curricula of the DM are tailored to their special needs. The medium of instruction of the small religious schools is adapted to the local or regional surroundings. The transmission of knowledge is therefore more effective as it is more immediate. With Urdu, a language spoken in Pakistan only by a part of the population,[87] the transmission of knowledge is achieved only indirectly.[88]

In fact many interviews[89] have shown that about 50 per cent of the boarding students of the DM formerly attended the primary stage of the formal education system. Due to poverty these students had to leave this system; their parents were not in a position to finance their schooling. On the other hand, they could not be put to work due to small holdings of land. In other cases the formal education was not consistent with the cultural attitudes of the parents, and the children were made to change over to the DM after passing the primary stage. Frequently, the parents sent their children to a madrasah because they had taken a vow that their child should attend a DM if a certain happening should materialize.

With the reform of the curriculum and the extension in the duration of the DM education from eight to sixteen years, parts of the formal primary education were incorporated into the DM. If the poorer strata of society affiliated to the traditional sector prefer the madrasah with its sixteen-year curriculum from the very beginning, this education could be established with an equal standing next to the formal education system.

As only very few students wish to attend a madrasah due to family tradition and even fewer of them wish to become a religious scholar[90] the

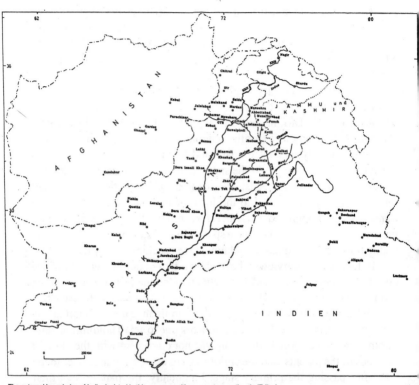

The external boundaries of India depicted in this map are neither correct nor authentic (Editor).

MAP 2: AREAS OF ORIGIN OF THE *MAWLÂNÂS*
(Drawn according to *The Times World-Atlas*, 1983)

usually social and economic causes favour or even necessitate the attendance in a madrasah. The drop-outs thus provide the DM with a large portion of their students.

It would be most revealing to inquire into the success of drop-outs in the DM and to find out how many actually become *mawlânâs*. The same is true of an inquiry into the drop-outs of the DM. One could establish the rate of *mawlânâs* having failed in the formal educational system. Such an inquiry is, however, not possible here as the poor data on the candidates for graduation and on the drop-outs as well as the meagre information on regional socio-economic conditions presently do not permit such an investigation.[91] We may, however, conclude that the declassification of the DM as schools for the poor and stranded, i.e. for the "marginalized" does not make this education an especially attractive one in the eyes of the modern sector. For a long time it was acceptable only for the lower strata within the social hierarchy.[92] This perception may, however, undergo a change under the new conditions created by the Zia administration.

NOTES

1. The candidates for graduation are generally young bachelor males between 20 and 27 years of age, preparing for the *dawrah-hadîth* examination (M.A. since 1981). The larger number of students passing the *mawqûf* stage (B.A. since 1981) has not been taken into consideration here.
2. The numbers differ partly due to insufficient book-keeping.
3. This is plausible as the Jâmi'ah al-Muntazar was registered only in 1983.
4. On the change of the northern areas due to the Karakorum Highway cf. Hermann Kreutzmann, "Die Talschaft Hunza (Northern Areas of Pakistan): Wandel der Austauschbeziehungen unter Einfluß des Karakorum Highway", in *Die Erde*, vol. 118, 1987, pp. 37-53.
5. Arbab Afridi Khan, *Manuscript*, op.cit., no pagination.
6. Many teachers are paid by the Saudi Government, who also offers free higher education in Saudi Arabia to the graduates of the Wafâq of the Ahl-e Hadith, with the prospect of a job either there or in some other Islamic country; for this information author is grateful to Muhammad Sarwar, Centre for South Asian Studies, University of Punjab, who had pointed this out in his studies on the DM of the NWFP. Afridi too had come to the same conclusions (interview with author, August 1987).
7. The year 1977 had been marked by internal political upheavals and only the Brelwis had presented themselves for graduation.
8. One has to keep in mind the exceptional situation in 1977 (when only the Tanzîm conducted final examinations), distorting the projected numbers.
9. This is based on the assumption that every village has at least one local religious scholar (*mullâ*).

10. The Zia administration had already been in existence for 11 years.

11. In the beginning of the fifties, Bhandaranaike had been able to take advantage of the Buddhist monks as catalysts for his victory in the elections and for his policies, with his campaign of indigenization (*Sinhala only*; 1953-56). Subsequent to this and parallel to the traditionalization of Sri Lankan politics, the number of students in the monasteries swelled. This was to have considerable political consequences. Bhandaranaike was not able to meet the expectations and thus disappointed the monks who were increasingly politicized and radicalized. Finally, a *bhikkhu* (Buddhist monk) assassinated Bhandaranaike in 1959. Cf. Urmila Phadnis, *Religion and Politics in Sri Lanka*, London, 1976, pp. 246-276; "Bhikkhu Pressure Groups and the Politics of Language", James Jupp, *Sri Lanka, Third World Democracy*, London, 1978; Kumari Jayawardena, "Ethnic Consciousness in Sri Lanka: Continuity and Change", in *Sri Lanka: The Ethnic Conflict*, ed. by Committee for Rational Development, New Delhi, 1984, pp. 160-173. For further hints I am grateful to Michael Roberts in Heidelberg (May 1987). On the recent history of Sri Lanka with a more political point of view cf. Thomas Prinz, "Die Geschichte der United National Party in Sri Lanka" (working title), Heidelberg (under preparation).

12. The radical forces are recruited from the traditional sector and from the sector oriented towards it, the Intermediary Sector I; they are socially rejected for their radicalization, especially by those who dispose of a latent readiness to de-traditionalize their areas of reproduction, i.e. persons belonging to the Intermediary Sector II.

13. The analysis is based on the data from the registers of the DM umbrella organizations of different years. It relies on photocopies of manually written, sometimes hardly readable documents. The evaluation of the data is done with the help of computerized statistical programmes.

14. With 280, 173, 394, 297 and 933 entries respectively.

15. The numbers sometimes differ from the data in Table 35 (2,166 examinees instead of 2,077). This is due to the incomplete access to the register. Thus, there were some minor differences in the analysis of data, without however, affecting the basic validity of the statements.

16. 40.9 per cent (850) out of 2,077; cf. also Diagram 4.

17. Cf. observations on migration below.

18. This is also evident from their large proportion in the total number of students in the DM of the NWFP (approximately 9 per cent); on the problem of Afghanistan cf. chapter VI.

19. 179 entries for 1963, 396 entries for 1974 and 997 entries for 1984 have been related to the respective numbers of inhabitants as taken from the census data of 1961, 1972 and 1982. We have received approximated statements on the number of candidates for graduation per 10,000 inhabitants.

20. About 100 entries could not be identified due to missing or unreadable photocopies. We may, however, suppose that the largest part of this data refers to the Peshawar DM

21. Appendix C, Table 46: Districts of graduation of the Deobandis (1963, 1965, 1974, 1975 and 1984).

22. Cf. important schools of graduation, and Dâr al-'Ulûm Haqqâniyyah, chapter VI.

23. Montstuart Elphinstone, *An Account of the Kingdom of Caboul and its Dependencies in Persia, Tartary, and India*, Graz, 1969 (first ed. 1815), vol. 2, p. 189.

24. Ibid., p. 216.

25. On the back cover of many issues of *al-Haq* one may often read: "KPT (Karachi Port Trust), the national port wants to support the economy by all means. KPT, in service of commerce and of the economy, etc." (translated from Urdu) or "On the High Crest of development with Commitment to Progress and Service KPT's major Programmes for Modernization and Development... KPT's accelerated efforts for meeting economic resurgence in the country, and the Government's future target for increased exports, Karachi Port, Gateway to Pakistan". Frequently, these are enriched with verses from the Koran: "Oh Prophet! Lo! We have sent thee as a witness and bringer of good tidings. And as a summoner unto Allah by His permission and as a lamp that giveth light" (sura 33/45-46).

26. 60.2 per cent of the emigrants from the NWFP (369,676, or 35 per cent of all the immigrants to Sindh), almost 7,000 from the FATA and 631,578 emigrants from the Punjab settled in Sindh, mostly in Karachi. From Sindh, on the other hand, not even 100,000 migrated to Punjab and only 16,135 went to the NWFP (data from different census reports of the Pakistan Population Census Report 1982).

27. Cf. Olaf Caroe, *The Pathans, 550 B.C. – A.D. 1957*, with an epilogue on Russia, Oxford, 1984, p. 19.

28. Mention may also be made of the Lahori Jâmi'ah Ashrafiyyah with 96 candidates (4.6 per cent), the Jâmi'ah al-'Ulûm al-Islâmiyyah in Karachi with 82 (4 per cent), the Mirâj al-'Ulûm in Bannu with 81 candidates (3.9 per cent) and the Dâr al-'ulûm Sarhad in Peshawar with 66 (3.2 per cent) candidates. These numbers refer exclusively to the five years under consideration here.

29. Thus, in 1963 the students from Mardan and Afghanistan preferred to attend the Jâmi'ah al-Islâmiyyah in Peshawar, while those from Dir and also from Mardan attended the Dâr al-'Ulûm Haqqâniyyah. The DM in Karachi, in contrast, took students from abroad, not only from Bangladesh, India and Iran, but also from the Sindhi hinterland. Only very few students from the NWFP graduated in Karachi.

In 1965 the candidates for graduation of the Dâr al-'Ulûm Haqqâniyyah came predominantly from the districts of Dir, Swat and Mardan, while the Peshawari students graduated from the Dâr al-'Ulûm Islamiyyah. The only madrasah in Karachi (Madrasah al-'Arabiyyah al-Islâmiyyah) presented only 18 candidates from abroad, Sindh and Mansehra.

In 1974 the Dâr al-'Ulûm Haqqâniyyah led with 127 examinees of whom many came from Afghanistan, Bannu, D.I. Khan, Mansehra, Peshawar, Mardan and Dir, while the Chitrali candidates presented themselves for graduation in the Dâr al-'Ulûm Sarhad. The two Karachi schools (Jâmi'ah Fârûqiyyah and Madrasah al-'Arabiyyah al-Islâmiyyah) had a large number of students from the northern frontier province (30 out of a total of 53) but only one from Peshawar.

In 1975 the two Karachi schools had only candidates from Swat, Occupied Kashmir, Baluchistan and from abroad.

In 1984 the DM in Karachi examined 224 candidates with the Jâmi'ah Fârûqiyyah and the Jâmi'ah al-'Ulûm al-Islâmiyyah. Most of them came either from Mansehra, Karachi or from abroad. Among the foreign students there were three Afghans. Of the 29 students from Mansehra, 27 were graduated from the Jâmi'ah al-'Ulûm al-Islâmiyyah.

The increase in candidates for graduation in Karachi becomes evident when considering the following data: in 1981 there were 111 candidates, in 1983, 220 and in 1984, 224 students were examined in Karachi. There were, however, no examinees from Peshawar.

30. There were 38 Afghan students out of a total of about 2,000 candidates for graduation.

31. The titles are specified as follows: *1. al-hâj, 2. hâjjî, 3. hâfiz, 4. qârî, 5. imâm, 6. khalîfa, 7. pîr, 8. ghâzî, 9. hakîm, 10. mawlânâ, 11. muftî, 12. sayyid, 13. shâh, 14. sharîf, 15. hadrat. 16. shaikh, 17. sâhib, 18. qâdî, 19. beg, 20. choudhrî, 21. mîr, 22. malik, 23. miyân, 24. mîrza.*

32. Cf. Appendix D, Table 47: Titles of fathers of Deobandi candidates for graduation in selected years (1963, 1965, 1974, 1975 and 1984).

33. According to a Hadith there is no genealogy in Islam (cf. Olivier Roy, *Islam and Resistance in Afghanistan*, p. 59. On the problem of the *Khân* see further below). This is why they are not mentioned in the registers either.

The more precise localization of the potential '*ulamâ*' down to the tehsil level makes it possible to undertake an ethnic classification. Thus among the Deobandi candidates the dominating tribes may be those of the *Bannuchi* (Bannu), *Marwat* (Lakki Marwat) and *Waziri* (Waziristan), *Daudzai* and *Safi* [Peshawar and Bajor on the *Safis* cf. also J.H.P. Evans-von Krbek, "The social structure and organization of a Pakhtun-speaking community in Afghanistan", Department of Anthropology, University of Durham, 1977 (unpublished)], *Gadun* (Mansehra, Hazara, Mardan), *Khattak* (Nowsherah), *Muhammadzai* and *Mundar Yusuf Zai* (Charsadda, Mardan), *Kundi, Lohani* and *Bhatini* (Tank), *Daur* (Miran Shah), *Babar* and *Khetiran* (DIK), *Mian Khel* and *Zamarai* (Kulachi) and *Muhammad Zai* (Swabi) [specification of the tribes according to Lt. Col. Muhammad Ihsan Allah (Retd.)], *Pashtûn Qabâ'il*, Lahore, 1984 (Urdu) and Olaf Caroe, *The Pathans*, pp. 15-24, and the map: "Tribal Locations of the Pathans", in O. Caroe, op.cit.

34. 19 out of 24 titles; cf. above.

35. The title of *mawlânâ* usually refers to a person having enjoyed a formal

religious education (sometimes a *Sûfî*), a person who therefore is an '*âlim* and generally belongs to a particular school of thought. He is thus set into a larger religious institutional context. The title of *mullâ*, in contrast, nowadays refers to a lower grade of religious scholar belonging to a village. He is usually economically and socially dependent on the villagers' contributions. Both, *mullâ* and '*âlim*, along with other religious dignitaries, form a professional group. The distinction between a "professional group" and a "clan" is of special significance in the tribal areas. The "professionals" do not belong to the "clan" and therefore are considered to be outsiders. Only those religious dignitaries possessing *barakah* (i.e. *sayyid*, *shâh*, *miyân* and *pîr*), enjoy an elevated status within the tribal society (cf. Olivier Roy, *Islam and Resistance*, pp. 23ff). The tribal law (*Pashtûnwalî*) in these areas is of special relevance, presumably giving little room to the Shari'a. Therefore, Roy argues, a *Khân* or his descendant would never undergo a religious education (cf. Roy, op.cit., p. 35). Outside the tribal areas, the *mullâ* and the *mawlânâ* enjoy the highest respect; they monopolize the rites of passage. Frequently they are the only ones with knowledge of reading and writing and of the Islamic jurisprudence.

36. Appendix C, Diagram 5: "Titles of fathers classified by groups".

37. This policy has increasingly enabled the well-to-do Pakistanis to undertake the pilgrimage to Mecca.

38. The other titles are not dealt with here as their numbers are insignificant.

39. Nine came from Karachi, seven from Muzaffargarh, fourteen from Multan, eleven from Peshawar and five from Quetta.

40. The *mawlânâs* of the NWFP mostly come from the districts of Peshawar (38), Mansehra (30), Mardan (29), followed by Bannu (29), Swat (15) and D.I. Khan (8). The *mawlânâs* of the Punjab come from the districts of Multan (12), Muzaffargarh (8), Bahawalpur and Bahawalnagar (6 each), and from D.G. Khan (5). From Karachi there are 11 and from Zhob 10 candidates for graduation, whose fathers were *mawlânâs*.

41. This is due especially to the fact that the clergy has a long egalitarian tradition in this area.

42. They are called "Arabs" by the local people, a term reflecting the high esteem bestowed on them in the seventies, prior to the emigration to Saudi Arabia.

43. At the district level the descendants of the Prophet are distributed as follows: Bannu 20, Chitral and Dir 19, Peshawar 15, Mansehra 8 and Mardan 5.

44. The title of *hâfiz* here does not necessarily require several years' religious studies.

45. This title implies a negative connotation in Punjab. *Hâfiz* is a person who, due to a mental or physical defect, is not able to earn his living by "normal means" but only by memorizing the Koran and its ornate recitation. The concept of "blind *hâfiz*" (*annâ hâfiz*) stands for a clumsy, helpless man.

46. Olivier Roy, *Islam and Resistance*, pp. 59ff et passim.

47. More than 108 candidates' fathers hold the title of *mawlânâ/maulwî/mullâ*. Only 38 *mawlânâs* from the district of Peshawar sent their sons to attend a madrasah. This suggests an exodus of the *mawlânâ* descendants from districts like Mardan, Mansehra, Swat and Zhob to Peshawar.

48. In 1963 there were 14 different titles; in 1965: 10, in 1974: 12, and in 1975: 13. In 1984 its number increased to 20 different titles.

49. Roy, *Islam and Resistance*, p. 35.

50. Ibid., pp. 23ff.

51. In 1963 there were 32 *Khâns*, in 1965: 20, 1974 already had 44, 1975: 37 and 1984 as many as 101 *Khâns*. The majority came from the Bannu area, the adjoining region of Waziristan (39 *Khâns*) and Peshawar (26).

52. In contrast to the analysis of the data on the Deobandis, the following analysis is undertaken without recourse to computerized programmes due to the small amount of data to be handled.

53. There were 140 fathers holding the title of *mawlânâ,* 59 *miyâns,* 51 *hâfizs,* 78 *hâjjis* and 47 were descendants of the Prophet.

54. For further explanation of the different districts concerning the labour market problems cf. below.

55. Only 1.5 per cent of all Brelwi examinees came from urban areas, such as Pakpattan and Daska (from a respective population of 50,000 and 100,000 inhabitants) estates.

56. Cf. chapter on religious endowments.

57. The founder of the Brelwi movement was, however, a Pakhtun.

58. Roy, *Islam and Resistance*, op.cit.

59. Cf. Saghir Ahmad, *Class and Power in a Punjabi Village*, London, 1977. A literary critique on the feudal situation in Punjab may be located especially in the short stories by Ahmad Nadim Qasimi. Cf. Afkar, *Nadîm nambar,* Karachi, 1975 (Urdu).

60. In scientific literature, frequently the movement under Shah Abd al-Aziz and Shah Ismail Shahid, is put on an equal footing with the Wahhabi movement in Saudi Arabia. On the problem of *Jihâd* in connection with British India cf. Rudolph Peters, *Islam and Colonialism: The Doctrine of Jihad in Modern History*, The Hague,1979, pp. 44-53.

61. With the partition of India in 1947, the *muhâjirîn* flowed into the districts close to the frontier as Montgomery (Sahiwal), Multan, Lyalpur (Faisalabad), Lahore and into the urban centres of Sindh. On the *muhâjirîn* cf. also T.P. Wright (Jr.), "Indian Muslim Refugees in the Politics of Pakistan," in *The Journal of Commonwealth Comparative Politics*, vol. XII, no. 2, July 1974, pp. 189-205 as well as Mohammad Arif Ghayur and J. Henry Korson, "The Effects of Population and Urbanization Growth Rates on the Ethnic Tensions in Pakistan," in Manzooruddin Ahmad, ed., *Contemporary Pakistan*, op.cit., pp. 204-227, esp. pp. 209-220.

62. S. Jamal Malik, "The Luminous Nurani".

63. Interviews in spring 1986 in the Hizb al-Ahnaf, in the Jâmi'ah Madaniyyah, Jâmi'ah Ashrafiyyah, Lahore and in the Jâmi'ah Salafiyyah in Faisalabad.

64. The administrative centre for examinations was relocated in 1980 from the Jâmi'ah Nizâmiyyah Ridwiyyah in Lahore to the Shams al-'Ulûm in Karachi.

65. See chapter VIII.

66. Unfortuantely, data for only these two years was available.

67. Author gathered this information in early summer of 1986 on a journey to Gilgit and Baltistan. There is a separate umbrella organization of the Shia located theie with its centre at Mahdiabad (about two hours by jeep from Skardu). The umbrella organization is not subordinated to the Wafâq of the Shia with its centre in Lahore, even though its chairman graduated there.

    The centre at Mahdiabad is a Waqf donated by a certain al-Haj Shaikh Hasan Mahdiabadi (1920-1985) who then lived in Kuwait, a Waqf of approximately 60 canals, called the Mohammadia Trust (founded in Feb. 1985, shortly before the death of the Sheikh). According to the information by the chairman in 1986, 25 DM with approximately 658 students aged between 10 and 22 were affiliated to the trust as well as another 106 madâris-dîniyyât (primary stage). The library of the Jâmi'ah Muhammadiyyah in Mahdiabad had large supplies of the latest school books from Iran, illustrating its influence.

    The influence of Iran—financial as well as ideological–is also remarkable in the schools in Gilgit. The teachers there received a monthly allowance of Rs. 1,200, and the students Rs. 60 if they passed an annual exam, usually taken in the presence of an Iranian scholar coming to Pakistan especially for this purpose once a year (information on 15.6.1986 in the Dâr al-'Ulûm Jafariyyah, Sikandarabad, Nagir).

    As Tables 34 (A-F) show, this trust will not be able to resist for long the growing attraction of the centre in Lahore. Besides this, students are also explicitly sent from Baltistan to Lahore and to Karachi.

    It is remarkable that the formal system of education in the Northern areas is mainly presided over and financed by the Ismaili community, whose medium of instruction is followed. There are about 120 Diamond Jubilee Schools, most of them for girls, as, according to a saying of the Agha Khan "priority should be given to the education of girls".

68. Even though Peshawar is the Northern centre of the Shiite political movement under the leadership of Arif Hussaini from Parachinar, up to 1985 there was only one religious teacher from Sialkot.

69. This contradicts the statement of Lawrence Ziring, according to whom "Sind contains the largest concentration of Shia Muslims..." Cf. Ziring, *Pakistan: The Enigma*, op.cit., p. 147.

70. This development is enforced especially by the improved infrastructure connecting the Northern areas since the opening of the Karakorum Highway.

71. Even the Ahl-e Hadith seem to have accepted a compromise when spreading their views. Thus, an application for registration (Reg. no. 1346 vom 8.3.1986) of the "Jamia Masjid Usmania Ahle Hadees" in Karachi 41, Orangi Town, Sector 11-E, reads that "*dhikr Allâh*" (meditative exercises of the *murîdî* and *pîrs)* are permitted, "*milâd al-nabî*" (birthday of the Prophet) will be celebrated and Hanafi regulations will be followed. All this is in contrast to their original ideas. This means that a strict implementation of ideological or theological views is not always possible. Frequently, the different schools of thought intermingle with each other.

72. Unfortunately, the data was not available in a complete form and access to the data was difficult due to "security measures". Nevertheless, some results can be presented.

73. The *Chaks* offer very little arable land and thus do not permit any traditional craftsmanship. In the times of the British they had served as administrative cells for the irrigation system of the cotton plantations. Today, there are landless peasants and labourers working for daily wages there. Cf. the contribution by Klaus Dettmann, "Agrarkolonisation im Rahmen von Kanalbewässerungsprojekten am Beispiel des Fünfstromlandes", in J. Hagedorn *et al.*, ed., op.cit., pp. 179-191. On further bibliographical data cf. chapter 3 of author's Masters Thesis, "Al- Mashraqi und die Khaksars".

74. Due to the incomplete data this percentage is only an approximation.

75. Fadl-e Haq Thekedar (the epithet *Thekedar* means entrepreneur) was not a *mawlânâ* in the accepted sense as he neither enjoyed any religious education nor was he a teacher in a madrasah. However, he preached regularly on Fridays.

76. According to some observers of the political scene in Lahore, the Jama'at-e Islami has been increasingly losing ground in this competition. The attempt on the life of the representative of the Ahl-e Hadith, Zuhur Illahi, in the summer of 1987 is said to reflect this competitive situation.

77. Large landholdings and cult of saints seem to be complementary to each other, as the latter legitimizes the feudal situation.

78. Before 1947 in the Punjab of today Pakistan had only 31 DM under the umbrella of the Brelwis (cf. *Ahmad I*, passim). Multan had 5 DM, Sahiwal and D. G. Khan 2 DM each and R. Y. Khan had 4 DM. Prior to the partition of India the Brelwis had two central DM in Lahore: the Dâr al-'Ulûm Jâmi'ah Nu'mâniyyah, established in 1887 and the Dâr al-'Ulûm Hizb al-Ahnâf, established in 1926. Both DM tried to broaden the area of influence of the Brelwis (cf. *Ahmad I*, pp. 447-450 and pp. 453-455).

79. This is also illustrated by the fact that leading Brelwi *'ulamâ'* and *muftîs* came from India, with almost no exception, mostly from the region around Muradabad. Mufti Abd al-Qaiyyum Hazarwi, chairman of the Tanzîm al-Madâris and leader of the Jâmi'ah Nizâmiyyah Ridwiyyah in Lahore, is an exception.

80. This is true with the exception of a few very influential Shiite bureaucrats and functionaries in industry and the media.

81. This is done especially with the help of the Tablîghî Jamâ'at, which is a branch of this school located in Raiwind, near Lahore.
82. Their proportion is about 15 per cent according to author's own estimates.
83. Cf. *Sargodha Report* of September 28, 1978, Islamabad (mimeo), p. 11.
84. The indicators applied here have been developed by the representatives of the modern sector of the society.
85. S.R. Khan, N. Mahmood and R. Siddiqui, "An Analysis of the School-level Enrolment, Drop-outs and Output in Pakistan, 1970/71, 1982/83" Islamabad, 1984. Mimeograph. The results are based on aggregated data of the Statistics Division.

    The rates of drop-outs differ from province to province: Baluchistan "had the most discouraging overall position on an absolute level . . .", while the "NWFP revealed the largest differentials by gender", i.e. the drop-out rates among girls were higher than those among boys (op.cit., p. 52). In Sindh, however, the rate of drop-outs was lower in the primary stage than in other provinces (op.cit., pp. 25f). This may be due to the fact that Sindh had—and obviously still has—the tradition to guarantee education to girls as well (cf. Sayyid Muhammad Salim, op.cit., p. 187). This is, however, not the place to discuss the specific aspects of different cultures which are responsible for the attendance of schools generally and by girls specifically. We may take it for granted that cultural factors have a strong influence on school attendance. Also, the economic situation of the family, which may permit or hinder the attendance in a formal school, has to be kept in mind.
86. As has been elaborated by Khan *et al.*
87. Only 7.6 per cent of all Pakistani households are Urdu-speaking (cf. *Population Census 1981, Pakistan*, Islamabad, 1984, p. 18). On the history of Urdu cf. Masud Husain Khan, Urdu, in Th.A. Seboek, "Current Trends in Linguistics", vol. 5, *Linguistics in South Asia*, Mouton, 1969, pp. 277-283. On the political role of Urdu in Pakistan cf. the contribution by Mohammed Arif Ghayur and J. Henry Korson, "The Effects of Population and Urbanization Growth Rates on the Ethnic Tensions in Pakistan", in Manzooruddin Ahmad, ed., *Contemporary Pakistan*, op.cit., pp. 204-227 and Mohammad Waseem, *Pakistan under Martial Law, 1977-1985*, Lahore, 1987, pp. 227-234.
88. Its character as "lingua franca" as well as its origin outside of the frontiers of today's Pakistan may be considered as the main reasons for the meagre dissemination of Urdu. Nevertheless Urdu is closer to the rural population, especially in Punjab and in Sindh than the colonial language which is still widespread in institutions of education and in the administration.
89. Interviews with open, non-standardized questions in Dâr al-'Ulûm Haqqâniyyah, Akora Khattak, Peshawar, in Dâr al-'Ulûm Jâmi'ah Na'îmiyyah, Garhi Shahu, Lahore, in Dâr al-'Ulûm Taqwiyyat al-Islâm, Shish Mahall Rd., Lahore, in the Jâmi'ah Ashrafiyyah, Ferozpur Rd., Lahore, in the Jâmi'ah Madaniyyah, Karimpark, Lahore, in the Madrasah Nusrat al-Haq, Nisbat Rd., Lahore, in the Jâmi'ah Ashrafiyyah, Nila

Gunbat, Lahore, in the Madrasah ʿAzîziyyah Hanafiyyah, Sadr Bazar, Lahore, in the Jâmiʿah Nizâmiyyah Ridwiyyah, Lahori Gate, Lahore, in the Jâmiʿah al-Muntazar, Model Town, Lahore, in the Jâmiʿah Salafiyyah, Faisalabad and in the Dâr al-ʿUlûm Jaʿfariyyah, Sikandarabad, Nagir in 1985/86.

90. Cf. the evaluation of the social background of the candidates for graduation.
91. It remains to be seen whether the reform of and official support for the DM is able to effectively counteract the problem of drop-outs.
92. There were similar conclusions in the contributions to the seminar on "Traditional forms of Education within a Diversified Educational Field: The case of Coranic Schools", Dec. 10-12, 1984, Paris (under the auspices of the UNESCO).

CHAPTER VIII

THE PROBLEM OF
THE LABOUR MARKET

The previous analysis of the districts of origin and social surroundings of the candidates for graduation and of the spatial distribution of the DM has shown that the various schools of thought have their strongholds in different parts of the country. The socio-economic characteristics of some districts have been pointed out. The frequently mentioned problems in the labour market resulting from the increasing numbers of 'ulamâ' in the context of the socio-economic conditions of the respective areas of recruitment will now be examined. We assume a significant relation between the (high) number of candidates for graduation of a region and its (low) degree of development.[1] In doing so, we will try to shed light on the problem of the labour market at the national as well as the regional level. The official measures concerned with employment of religious scholars, such as the introduction of the Arabic as a compulsory language, the mosque schools and the LAMEC initiative will also be considered.

THE SOCIO-ECONOMIC CONDITIONS IN THE AREAS OF ORIGIN OF THE GRADUATES

The future 'ulamâ' originate from only a few regions of Pakistan.[2] Also, the Deobandis mostly originate from the regions of the NWFP and from the tribal areas, while the Brelwis, the Ahl-e Hadith and the Shia mostly originate from the Punjab.

THE NWFP AND THE TRIBAL AREAS

Land ownership is well spread in this area; about 80 per cent of the peasants own more than 5 acres each i.e. more than 41 per cent of the land. On an average, each peasant owns 4 acres.[3] The agrarian structure of the NWFP is relatively egalitarian. The reason for this lies in the social structure of the northern frontier province; "... a system of land tenures rooted in tribal equality and so favouring the peasant proprietor...".[4]

By modern standards, the areas of the NWFP, especially Hazara and Bannu, are not only "agriculturally weakly structured" but also have only a poorly developed degree of industrialization, urbanization and education.[5] The exceptions are Peshawar, D.I. Khan, Mardan and Quetta.

The analysis by Khan and Iqbal[6] is of special significance in this analysis. According to them the "most developed" region of the NWFP is Peshawar while Mansehra, Bannu, and D.I. Khan—to name a few of the main districts of recruitment for the 'ulamâ'—are either "moderately" developed or "least developed".[7]

The lack of job opportunities in industry and commerce and low degree of development with a simultaneously high density of population are the main reasons for the exodus from the mountainous regions of the NWFP.[8] "The entire tribal areas" are said to be "least developed".[9]

The tribal areas had been left to themselves between 1947 and 1972 and had not been integrated into the national mainstream. They were an autonomous territory which was not yet completely connected to the world economy and thus still had remains of a subsistence economy. With the takeover by the Bhutto administration, however, these areas were connected to the Central Government. Reacting to the increasingly stronger Soviet influence in Afghanistan, the People's Party (PPP) under Bhutto brought about bureaucratic, economic and infrastructural changes, which were also meant to create new job opportunities.[10]

If we take the rate of migration as an indicator for the degree of development and for the economic profitability of a region, the thesis of Zingel may be accepted. According to him, the tribal areas and the NWFP were weakly structured and therefore were areas of exodus. The majority of the migrants in fact originate from the NWFP and especially from the tribal areas. These regions have a functioning, traditional, hierarchically structured system of law and order, which may, however, disintegrate in the course of "social and economic changes".

In this context the typology suggested by Charles H. Kennedy can be referred to. According to him one may distinguish between the traditional and modern sectors within the Pakistani agrarian structure. Thus, the area of recruitment of the Deobandis may be considered to be a pronouncedly traditional agrarian area, as, according to Kennedy, it has a low degree of mechanization and a high number of small peasants (especially Bannu, Swat, Zhob, Mansehra and Chitral).[11]

A further cause for the disintegration of the traditional systems of order may be the large number of candidates for graduation, especially from the areas of Bannu, Hazara, Bajor and the area surrounding Peshawar to the south. For these candidates, migration is one of the few opportunities to enter the modern sector of production. This means that either Bhutto's measures did not contribute in a positive way to the solution of the problems in the labour market or that there must have been some other reason behind the large number of migrants, in this case, the clergy. In evaluating the exodus the effects of the "Saur Revolution" of 1978 on this frontier region should not be neglected.

Another reason for migration may be the fact that Bajor and Mohmand are populated by the tribe of the *Sâfîs*. This is one of the last tribes converted to Islam "and for that reason [they] are among the most fruitful in the production of fervent exponents of the faith, even in these latter days". They provide many students of theology.[12] The "religiousness" of a tribe together with its shared frontiers with Afghanistan may be a reason for the large number of religious students flowing into the urban centres. Even if this does not totally negate the direct relation between the lack of job opportunities and a high number of religious scholars it would certainly challenge this correlation. On the other hand, the limited prospect for landed property for the descendants frequently causes the majority of the people settled there to designate at least one of their sons to the profession of an Islamic scholar.[13]

The Agrarian Punjab

In the Punjab, ownership of landed property differs from that of the NWFP, especially in the areas of the so called canal colonies, Multan, Sahiwal and Faisalabad—a region where prior to partition Sikh feudal lords and peasants used to live. The migratory movement of 1947 led to a redistribution of the land and of property. The refugees from India (*muhâjirîn*) settled on the land in the canal colonies,[14] soon resulting in an overpopulation of these areas. It was only in 1954 that landed property in Pakistan was distributed according to the old possessions of the *muhâjirîn*. Due to the limited access to land and the large peasant population, the majority of the peasants had to sell their labour. In the course of an increasing modernization of the farming sector labour-intensive agriculture was substituted by the feudal lords in favour of modern technology. This resulted in further loss of jobs and in a rural exodus.[15] This development suited the feudal lords who wished to extend their political power.[16] This was reinforced by the "green revolution" pushing the small and landless peasants increasingly into the urban areas as they were more and more marginalized in the rural areas.[17]

The agrarian structure in the Punjab reveals the trends of migration and the concentration of the candidates for graduation in certain areas. The development of the Punjabi agriculture is described below.[18]

In the seventies, the Punjab witnessed an increase in the output of agricultural produce, especially in the districts of Mianwali, D.G. Khan and Muzaffargarh (western region), mostly in cash crops.[19] This was due to the high input of fertilizers and irrigation, as well as the increase in the cultivated area. Landed property was more concentrated here, the average farm was larger. In contrast, the districts of Faisalabad, Sahiwal and Multan (central region) as well as Sialkot, Lahore, Rawalpindi and Jhelum had the lowest concentration of landed property. Nevertheless, the number of peasants had increased in all the districts of the Punjab. This reflects the accumulation of landed property among the small peasants, and a reduction in the "top-concentration", resulting again in an increase of the "medium-size holdings" (12.5 acres to 25 acres).[20] Also many of the feudal landlords with more than 150 acres in all districts of the Punjab[21] cultivated their land themselves. As the access to land for cultivation became increasingly difficult for the marginalized and the small peasants,[22] they in turn rented out land or leased it to the medium and large landowners, i.e. to the groups profiting from the official policies.[23]

The following factors contributed to the rise of poverty in the rural areas:

1.   increase in concentration of land among the feudal lords;
2.   increased cultivation of the land by the large landowners them-selves;
3.   increase in areas under cultivation with the simultaneous incentives to large landowners;
4.   increased intensity of capital in agriculture;
5.   the land reforms were not carried out consistently;
6.   an increased division of the land; and
7.   the increase of marginalized peasants and small peasants.

Seen in the light of these facts, one observes that the Brelwis originate from areas in which marginalized peasants and small peasants lease out their land to medium and large landowners and in which there is a high degree of modernization and a progressive concentration of ownership. In their own districts, the marginalized and the small peasants have no access to more land. They have little opportunity to improve their material condition. This is consistent with the typology of Kennedy,[24] according to which the candidates for graduation of the Brelwis and of the Ahl-e Hadith were to be looked for in districts with a high degree of modernization. This also explains the willingness for reform among the representatives of the Tanzîm al-Madâris when it comes to normative, i.e. curricular innovations.[25]

The districts populated by the Shia candidates for graduation, Sargodha and Jhang, seem to be structured similarly to the areas of recruitment of the Deobandis.[26]

INDUSTRY IN THE PUNJAB

According to the indicators of Zingel, Pasha and Hasan[27] the districts of origin of the Brelwis are mostly "industrial districts",[28] which may be considered relatively well developed.[29] The districts of Sahiwal and Multan are neither marked by any signs of "underdevelopment" in the industrial sector nor are there large number of marginalized peasants from whom the candidates for graduation mainly originate. This contradicts the correlation between a low standard of development and a high number of mawlânâs.

More and more students receive a formal education to become mawlânâs. This points to the fact that the "areas labelled districts of industry" do not provide sufficient jobs for the regional population and that the profession of the clergy is not a redundant one.

When applying the criteria of Khan and Iqbal, we arrive at similar conclusions.[30] According to them, the "most developed" districts are located in the central and eastern parts of the Punjab,[31] while Multan, Sargodha, Mianwali, and the northern Punjab are "moderately" developed.[32]

As the most urbanized group, the school of thought of the Ahl-e Hadith is located in those regions, which are characterized by large estates and good access to the regional and supra-regional markets (or by transsectoral trade). They are located in the so called "relatively developed"[33] or "most developed"[34] districts. There has, therefore, been hardly any migration of these 'ulamâ' to urban centres. One may, however, observe a migration to Saudi Arabia as well as the exodus of Shia candidates for graduation to Qom or to Najaf.

Rural exodus frequently remains the only hope to escape from social and economic misery in the short run. The urban economy is, however, not capable of absorbing the migrants.[35] As a result, a potential of conflict is slowly buliding up; the processions and other forms of protest are now frequent in the large urban centres of Pakistan. The type and manner of the cultural articulation of conflict and its specific solution depends on the degree of integration of the particular sector into a complex society.[36]

QUO VADIS, OH *MULLA*?

Previously, the graduates of the religious schools traditionally worked as religious teachers or as religious scholars in small localities or in urban areas. They generally eked out only a modest living. Earning money had not been a priority for the umbrella organization and for the *mohtamims*. In contrast, they mainly concentrated on their graduates as representatives of their interests, so that they would act as a multiplying factor for their school of thought. At best, a graduate would establish his own religious school. The practice of crafts is not widespread among the *mawlânâs*.

The religious scholar was able to make use of his knowledge about Islam by finding solutions to daily problems, as Islam offers numerous suggestions and rules for different strata of society, thus interweaving the profane and the sacred spheres. In doing so, the clergy held a monopoly, which hardly led to a wealthy life-style.[37] The exceptions are some '*ulamâ*' and saints of shrines who are counted among the richest persons of the nation.

Access to secular institutions had been barred to the clergy due to their lack of knowledge in secular subjects, especially in the field of accounts and English, basic qualifications for higher postings in the bureaucracy. In this they resemble the graduates of the Al-Azhar University in Cairo.

There was no parity between the incomes of the higher '*âlim* in Pakistan and the bureaucrats. The religious scholars employed by the Auqaf Department did not exceed grade 12[38] in spite of their frequent demands for a raise in pay. In 1978, the CII had proposed to adjust the salary for a teacher of oriental languages (graduates of religious schools) to that of a teacher of English.[39] In the beginning of 1979, as part of the process of Islamization, the Ministry of Religious Affairs refixed the salaries of *khatîb*, *imâm* and *mu'adhdhin*. This applied, however, exclusively to those religious scholars affiliated to the Ministry of Religious Affairs, i.e. to the Auqaf Department.[40]

The Shari'a courts in Pakistan do not offer a sufficient number of job opportunities as the Government employs only very few judges every year.[41] Therefore, the '*ulamâ*' frequently have to fall back on the poorly paid job in a mosque, mostly in rural areas. Here, they frequently meet with rejection from the local population who prefer their *own* candidate instead of some '*âlim* allocated to them from outside.

The job opportunities are reduced to the position of a religious scholar in a mosque or the traditional profession of a teacher. The most sought after jobs are of teachers in the Arabic language, for which most graduates are over-qualified. Further job opportunities can only come from formal institutions which employ an *'âlim* as a teacher, much in the same way as does the traditional institution.[42]

There have been similar employment problems for the graduates of the Al-Azhar University in Egypt.[43] Only a very small fraction of the *'âlamiyyah* graduates were accepted in governmental positions.[44]

Due to low salaries, lack of prestige and job opportunities, the *'ulamâ'* are increasingly sending their sons to formal schools, colleges and universities in order to improve their chances. Their studies in the madrasah continue side by side, so as to keep up the tradition and their claims on the religious institutions.[45] The *Azharis* were also forced to modernize their curriculum and to adjust to the new conditions in the labour market, without necessarily improving their economic situation. On the contrary, they were in danger of becoming indebted to the state.[46]

The Zia administration tried to integrate the surplus of *mawlânâs* it created by offering them job opportunities through several measures. The problem of how to integrate the graduates into the working process, which had not been given due attention in the *Halepota Report,* has been recognized only lately.

ARABIC AS AN EMPLOYMENT SCHEME

During the seventies, an attempt was made to win over teachers from the DM. The need arose when the Bhutto administration in its efforts at rapprochement with Arabic and Islamic countries[47] introduced Arabic as an optional subject in grades 6 to 8.[48] Preference was given to teachers qualified as *fâdil 'arabî* and *fâdil dars-e nizâmî*. They were given a posting equivalent to that of teachers in the formal education system.[49]

In the course of the Islamization process, this idea was taken up again and finally, in 1982, Arabic was adopted as a compulsory subject, starting from grade 6. This measure was legitimized from the ideological, religious and purely pragmatic points of view.[50]

According to the National Education Policy (NEP) of 1979 Arabic was given attention because of its connection with the Pakistani ideology of state and with Islam.[51] This view of NEP followed the National Education Conference of 1977 where, besides ideology, pragmatism had been preached as well. This was also pointed out in 1982 by a representative of the Task Force:

A further factor (for learning Arabic–besides its religious character) and one specially relevant to the working class Pakistani, is the economic opportunity represented by the nearby Arabian Gulf.[52]

In order to promote the learning of Arabic, the NEP proposed in 1978 to set up Arabic language centres which were to be coordinated by the Allamah Iqbal Open University (AIOU).[53] According to the NEP, these centres were to be established in those towns from where the majority of the so-called overseas workers were recruited. This meant giving official support to export of manpower. In fact arrangements were made for a "functional course for illiterates, particularly those intending to serve in the Middle East".[54] It seems unlikely that workers, who are not part of the traditional sector would have any inclination to learn Arabic from a *mawlânâ*.

Arab countries, obviously interested in disseminating their language, had declared their readiness to finance the materials for instruction as well as the teaching body (about Rs. 44.32 million): "Arab countries have promised to provide books and reading materials . . . and teachers and arrange their training".[55]

Besides the urge of these states to spread the Arabic language, the CII also proposed to give more weight to this language. This would help secular judges to win access to Islamic sources of law. Since 1977, the CII has insisted on granting the Arabic language the compulsory status from secondary stage onwards.[56]

In order to implement the instruction of Arabic at the national level, several plans were drawn up. The first was to educate a sufficient number of Arabic teachers. This, however, did not prove practicable, so the question arose whether graduates of the DM could be employed for this purpose. In order to do so, the rules of recruitment were amended. However, this was not well received by the bureaucracy:

Reservations were voiced by various officials of the provincial departments of education about recruiting Maulanas for the schools on the suspicion that they would divide the students on the basis of their own preferences for a particular Maktab-i-Fikr.[57]

The AIOU is one of the few institutions responsible for the training of teachers in Arabic. Those admitted to its Arabic Teacher Training Courses were teachers of Arabic from formal schools and colleges.[58]

The demand for teachers of Arabic rose quickly. It is estimated that in 1982 there was a demand for 6,000 teachers in order to introduce the subject on a compulsory basis in Pakistan. There were only 2,500 teachers available at the time.[59] Within four years, the gap (3595 trained teachers) had been filled.[60]

Most teachers of Arabic came from Peshawar, an area with a large number of DM students.[61] To meet the demand for a growing number of graduates from the DM the *mawlânâs* could have been integrated in a meaningful way. But instead of using the existing potential from the DM, the new teachers were recruited from the formal system of education. This deprived the *mawlânâs* of an important job opportunity. As we have seen, the Pakistani bureaucracy has an inclination to support secular manpower as against religious manpower. It does not look as though the *mawlânâs* stand much chance in the future.[62]

Only in the backward areas as in NWFP and in Baluchistan are a large number of DM graduates employed as teachers of Arabic. Thus, the education in the DM continues to be an education system for the poor.

STUDY OF KORAN IN FORMAL INSTITUTIONS

In 1982, the Task Force had proposed to introduce Koran courses in the formal schools.[63] The aim of these Koran courses was to acquaint students and teachers with the principles of Islam by reading the original texts.[64] As the Task Force report found the teaching of Koran in formal schools unsatisfactory, Koran classes were given by graduates of the DM:

... teachers may be had, for both the teaching of Arabic and Islamiyat at the middle level, from among the graduates of the various Deeni Madaris . . . the important thing to note is that the human resources are available. With their specialized training, graduates of Deeni Madaris would make particularly good teachers at this level. Those graduates who have further qualified in the general education stream at the Inter, B.A. or M.A. levels could easily assume the responsibility of teaching in the higher schools and colleges.[65]

Persons with the title of *hâfiz* were to be employed in higher stages of education also.[66] For the first time a serious proposal for the meaningful integration of the surplus DM students was made by employing them in the official programmes. According to a leading functionary of the Deobandi Wafâq al-Madâris, Mufti Anwar Shah, a considerable number of DM graduates were employed as Koran teachers despite the reluctance of the bureaucracy.[67] A systematic integration of the *'ulamâ'* as teachers of Koran has not been achieved to this day. In view of the attitude of the bureaucracy, an adequate integration in the near future seems unlikely.

LAMEC

In the course of Islamization, the widespread illiteracy was to be eradicated. It is one of the foremost duties of a Muslim to make sure that his
fellow beings know how to read and write, so that he may read God's word
in the Arabic original, even if he does not fully understand it. With this in
mind, a literacy drive called the Literacy and Mass Education Campaign
(LAMEC) was launched.[68]

Besides its purely functional aims of teaching how to read and write,
LAMEC was meant to illuminate Islamic values,[69] national history and
culture and to transmit knowledge of productive skills—especially in the
agrarian sector.[70]

Among its other projects, LAMEC developed the Literacy Mosque
Centres in mosques and DM. They were to teach Urdu.[71] An official
supervision and control of the centres at the district level was useful in the
implementation of the scheme.

According to the scheme, 2,000 DM would inaugurate the Iqra
Centres (Centres of reading) in 1984/85. In order to achieve this goal,
LAMEC wrote to 2,500 chairmen of DM.[72] The prerequisites for the
establishment of an Iqra Centre were:

   (1) it should be located in a mosque or in a madrasah;
   (2) there should be two hours of daily instructions;
   (3) an Alim or someone delegated by him should teach;
   (4) adult men were to be taught by male teachers while children and
        women should be taught by elder ladies;
   (5) the teacher would have to know Islamic injunctions and act
        accordingly;
   (6) after a five months course, an examination is to be held by an
        external teacher on the basis of an examination paper supplied
        by LAMEC;
   (7) two groups would be taught in the course of one year;
   (8) LAMEC would receive a monthly report on the basis of a
        prescribed form;
   (9) successful examinees would receive a certificate;
   (10) good students and teachers would receive presents; and
   (11) a class would have a minimum of 20 students.

As the Iqra Centres were controlled by the members of the corresponding Local Zakat Committees *Nâzim-e Salât* groups (these were
installed in 1984, to perform prayers, like a person officially responsible

for maintaining order) to guarantee the cooperation between the LAMEC centres and the DM, the DM increasingly lost their autonomy. The catalogue of prerequisites had opened up one more entry for the state to infiltrate the autonomous supporters of the Islamic culture. As far as the course contents were concerned, a modernization of the curriculum was aimed at. The Local Government, Rural Development Punjab, National Farm Guide Trust of Pakistan supplied the necessary publications for this purpose.

At the end of 1984 LAMEC achieved its first success: within one year, 841 Iqra Centres had been established; however, 80 per cent of them located in the Punjab while in other provinces, such as in Baluchistan, they had not been able to gain a foothold.[73]

One explanation for this may be that the allocation of resources was made in favour of Punjab by the dominant Punjabi bureaucracy, who neglected other provinces. It is, however, also possible that the 'ulamâ' of the other provinces rejected any interference of the Government in their affairs. An integration into the LAMEC initiative would have inevitaby involved a control over the DM. This assumption is backed up by the fact that there are some areas with many Iqra Centres, while in others, there are none at all. Divisions like Lahore, Gujranwala, Multan and Bahawalpur, with many centres have more DM of the Brelwi than of the Deobandi, as well as schools of the Ahl-e Hadith. If, in fact, the consent of the DM chairman was a prerequisite for the establishment of an Iqra Centre one may well suppose that a large number of the Deobandis—and this is especially true of Sindh—refused to give their consent. This may explain the regional concentration of the Iqra Centres.[74]

One may suppose that the DM with an attached Iqra Centre may be also the ones responsible for the "mushroom-growth".[75] The reasons behind the establishment of these centres were financial rather than educational. Furthermore, the LAMEC programme implies a secularization of the religious schools by a functionalist orientation of the curriculum just like the Mosque School Scheme (cf. below). This de-Islamization of autochthonous institutions is hardly in accordance with the aims of its supporters, especially as the Literacy Mosque Centres Programme provides the graduates of the DM with poorly paid positions.[76] Even here students from the formal education system were preferred as teachers.

MOSQUE SCHOOLS

Even the smallest social entities of Islamic culture were to be mobilized in the course of the Islamization process and were to be finally attached to the colonial sector. As a social centre the mosque is one of the most important elements of an Islamic community, and, like the shrine, it is the microcosm of the traditional culture. At all times, the mosque has been the centre for elementary instruction,[77] not infrequently leading to the study of "Islamic sciences". The *maktab* (literally the place of writing) attached to the mosque is oriented towards the memorization of the Koran (*hifz*), a task which takes about four years.[78] Besides this, Islamic rites are studied and practised, stories from the times of the Prophet are told and basic knowledge of arithmetic and writing are transmitted. This may be followed up by two to three years of religious instruction and grammar of the Arabic language.[79] For the mosque schools there seems to be no clear-cut pedagogical concept; the holy act of transmitting knowledge and of adopting knowledge guarantees, however, the unquestioned authority of the teacher. The scope for any initiative by the student therefore is quite reduced.

The authors of the NEP of 1979 agreed that the mosques as institutions of education were able to take up the fight against illiteracy, overcome the problems of the shortage of school buildings and were capable of setting free new energies.

According to this scheme, schools were to be established where few formal schools existed, such as in the rural areas: "Backward areas of the country will be allocated more (mosque) schools".[80] The curricula, however, were not "Islamic", but adjusted to the formal sector, enriched with the reading of the Koran (*nâzirah*).[81] The basic objective was to put up a cheap and effective primary education in the rural areas. Rs. 104.35 million had been allocated for 5,000 mosque schools, i.e. Rs. 21,000 per school.[82] Personnel expenses accounted for the largest share of the project. Each school was to employ one *imâm*[83] and one teacher from the secular education system. In order to make the project attractive for teachers with a Primary Teaching Certificate (PTC) they received a monthly amount of Rs. 528,[84] while the *imâm* only received Rs. 150. It was not always easy to find PTC teachers,[85] as they had to share the ideological affiliation of the respective village or mosque.

The first mosque schools were established in 1982/83. During the following year, the number of newly established schools declined rapidly,[86] as the Central Government had reduced the financial aid.[87] The distribution of funds through the Central Government usually led to an arbitrary location of schools by the Provincial Governments. It is especially remarkable that the number of mosque schools per district is always between 491 and 498,[88] even though the differences in the development in different districts are enormous; Faisalabad, relatively "modernized" and well-connected through its infrastructure, has as many schools as

Bahawalnagar which is barely "modernized" and poorly connected. In Punjab this has resulted in a situation where 25 per cent of these schools are situated in urban areas and 70 per cent in rural areas which already have formal schools. Only 5 per cent of the mosque schools are in those rural areas where primary schools are more than 1 kilometre away from the village.[89]

Areas actually in need of mosque schools were neglected. The mosque school scheme had thus failed in its objectives.

Reasons given by the National Education Council were:

(1) disputes among supporters of different sects;
(2) soiling of mosques by small children;
(3) the prohibition of children to use the main room of the mosques by the *imâm*;
(4) the poor level of the mosque schools;
(5) the comparatively bad living conditions for the teachers;
(6) lack of a summer vacation; and
(7) inadequate education of the inspectors in some provinces.

Therefore, the project according to the National Education Council had to be formalized, the *imâm* was to receive a monthly pay of Rs. 300 and the same fringe benefits as the teachers of the formal education system.[90]

The mosques were a means for the integration and dynamization of the traditional sector.[91] Instead of employing the proposed DM graduates, teachers of the formal education system were recruited. If instead of these teachers thousands of '*ulamâs*' had found places in mosque schools not only would the problem of the different schools of thought have been resolved, each village could have a *mawlânâ*. The rising potential of conflict among the *mawlânâs* in urban centres could have been diverted to the rural areas and so might have been defused.

Considering the fact that about 60,000 mosques in Pakistan are more or less autonomous bodies (an estimate which is rather modest as there are approximately 40,000 villages) and are not subject to any governmental control, it may be most urgent for the Government to take hold of these centres. This control is effected by a strong bureaucratization of the mosques through the Deputy Commissioner and the active control of the backward *mulla* through a secular teacher who is to transmit the values of the national state of Pakistan.[92] The introduction of educated religious scholars might have turned the mosques and mosque schools into important centres of the different schools of religious thought. They would then have been subordinated to an umbrella organization or a religious party.

Under these circumstances the curtailment of job opportunities for religious scholars by the administration is understandable.

The transmission of modern secular values by the curricula of the colonial sector[93] into hitherto untouched areas, induces social change which could bring about far-reaching upheaval. The relatively low priced mosque schools[94] might be able to raise the level of literacy; in the long run, however, this will cause problems: imported curricula give rise to needs which only the elite is able to afford.

THE ARMY AS SAVIOUR?

For the present, the army has turned out to be the "saviour" of the religious scholars. It showed special interest in these scholars and tried to integrate them into the colonial heritage, to be sure only up to a certain degree.

It is not only the newspaper dailies who have recently been calling on the DM graduates to join the army; the monthly magazines of the religious schools also increasingly feature advertisements of the army. These advertisements do not publicize the joining as a simple soldier. Several job opportunities are offered to the *mawlânâs*.[95] The offers cover everything from service as an army medical doctor[96] and P.M.A. Long Course for a Commission in the army[97] or a Junior Commissioned Officer *khatib*[98] to the service as a religious teacher with the Pakistani marines.[99]

The access of *mawlânâs* to the army still seems to be limited. According to military circles, however, the number of graduates from religious schools seems to have increased rapidly over the last eight years.[100] This might lead to new problems within the military, as the majority of the soldiers can be mobilized by Islamic ideas and institutions, especially if their superiors do not abide by the principles of Islam.

In spite of the attempts by the army to offer to religious scholars a new sphere of work, however modest, one may consider this to be inadequate for the economic integration of the clergy; supporters of Islamic traditions will not easily become a part of the colonial sector.

SUMMARY

The bureaucracy has not only always objected against the recognition of the clergy[101] but has also tried to deny them any opportunity to establish themselves in the labour market. By doing so the bureaucratic elite literally took the wind out of the sails of the *mawlânâs*.

In the end, the aim of the official programmes seems to pacify the trouble spots and to control them and, to open up new markets. It is difficult to understand why the clergy has not been integrated into the expanding colonial sector in a more systematic way. By this time, about 20,000 graduates could have been employed in various projects in the course of the Islamization process (12,500 in the mosque schools; 6,000 as teachers of Arabic; 850 as directors or teachers in the Iqra Centres). Instead, the bureaucracy systematically tried to cut down on the job opportunities for religious scholars and to allocate their traditional jobs as teachers to members of the colonial sector or of the intermediary sector. Thus, the *mawlânâs* hardly had a chance to find an acceptable role in the Islamization process.

This policy of marginalization of the *mawlânâs* may well be the intention of the regime. If, in fact, education in the DM were profitable, not only due to its low cost for the students but also for chances to find jobs, these schools would soon be overcrowded. The socially backward masses would send their children to these schools, free of charge and with the prospect of an assured job afterwards. Along with the integration of the traditional sector there would also be participation. The Government has little interest in seeing that this should be the case. The Government therefore prefers mere integration. The '*ulamâ*' for the time being will remain only the ones receiving the usufruct of the Zakat system.[102] In this sense the Tanzîm al-Madâris is quite right to complain in 1985 that the equalization of the degrees of the DM is merely formal, while in reality "nothing has changed".[103]

NOTES

1. When measuring the standard of development we refer to: M.H. Khan and M. Iqbal, "Socio-Economic Indicators in Rural Pakistan: Some Evidence", pp. 93-108 and H.A. Pasha and T. Hasan, "Development Ranking of Districts of Pakistan", in Ijaz Nabi, ed., *The Quality of Life in Pakistan*, pp. 47-92, Lahore, 1986, pp. 47-92. Also, Wolfgang-Peter Zingel, *Die Problematik regionaler Entwicklungsunterschiede in Entwicklungsländern*, Wiesbaden, 1979. These parameters with their background in the theory of modernization are applied here despite some doubts. Unfortunately, till now, parameters with indigenous characteristics have not been developed nor applied in socio-economic studies on Pakistan. The parameters, as they are, nevertheless make it possible to classify the types of districts. We have not undertaken any correlational tests here.
2. As an example, we will consider below the Deobandis.
3. The accumulation of landed property in Punjab and especially in Sindh is

much higher, cf. M.H. Khan, *Underdevelopment and Agrarian Structure in Pakistan*, Lahore, 1985, pp. 73f.

4. Olaf Caroe, *The Pathans,* op.cit., p. 429; further details on the agrarian structure in Dir, Bajor, Swat and Utman Khel may be located in R.O. Christensen, ed., *Report on the Tribes of Dir, Swat and Bajour together with the Utman-Khel and Sam Ranizai*, Peshawar, 1981 (first ed. 1901), pp. 40ff and Akbar S. Ahmed, *Social and Economic Change in the Tribal Areas*, Oxford, 1977, esp. pp. 13ff.

   Elements of a caste-structured society are, however, also evident in these regions, such as in the social organization of the Sayyids, the Swatis and the Gujjars. Cf. M.Z.I. Khan, "Land Tenure System in Mansehra District NWFP Pakistan", Master's Thesis, Department of Anthropology, Quaid-i-Azam University, Islamabad, 1981 and A.K.H. Qazilbash, "Authority and Power Structure in Konsh Valley Distt. Mansehra, NWFP", Master's Thesis, Department of Anthropology, Quaid-i-Azam University, Islamabad, 1981.

5. Zingel, *Problematik,* op.cit., p. 332; similar results cf. Pasha and Hasan, "Development Ranking, etc.", op.cit., p. 70.

6. There are 22 socio-economic indicators concerning the standard of living in rural areas, subdivided into two groups:

   Group A. 1. Possibility of irrigation, 2. Cottage-industries, 3. Drinking water, 4. Electricity, 5. Tractors, 6. Tubewell. Group B. 1. Paved roads, 2. Station, 3. Post-office, 4. Grain market, 5. Fertilizer warehouse, 6. Office of the field assistant, 7. Tehsil-Main office, 8. Police station, 9. Gas-oil pump, 10. Tractors repair facilities, 11. Veterinary hospitals, 12. Hospitals, 13. Banks, 14. Primary schools, 15. Middle schools, and 16. High schools.

   Group A reveals the degree of access to the indicators and is meant to offer information on production and job opportunities in the respective district. Group B reveals the distances from a village of a district to these indicators which have to be covered in order to reach these indicators and to the job opportunities. All indicators are considered to have equal value; cf. M.H. Khan and M. Iqbal, "Socio-Economic Indicators in Rural Pakistan", op.cit., pp. 94f.

7. M.H. Khan and M. Iqbal, op.cit., pp. 102ff.

8. Zingel, *Problematik*, op.cit., p. 354; this area comprises the districts of Chitral, Dir, Swat, Malakand Protected Area, Hazara, Mardan, Peshawar, Kohat and the adjoining tribal areas as well as parts of the D.I. Khan district. Mining areas are also located in the districts of Rawalpindi, Attock and Jhelum, as well as in Quetta, Zhob, Loralai and in North-Kalat and in North-Sibi.

9. Cf. Zingel, op.cit., p. 334; for a microanalysis cf. Herbert Albrecht, *Lebensverhältnisse ländlicher Familien in Westpakistan; Sozialökonomische Schriften zur Agrarentwicklung*, Saarbrücken, 1971.

10. Not only did they construct streets and push ahead electrification and energy supply; they also extended the arable land and increased the production of

the agrarian sector; cf. Caroe, *The Pathans*, op.cit., p. 527ff and A.S. Ahmed, *Social and Economic Change*, op.cit., pp. 53ff and 61-66.

11. Both indicators were applied by Charles H. Kennedy in order to ascertain the degree of "modernity" in the agrarian structure on the district level; cf. Kennedy, "Rural Groups and the Stability of the Zia Regime", in Craig Baxter, ed., *Zia's Pakistan: Politics and Stability in a Frontline State*, Lahore, 1985, pp. 23-46.

12. Cf. Caroe, *The Pathans*, op.cit., pp. 19f and 362, footnote 4 and Lt. Col. Muhammad Ihsan Allah, *Pashtûn Qabâ'il*, op.cit., pp. 98f. For *Sâfîs* in Afghanistan cf. also J.H.P. Evans-von Krbek, "The social structure and organization of a Pakhtun speaking community in Afghanistan", op.cit.(unpublished).

13. This reveals the strong influence of the *Pakhtûnwalî*, the secular Pakhtun habitual law. In Islam, in contrast, the law of inheritance is canonically laid down.

14. True to the motto of one acre land per head.

15. Hamza Alavi, "The Rural Elite and Agricultural Development in Pakistan", in R.D. Stevens and H. Alavi and P.J. Bartocci, eds., *Rural Development in Bangladesh and Pakistan*, Honolulu, 1976, pp. 317-353; pp. 322ff.

16. "The more land that he [the landlord] would bring under his control, the larger was his constituency and the greater his political power"; S.J. Burki, "The Development of Pakistan's Agriculture: An Interdisciplinary Explanation", in R.D. Stevens et al., eds., *Rural Development in Bangladesh and Pakistan*, op.cit., pp. 290-316; here p. 303.

17. This may be considered a result of dependent reproduction: the production of food stuffs for internal use stagnates, while the production of goods for the world market increases. The export-oriented sectors of the national economy (represented here by the large landlords) have easy access to fertilizers, pesticides, seeds, water, credits and official subsidies, while the sector focused on the production of food for personal needs (represented here by small peasants and landless sharecroppers) does not have such opportunities. (One must add here that there is hardly any subsistence economy areas in Pakistan.) Simultaneously the latter is necessary for the economy, as it provides the externally oriented sector and the industry with raw material and cheap labour (cf. Senghaas, *Weltwirtschaftsordnung und Entwicklungspolitik: Plädoyer für Dissoziation*, Frankfurt a.M., 1978, esp. pp. 189-195; In this context, Senghaas uses the term of *Agrarian Paradox*).

18. This is based on the premises made above and in reference to the contribution by M.H. Khan, *Underdevelopment and Agrarian Structure in Pakistan*, op.cit.

19. This shows the dependency from the money markets.

20. This is especially obvious in the districts of Sahiwal, Faisalabad, Multan, Lahore, Mianwali and Muzaffargarh; cf. Khan, *Underdevelopment*, op.cit., pp. 61ff and 92.

21. With the exception of Attock and D.G.Khan.
22. Especially in Sahiwal, Faisalabad and Multan, where most farms are run by landlords. In Sindh, access to land is easier; cf. Khan, *Underdevelopment*, op.cit., p. 97.
23. Ibid., pp. 219-241.
24. Cf. Kennedy, "Rural Groups and the Stability of the Zia Regime", in Craig Baxter, ed., *Zia's Pakistan*, op.cit., pp. 23-46, esp. 32ff.
25. By contrast, the curricular changes undertaken by the Deobandis are less enthusiastic about reform; cf. the curricular discussion in chapter VI.
26. Cf. Kennedy: "Rural Groups and the Stability", op.cit., p. 32ff.
27. Cf. Zingel, *Problematik*, op.cit.; Pasha and Hasan, "Development Ranking", op.cit.
28. This refers mainly to the districts of Sahiwal, Multan and Sargodha.
29. Sargodha (important for the classification of the Shia), Sahiwal and Mianwali are "rather more rurally structured"; cf. Zingel, *Problematik*, op.cit., p. 332.
30. Cf. M.H. Khan and M. Iqbal, *Socio-Economic Indicators in Rural Pakistan: Some Evidence*, op.cit., pp. 94f.
31. Most developed areas are located in the Punjab if we go by the criteria of production and job opportunities as well as by the criteria of distance from the factors of production. While group A (possibilities for the input) includes also the districts of Peshawar, Quetta and some districts of Sindh, those of group B (distance to the indicators) includes the "most developed" districts of Gujrat, Faisalabad, Sialkot and Sahiwal (cf. M.H. Khan and M. Iqbal, *Socio-Economic Indicators*, op.cit., p. 104); cf. also value chapter IV on Zakat.
32. M.H. Khan and M. Iqbal, *Socio-Economic Indicators*, op.cit., pp. 102ff.
33. These terms have been taken from Pasha and Hasan, "Development Ranking", op.cit., p. 70.
34. These terms have been taken from M.H. Khan and M. Iqbal, *Socio-Economic Indicators*, op.cit.
35. In the sometimes highly specialized industry developed skills are a necessity.
36. Cf. the theoretical classification, chapter I.
37. The position of a village-*Mullâ* is very well portrayed in the short story "*Al-Hamd lillâh*" by Ahmad Nadim Qasimi, *Sannatâ*, Lahore, 1959 (Urdu), pp. 133-167.
38. This was equal to the salary of an assistant-in-charge (from Rs. 750 to Rs. 1,550 per month) (cf. Charles H. Kennedy, *Bureaucracy in Pakistan*, Oxford, 1987, p. 11).
39. CII, *Recommendations on the Education System*, op.cit., pp. 36f, which reads: "Their salary should be adjusted to that of a English graduate as prior to the establishment of Pakistan.They are to receive equal treatment in other matters as well".
40. The salary was classified into four grades:
    1. Grade 12 for those who could prove their graduation by one of the four

DM umbrella organizations and thus were *fârigh al-tahsîl*.

2. Grade 9 (Rs. 620 to 1,200 per month; salary of a stenotypist) for those who had graduated in some other madrasah (*farâghat*).

3. Grade 6 (Rs. 540 to 940 per month; salary of an office employee) for those who had had their final examination in some unknown madrasah.

4. Grade 2 and 4 (Rs. 460 to 700 per month and Rs. 500 to 820 per month respectively) for those having reached only the *hifz al-qurân* [as stated in *Jurat* (R) 1.1.1979 (Urdu)].

The students of some listed DM enjoyed the same reduction in public transportation fares as the students of the formal education system. To qualify for a reduction, the student needed an identification card, issued by the corresponding DM.

This regulation was, however, not a new one; under Bhutto the Tanzîm al-Madâris had written to the departments of Auqaf, military, transport as well as to the department of education and had achieved a reduction in public transport fares for their DM students [cf. *Lâhah-e 'aml 1974, Tanzîm al-madâris al-'arabiyyah*, Lahore, 1974, pp. 9 and 11 (Urdu)].

41. In Egypt there is a similar trend. Cf. A. Chris Eccel: *Egypt, Islam and Social Change: Al-Azhar in conflict and accommodation*, Berlin, 1984, pp. 251ff and the chapter "Specialization for the Job Market". Judges of secular courts in any case receive a higher salary than the Shari'a judges.

42. Lately the army have started employing graduates of religious schools as *khatîb* and as *imâm*. This might result in the development of a new alliance between the army and the religious elite (cf. below).

43. There too the monthly salary of an *'alim* was not above that of an official bureaucrat; cf.Eccel, *Egypt, Islam and Social Change*, op.cit., pp. 251ff.

44. Till today, no *'alim* is employed in the federal bureaucracy of Pakistan (cf. Kennedy, *Bureaucracy*, op.cit., p. 135).

45. Thus, Sayyid Ridwi (Hizb al-Ahnaf, Lahore; member of the CII and of the 'Ulamâ' Committee of the PZC), Mufti Abd al-Qaiyyum Hazarwi (Jâmi'ah Nizâmiyyah Ridwiyyah, Lahore; member of the 'Ulamâ' Committee of the PZC) and Mufti Naimi (Jâmi'ah Na'îmiyyah, Lahore; member of the CII) sent their sons to formal schools. As legal heirs of their fathers the sons followed them as *muhtamim* or as *sadr mudarris*, etc. In Egypt it was the same, cf. Eccel, *Egypt, Islam and Social Change*, op.cit., pp. 292 and 314. Or "While still training religious scholars, its graduates now can compete equally with those of the other universities", Derek Hopwood, *Egypt: Politics and Society 1945-1981*, London, 1982, pp. 95-99.

46. Cf. Eccel, op.cit., pp. 230ff and 267ff. The reorganization of *al-Azhar* in 1961 provide for an integration of secular subjects in order to break the influence of the conservative teachers. On the secularization of *al-Azhar*, cf. Hopwood, op.cit., pp. 95-99.

47. There has been a long debate over whether Arabic should be classified as a compulsory subject, as a medium of instruction and even as the national language.

48. This step was justified with reference to Islam being the ideological basis of a state like Pakistan. Its citizens therefore supposedly had a strong affiliation to the Koran and Sunna and kept in close touch with the Arabic world.

49. GoP; Ministry of Education, Curriculum Wing, *Arabic Curriculum*, Islamabad, 1975, p. 20 (Urdu). The curriculum drawn up in 1975 still served as the point of reference for the instruction of Arabic in 1986. The majority of the members of the committee for setting guidelines for the instruction of Arabic did not know Arabic themselves!

50. The pragmatic aspect had already been pointed out by Abul Ala Mawdudi in 1963: Arabic was to be taught in technical institutes, as most Pakistani medical doctors and engineers would like to work in Saudi Arabia and needed to speak Arabic (cf. *PT*, 18.9.63). As many other advocates of Arabic, the ideological argument was only secondary.

51. NEP, 1979, op.cit., p. 48.

52. Yusuf Talal, *Draft chapter on Islamic Education for inclusion in the Report of the President's Task Force on Education*, Islamabad, 1982 (mimeo), p. 8 (hereafter cited as *Draft chapter on Islamic Education*).

53. This institution is comparable to the system of "Volkshochschulen" in the Federal Republic of Germany.

54. Cf. NEP, 1979, op.cit., p. 49, IX and X.

55. Ibid., p. 49, XII and XIII; cf. also numerous "Letters to the editor" in *D*, and *TM*. In the last few years Arabic news is read on TV for a few listeners. The influence of Arabic countries on Pakistan has been dealt with by Feroz Ahmad (cf. Feroz Ahmad, "The New Dependency", etc.). The function of Pakistan as a "super-mercenary" for many Arabic states is especially remarkable.

56. *CII, Recommendations on the Education System*, op.cit., pp. 28f. The intention to enrich the curriculum already overloaded with languages (at present more than 40 per cent of the total teaching time) is evidence of the lack of a well-planned pedagogical strategy. It proves that there is the strong Arabic interest especially from 1977 onwards. Arabic scholars on law and specialists on Islamization had visited CII on a number of occasions.

57. Talal, *Draft chapter on Islamic Education*, op.cit., p. 6. Talal further explained: "These suspicions, however, were proved in the field to be unfounded. Such suspicions should never be allowed to affect the making of educational policy at any level".

58. These teachers were to have command of the Arabic language within 397 hours or in six months (16 hours per week); cf. manuscript of the AIOU on courses of Arabic (mimeo), Islamabad, n.d.

59. Talal, *Draft chapter on Islamic Education*, op.cit., p. 11.

60. Author's calculations on the basis of the manuscript of the AIOU on the courses of Arabic (mimeo), Islamabad, n.d.

61. Ibid.

62. This discriminative policy by the administration is especially evident in the

fact that 20 per cent of the 3,595 teachers of Arabic originate from formal institutions of the Peshawar Division. Those responsible for the selection of primary teachers in the subject "Reading of Koran" are the so-called District Education Officers!

63. Similar proposals had been presented by the CII on March 17, 1982; cf. CII, *Recommendations on the Education System,* op.cit., pp. 51f.

64. Thus, the American Muslim and adviser to the Ministry of Education for religious education held the following view: "Such a course would accustom the student to making direct reference to the Holy Quraan on all matters pertaining to his Deen", Talal, op.cit., p. 5. What is remarkable about this response is its fundamentalist approach.

65. Talal, op.cit., pp. 2f and 6; there one reads: "The fact is, that only a very small percentage of our primary school teachers are themselves able to recite the Quraan properly".

66. The Task Force report reads: ". . . the Government might consider setting aside a certain number of seats in its institutions of higher learning, particularly in Medical and Engineering colleges for qualified students who have memorized the entire Quraan" (Talal, op.cit., p. 4).

67. According to the person in charge of educational matters of the Wafâq al-Madâris al-'Arabiyyah (Mufti Anwar Shah) in 1985 a large part of the approximately 600 teachers for Koran in Baluchistan came from the DM as was the case in NWFP. We have not been in a position to verify these statements.

68. The criteria for literacy was the ability to read a simple text in the national language Urdu or in a regional language. As the name LAMEC indicates, the initiative for its establishment came from the colonial sector of the society.

69. In the sense of a fundamentalism with an integrationist character.

70. See LAMEC, *Literacy: A new thrust,* by Dr. A.R. Chaudhary, Chairman LAMEC, GoP, Islamabad, n. d.

71. LAMEC was responsible for eight programmes. The explanations here concern the programme of reading circles in the mosque schools (cf. LAMEC, *Literacy,* op.cit., pp. 3 and 10). The Literacy Mosque Centres were to satisfy the demand by Zia to make the Koran intelligible to all students and to teach them to read.

72. Cf. LAMEC, *Literacy,* op.cit., p. 17, as well as *TM,* 21.2.85: "Madarasas to promote religious education". The initiative was by LAMEC which had only two (secularist) *'ulamâ'* members. LAMEC proposed to the *'ulamâ'* and *mashâ'ikh* of the DM to teach the students Koran and Hadith in order to take the Islamization ahead. Financial incentives were to support the LAMEC programme. In the programme of establishing Iqra Centres in the DM the *'ulamâ'* received course books for the students, guidelines for the teachers as well as Rs. 250 per month for the teacher who did not necessarily have to be a *mawlânâ* himself.

73. Summary from the "dini madaris projekt", LAMEC of 1984, Urdu, mimeo.

74. Besides these inter-provincial aspects no pattern of distribution for the Iqra Centres can be made out. In the NWFP and in Sindh only those districts have been mobilized for the programme which were easily accessible, such as Peshawar, Hayderabad and Karachi, or those where a sufficient number of conformist forces were available as in Hayderabad.

75. Cf. chapter VI.

76. Only Rs. 250 per month.

77. On the functions of a mosque cf. S.M. Imamiddin, "Mosque as a centre of education in the early Middle Ages", in *Islamic Studies*, vol. 23, no. 3, 1984, pp. 159-170.

78. As the recitation of Koran is a holy act—it is, in fact, God's word which is recited—every incorrect pronunciation is considered a sin.

79. M.A. Quraishi, *Some Aspects of Muslim Education,* Lahore, 1983 (completed in 1970), pp. 14f.

80. NEP, 1979, op.cit., pp. 8f.

81. Ibid. The World Bank, as the main supporter of the scheme, carries the primary responsibility for the secular character of the mosque schools. According to statements of a leading technocrat of the Education Project, Lahore the representatives of the World Bank at first were sceptical about Islam and mosques. It had been clear that the World Bank did not want any "church schools" but emphasized secular education. For pragmatic reasons the Pakistani functionaries therefore stressed that the mosque school scheme only relocated the programme without changing its curricular content and they affirmed that there was no intention of imparting a religious education. The secular character of the mosque schools was thus laid down in advance. A similar tendency of de-Islamization or de-Traditionalization is also evident with the Iqra Centres.

82. NEP, 1979, op.cit., p. 10. This sum was raised to Rs. 400 million in the course of the Special Priority Development Programmes (SPDP).

83. The intention was not to employ a special *imâm* for the purpose but to rely on the local *imâm*.

84. A basic salary of Rs. 315 plus Rs. 150 allowance, and Rs. 63 house rent.

85. The teacher was appointed by the respective District Deputy Commissioner. He also presided over the District Implementation Committee and thus decided on the establishment of schools and mosque schools in his district.

86. Press articles even read: "No mosque school opened last year (1983/84) in Punjab", *Dawn*, 7.6.85, p. 2.

87. Ministry of Education, *Mosque Schools Programme 1982/83: Materials for Supplementaries,* Islamabad, 1985 (mimeo), pp. 3f. As a result, the teachers of the mosque schools did not receive their salary "due to administrative difficulties since five months", thus *NW*, 26.11.83 and *J,* 5.12.83.

88. Ministry of Education, *Mosque Schools Programme 1982/83,* op.cit.

89. Ruhi T. Humairah, *Ta'lîm-e 'âmah mêñ masjid skûl skîm kâ jâ'izah,* Masters Thesis in IER, 1984, no. 2596.

90. National Education Council: *Report of the Meeting of Primary School Teachers and Administrators*, Islamabad, 1984, pp. 18f.

91. Already in the sixties there had been a similar attempt in connection with the modernization policy of the Auqaf Department under Ayub Khan. The intention had been to implement the official ideology with the help of the *mullâ* at the social micro level: "Literacy centres in mosques: The idea is to convert the imams and khatibs to the concept of the (literacy) campaign and get them committed to the level of active participation" (*D*, 25.6.68). Or: "Auqaf progress: The aims ... should be to tell them (imam and khatib) how to help the people to lead a more dynamic life in the light of their religion ... and to make them participants more actively in the national development effort. It must be remembered that the imams command great and attentive audience: this power should be profitably utilized ... the research and publication programme should ... try to lend vitality and comtemporary relevance to the old classics of Islam" (*PT*, 10.8.67).

92. A statement by the CII shows that the teachers of the formal schools had to present the right ideology. In 1981, the council had been asked by the Ministry for Education to define the ideology of Pakistan especially with regard to the employment interviews with future teachers. This task had not been accomplished by 1982 (cf. letter of the CII, no. F. 8(21)/81-R-CII 3565).

93. The curricula are usually chalked out exclusively by representatives of the colonial urban sector, preferably by British and American specialists.

94. UNESCO: International Institute for Educational Planning, K.A. Khan, "The Mosque Schools in Pakistan: An experiment in integrating non-formal and formal education", Paris, 1981.

95. We have analysed the advertisements in *Al-Haq* (Akora Khattak, Peshawar),which is representative of the advertisements of the Pakistani army and have been placed in this monthly at least since 1983.

96. The precondition for this is a degree of MBBS, which is not obtainable in a madrasah (cf. *Al-Haq*, 19/3, Dec. 1983, p. 64).

97. A precondition for this is an Intermediate exam or a corresponding degree, status of a bachelor and aged between 17 and 23 years (cf. *Al-Haq*, 19/5, Feb. 1984, p.14).

98. A precondition for this is a degree of *dars-e nizâmî* and a matric degree as well as fluent knowledge of Arabic. The age should be between 20 and 25 years (*Al-Haq*, 21/1, October 1985, p.14).

99. The age limit was 35 years, and the minimum qualification a degree of *dars-e nizâmî* and matric. Recognized degrees were only those of the *shahâdah al-'âlamiyyah* of the Wafâqs of the Deobandis, of the Ahl-e Hadith and of the Shia as well as those of the Tanzîm of the Brelwis (cf. *Al-Haq*, 20/12, 1985, p. 16).

100. Due to security reasons the exact number could not be ascertained. As Stephen P. Cohen stated, the curriculum of the Command and Staff Colleges

had a larger number of Islamic subjects since the rise to power of Zia ul Haq. There was an attempt to reserve for the clergy a number of recognized positions; cf. Cohen, *The Pakistan Army*, op.cit., pp. 95f.

101. We may recall here the discussion on the formal recognition of degrees of the clergy and the personal intervention of General Zia ul Haq.

102. The stigma of those receiving Zakat often attaches to them.

103. *Annual Report of the Tanzîm al-madâris 1985*, Lahore, 1985 (Urdu), p. 22.

CHAPTER IX

CONCLUDING REMARKS

Most of the literature available on modern Islam in general and Islamization in particular has hardly contributed to clear understanding of Islam as a political force, thus giving a rather distorted picture, and thereby nourishing the already existing prejudices specially among Western readers.

While most anthropological studies seem often to concentrate on local Islam, focusing on the micro-level, sociological and political studies confine themselves to investigating Islamization in terms of macro-level issues. Neither attempts to bridge the two levels in order to develop a coherent understanding of what Islamization really is. Only few socio-historical studies have shown a deeper insight on the basis of a theoretical approach to this subject.

A theoretical framework is necessary because Pakistani society is not only complex in terms of different Islams prevalent but also in terms of its urban, rural, traditional and colonial sectors. The representatives of the different sectors and their interaction have to be identified in order to understand the increasing complexity of the society. Proceeding socio-historically, a framework was taken into account in which different Muslim discourses and the different social groups were placed. Thus, it was possible to locate the supporters and architects of what we consider to be Islamization.

As the subtitle of the book suggests, Islamization is an approach to curb autonomous and autochthonous institutions that have not only hitherto existed and functioned more or less peacefully but have also given identities to the masses.

One may very well ask, what is to be Islamized in a country which, by its *raison d'étre,* is supposed to be Islamic and has been created for the Muslims of the subcontinent? The study of the sociological basis of the supporters of Islamization points to the fact that only a small religious elite and those integrated into a (post)-colonial system are busy defending *their* State through this policy.

These social groups differ with regard to their respective integration into the international system, the structures of which were laid down during the colonial rule. The degree of the social sectors' integration into this broader colonial system is reflected in their respective cultural articulation of social and economic conflicts. Paradoxically, the more the supporters of a certain kind of Islamization are secularized by virtue of their socio-economic background and enjoy the benefits of modern life, the more they tend towards an "integrationist" interpretation of Islam. In other words, their conceptualization of Islam is ideologized and aims at changing the society as a whole—*hic et nunc*. They are bound to draw their perceptions of State and society not only in contrast to Western ideologies but also in conformity with them. They are committed to a *Weltanschauung* which can cope with the West, not by abolishing the given structures but by enlarging the sphere of the State from which they receive their identities and in which they reproduce themselves. We may observe this approach in the postulates of the Islamic *avant-garde* and the religious elite.

Contrary to this conceptualization, "isolationist" interpretations are reflected in the positions of some Islamic scholars, the *'ulamâ'*, and the representatives of *Folk*-Islam, the *mashâ'ikh*, who tend towards a more theological interpretation with a considerable degree of autonomy. They make little claim to change the society and are hardly concerned with the present.

Between these integrationist and isolationist or *colonial* and *traditional* poles, there are *intermediate sectors* which reflect the potential for the mobilization of the Islamization. The roots for this state of affairs can be found in the social history of the different social sectors.

In Pakistan we may observe the integrationist strategy attempting at integrating Islam, or better, certain aspects of the Shari'a and *Tarîqah*-Islam, into the existing system, a system which rely heavily on colonial heritage that led to a split-up of different spheres of life, primarily at the level of production and reproduction, thereby causing increasingly societal tensions.

The main thesis is that the Islamization of the Zia regime proved to be a means of state control in order to guarantee stability and continuity, projecting thereby a particular notion of Islam. The policy of Islamization is analysed in terms of the different mechanisms of integration as pursued by the State and the reactions and results within the complex Pakistani society.

The Islamization is paradigmatically demonstrated in a historical context: first, in the role of the Council of Islamic Ideology as a main catalyst for Islamization; secondly, in the process of nationalization of the Islamic endowments (Waqf); thirdly, in the elaboration of the Zakat and

Ushr system as it was implemented in 1980; and finally, in the interaction between the Islamic scholars and their places of learning (Dînî Madâris) in the context of official policies.

The Council of Islamic Ideology was created in order to change the colonial structures to conform with Islam. Accordingly, its suggestions were conformist, and its members were mostly recruited from the colonial sector or at least from the intermediate sector, which is oriented towards colonial norms. By the end of the Bhutto regime the composition of the Council was slightly changed, showing an increase in the representatives of the religious elite and pursuing a different policy. The aim was to integrate Islamic norms into the social and economic discourse, without, however, any interest in changing the existing system. Under Zia, the CII's composition changed drastically and Islamic scholars had the upper hand. But still very few revolutionary suggestions were made. Nevertheless, an opposition slowly emerged, which was visible in some members' resignations. Critical remarks, and thus a *isolationist* approach, on the Islamization were not too seldom. But, since the Council is an advisory body, its suggestions had little influence. Because the coopted members represented different schools of thought, they could not stand up on a common platform and the opposition remained at an individual level. In this way, the State was able to ignore *traditional* Islamic corporations seeking support from a loyalist group.

By the sixties, the representatives of the *traditional sector* became victims of State intervention. In contradiction to the text of the Mussalman Wakf Validating Act, 1913, which the "father of the nation" had pushed through, the State from 1960 onwards nationalized (profitable) religious endowments in order to further its interests. The Auqaf Department was thus able not merely to employ its supporters, but also to localize and bind down "subversive" and "un-Islamic" tendencies. The administrative tying up of autochthonous institutions was accompanied by a transformation of the foundations in substance. Thus, the central and sacred position of the shrine-holder (*pîr, mujâwir,* etc.) was apparently replaced by the anonymous State and its agents. Similarly, the bureaucracy and the military attempted to transform religious education in the endowments through alterations in the curricula.

These changes, however, affected the attitude of the followers (*murîdîn*) and the pilgrims sanctioned the official policy of integration by reducing their contributions to shrines and setting up new ones. But the rejection of State power hardly takes any other form than individual protest, as in the case of the Council. In the face of this the State can afford to restrict its investments to those endowments which earn large incomes. Modern institutions were built in profitable shrines, while other foundations decayed. The installation of cash-boxes in shrines proved very profitable for the Auqaf Department. Their contributions to its annual receipts are almost 50 per cent. The structure of income differs in different areas and reflects their respective social environments.

Sectarian conflicts increased under Zia ul Haq. This gave the State the excuse to nationalize more foundations and to strengthen its control in those already nationalized. In this way the colonial sector successfully absorbs autonomous institutions. It enriches itself, pushes through its ideology and legitimizes it Islamically. At the same time, traditional organizational structures are dissolved without being adequately replaced.

The introduction of the Zakat and Ushr system in 1980 had its roots in the sixties, when this subject was first brought up. But it was only under Zia that it was introduced. The highly sophisticated system of deducting Zakat at source from all but current accounts was elaborated by secularized forces rather than by Islamic scholars. Its sudden implementation produced a lot of resentment among different sections of society. The system aims at extracting resources from a certain part of the society, namely the middle class, and leaves the upper and lower ends of the social hierarchy untouched, as also the Non-Muslim, Shia and Non-Pakistani groups. It has also created a vast army of loyalists employed in the system. Furthermore, there is evidence of evasion of Zakat and growing conversion of Sunnis to Shias, as the latter do not need to pay Zakat to the State.

The procedure of disbursing the money deducted gives a picture of similar distortions. Instead of spending the money on the poor and the needy, a significant amount flows to the bureaucracy, stabilizing the main pillar of the State. The money is disbursed on the basis of the numbers of population instead of the degree of development or poverty of a district, bringing into focus the effects of what is called an Islamic Welfare System. And, since the Zakat system requires an administrative network from Islamabad down to the local level, control of every corner of the society seems to be guaranteed, breeding a great deal of corruption and conferring political power on those administering the scheme. Politically non-conformist forces are punished by withdrawal of Zakat money. This is specially true for the *mustahiqûn* studying in religious schools. Moreover, instead of questioning and abolishing the colonial system of taxation, it is now legitimized by the introduction of an Islamic tax. In addition to this, the social service existing as part of the traditional society is gradually eliminated but not replaced by alternatives.

As has been seen during the *tahrîk-e nizâm-e mustafâ* in 1977, religious schools and their leaders had played a significant role in mobilizing a considerable part of the society. Hence, religious schools inherited the potential of upheaval especially as they were self-sufficient and autonomous. In order to gain control over these autochthonous institutions, several attempts have been made by the Government, starting with the Awqâf scheme of the Ayub era. But just on the eve of the Waqf Ordinance 1960 the theologians of different schools of thought built up umbrella organizations in order to safeguard their interests. On a common platform they could oppose the integrative policy of the colonial sector. Hence, a takeover of religious endowments in the shape of religious schools was not easy.

In order to get hold of the '*ulamâ*' and other representatives of the traditional sector, the administrative integration was accompanied by reforms regarding the traditional curriculum, the *dars-e nizâmî*. An integration of "modern" and "old" subjects was envisaged in the sixties, but not really followed up due to opposition.

The Bhutto regime was the first to recognize the hitherto "backward" Islamic scholars when formalizing their degrees. The recognition did not, at certain places only lead to any significant changes due to resentment among the bureaucracy and the intellectuals. The issue became acute under Zia, who had postulated an Islamic system. Without a reasonable backing of the '*ulamâ*' he was not able to carry out his reforms. Accordingly, the regime has tried several steps to bring the holders of Islamic tradition under state control, although, with only partial success. The means employed to regularize the "clerical" entities and their leaders were many: starting from the reconstitution of the Council of Islamic Ideology in 1977, the 'Ulamâ' and Mashâ'ikh-Conventions in Islamabad, the Zakat and Ushr Ordinance 1980, the Awqâf schemes and the Federal Shariat Court, etc.

One of the main issues was, however, to modernize the clergy's places of learning and to integrate them accordingly. The state once more undertook various reforms compromising the traditional curriculum of the religious schools, their administrative set-up as well as their financial resources, displaying a strategy of limited participation.

The members of the National Committee on Religious Schools 1979, comprising the religious elite, intellectuals and bureaucrats, produced a report showing the economic situation of the institutions of different schools of thought, their respective curricula and their area of operation. A reform was recommended, like in the sixties, which was agreed upon by all members. However, the proposals could not materialize due to strong opposition of the Deobandis, who launched a nationwide campaign. Their reaction to the colonial rule in the nineteenth century was repeated. Although the proposals of the committee had to be abandoned for the time being, there were still other means to consolidate—or rather to "Islamize"—the 'ulamâ'.

The Zakat and Ushr Ordinance 1980 had a large impact on the religious schools. By virtue of this scheme, their students were entitled to receive Zakat through the "headmasters". It is, however, only disbursed to schools which follow the official policy. Although a section of the Deobandi schools rejects Zakat money, the majority of the 'ulamâ' and the Dînî Madâris do benefit from the money disbursed by the Provincial Zakat Councils. Connected with the disbursement of Zakat are requirements of registration and book-keeping, obligations disliked by the 'ulamâ' as they consider them to be attempts to curb their autonomy. This is specially true since the leaders of the religio-political parties are mainly recruited from theological seminaries and thus represent a considerable part of the political opposition. The boycott has, however, a political undertone and prevails in one province only: the Deobandi schools identify themselves with regional nationalism in Sindh, referring to a fatwâ of Mufti Mahmud. Thus, the religious schools can be regarded as vehicles of nationalist movements against State Power, which seems to come from the Punjab suppressing all efforts of regional autonomous movements.

The Government, in order to resolve the national struggles, has been introducing Zakat to the more conformistic religious groups, namely the Brelwis, Ahl-e Hadith and Jama'at-e Islami, especially in Sindh and Baluchistan. In so far the Government was in the position to play off the different supporters of a traditional society by well aimed measures of divide and rule. The new system is thus used as a political tool rather than a means to build up a social welfare system. While a large number of the small religious schools are benefiting from the Zakat scheme, huge amounts are being allocated to higher spheres of religious learning and big urban schools serving elitist purposes.

The official Zakat disbursements amount to more than one-fourth of the annual receipts of religious schools, leading to a considerable dependency. Moreover, new requirements are conspicuous among the 'ulamâ', who can only be satisfied through Zakat money. In addition to this dependency, the scheme has led to the establishment of new religious schools, resulting in their "mushroom-growth". These new schools are frequently seen in rural areas, set up in response to the demands of the poorer sections of the society. Apparently, the State is able to control the development of these institutions.

The next step of integration was the recognition of the religious schools' degrees, bringing the 'ulamâ' at par with the formal education system, which is based on the colonial legacy. The equivalence scheme was pushed through by Zia ul Haq on his personal initiative, contrary to the ambitions of the secular forces, thus giving the representatives of the traditional sector a chance to establish themselves alongside the other State organs, at least formally. This measure was, however, tied to the condition to set up a reformed curriculum integrating "modern" and "old" subjects of sixteen years duration, instead of the present eight year syllabus, reflecting the proposals of the National Committee on Religious Schools 1979. The setting up of the new curriculum witnessed a conflict between the jayyid 'ulamâ' and the old regime among the Deobandis resulting in a compromise. Other schools of thought were keen on producing a reformed syllabus.

The policy of integration has shown a spectacular increase of graduates, thus giving rise to a potentially explosive situation in the nineties.

The recognition of the degrees and the Zakat scheme resulted in organizational changes within the different schools of thought. The strengthened organization of the 'ulamâ' and the religious schools has the potential to both benefit and damage the Government. While the benefit lies in making these schools and their students more identifiable, the potential damage arises from their cohesiveness, bringing new problems for the State.

Certain areas of origin can be identified for each school of thought as well as their particular geographical concentration, thus indicating particular social, economic, spatial and ethnic as well as the familiar background of the 'ulamâ'. Accordingly, the more trade-oriented Ahl-e Hadith are concentrated in the commercial centres of Pakistan, while the more peasant oriented Brewlis are mostly found in the rural areas of Punjab. The Deobandis, as the largest group, are specially strong in the NWFP, in Sindh and in Baluchistan. The stronghold of the Shia is the Northern Areas, some parts of Punjab and urban Sindh. The Jama'at-e Islami as the representatives of the Islamic avant-garde are to be found in urban centres as well as in politically sensitive areas. Besides these developments, some religious schools and scholars have proved to be important elements in the Afghan crisis and the Jihâd. Especially the Dâr al-'Ulûm Haqqâniyyah turned out to be a useful centre for the men and material for the holy war. It remains to be seen how far the colonial sector will be capable of maintaining its dominance over the increasingly stronger traditional and intermediary sectors.

Accordingly a section of the religious scholars can be integrated in the *Jihâd* issue. The majority, however, are now waiting to be integrated in the national economy, since they are "equivalent". It is suggested that, because of the bureaucracy's inability to provide them with jobs, although some new literacy programmes have been implemented, thousands of M.A.-*fudalâ'* will soon constitute a problem for the Government.

To sum up, the official policy towards religious and autochthonous institutions has led to growing divergence between influential sections of the "clergy", who have mass support, and the Government. There has been a resurgence of religious schools and an overproduction of *fudalâ'*, as a result of modernization strategies which serve political ends and try to control indigenous institutions rather than to Islamize a Muslim society.

The reconciling, unifying and integrationist Islamization in Pakistan cannot succeed due to the prevalence of different schools of thought in different regions. In contrast to the somewhat modernist interpretation of official Islam on the basis of *ijtihâd*, there are the traditionalists who mostly adhere to *taqlîd*. The isolationist tendencies of the latter can be regarded as quite legitimate reactions, carrying a potential for conflict not to be tackled easily by integrationists.

EPILOGUE

The "projected numbers of *mawlânâs* indicate the potential of social and political conflict set in motion under the Zia regime. There is a very high probability that the Government will be faced with an enormous problem in the next five to ten years to come." (pp. 230, 232) When I wrote these words in 1987 I had not realized that the dimension of the suggested social and political conflict would rise at the speed we have been witnessing during the last years.

The intensity of the tussle between what I have deliberately called the colonial sector[1]—by which I mean ideally the representatives of colonial legacy, e.g. the higher ranks of civil service and military, and capital—and traditional sector has increased particularly after the death of Zia ul Haq. The main reason of this serious development is mainly to be found in the programmatically half-hearted attempts or rather programmatic neglegence on the side of the Government to integrate the prime representatives of the latter sector, e.g. religious dignitaries, into the national progress and process in a reasonable way. Indeed, as recent data suggest, it seems quite unlikely that the State will be able to further stabilize its position and continue suppressing the revolution of rising expectations which it itself has been creating by means of a variety of Islamization measures, covering Islamic banking, Islamic ideology, Islamic social structure and Islamic education.

I argued that Islamization was a major tool for legitimizing Zia ul Haq's rule, a rule supported by and large by the representatives of the colonial sector and by those affiliated more or less to what has been called the intermediary sectors—the main protagonists of Islamization. Connected with this was the attempt to internationalize the internal market, in accordance with the imperatives of the world-market.

The legitimizing function of this policy again became most evident in the ominous referendum held by Zia in December 1984, in which Islam was to be a major issue, and in several Constitution Amendment Orders.[2] They all authorized him to stay in power for the next several years to come. Notwithstanding Zia's quasi-integrative policies *vis-a-vis* the *'ulamâ'* and

Sûfîs and their considerable support—which he went on persuing during several 'Ulamâ', Ma<u>sh</u>â'i<u>kh</u> and Nizam-e Islam Conventions—he never really looked for them to participate in the overall national political business. This marginalization of '*ulamâ*' has its roots in the colonial tradition and can still be observed today clearer than ever before.

Apart from certain paradigms of Islamization which have hitherto attracted so much foreign attention, like the Islamic banking system, implementation of Sharî'a courts and *hudûd* punishments as well as political opposition and the impact of such policies on minorities and women,[3] I argued—and I still do so—that the main changes, indeed, have occurred in areas which until recently have been quite neglected by scholars of Muslim countries and social scientists. This is the field of scholars and students of religious schools, their scholarship and institutions, and, unvariably connected with them, the dissolution of autochthonous structures, which have a long evolutionary tradition in a Muslim environment, as well as the serious reactions manifested by the upholders of Islamic tradition.

What actually has happened in this field of enquiry during the last ten years, what kinds of changes—if at all—have occurred especially after 1988 and finally why the religio-political and socio-economic situation has become so unbearably aggressive? Answers to these pertinent questions cannot be given in detail; however, on the basis of the existing research and results brought forward so far one may at least raise some main issues, draw a number of main lines and observe some trends. Firstly, we will look at the political scenario, then we will focus our attention on a few Islamization measures and finally we will turn our attention towards the religious scholars and their institutions.

To start with, even if the enigmatic death of Zia ul Haq in August 1988 had opened up a new chapter in Pakistan's political culture, the Islamization drive was not altered severely. Public elections were held in which Benazir Bhutto won the day albeit for a short while.[4] The interlude ended when the prime minister was dismissed in 1990 by the then President Ghulam Ishaq Khan, a close friend of Zia ul Haq.

Meanwhile, Zia's protege Nawaz Sharif, who in 1985 had managed to become prime minister of Punjab and who presently is the opposition leader, pursued, like Zia, a similarly pragmatic tactic. He integrated a large opposition front against the PPP in the Islamic Democratic Alliance (IJI). Again, Islam became the main slogan for political and social mobilization. Consequently, Nawaz won the election in 1990 but at least had to give 15 mandates to the religious parties which had supported him. In May 1991 he passed the Enforcement of Shariat Act and a Blasphemy Bill, which Zia had proposed some years before. This was to pacify some uneasy *'ulamâ'* who ever since had been shouting for the establishment of an Islamic—albeit Sunnite—State and who had always been told that once this was established, their predicaments were reduced, better undone, perdicaments they had been facing at least since the days of British raj. According to them, *Pâkistân ka matlab kiyâ, lâ ilâha illâ Allâh* never had a chance to work in the new country. Naturally, it was absolutely unlikely that the colonial sector would ever Islamize its own existence in the sense the diversity of the *'ulamâ'* took it to be. The fact that religious scholars never have been representing an islamically monolithic block, was a most wellcome excuse for the politically dominant sector to belittle the interests of the dignitaries. Hence, then and now, the parlamentary system, the rights of women and religious minorities as well as the financial system were clearly exempted from the Shariat Act. Again, Islamization was reduced to a ritual affair, the *mullas* being mocked at. Thus, the religo-political parties gradually resigned from the Alliance (IJI), one by one, and for the first time they stood up against the PPP and the Pakistan Muslim League (PML) in the 1993 election as a third force.

Admittedly, the PPP won the elections clearly with a rather secular manifesto, heavily stressing on what it called the new social contract, producing rather too high an expectations. However, Islam was one of its four principles at least, enlighted and free. "We believe in IJMA; We are not clericks . . . Islam . . . is a Religion without discrimination . . . of Fundamental Rights . . . of Revolution . . . of Equity . . . of Tolerance . . . of Liberation" declares the manifesto, which wants to produce inter alia "a programme to restore the dignity of the people".[5] The *'ulamâ'* seem to be exempted, though. Islamization is hardly mentioned in the manifesto, except the proclamation that "Ushr collection will be streamlined. We expect to get more than Rs. 4 billion through this method. Half the money will go to the provinces and half to the local bodies." Notice that again a tendentious urban policy can be observed, instead of a fair redistribution of the whole amount among the local—rural—bodies. Islamic slogans are utilized. Business as usual. The same seems to be true in the case of parliament which is regarded as the agent of Allah's trustees: "Thus the sanctity of parliament is the sanctity of Allah's will as expressed through the ballot box." This is not too far away from Maududian perception, a kind of *hizb Allâh*, the party of God.

The loosers, the PML, had stressed in a similarly eclectic manifesto the process of Islamic renaissance and consequently represented even more Islamic rhetorics. They, however, did not stop challenging Benazir, and again, '*ulamâ*' became tools in this battle for power. Alliances with religio-political parties seemed to be an approved way of increasing the base of Nawaz Sharif. But as we will elaborate in what follows, the '*ulamâ*' meanwhile have become quite a force: When in July 1994 the Minister of Justice—Iqbal Haider—attempted to modify the Blasphemy Bill to avoid its abuse by different Islamic groups, he was threatened by religious scholars. They succeeded in pushing through their demands.

The background of these increasing home-political problems can not only be gathered from the policies persued by Islamabad during the last few years, but one can also say that there is little difference in these particular issues between the former regimes and the young PPP politicians. As far as the Islamization is concerned certain aspects may be mentioned which have furthered these serious developments:

It may be true that the Council of Islamic Ideology (CII) was reconstituted after 1988, but the fact remains that its task is to legitimize state policy in what is thought to be Islamic. The members were chosen by the centre according to their loyalist stand. The Council has also recently started publishing some of its sometimes controversial reports but the ·suggestions therein have not been realized though they were far away from what the Islmaic *avant-garde* and the religious elite—members of the intermediary sectors—consider to be in accordance with Islamic injunctions.

In recent years the same tenditious policy has been pursued in respect to nationalized religious endowments, some of which have become the main centres for the dissemination of State ideology, like the exciting building of the shrine of Data Ganj Bakhsh in Lahore. The urban features of Islamabad's policy can be observed here very clearly, stabilizing the administrative set-up of the colonial sector which has been expanding quite successfully in certain virgin areas, enriching itself and pushing through its ideological objectives. This policy is justified throughout in Islamist terms, e.g. in the modernistic sense of Javed Iqbal, the author of *Ideology of Pakistan*. In contrast to this, more and more traditional structures are being dissolved without properly being replaced.

Similarly, the Zakat and Ushr system turned out to be a physical expression of the colonization of traditional systems and values. Because of its perennial income it was welcomed by the successor Governments and meanwhile it has widened its impact considerably. While in the beginning—1980/81—the collected amount was mere Rs. 844 millions, in 1987/88 it had increased to nearly Rs 2,000 millions. And by 1993 the PPP was expecting "to get more than Rs. 4 billion through" Ushr collection alone. Formerly, this tool of State control was not well accepted by the majority of Zakat payers and by politically sensible religious scholars as well as by Shiites. But, meanwhile, those liable to paying Zakat have become accustomed to this Islamic tax; the number of avidavits presented to the deduction agencies has decreased—even among the Shiites—leaving the Zakat administration with an increasingly handsome income. Nevertheless, disbursement problems, corruption and nepotism, especially among those involved in the Zakat system, have not vanished leaving considerable room for political manouvering.[6]

It is true that the official Zakat system has provided the scholars with some good amounts and also made them in several instances responsible for distribution of Zakat to the poor at the local level. For example, in rural areas some of them even became Ushr collectors which in turn changed their status to some degree enabling them to be in direct contact with the representatives of Islamabad—the district administration and local Government department agents; and after the party-less elections in 1985,[7] the Zakat and Ushr system has elevated their status giving them some amount of social and political power. This the 'ulamâ' in turn use for their own political or religious interests, as other politicians and economic magnates do. Inspite of this growing political power and rising expectations the 'ulamâ' are kept aloof arbitrarily from the national political and economic process. This is especially true in rural or backward areas where the number of religious schools and hence of sectarian clashes has increased dramatically. We will turn to this problem in a minute.

Connected with these measures of Islamization are the issues related to the changes concerning religious schools, their teachers and students, the main focus of this study:

One way of the dissemination of "Islamic thought" from the centre was and is persued by the International Islamic University in Islamabad which was founded in 1980.[8] Its notorious Da'wah Academy is of particular importance, because it is thought to be a melting pot of all different branches of Islamic discourse in Pakistan, dominated, however, by the Jama'at-e Islami and by the *salafi* branch of the Deobandi school of thought. The Academy has a wide range of programmes, from *a'immah* and correspondence courses to international tarbiya camps and scout leaders programmes etc.; literature such as Sayyid Qutb, Maududi, Islahi, Shibli, Nadwi, etc. One of the Academy's aim is to bring about religious harmony in Pakistan. In a draft paper such hopes are expressed thus: "If the course continues it is hoped that this will eventually be able to minimise the religious differences among Ulama in Pakistan and at the same time create a better image of Pakistan abroad."[9] Newly established goods terms with institutions in other Muslim regions such as in the former USSR and Al-Azhar in Egypt facilitate trans-national missionary activities. Besides selected graduates of the umbrella organizations of religious schools— primarily the Deobandi Wafâq—members of the Pakistan Army and of the Auqaf Departments also have started joining the diverse programmes. Hence State ideology, combined with Islamic internationalistic ideology, is being disseminated, not only through traditional institutions of Islamic discourse, like mosques, madâris and waqf, but also through modern institutions such as the army and formal education. The Academy wants to "create awareness of Islamic identity in Muslims living (also) in Non-Muslim surroundings and to develop an ideoloogical consciousness" which ultimately should lead to Muslim unity. With regard to the growing number of students in the Academy and the University (also from Southeast Asia and Africa) one may consider these activities to be the right supply for a demand prevalent among certain social urban groups, particularly the lower and middle classes, which have become more and more victims of a mis-match. The growing demand for such Da'wah courses is also reflected in the fact that even during the interlude of the PPP in 1988/89, the budget of the Academy was increased considerably. While it amounted to Rs. 3.2 million in 1985-86[10] and Rs. 8.05 million in 1987-88, it increased to Rs. 21.4 million in the year 1988-89.[11] This not only shows the impact of the Islamization policy lobby in Government agencies and the educational sector, it also sheds light on the impressive impact of the Academy and its activities in Pakistan as well as abroad.

The handsome support of this institution, however, cannot deny the fact that the colonial sector does not stop to subject leaders and institutions of the traditional sector in each and every way. And this has led to the crisis which was produced by the shortsighted policy of several regimes, including the present.

The Academy's desired attempt to create a harmonious Pakistan may also be seen behind the religious controversies that have become increasingly popular, including such an issue as Lady Diana's knee in September 1991. The background behind the controversy was the tussle between different religious groups: while the Khatîb of Lahore's largest mosque—which is held by the Auqaf Department—who is a Deobandi, on the one hand, allowed Lady Diana to enter the holy premises without "proper" garments, on the other hand, he had declared Benazir Bhutto's Government unlawful. For his "unislamic" behaviour legal proceedings were instituted against him, led by Brelwis and supported by members of the PPP.

The path of religious controversies is paralleled by the emergence of a variety of new identities and organizations. Government was not inactive in creating them. It created counter forces against regional nationalist movements, like, e.g. in the case of loyalists Zakat receivers in Sindh. Similarly, the Muhâjir Qawmî Mahâz (MQM), which was to counterbalance the PPP, was a creation of the politically dominant sector. The rise of the MQM was paralleled by bloody upheavals in Karachi and in urban Sindh, so that in 1992 when Sindhi nationalism was on its height and the state looked like disintegrating, the army had to intervene massively. It is said, that thereafter Islamabad also created a competitive organization called the MQM-Haqqiqi group. The rise of this rival organization has increased the problems tremendously. Similar tactical steps were taken by other religio-political organizations, like the JUI and the JUP which split in 1990.[12] Some of the new groups are most militant, like the Anjuman-e Sipâh-e Sahâba. This wing of the Deobandi JUI was created in 1985 particularly for the elimination of the Shia minority which after all constitutes 14 per cent of the Pakistani population. However, since the Iranian Revolution, the Pakistani Shiites have become more self-confident and have organized themselves in the Tahrîk-e Nifâz-e Fiqh-e Ja'farîya[13] and have recently established an Anjuman-e Sipâh-e Muhammad whose leader, Rada Naqwi, was trained in Iran ideologically and in Afghanistan militarily. Both *Anjumans* are the most brutal manifestation of cultural articulations of marginalized urban young men. They also mirror the prolonged conflict between Iran and Saudi Arabia in Pakistan. As is well known by now, these young men usually originate from religious schools, where they obtained degrees. They are now pushing into the job market.

Apparently all this happened because the number of religious scholars and their institutions has increased in a spectacular way. But the madrasah student is dismissed from the process of national integration. Leaving him with high expectations, he is left without a job. The only source of income for the jobless consequently may be the founding of new religious schools. In this way the graduate further would support exclusive identities and strengthen the network of his respective *maktab-e fikr*. This in turn increases the problems, especially competition with other schools of thought often leading to what is called sectarian clashes. According to a recent report, "746 religious institutions [are] fanning sectarianism in Punjab".[14] This is nearly one third of the 2,500 religious institutions in the province, some 900 (36 per cent) of which are receiving Government aid.[15]

This increasing sectarian problematic has led to the PPP Government recently (Dec. 1994) to the decision to increase the control of religious schools, their registration, and their financial resources. One step in this direction was to stop paying Zakat via Provincial Zakat Councils to religious schools or at least to examine their administration and to prohibit the *mulla's* use of loud-speakers. Understandably, this has caused great resentments and has been called *mudâkhalat fi al-dîn* by religious dignitaries. As many religious schools are centres of religio-political activities and as they are recruitment centres for religio-political leaders it is but natural that the *'ulamâ'*—even if they are in opposition to each other— stand up united in this issue against Benazir challenging her status severely. Indeed, Deobandis, Brelwis, Ahl-e Hadith and Jama'at-e Islami gathered in a Brelwi Dâr al-'Ulûm (Jâmi'ah Na'îmiyya) in Lahore on January 1, 1995 under the leadership of the Deobandi Sami' al-Haqq from Akora Khattak to convene the *kull Pakistan tahrîk-e tahaffuz-e masâjid wa dînî madâris*. This exclusive Sunnite convention in its nine points was of the view that Government should not intervene in the running of religious institutions, otherwise—they threatened—there would be a nation-wide crisis. Moreover, the rather docile Brelwis have started to talk self-confidently about an ideologized Islam; Sarfaraz Naimi, successor and son of Mufti Naimi, stood for a transformation of the whole society. It is but natural that the religious schools will not give in and will resent the obligation to open their cashbooks for accountablity. This is especially true, since in recent times more and more of them have equipped themselves with weapons and the latest technology: computers. This is an indication of their elevated self-confidence, on the basis of which they foster isolationist tendencies, which under the given marginalizing circumstances seem to be quite legitimate. Considering their economic and social situation—a mulla reports that after Zia's death the degrees once equivalent to M.A. Islamiyyat or M.A. Arabic, in practice have stopped being given this status[16]—this might be, indeed, the only way to deal with the power-holders.

Again, instead of trying to integrate the *'ulamâ'* and provide jobs for them, they are rejected, utilized and stigmatized, as the manifesto of the PPP implicitly reminds: "We are not clerics", the dignity of the *'ulamâ'* is not restored. Fed up with this official approach they have taken up arms only recently. As can be traced in the newspapers, militarization has become quite easy in Pakistan nowadays—one speaks of Kalashnikov-culture. Especially for students and teachers of religious schools provision of weapons poses hardly any problems; their centres of learning have been receiving quite some amounts from Islamabad since the students have been active in the *Jihâd* for Afghanistan. It is no secret that many *mujâhidîn*—not to speak of the recently established militia called *Tâlibân* (e.g. students)—were students or graduates of madâris. They were trained also in other battlefields like Kashmir, Tajikistan, Chechnya, etc. When back to Pakistan more and more of these scholars and students began to set up their own organizations like the Sipâh-e Sahâba, whose chief Azam Tariq[17] seems to be well equipped with quite some heavy weapons, like stinger-rockets. Presumably every religio-political party has a sizeable number of Afghan war veterans in its rows.

Until recently, scholars and students of madâris usually refrained from threatening the State physically, although they had shown their mobilization potential during several demonstrations and were helpful in overthrowing Government in 1977. But now they have started to show a growing aggressiveness by severely threating the stability of the State. The episode in Malakand in November 1994 when hundreds of Islamic hardliners took up arms to enforce Shari'a in this area may be a clear indication of the ever-growing problem which could only be crushed with military intervention, leaving some hundred people dead. Their demands, however, were sanctioned: secular jurists were replaced by *qâdîs*. The polarization of society again became perceivable during the so-called *"dandâ* action" of the *mullas* and their students on 31 December 1994/ 1 January 1995. This was but a clear denouncement of the colonial sector's rituals by frustated forces. It is curious that its representatives living in cantonments and civil lines, etc., were quite worried and several new-year parties had to be cancelled. These successes have naturely elevated the self-confidence of the representatives of traditional order.

Hence, *'ulamâ'* have radicalized and militarized themselves during the last few years. Against this increasingly aggressive background, it is interesting to note that recently English language media—the colonial sector so to speak—has started to report on the "mulla" regularly; as could be presumed, he is portrayed in a negative way, usually called Islamic militant. His way of studying is pillorized and his standard of knowledge is ridiculed, but no attempt is made to understand or analyze his problems and the humiliation he has undergone. One may sense the arrogance and ignorance among the English media in Pakistan not only in this regard. One report, e.g., rather mixes up issues, calling madrasah students *per se* fundamentalists, and the Wafâq al-Madâris a Government institution. We know that very few madrasah students can be called fundamentalist, and that the Wafâq is not a Government institution but the umbrella organization of the Deobandi schools. The report further opines that "the students are taught to defend their dogma with their lives. They are the ones who go chanting to the streets and religious-political processions and meetings of the mullahs. For them death is matyrdom and life is living like a ghazi." It is said that they are being prepared for a global Islamic revolution after which Mecca will be the capital of the world.[18] Other journalists have pillorized, that in their madâris the *mullas* teach, among others, "alif for Allâh, bah for bandûq, j for jihâd, kh for khûn and tah for talwâr" etc. These perceptions are deeply intrenched in the minds of those representing Western media. They usually point to the militancy of these scholars and students—the *mullas*—as a collective individual with a collective consciousness. Thus, they create a new enemy image. But it should be made very clear that even in formal or ordinary schools similar ideas and images are being taught. For that matter, it is not only in the madâris that the "militant" is produced, there is also a long history of his production in institutions of the colonial sector as well which has hitherto escaped the attention of scholarly discourse.[19]

The impact of religious scholars and their students should not be ignored, since religio-political parties do dominate the Islamic public, although in the political public they are still not that popular. During the last elections in October 1993 the twelve different Islamic parties gained only nine out of 207 mandates, less than the number of mandates for non-Muslim minorities. This for the time being shows that the *'ulamâ'* have to give way to the professional politicians who are, however, increasingly held responsible for the desolate and corrupt situation in the country and are blamed for the decaying political culture. Even if the "mulla"-parties are competing with each other severely they are united in the sense that neither the PPP nor its opponent, the PML, are interested in setting up a real Islamic state which, according to the *'ulamâ'*, was promised by the father of the nation. However, the pertinent question is: what ingrediences are needed to establish an integrating system which would restore the dignity of all people, guarantee social and economic security, and stand for absolute freedom of expression, be it Islamic or Muslim.

To sum up, the withdrawal of the traditional sector into marginalization has obviously reversed now: Islamabad's forced image of a particular brand of Islam aiming at modernizing development strategies and at internationalization of the internal markets has led to an increasing radicalization among the bearers and protagonists of tradition and those dwelling between the two poles, modern and traditional. Their more or less isolationist stand seems to be their only possible and legitimate way of self-defence and self-preservation. It is true though that these are opposing divisions among them for the time being, as the ever increasing number of sectarian and ethnic clashes indicates. The motives behind these clashes are competing economic and political interests and socio-psychological processes which have come about in the wake of the expanding disintegration of traditional cultures and patterns of social order.

These primarily urban clashes are gradually spreading to the rural hinterland giving rise to regionalism and threatening the rests of the colonial state. Insofar the policy of Islamization has turned out to be a boomerang not easy to handle, especially since these problems were not anticipated by the Islamists: "The spirits that I called . ."

As long as the traditional and intermediary sectors are subject to Islamabad's interests alone without any mutual understanding and co-operation, the intensity of the struggle will go on increasing. This is particularly true in a region where the vast majority of citizens live in miserable socio-economic conditions and where utopian declarations are rife. In a society full of growing intra-societal conflicts such declarations foster a feeling of solidarity and identity which is articulated in an Islamic symbolism, as indicated the cases of Salman Rushdie and Taslima Nasrin. The revolution of increasing expectations created by Islamabad can only be crushed by severe interventionism in order to secure its "own" state, a state which has little to do with the masses.

In view of the cultural, religious, economic and infrastructural poten-tial of traditional institutions in general and religious schools in particular, those who run these establishments may in the long run be able to make a constructive contribution to indigenous developmental processes designed to fit the needs of the local population. In this way, the most important connection between official ideology (Islam) and the social mass base (religious scholars) could ultimately be established. This would, however, imply most probably that 'ulamâ' and their places of learning would become not only the local or regional representatives of the people but also would be present in trans-national fora and determine national and international politics. Similar trends can be observed in the Middle East, where neo-colonial systems try, by authoritarian means, to subdue autoch-thonous movements and institutions.

NOTES

1   The capital of Pakistan, the city of Islamabad proper, is one obvious example of the establishment of what is meant by colonial sector. It is isolated from the rest of the society. Consequently the city border starts with what is called the Zero-Point which really opens up a new world.

2 See Riaz Ahmed Syed, *Pakistan on Road to Islamic Democracy, Referendum*, 1984, Islamabad, 1985; Mohammad Waseem, *The 1993 Elections in Pakistan*, Lahore, 1994, Appendix A.

3 See, e.g. Rubya Mehdi, *The Islamization of the Law in Pakistan*, Richmond, 1994; Seyyed Vali Reza Nasr, "Islamic Opposition to the Islamic State: the Jama'at-i Islami, 1977-78", in *International Journal of Middle Eastern Studies*, 25 (1993), pp. 261-283; Mushahid Hussain, *Pakistan's Politics: The Zia Years*, Lahore, 1990; Dale F. Eickelman (ed.), *Russia's Muslim Frontiers: New Directions in Cross-Cultural Analysis*, Bloomington, 1993.

4 See Tariq Ismail, *Election 88*, Lahore, 1989.

5 See Waseem, *The 1993 Elections*, Appendix B, here pp. 254ff.

6 See Government of Pakistan, Ministry of Finance, Central Zakat Administration, *Qânûn-e Zakât o 'Ushr: chand shubahât kâazâlah*, Islamabad, Dec. 1990.

7 For the elections in 1985 see Hasan Askari Rizvi, "Third General Elections in Pakistan 1985", in *Pakistan Journal of Social Sciences*, XI & XII (1985-86) (Islamabad), pp. 1-21.

8 For this institution see J. Malik, "International Islamic University, Islamabad", in J. L. Esposito et al. (eds.), *The Oxford Encyclopedia of the Modern Islamic World*, vols. 1-4, New York and Oxford, 1995, vol. 2, pp. 209-211.

9 International Islamic University, Da'wah Wing: *National Programmes* (mimeo) Islamabad, 1989, p. 3.

10 See International Islamic University, Da'wah Wing: *Progress Report*, p. 21.

11 Personal informations.

12 See *Viewpoint* (Lahore), XV/29, March 1, 1990, pp. 8, 17. For these parties see now Mujeeb Ahmad, *Jam'iyyat 'Ulama-i-Pakistan 1948-1979*, Islamabad, National Institute of Historical and Cultural Research, 1993, and Charles H. Kennedy and S.V.R. Nasr, in Esposito (eds.), *The Oxford Encyclopedia*, vol. 2, pp. 364f and 365ff, respectively.

13 The Shia was organized by leading Shiite scholars in the Tahrîk-e Nifâz-e Fiqh-e Ja'farîya (TNFJ). It has since been split into two seperate branches that persue different political approaches; see Afak Haider, "The Politicization of the Shia and the Development of the Tehrik-e-Nifâz-e-Fiqh-e-Jafria in Pakistan", in Charles H. Kennedy (ed.), *Pakistan 1992*, Boulder, 1993, pp. 82-88.

14 See *The News* (Islamabad), 7.3.95, p. 11.

15 It is not clear what kind of schools were meant in the report. It seems, however, that the report has considered smaller institutions and *maktabs* as well. Accordingly their number is relatively high compared to the data given in Table 34: "Dînî Madâris according to their School of Thought", (pp. 198-200). For the rise of sectarianism in the Northern Areas see Andreas Rieck, "Sectarianism as a political problem in Pakistan: The case of the Northern Areas", in *Orient*, 1995 (Opladen) (in press).

16 As quoted in *Home News*, Jan. 12-18, 1995, p. 7.

17 Azam Tariq was also present at the meeting of religious scholars in Lahore on Jan. 1st, 1995.
18 *Home News*, Jan. 12-18, 1995, p. 7.
19 See, however, K.K. Aziz: *The Murder of History*, Lahore, 1993; Ayesha Jalal, "Conjuring Pakistan: History as Official Imaging", in *International Journal of Middle Eastern Studies,* 27 (1995), pp. 73-89.

APPENDIX A

MEMBERS OF THE ADVISORY COUNCIL OF ISLAMIC IDEOLOGY AND THE COUNCIL FOR ISLAMIC IDEOLOGY 1962-1984*

1962

		Languages
Justice (Retd.) Abu Saleh Muh. Akram[1]	(Chairman)	E,B,U
Justice Muh. Sharif[2]	(resigned 64)	E,U
Maulana Akram Khan[3]	(resigned 64)	E,B,U,A
Maulana Abdul Hamid Badayuni[4]		U,A,P
Maulana Hafiz Kifayat Husain[5]		U,A,P
Dr. I. H. Qureshi (IRI)[6]		E,U
Abdul Hashim (Islamic Academy Dacca)[7]		E,B,A,U
Maulana A.H. Muh. Abdul Hai[8]		B,U,A

Councellors

Mr. Akhtar Husain (Ex-Governor of West Pakistan)
Governor of State Bank of Pakistan
Deputy Chairman, Planning Commission

(Explanation cf. Table on the period covering 1981-84)

1964/65

Allamah Alauddin Siddiqui[1]	(Chairman)	*Languages*
(Islamic Studies dept., University of Punjab)		E,U,P,A
Justice (Retd.) Abdul Jabbar Khan[2]	(resigned 65)	E,B,U
Maulana Vilayet Husain[3]		B,A,U

* The names of members do not follow the transcription used up to this point. In the text below I have followed the transcription of names as given in the English newspapers and magazines of the country as well as those in the Pakistan Gazette.

		Languages
Maulana Abdul Hamid Badayuni[4]		U,A,P
Maulana Hafiz Kifayat Husain[5]	(ended 65)	U,A,P
Dr. I. H. Qureshi[6]	(resigned 64)	E,U
Ch. Muh. Ali (Peshawar University)	(resigned 65)	E,Pa,U
Abdul Hashim (Islamic Academy, Dacca)[7]	(ended 65)	E,A,U
Maulana A.H. Muh. Abdul Hai[8]	(resigned 65)	B,U,A
Dr. Fazlur Rahman (IRI)[9]		E,U,A,G, L,Pu,P

New nominations for the resigned members

Dr. A.B.A. Haleem (University of Karachi)	E,U
Dr. Syed Moazzam Husain (University of Dacca)	E,B,U,A
Maulana Abdul Mannan[10]	B,U,A
Mufti Jafar Husain[11]	U,P,A
Secretary, Ministry of Law and Parliamentary Affairs	E,U

Additional four councellors

Mr. M.M. Ahmad, S. Pk. CSP, Deputy Chairman Planning Commission (ex-officio)

Mr. M. Rashid, S. Pk. S.K., Governor of State Bank Pakistan (ex-officio)

Mr. Akhtar Husain, H. Pk. CSP (Retd.), Ex Chairman, National Press Trust

Mr. S.A. Hasnie, H.Q.A. S.Pk., Ex Governor, State Bank of Pakistan[12]

(Explanation cf. Table on the period covering 1981-84)

1969/1970

		Languages
Allamah Alaudin Siddiqui[1]	(Chairman)	E,U,P,A
Maulana Vilayet Husain[2]	(ended 70)	B,A,U
Maulana Abdul Hamid Badayuni[3]	(died 70)	U,A,P
Khalid M. Ishaque (Advocate)[4]	(from 70)	E,U,A,S
Dr. Serajul Haque (University of Dacca)	(from 70)	E,B,U,A
Abdul Hashim (Islamic Academy of Dacca)[5]		E,A,U
Dr. Fazlur Rahman[6]	(resigned 69)	E,U,A, G,Hug,Pu,P

	Languages
Justice (Retd.) Aminul Islam[7]	E,B,U
Dr. A.B.A. Haleem (University of Karachi)	E,U
Dr. Syed Moazzam Husain (University of Dacca)	E,B,U,A
Dr. A. W. J. Halepota (University of Sindh)[8]	E,S,U,A
Mufti Jafar Husain[9]	U,P,A
Secretary, Ministry of Law and Parliamentary Affairs	E,U

(Explanation cf. Table of the period covering 1981-84)

1974

		Languages
Justice Hamoodur Rahman[1]	(Chairman)	E,B,U
Justice Muh. Gul, S.Q.A. Law Sectretary		E,U,Pu
Justice (Retd.) Jamil Husain Rizvi[2]		E,U,Pu
Justice (Retd.) Qadir Nawaz Awan		E,U,S
Justice Muh. Afzal Cheemah[3]		E,U,Pu,A,P
Maulana Muh. Hanif Nadvi[4] (IRI)		U,E,A,Pu
Maulana Irshadul Haqq Thanvi[5]		U,A,E
Maulana Muh. Bakhsh Muslim[6]		E,Pu,E,A
Maulana Najmul Hasan Kararvi[7]		E,Pa,E,A
Maulana Muh. Idris Kandhalvi[8]		U,A,P
Dr. Prof. Shamim Akhtar (Islamabad University)		E,U
Dr. Miss Kaniz Yousuf (Islamabad University)		E,U
Dr. A.W.J. Halepota[9] (IRI)		E,S,U,A

No councellors

(Explanation cf. Table of the period covering 1981-84)

1977

		Languages
Justice (Retd.) Muh. Afzal Cheemah[1]	(Chairman)	E,U,Pu,A,P
Justice (Retd.) Salahuddin Ahmad[2]		E,B,U
A. K. Brohi (Advocate)[3]	(resigned 78)	E,S,U,A
Khalid M. Ishaque (Advocate)[4]		E,U,A,S
Maulana Muh. Yousaf Binori[5]	(died 78)	A,U,Pa,P
Khawajah Qamar ud-Din *pîr* of Sialwi[6]		E,Pu,A,P
Mufti Sayyahuddin Kakakhel[7]		U,A,Pa,P

		Languages
Mufti Muh. Husain Na'imi[8]	(resigned 80)	U,P,A,Pu
Maulana Zafar Ahmad Ansari[9]		U,E,P,A
Maulana Taqi Uthmani[10]		U,A,E,P
Mufti Jafar Husain[11]	(resigned 79)	U,P,A
Maulana Muh. Hanif Nadvi[12]		U,E,A,PuDr.
Ziauddin Ahmad[13] (Governor of State Bank)		E,U
Tajammul Husain Hashmi[14]	(resigned 78)	E,U

*In 1978 the following persons completed the Council or took over the seats
vacated by their predecessors:*

		Languages
I. H. Imtiazi[15]		E,U,Pu
Maulana Shamsul Haq Afghani[16]		U,A,Pa,P,E
Allamah Sayyid Muh. Razi[17]	(resigned 80)	U,A,P,E
Dr. Mrs. Khawar Khan Chishti[18]		E,U,Pu

No counsellors but several "Panels"

(Explanation cf. Table of the period covering 1981-84)

1981-1984

		Languages
Justice Dr. Tanzil ur Rahman[1]	(Chairman)	E,U,P,A
Justice Syed Jamil Husain Rizvi[2]	(died 81)	E,U,Pu
Allamah Ahmad Saeed Kazmi[3]	(resigned 81)	U,P,A,Pu
Maulana Muntakhib ul Haq Qadri[4]		U,P,A
Maulana Mahmud Ahmed Rizvi[5]		U,P,A
Khawajah Qamar ud-Din *pîr* of Sialwi[6]		U,Pu,A,P
Mufti Sayyahuddin Kakakhel[7]		U,A,Pa,A
Maulana Shamsul Haq Afghani[8]		U,A,Pu,P,B
Maulana Zafar Ahmed Ansari[9]		U,E,P,A
Maulana Muh. Ubaidullah[10]		U,P,A
Maulana Abdul Ghaffar Hasan[11]		U,A,P
Qazi Sa'ad Ullah Muh. Hasni[12]		U,A,P,B
Dr. Ziauddin Ahmad[13] (Governor of State Bank)		E,U
Allamah Ali Ghaznafar Karrarvi[14]	(resigned 81)	U,A,P,Pu

	Languages
Dr. Sharafat Ali Hashmi[15]	E,U
Dr. A. W. J. Halepota[16] (IRI)	E,S,U,A
Ghias Muhammad[17] (ex-Attorney)	E,U,Pu
Dr. Mrs. Khawar Khan Chishti[18]	E,U,Pu
Abdul Malik Irfani[19] (Advocate)	Pu,U,E,A,P

Sources: The names of the members are taken from: "Extract from A Brief Account of the Activities of the Advisory Council of Islamic Ideology", January 1964, December 1970, pp. 2, 3, 4 and 5 (copy received for information by the CII); *The Gazette of Pakistan,* Extraordinary Part II, February 1974, Islamabad: 1974, pp. 165f, *The Gazette of Pakistan,* Extraordinary Part III, May 31, 1971, Islamabad, pp. 247f as well as *Annual Report* of the CII for 1977-78, GoP, Islamabad, 1979, pp. 6f.

Explanation:

IRI	=	Islamic Research Institute
from	=	beginning of the nomination
end.	=	end of the term as memeber
U	=	Urdu
E	=	English
A	=	Arabic
P	=	Persian
Pu	=	Punjabi
Pa	=	Pashto
S	=	Sindhi
B	=	Bengali
G	=	Greek

The best language is given first, the second best as second, etc. All data on the knowledge of languages of the members have been conveyed to me by Mr. Hafiz Muhammad Latif (Chief Research Officer, CII) on 27.2.85 in the CII in Islamabad. It is quite possible that this data may not correspond completely to the factual position. They are, however, sufficient to state the educational orientation of the different members.

NOTES ON THE MEMBERS OF THE COUNCIL

1962

1. Member of the Muslim League; resigned in February of 1964.
2. Resigned in February of 1964.
3. Bengali; President of the provincial Muslim League; also resigned in February of 1964.

4. Born in 1898 in Badayun in U.P.; member of the 'Ulamâ' Convention 1951 and active in establishing the 22-*Points*; former President of the JUP; affiliated to the *Qâdiriyyah*. An early advocate of the idea of Pakistan. And in 1940 had been a close adviser to M.A. Jinnah. From 1914 he had been active in the Khalifat movement, building up branches of this movement. From 1937 he was a member of the Muslim League. From 1947 he was the President of the JUP in the Sindh/Karachi area. In Karachi he founded a religious school called Ta'limat-e Islamiyyah with modern and traditional education (*muhâjir*; Brelwi). Muhammad Sadiq Qasuri, *Akâbir-e tahrîk-e Pâkistân*, vols. I (vol. I, pp. 51 and 105ff) and II, Lahore, 1976 and 1979 (henceforth *ATP*). See also Muhammad Din Kalim Qadiri, *Tadhkirah-e Mashâ'ikh-e Qâdriyyah*, Lahore, 1985, pp. 279ff (Urdu).

5. 1898-1968. Member of the 'Ulamâ' Convention 1951 and co-author of the 22-*Points*. In 1910 he had enjoyed a madrasah education in Lucknow and in 1916 he had passed the *fâdil 'arabî* of the Punjab University. In 1920 he lived briefly in Peshawar where he dedicated himself to Tabligh and in 1925 he became Qazi-e Shari'at of the Sarhad Government. In 1942 he resigned and stayed on in Lahore from 1947 onward. In 1957 he became a member of the Law Commission and in 1962 a member of the Auqaf Board (*mujtahid*; *muhâjir*; Shia). Sayyid Husain Arif Naqwi, *Tadhkirah-e 'Ulamâ'-e Imâmiyyah (TUI) Pâkistân, Markaz Tahqiqât Fârsî wa Pâkistân*, Islamabad, 1984, pp. 249-251.

6. From India; an important political activist of the Muslim League. Studied in Delhi and in Cambridge. He was member of the Basic Principles Committee. After his guest professorship for Pakistan Studies at the Columbia University he became the Director of the Institutes of Islamic Research in 1960. As Chairman of the IRI he held the opinion that: "the most important task of the Institute was the explanation of Islam in the context of modern life and scientific criteria..." Cited by Muh. Khalid Masud in IS, op.cit., p. 36.

   Thus Qureshi clearly is to be counted among the Islamic *avant-garde*. Author of several books (*muhâjir*).

7. Bengali; prior to partition he had been the General Secretary to the Muslim League.

8. Bengali from Naokhali.

1964/65

1. Born in Lahore in 1907; died in 1977. Enjoyed a madrasah education as well as a formal education; member of the Muslim League. Rahi, Akhtar. *Tadhkirah 'Ulamâ'-e Punjab*, Lahore, 1980, vol. I, pp. 385ff.

2. No data.

3. Bengali; head of the modernist Madrasah-'Alia, Dacca.

4. See 1962 No. 4 (*muhâjir*; Brelwi).

5. See 1962 No. 5 (*muhâjir*; Shia).

6. See 1962 No. 6. He resigned when he accepted the chairmanship of the IRI.
7. See 1962 No. 7.
8. See 1962 No. 8.
9. Ph.D. from McGill University, Canada. Supposedly returned to Islam via the scriptures of Ibn Taymiyyah. Could not push through with modernist views. There was a conflict between him and the '*ulamâ*'. The critique by Yusuf Binori was especially vivid, demanding the '*ulamâ*' to propagate against F. Rahman. Al-Bayanat, *Binorî nambar*, Karachi (Urdu), pp. 49, 318-323.
10. Member of the JUI. Signed the Resolution of 1969 (Deobandi).
11. Born in 1914 in Gujranwala into a traditional religious family. In 1928 was in Lucknow (Madrasah Nizâmiyyah). After graduating from the Lucknow University, he also passed *Fâdil 'Arabî* and *Fâdil Hadîth*. Later went on to Najaf. From 1949, member of the Ta'lîmât-e Islâmî Board. Was active in 1977 in the PNA and in 1979 was Qâ'id-e millat Ja'fariyyah in the Bhakkar Convention. In 1979 founded the Jâmi'ah Ja'fariyyah in Gujranwala. He was also member of the 'Ulamâ' Convention 1951 and co-author of the *22-Points* (*mujtahid*; Shia). *TUI*, pp. 73-76.
12. Cf. CII, *Annual Report*, 1967, p. 2.

1969/1970

1. See 1964 No. 1.
2. See 1964 No. 3.
3. See 1962 No. 4 (*muhâjir*; Brelwi).
4. Today a leading intellectual personality of Pakistan.
5. See 1962 No. 7.
6. See 1964 No. 9.
7. Bengali; High Court, Dacca.
8. Formal and madrasah education. Member of several Silsilahs (tendency towards the Deobandis).
9. See 1964 No. 11 (*mujtahid*; Shia).

1974

1. Member of the Muslim League; Justice at the High Court of Pakistan from 1970-1981; was Adviser on Constitutional Affairs to the CMLA, from which he resigned. Was member of the Mu'tamar al 'alam al islamî (Islamic World Congress).
2. Formal and madrasah education; see also 1981 (Shia).
3. From Faisalabad. Studied Law at the Punjab University. Member of the Nizâm-e Islâm party and the 1962 Member National Assembly (MNA). Was for some time, Deputy Speaker. Justice at the High Court Punjab; Secretary, Ministry of Law and Justice of the Supreme Court. Today delegate of the

Mu'tamar al 'alam al Islâmî in Pakistan.

4. Studied at the Nadwat ul 'Ulama in Lucknow; was employed at the Institute of Islamic Culture, Lahore (Ahl-e Hadîth).

5. (*Muhâjir*; Deobandi)

6. *Khatîb* of the Jâmi'ah Moschee in Lahore (affiliated to the Ministry of Auqaf, Deobandi).

7. Born in 1918 in Allahabad. From 1927 studied at the Madrasah Nizâmiyyah in Lucknow. In 1933 studied formal subjects (Arabic, Tibb and Islamic Law) at the Lucknow University; from 1947 in Peshawar. Member of the Muslim League and a political activist. Died in July 1982 (*muhâjir*; Shia). Cf. *TUI*, pp. 406ff.

8. Born in 1899 in Bhopal. Former student of Ashraf Ali Thanwi. Later went to Deoband and was active at the Jâmi'ah Islâmiyyah in Bahawalpur (affiliated to the Ministry of Auqaf) from 1949. Since 1951 at the Jâmi'ah Ashrafiyyah in Lahore. Also signed the *22-Points* (*muhâjir*; Deobandi). Cf. Akhtar Rahi, *Tadhkirah* op.cit., vol. II, pp. 609 ff and Hafiz Muhammad Akbar Shah Bukhari, *Akâbir-e 'Ulamâ'-e Deoband*, Lahore, n.d. (*AUD*), pp. 177ff.

9. See 1969 No. 8 (has a tendency towards the Deobandis).

1977

1. See 1974 No. 3.

2. No data.

3. From 1978 Minister for Religious Affairs.

4. See 1969 No. 4.

5. Sayyid; born in 1904 in Peshawar. His father was an expert on Islam, and a merchant and Shaikh of the *Naqshbandi*. Educated in madrasah in Kabul. In 1930 became *maulwî fâdil* at the Punjab University; in 1945-47 in Deoband; *khalîfah* and *majâz* of the Ashraf Ali Thanwi; in 1951 *hijra* to Pakistan; followed Shabbir Ahmad Uthmani to Dabhil and there became the *sadr mudarris* of the Jâmi'ah Islâmiyyah Tando Allah Yar near Hyderabad, Sindh. Later established madrasah in Karachi. Member of the 'Ulamâ' Convention 1951 and co-author of the *22-Points*; Member of the JUI; Against the concepts by Ayub Khan, Parvez, Fazlur Rahman and Maududi on Islam. In Peshawar, President of the JUI Peshawar (Deobandi). *AUD*, pp. 234f; Al-Bayanat, *Binorî nambar,* Karachi (Urdu), pp. 10f, 51, 83, 312ff.

6. Born in 1906 in Sargodha District. Madrasah education in Muradabad. Member of the Banaras All India Sunni Conference in 1946. In 1946 worked for the Muslim League. Of important political influence due to his powerful *gaddî* (seat of a *pîr*; literally cushion). He is considered a high-ranking mystical personality and one of the most important representatives of the *mashâ'ikh*. President of the JUP from 1970. Resigned from this post in 1973. Then supporter of Shah Ahmad Nurani. Died in 1981 (Brelwi). Muh.

Saddiq Hazarwi, *Ta'âruf-e 'Ulamâ'-e Ahle Sunnat (TUAS)*, Lahore, 1979, pp. 268-271, *ATP*, vol. I, pp. 51 and 200ff.

7. Born in Peshawar. Taught in Faisalabad and has studied in a Deobandi madrasah. Today legal advisor to the International Institute for Islamic Economics (IIIE). Leans towards the Jama'at-e Islami.

8. Born in 1923 in a merchant family in Muradabad. Taught from 1948 to 1953 in the Dâr al 'Ulûm Anjuman-e Nu'mâniyyah in Lahore. Established a madrasah in Lahore. Member of the JUP. During the sixties member of the Auqaf Department. Has been very active since 1977 in the *'nizam-e mustafâ'* movement (*muhâjir*; Brelwi). *TUAS*, pp. 286-290, *Wafâq* (RP), 30.7.80 (Urdu).

9. Born in 1905 in Allahabad. No madrasah education; studied Philo-sophy; member of the JUH, later member of the Muslim League; today inclined towards the Jama'at-e Islami; signed the *22-Points* and was one of the members of the Ta'limat-e Islami Board (*muhâjir*; Deobandi).

10. Born in India. Law degree of Karachi University; M.A. in Arabic; madrasah education; Chairman of the Dâr al 'Ulûm in Karachi; member of the JUI; Justice of the Shariat Court (*muhâjir*; Deobandi).

11. Studied in Najaf and in Lucknow. Resigned in April 1979; see also 1964 (*mujtahid*; Shia). *TUI*, pp. 73-76.

12. Studied in the Nadwat ul 'Ulamâ; employed in the Institute of Islamic Culture. Originally from Gujranwala (Ahl-e Hadith).

13. Born in India. Studied abroad and graduated from Harvard. Inclined towards the Jama'at-e Islami. Currently Director of the IIIE (*Muhâjir*).

14. Secretary for Religious Affairs.

15. Federal Minister. From 1980 Administrator for Zakat.

16. Born in Peshawar. In Deoband during 1920-29; *ba'iah* by Ashraf Ali Thanwi, *khalîfah* and *majâz* by Mufti Muhammad Hasan Amratsari, Founder of the Jâm'iah Ashrafiyyah, Lahore; taught at the Bahawalpur University from 1963 to 1975. Chief Justice and Minister of Education in Qalat State. Member of the 'Ulamâ' Convention 1951 and co-author of the *22-Points* (Deobandi). *AUD*, pp. 283-284; see also Ridwi, *Tarîkh Dâr al-'Ulûm*, etc., op.cit., vol. II, pp. 123ff.

17. Originated from Lucknow; now in Karachi. Resigned in May 1979 as the Government planned to introduce Sunni *fiqh* (*muhâjir*; Shia). *MN*, 5.5.79.

18. Originated from Lahore. Chairman of a Women's, College. Ph.D. USA.

1981-1984

1. Originated from U. P., now in Karachi. Ph.D. in Islamic Law from the University of Karachi. No madrasah education (*muhâjir*).

2. See also 1974 No. 2; Formal and madrasah education (Shia).

3. Born in 1913 in Muradabad into a traditional religious family; madrasah education in Muradabad; built up a madrasah in Multan. *Murîd* of Khawajah

Muinuddin Chishti Ajmeri in Multan. Established the Anwar al 'Ulûm in Multan in 1935; Member of the Muslim League. 1946 Member of the Banaras All India Sunni Conference; strong Pakistani-nationalist. Founder of the JUP and of its *Nazim-e 'ala.* 1978 Chairman of the Tanzîm al Madâris. 1978 President of the JUP. Under his chairmanship, the All Pakistan Sunni Conference in Multan was held. Taught also at the Bahawalpur University. Resigned in 1981 stating that the work of the Council was in vain; member of the Central Zakat Council (*muhâjir*; Brelwi). *TUAS* pp. 26-30; *ATP*, pp. 51f. and *NW*, 13.5.81; see also CII, *Annual Report,* 1981/82, op.cit. (Urdu), p. 293.

4. Born in 1910 in U.P. Madrasah education in Deoband and in Muradabad. Member of the JUP; settled in Gulshan-e Iqbal, Karachi (*muhâjir*; Brelwi).

5. Born in 1924 in Agra (India) into a traditional religious family. Madrasah education. Built up the Hizb al Ahnâf in Lahore; advocates an Islâmic pluralism, as there cannot be, according to him, one Islâm for the entire country; also lamented the Zakat regulation and the nationalization of the religious endowments (*muhâjir*; Brelwi). *TUAS*, pp. 342-345; for a critical statement see '*Ulamâ' Kanwenshan,* 1980 (Urdu) op.cit., pp. 29f.

6. See 1977 No. 6 (Brelwi).

7. See 1977 No. 7 (Deobandi; Jama'at-e Islami).

8. See 1977 No. 16 (Deobandi).

9. See 1977 No. 9 (Deobandi; Jama'at-e Islami).

10. Madrasah education. Chairman of the Jâmi'ah Ashrafiyyah in Lahore. Member of the JUI. Supposedly has family ties with Zia (Deobandi).

11. Madrasah education. Taught in Faisalabad. His son, S. Abdul Ghaffar Hasan is said to collaborate with the Jama'at-e Islami (Ahl-e Hadith).

12. Born in 1924 in Baluchistan. Madrasah education (Deobandi).

13. See 1977 No. 13 (Inclined towards the Jama'at-e Islami)

14. Born in U. P.; Ph.D. from Harvard University; resigned in June 1981, due to personal reasons. He was substituted by Allamah Talib Jauhari from Karachi (*muhâjir*; Shia). CII, *Annual Report,* 1981-82, op.cit. (Urdu), p. 16.

15. Born in 1924 in Aligarh. Taught economics at Aligarh and studied Business Administration in California (*muhâjir*).

16. See 1969 No. 8 and 1974 No. 9; born in Sindh; madrasah education and Ph.D. in Oxford (inclined towards the Deobandis). Holds the chairmanship of the CII since 1985.

17. Originally from Hoshiarpur. Formal education in Lahore (*muhâjir*).

18. See 1977 No. 18.

19. Originally from Gujrat. Said to be a paid employee of the Jama'at-e Islami (inclined towards the Jama'at-e Islami).

APPENDIX B

"NOTIFICATION" FOR THE EQUIVALENCE

UNIVERSITY GRANTS COMISSION
SECTOR 5-9,
ISLAMABAD
(Academic Division)

No: 8-418/Acad/82/128

Dated: Nov 17, 1982

NOTIFICATION

Subject: EQUIVALENCE OF DEENI ASNAD WITH UNIVERSITY DEGREE

The decision of the University Grants Commission on the subject, is reproduced below for information and implementation

> Ashahadat-ul Fazeela ....
> Sanad awarded by Wafaq-ul-Madaris; Ashahadat-ul-Faragh ....
> .... Sanad awarded by Tanzeem-ul-Madaris,
> Ashahadat-ul-Alia .... Sanad awarded by
> Wafaq-ul-Madaris-ul-Salfia (Ahl-e-Hadis) ; and Sultan-ul-Afazil
> .... Sanad awarded by Wafaq-ul-Madaris, Shia
> after Dora-e-Hadis be considered equivalent to the M.A.
> Arabic/Islamic Studies for the purpose of teaching
> Arabic and Islamic Studies in colleges and universities
> and for pursuing higher studies in Arabic and Islamic
> Studies. For employment in fields other than teaching,
> however, such Sanad holders would be required to qualify
> in two additional subjects other than Arabic and Islamic
> Studies at the B.A. level from a university. They would also
> have to qualify in the recently introduced elective Pakistan
> Studies and Islamic Studies paper at the B.A. level.

To bring uniformity to the nomenclature of the Asnad issued by different schools of thought, it was decided that henceforth the final Sanad (degree) recognised as equivalent to M.A. in Arabic and Islamic Studies will be known as "Shahadat-ul-Almiyya Fil Uloomil Arabi Wal Islamia".

(Mohammad Latif Virk)
Director Academics

APPENDIX C

TABLE 46: DISTRICTS OF GRADUATION OF THE DEOBANDIS IN SELECTED YEARS
(1963, 1965, 1974, 1975 AND 1984)

District of Graduation	Number	Percentage
No data	127	—
Abbottabad	9	0.5
Attock	22	1.1
Azad Kashmir	8	0.4
Bannu	127	6.5
Bahawalpur	11	0.6
Bahawalnagar	4	0.2
Faisalabad	32	1.6
Gujranwala	34	1.7
Hayderabad	9	0.5
Karachi	379	19.4
Kohat	91	4.7
Lahore	139	7.1
Muzaffargarh	11	0.6
Multan	281	14.4
Mansehra	2	0.1
Mardan	16	0.8
Peshawar	669	34.3
Quetta	13	0.7
Rawalpindi	27	1.4
Sialkot	5	0.3
Sahiwal	38	1.9
Swat	10	0.5
Thatta	7	0.4
Toba Tek Singh	6	0.3

TABLE 47: TITLES OF FATHERS OF DEOBANDI CANDIDATES FOR GRADUATION
IN SELECTED YEARS (1963, 1965, 1974, 1975 AND 1984)

Title	Number	Percentage
No data	1320	—
Al-Hâj	46	6.1
Beg	3	0.4
Chaudhrî	3	0.4
Faqîr	3	0.4
Ghâzî	2	0.3
Hâjjî	78	10.3
Hakîm	7	0.9
Hadrat	3	0.4
Hâfiz	41	5.4
Imâm	2	0.3
Khalîfah	1	0.1
Mawlânâ	342	45.2
Mîr	28	3.7
Malik	6	0.8
Mirzâ	21	2.8
Muftî	3	0.4
Mîrzâdah	2	0.3
Pîr	3	0.4
Qâdî	2	0.3
Sâhib	19	2.5
Sayyid	53	7.0
Shaikh	8	1.1
Sharîf	5	0.7
Shâh	67	8.9

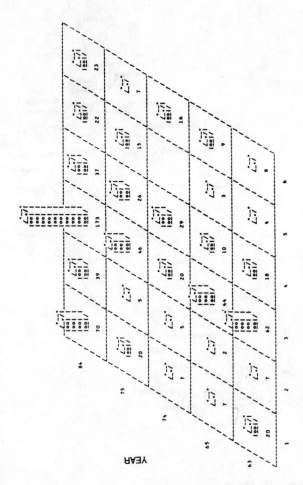

TITLES OF FATHERS

DIAGRAM 5: TITLE OF FATHERS, CLASSIFIED BY GROUPS

Explanation:

1 = Al-Hāj, Hājjī

2 = Hāfiz, Qārī, Imām, Khalīfah, Pīr, Ghāzī, Hakīm

3 = Mawlānā, Muftī

4 = Sayyid, Shāh

5 = Sharīf, Hadrat, Shaikh, Sāhib, Qādī

6 = Beg, Chaudhrī, Mīr, Malik, Mirzā, Mirzādah

APPENDIX D

The external boundaries of India depicted in this map are neither correct nor authentic (Editor).

MAP 3: ADMINISTRATIVE BOUNDARIES OF PAKISTAN, 1973

Source: *W.P. Zingel: Die Problematik regionaler Entwicklungsunterschiede in Entwicklungsländern*, Wiesbaden, 1979, p. 211.

PAKISTAN

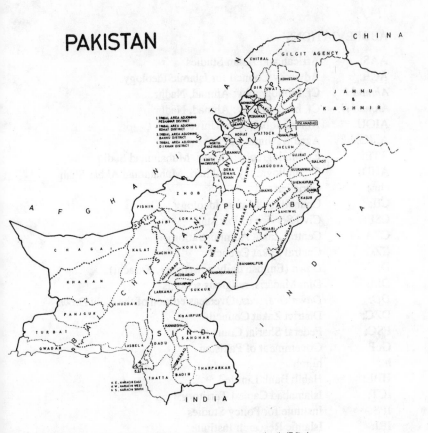

MAP 4: ADMINISTRATIVE BOUNDARIES OF PAKISTAN, 1982

Source: GoP, Statistics Division, Population Census Organisation, *1981 Census Report of Pakistan*, Islamabad, 1984, p. 199.

ABBREVIATIONS AND GLOSSARY

ABBREVIATIONS

AAS:	African and Asian Studies
ACII:	Advisory Council for Islamic Ideology
Ahmad I:	Cf. bibliography: Ahmad, Nadhr
Ahmad II:	Cf. bibliography: Ahmad, Nadhr
AIOU:	Allama Iqbal Open University
A. Kash.:	Azad Kashmir
ATP:	Cf. bibliography: Qasuri, Muhammad Sadiq
AUD:	Cf. bibliography: Bukhari, Muhammad Akbar Shah
chr.:	Christian
CII:	Council for Islamic Ideology
CSP:	Civil Service of Pakistan
CZA:	Central Zakat Administration
CZC:	Central Zakat Council
D:	*Dawn* (English daily newspaper, Karachi)
DM:	Dînî Madâris, religious schools
DO:	*Dawn Overseas*, Overseas edition of the daily *Dawn*
DZC:	District Zakat Council
FSC:	Federal Shariat Court
GoP:	Government of Pakistan
h.:	hijrah
HBL:	Habib Bank Limited
ICT:	Islamabad Capital Territory
IPS:	Institute for Policy Studies
IRI:	Islamic Research Institute
IS:	Islamic Studies, Islamabad
J:	*Jang* (Urdu daily newspaper, Lahore)
JI:	Jamâ'at-e Islâmî, religio-political party
JMP:	Jam'iyyat al-Mashâ'ikh Pâkistân
JUH:	Jam'iyyat-e 'Ulamâ'-e Hind, religio-political party in India, established prior to the partition of 1947 (Deobandi)
JUI:	Jam'iyyat-e 'Ulamâ'-e Islâm, religio-political party (Deobandi, established 1945)

JUP:	Jam'iyyat-e 'Ulamâ'-e Pâkistân, religio-political party (Brelwi, established 1947)
K:	Karachi
L:	Lahore
LAMEC:	Literacy and Mass Education Campaign
LZC:	Local Zakat Council
M:	*Mashriq* (Urdu daily newspaper)
Mad.:	Madrasah
MAS:	*Modern Asian Studies*
MC:	Mashâ'ikh Convention
MCG:	*Military and Civil Gazetteer*
ML:	Muslim League
MN:	*Morning News* (English daily newspaper, Karachi)
MRD:	Movement for the Restoration of Democracy
MS:	Mosque Schools
N. Areas:	Northern Areas
NBL:	National Bank Limited
NCDM (P):	National Committee for Dînî Madâris (Pakistan)
NEC:	National Education Council
NEP:	National Education Policy
NIDMP:	National Institute for Dînî Madâris (Pakistan)
NIT:	National Investment Trust
NLA:	National Language Authority
NW:	*Nawâ'-e Waqt* (Urdu daily newspaper, Lahore)
NWFP:	North West Frontier Province
NZF	National Zakat Foundation
n.d.:	no data
PID:	Press Information Department
PNA:	Pakistan National Alliance
PPP:	Pakistan People's Party
PS:	Private Schools
PT:	*Pakistan Times* (English daily newspaper)
PZC:	Provincial Zakat Council
QAU:	Qaid-e Azam University, Islamabad
RP:	Rawalpindi
TM:	*The Muslim* (English daily newspaper, Islamabad)
TUAS:	Cf. bibliography: Hazarwi, Muhammad Sadiq
TU:	Cf. bibliography: Naqwi, Sayyid Husain Arif
UBL:	United Bank Limited
UC:	'Ulamâ' Convention

UGC: University Grants Commission
ZUO: Zakat and Ushr Ordinance 1980

GLOSSARY

adîb 'âlim and *adîb fâdil*

> second and third stage of secular language studies in the English tradition. The subject matter is one of the "Islamic" languages, in this case Urdu, without reference to any religious elements. The first stage is simply called *adîb*. During the three years of study the student has to pass an examination after each year in six subjects: Morphology, Literature, Logic, Law, Translation as well as an oral examination. *Adîb* corresponds to the level of Matriculation, *adîb 'âlim* to the F.A. level and *adîb fâdil* to the B.A. level

'allâmah

> scholar, savant

'âlim, pl. *'ulamâ'*

> Islamic scholar; requires an education of several years in a religious school

'âlim 'arabî

> (cf. also *fâdil 'arabî*) (literally, expert of the Arabic language) This is the first stage of a three tier education in the Arabic language. This kind of instruction in language was introduced by the colonial ruler during the last century. The subject matter is secular (cf. also *adîb 'âlim*)

amîr, pl. *umarâ'*

> leader, guide

'aqâ'id

> religious beliefs, creedal statements

'attiyyât

> alms, excluding Zakat

awliyyâ'

> holy men, similar to *pîrs*

bai'ah

> a vow of alliance to a *pîr*.

barakah

> blessing, spiritual power

B.ed.; M.ed.

> Bachelor of Education; Master of Education

bid'ah
    innovation
da'wah
    peaceful mission in Islam
dâr al-'ulûm
    higher religious school
darjah-e fawqâniyyah
    higher level of religious education
darjah-e ibtedâ'iyyah
    primary level of religious teaching
darjah-e mutawassatah
    intermediate level of religious teaching
darjah-e takhassus
    special course in religious school, following the *dars-e nizâmî* in
    case it is actually offered
darjah-e wustânî
    cf. *darjah-e mutawassatah*
dars-e nizâmî
    traditional curriculum of religious schools
dars-e qur'ân
    instruction on Koran
dawrah-e hadîth
    highest stage of theological qualification
"Degree" level
    level of education which ends with a certificate of graduation;
    usually from grade 12 onwards, also B.A. (Bachelor of Arts)
dîniyyât
    Science of Islam, usually lower stage
Establishment Division
    administrative body vested with extensive powers, deciding,
    among others, posting within the civil service
fâdil, pl. *fudalâ'*
    graduate
fâdil 'arabî, pl. *fudalâ' 'arabî*
    (cf. also *'âlim 'arabî*) (literally expert of the Arabic language)
    Here the third and highest stage of the secular course on the
    Arabic language.
faqîh, pl. *fuqahâ'*
    Islamic scholar of jurisprudence; expert on Islamic law (*fiqh*)

farâ'id
> law of inheritance

fatwâ, pl. *fatâwâ*
> Islamic judgement on questions of Islamic law

fiqh
> Islamic law

fitnah
> apostasy

hadd, pl. *hudûd*
> literally limit; term for some punishments prescribed in the Koran

hadîth
> sayings of the Prophet Muhammad, compiled in several collections of *Hadîth*, with a normative character for the Muslims. The authenticity of such a Prophetic Norm and tradition varies for each Muslim according to the school of law he adheres to. The elements of a *Hadîth* are the *isnâd* (the chain of traditions) and the *matn* (the text)

hâfiz, pl. *huffâz*, English plural: *hâfizs*
> someone knowing the Koran by heart. It usually takes three to four years to achieve this

hajj
> the annual pilgrimage to Mecca

hâjjî, pl. *hujjâj*, English plural: *hâjjîs*
> pilgrim performing *hajj* or a person having performed *hajj*

hijrah
> Muhammad's migration from Mecca to Medina;
> beginning of the Islamic chronology; A.D. 622

hîlah or *hiyal*
> legal stratagem; method frequently employed to circumvent the Shari'a

hifz
> the art of knowing the Koran by heart

'ibâdah
> obligation by man to God, in contrast to *mu'âmalah*, prescribing the social behaviour and conduct among men

'îd
> a festival and Islamic holiday

ijâzah
> permission to a student to teach the teachings of a scholar

ijmâ'
> the method of arriving at a consensus in an Islamic judicial trial

ijtihâd
> the solving of a problem of law by reference to the individual inquiry according to Islamic principles

imâm, pl. *a'imma*, English pl. *imâms*
> head of a mosque, leading the communal prayer. In Shia tradition he is, at the same time, the head of the community

iqrâ'
> invitation to read or recite (literally, recite!)

isnâd
> pl. of *sanad*

itâ'ah
> absolute obedience

jayyid 'ulamâ'
> the modernist forces among the religious scholars

jihâd
> holy war in Islam, spiritual struggle against one's lower instincts as well as war against non-Muslims

khalîfah, pl. *khulafâ'*
> literally, successor; title of those who presided the Islamic imperium after the death of Prophet Muhammad. In mystical terminology the successor of a *Sûfî shaikh*

khatîb, pl. *khutabâ'*, English plural: *khatîbs*
> head of a mosque, delivering the Friday sermon (*khutbah*)

khums
> literally, one fifth; religious tax payed to the Prophet. Among the Shia the *khums* is delivered to the current head of the Shia community

khutbah
> Friday sermon

madâris
> cf. *madrasah*

madrasah, pl. *madâris*
> religious school with a special curriculum, characterized mainly by the studies of Koranic teachings and rational sciences

mahkamah
> department

majâz

someone who has received the permission of a *pîr* to disseminate his teachings

majlis

meeting, convent

maktab

place of memorizing and reading the Koran; limited to pre-school and primary knowledge

maktab-e fikr, pl. *makâtîb-e fikr*

a school of thought. Some schools of thought do not differ from each other in a theological sense. In contrast to this one may mention the "*madhâhib*" (sing. *madhhab*) (schools of law) with considerable differences in their principles of interpretation of the Islamic law

Maktab-Scheme

a programme taken up by the Government during the sixties in order to spread literacy, especially among the rural population. It was to be implemented via mosques and *maktabs*.

mandîs

small local markets

ma'rifah

gnosis

markaz

literally, centre

mashâ'ikh, pl. of *shaikh*

Islamic mystic and leader of an order

Matriculation (matric)

stage reached after ten years of school

maulwî

Islamic scholar; in contrast to the *mawlânâ* the *maulwî* holds a lower academic level

mawlânâ

(literally, our lord) usually the title of a Sunni religious scholar with a formal theological schooling; hardly applied in the Arabic world

mawqûf (*'aliyyah*)

the level between the primary and a higher stage of the religious schools, today equal to B.A. degree

mîr

in most cases the same meaning as *sayyid* (descendant of the

Prophet); on the Indian subcontinent also an ethnic group

mohtamim or *muhtamim*

manager or/and head of a religious school

mu'adhdhin

the person calling the believers to their daily prayers with the *'adhân*

muftî

high Islamic scholar, authorized to deliver a *fatwâ*

muhâjir, pl. *muhâjîrûn*

originally someone who had taken part in the *hijrah*, the exodus from Mecca to Medina; today general expression for refugee; in the Indian-Pakistani context someone who left India or Pakistan in order to settle in the new state. The *muhâjirs* in Pakistan usually originate from northern India.

mujâwir

person administering a heritage

mujâhid, pl. *mujâhidûn*

holy warrior; someone fighting for Islam

mujtahid

someone authorized to practise *ijtihâd*

mullâ or *mulla*

in most cases, a term for the local theological authority, in contrast to the *mawlânâ* and *maulwî*; nowadays, however, without formal religious education or qualified theological studies; holds a negative connotation in popular speech. In the eighteenth and nineteenth century, the title of *mulla* had been held in high esteem.

murîd

disciple, usually of a *pîr*

murshid

leader, usually of a mystical order, cf. *pîr*

mustahiq, pl. *mustahiqûn*

needy persons, entitled to Zakat according to Islamic law

mutawallî

someone who takes care and is in charge of an endowment

nâzim

leader, director

nâzirah

the reading of Koran

nadhrânah
> alms

nisâb
> curriculum, but also a certain limit, the limit of wealth beyond which one has to pay Zakat

pîr
> mystical leader, *sûfî* master

qâdî
> religious scholar

qârî
> someone able to recite the Koran according to certain prescriptions

qiyâs
> determining the applicability of law in Islam; conclusion or analogy

qirâ'at
> the artistic recitation of the Koran according to certain prescriptions

sadaqah
> voluntary donation of alms

sâhib
> title of respect; address

saiyyid, pl. *sadât*
> usually a descendant of the Prophet

sajjâdah-nashîn
> successor to the leadership of a *pîr*

salaf
> literally, predecessor; *al-salafiyyah* refers to an Islamic reform movement of Muhammad Abduh (1849-1905) in Egypt; here, movement practising *ijtihâd*, following the ancestors but not the schools of law

sanad, pl. *isnâd*
> degree, certificate; in the Sciences of *Hadîth* also the chain of tradition

shâh
> a descendant of the Prophet or His family

shahâdah
> degree, also martyrdom

shaikh, pl. *shuyyûkh*
> an Islamic dignitary, often a *pîr*

shaikh al-islâm
>   high Islamic scholar, dominating a court of justice

shaikh al-hadîth
>   an expert on the tradition of the Prophet

shirk
>   blasphemy by polytheism

shurâ
>   body of Islamic and other authorities

silsilah
>   literally, chain; here the chain of ancestors of a saint or an order

sîrat
>   biography; mostly biography of the Prophet

tablîgh
>   mission in Islam

tafsîr
>   interpretation of Koran, exegesis of Koran

tahtânî
>   stage of religious education prior to _mawqûf_, but still above the
>   primary stage

tajwîd
>   the art of pronouncing the Koran correctly; also a subject in
>   religious schools

tamlîk
>   here the transfer of Zakat into the property of the _mustahiq_

tanzîm
>   organization, here referring to the umbrella organization of the
>   religious school of the Brelwis

taqlîd
>   literally, imitation; here, the imitation of a recognized school of
>   law; in contrast to _ijtihâd_

tarîqah, pl. _turuq_
>   literally, way; here, mystical way or order

tawhîd
>   the belief in the unity of god in contrast to _shirk_, where Allah is
>   accompanied by other gods

tawhîn-e rasûl
>   offence to the Prophet

thâniyyah
>   second, secondary

ulâ
>   first, primary

'ulûm-e 'aqliyyah
> the so-called acquired or rational sciences˙

'ulûm-e naqliyyah
> the so-called traditional sciences; they are of a transcendent nature

ummah
> community of all Muslims

University Grants Commission (UGC)
> body established in July 1973 to coordinate the academic pro-grammes of the universities of the country and to finance them. The UGC has three main fields of activities: Centres of Exellence; Area Study Centres; Pakistan Study Centre. Furthermore, basic works as educational campaigns on Islam via the media, revision of books as well as their publication were to be offered by the UGC·. The education plan of 1979 has extended the scope of the UGC in some fields.

'urf
> customary law

'urs
> literally, the marriage; on the Indian subcontinent refers to the anniversary of a saint's death; annual celebrations at a shrine

'ushr
> literally, the tith; compulsory annual tax on agricultural produce; Zakat

usûl
> principles

wafâq
> organization, here umbrella organization of religious schools

wâqif
> someone donating a *waqf*

waqf, pl. *awqâf*
> religious endowment

zakat
> literally, purification, from the Arabic *'zakâ'*; annual tax on the annual savings (2.5 per cent) compulsory for each Muslim

1 *lac*
> = 100,000

1 *tolâ*
> = 11.664 gram

1 *acre*
> = 0.4047 hectare

BIBLIOGRAPHY

Abdullah, Mahmud Muhammad. *Al-lughat al-'arabiyyah fî Bâkistân*, vol. I, Islamabad, 1983 (Arabic).

Askari, Muhammad Hasan. *Jadîdiyyat*, Lahore, 1979 (Urdu).

Adorno, Th. et al. *Der Positivismusstreit in der deutschen Soziologie*, Darmstadt, 1982.

Afridi, Arbab Khan. "Manuscript on the Dînî Madâris in NWFP", Institute of Education and Research, Peshawar, 1984. Mimeograph (Urdu).

Afzal, Mohammad. "Integration of Madrasah Education with the formal System of Education at Secondary Level", Master's Thesis, Islamabad, 1985.

Ahmad, A. and. V. Grunebaum, G.E. eds., *Muslim Selfstatement in India and Pakistan, 1857-1968*, Wiesbaden, 1970.

Ahmad, Aziz. *Islamic Modernism in India and Pakistan*, Oxford, 1967.

———. *Studies in Islamic Culture in the Indian Environment*, Oxford, 1964.

———. "The Conflicting Heritage of Sayyid Ahmed Khan and Jamal Ad-Din Afghani in the Muslim Political Thought of the Indian Subcontinent", in *Trudui XXV Mezdhunarod. Kongres Vostokovedov 1960*, vol. IV (1963), pp. 147-152.

Ahmad, Feroz. "Pakistan: The New Dependence", in *Race and Class*, vol. XVIII, no. 1, 1976, pp. 3-22.

Ahmad, Hafiz Nadhr. *Hamârî Darsgâhôñ mêñ dînî ta'lîm*, presented at the conference Kull Pâkistân Mu'tamar 'Arabî wa 'Ulûm Islâmiyyah in Peshawar, 1955. Mimeograph (Urdu).

———. *A preliminary survey of madaris-i-deeniyyah in East & West Pakistan*, presented at the first Pakistan Oriental Conference, December 1956. Mimeograph (Urdu).

———. *Jâ'izah-e madâris-e 'arabiyyah Islâmiyyah maghribî Pâkistân*, Lialpur, 1960 (Urdu) (*Ahmad I*).

———. *Jâ'izah-e madâris-e 'arabiyyah maghribî Pâkistân*, Lahore, 1972 (Urdu) (*Ahmad II*).

Ahmad, Imtiaz. ed., *Ritual and Religion among Muslims of the Sub-continent*, Lahore, 1985.

Ahmad, Khurshid and Zafar Ishaq Ansari. eds., *Islamic Perspectives: Studies in honour of Mawlânâ Sayyid Abul A'lâ Mawdûdî*, London, 1979.

Ahmad, Mohammad Akhlaq. *Traditional Education among Muslims: A study of some aspects in modern India*, New Delhi, 1985.

Ahmad, Zahid. "*Pâkistân mêñ chapnê wâlê dînî rasâ'il o jarâ'id kâ aik jâ'izah*", M.A. Islamic Studies Department, Lahore, 1984 (Urdu).

Ahmed, Akbar S. *Social and Economic Change in the Tribal Areas*, Oxford, 1977.

Ahmed, Manzooruddin. ed., *Contemporary Pakistan: Politics, Economy and Society*, Karachi, 1982.

———. "The Political role of the 'Ulama' in the Indo-Pakistan Subcontinent", in *Islamic Studies*, vol. 4, no. 4, 1967, pp. 327-354.

Ahmed, Munir D. "Muslim Education prior to the Establishment of Madrasah", in *Islamic Studies*, vol. 26, no. 4, 1984, pp. 321-349.

Ahmed, Munir. "The Shi'is of Pakistan", in Martin Kramer, ed., *Shi'ism: Resistance and Revolution*, London, 1987, pp. 275-287.

Ahmed, Saghir. *Class and Power in a Punjabi Village*, New York, 1977.

Al-Attas, S. Muhammad. *Aims and Objectives of Islamic Education*, Jeddah, 1979.

Al-Baiyanât. "Binorî nambar", Jâmi'ah al-'Ulûm al-Islâmiyyah Karâchî, Karachi, 1978 (Urdu).

Al-Ghazzali. *The Book of Knowledge*, trans. by Nabih A. Faris, Sh. Muh. Ashraf, Lahore, 1974 (1st English edn. in 1962).

Al-Haq, monthly from Akora Khattak, Peshawar (Urdu).

Al-Rahman. "Muftî Mahmûd nambar", Lahore, n.d., pp. 43-46 (Urdu).

Al-Wafâq. *Wafâq-e 'ulamâ'-e shî'iyyah Pâkistân kê chothe sâlânah ijtimâ' kî tafsîlî repôrt*, Lahore, 1985 (Urdu).

Alavi, H. and T. Shanin, eds., *Introduction to the Sociology of Developing Societies*, London, 1982.

Alavi, Hamza. "Class and State", in H. Gardezi and J. Rashid, eds., *Pakistan: The Roots of Dictatorship*, London, 1983, pp. 40-93.

———. "The State in Postcolonial Societies: Pakistan and Bangla Desh", in K. Gough and H.P. Sharma, eds., *Imperialism and Revolution in South Asia*, New York, 1973, pp. 145ff.

Albrecht, Herbert. *Lebensverhältnisse ländlicher Familien in West Pakistan; Sozialökonomische Schriften zur Agrarentwicklung*, Saarbrücken, 1971.

Amad wa Kharch, al-Jâmi'at al-salafiyyah 1984, Lahore, 1984 (Urdu).

Ansari, Muhammad Fazl ur-Rahman. *The Qur'anic Foundations and Structure of Muslim Society*, Karachi, 1977.

Ansari, Sarah F.D., *Sufi Saints, Society and State Power: The Pirs of Sind, 1843-1947*, Ph.D. dissertation, Royal Holloway and Bedford College, London, 1987.

Arshad, Abd al-Rashid. *Bîs barê musalmân*, Lahore, 1986 (Urdu).

Aziz, K.K. *A History of the Idea of Pakistan*, vols. I-IV, Lahore, 1987.

Aziz, K.K. *Rahmat Ali: A Biography*, Lahore, 1987.

Bahadur, Kalim. *The Jama'at-i-Islami of Pakistan*, Lahore, 1983.

Baljon, J.M.S. *Modern Muslim Koran Interpretation 1880-1960*, Leiden, 1961.

Batalwi, Arif. *Jinnah sê Diyâ' tak*, Lahore, n.d. (Urdu).

Baxter, Craig. ed., *Zia's Pakistan: Politics and Stability in a Frontline State*, Lahore, 1985.

Baqi, Muhammad Fuad Abdal. *Al-mu'jam al-mufâhras lî alfâz al-qur'ân al-karîm*, al-Qâhira, 1363 h. (Arabic).

Bennigsen, A. and M. Broxup, *The Islamic Threat to the Soviet State*, Rawalpindi, 1983.

Binder, Leonard. *Religion and Politics in Pakistan*, Berkeley, 1961.

Bibi Sakina. *Dâr al 'Ulûm Haqqâniyyah, Akôrâ Khattak, Peshâwar, IER,* University of Peshawar, Master's Thesis, 1985, Mimeograph (Urdu).

Blake, Stephen P. "The Patrimonial-Bureaucratic Empire of the Mughals", *Journal of Asian Studies*, vol. 39, no. 1, 1979, pp. 77-94.

Bray, Mark. "Universal Education in Pakistan", *International Review of Education*, vol. 29, no. 2, The Hague, 1983, pp. 167-178.

Brohi, A.K. "Islamic University of Islamabad: Principles and purposes", *Pakistan Studies*, vol. 1, no. 2, London, 1982.

Buddenberg, Doris. "Islamization and shrines: An anthropological point of view", presented at the 9th European Conference on Modern South Asian Studies, Heidelberg, July 9-12, 1986. Mimeograph.

Bukhari, Hafiz Muhammad Akbar Shah. *Akâbir-e 'Ulamâ'-e Dêôband*, Lahore, n.d. (Urdu).

Burki, Sh. Javed. *Pakistan under Bhutto*, New York, 1979.

Caroe, Olaf. *The Pathans: 550 B.C.–A.D. 1957, with an Epilogue on Russia*, Karachi, 1984.

Chaudhry, A.G. *Some Aspects of Islamic Education*, Lahore, 1982.

Choudhury, G.W. *Constitutional Development in Pakistan*, Lahore, 1969.

Christensen, R.O. ed., *Report on the Tribes of Dir, Swat and Bajor together with the Utman-Khel and Sam Ranizai*, Peshawar, 1981.

Chughtai, Muhammad Abd Allah. *Qîâm dâr al-'ulûm dêôband*, Lahore, 1980 (Urdu).

Clark, T. W. ed., *The Novel in India*, London, 1970.

Cohen, Stephen P. *The Pakistan Army*, Berkeley, 1984.

Cole, J.R.I. *Roots of North Indian Shî'ism in Iran and Iraq: Religion and State in Awadh, 1722-1859*, Berkeley, 1988.

Dettmann, Klaus. "Agrarkolonisation im Rahmen von Kanalbewässerungsprojekten am Beispiel des Fünfstromlandes", in J. Hagedorn, J. Hovermann and H.J. Nitz, eds., *Landerschließung und Kulturlandschaftswandel an den Siedlungsgrenzen der Erde*, Göttingen, 1976, pp. 179-191.

Directory Federal Councillors of Pakistan, Karachi, n.d.

Diya, Shakil Ahmad. *Sindh kâ muqaddimah*, Karachi, 1986 (Urdu).

Eaton, R.M. *Sufis of Bijapur 1300-1700*, New Jersey, 1978.

———. "The Political and Religious Authority of the Shrine of Bâbâ Farîd", in B.D. Metcalf, ed., *Moral Conduct and Authority*, op.cit., pp. 333-356.

Eccel, A. Chris. *Egypt, Islam and Social Change: al-Azhar in conflict and accommodation*, Berlin, 1984.

Elphinstone, Mountstuart. *An Account of the Kingdom of Caboul and its Dependencies in Persia, Tartary, and India, Graz,* 1969, vol. 2, chapter IV.

Ende, W. and U. Steinbach, eds., *Der Islam in der Gegenwart*, Munich, 1984.

Ende, W. Waren, "Ğamâladdîn al-Afġânî und Muhammad 'Abduh Agnostiker?" in *Zeitschrift der Deutschen Morgenländischen Gesellschaft*, Supplementa I, XVII. Deutscher Orientalistentag, Vorträge Teil 2, Wiesbaden, 1969, pp. 650-659.

Esposito, John L. ed., *Voices of Resurgent Islam*, Oxford, 1983.

Ewing, Katherine. "The Politics of Sufism: Redefining the Saints of Pakistan", *Journal of Asian Studies*, vol. XLII, no. 2, February 1983, pp. 251-268.

————. "Malangs of the Punjab: Intoxication or Adab as the Path to God?" In B.D. Metcalf, ed., *Moral Conduct and Authority*, op.cit., pp. 357-371.

Faruki, Kemal A. *The Evolution of Islamic Constitutional Theory and Practice*, Karachi, 1971.

Faruqi, Ziya-ul-Hassan. *The Deoband School and the Demand for Pakistan*, Lahore, 1963.

Fihrist-e maqâlât, idârah-e 'ulûm-e islâmiyyah, Punjab University, M.A. Thesis 1952-1984 (Urdu).

Findley, C.V. "The Advent of Ideology in the Islamic Middle East", in *Studia Islamica*, 1982, vol. 50, pp. 143-169, and 1982, vol. 51, pp. 147-180.

Flügel, Gustav. *Concordance of the Koran*, Karachi, 1979.

Friedman, Yohannan. "The attitude of the Jam'iyyat al-'Ulama'-i Hind to the Indian national movement and the establishment of Pakistan", in *AAS* 7, 1971, pp. 157-180.

————. "The Jam'iyyat al-'Ulama'-i Hind in the Wake of Partition", in *AAS* 11, 1976, pp. 181-211.

Gankovski, Yu.V. and V.N. Mosalenko. *The Three Constitutions of Pakistan*, Lahore, 1978.

Gankovski, Yu.V. and L.R.G. Polonskaya. *A History of Pakistan, 1947-58*, Lahore, n.d.

Gardezi, H. and J. Rashid eds., *Pakistan: The Unstable State*, Lahore, 1983.

————. *Pakistan: The Roots of Dictatorship*, London, 1983.

Geijbels, M. "Aspects of the Veneration of Saints in Islam with special reference to Pakistan", in *Muslim World*, no. 68, 1978, pp. 176-186.

Ghafoor, R.A. *Manual of Waqf Laws*, Lahore, n.d.

Ghani, Ashraf. "Islam and State-Building in Afghanistan", in *Modern Asian Studies*, vol. 12, 1978, pp. 269-284.

Ghayur, Mohammad Arif and J. Henry Korson. "The Effects of Population and Urbanization Growth Rates on the Ethnic Tensions in Pakistan", in Manzooruddin Ahmed, ed., *Contemporary Pakistan*, op.cit., pp. 204-227.

Gieraths, Christine and Jamal Malik. *Die Islamisierung der Wirtschaft in Pakistan unter Zia ul Haq*, Bad Honnef, 1988.

Gieraths, Christine. "Pakistan: Social Welfare through Islamization. Assessment and Evaluation (1979-84)", *ASIEN*, no. 31, April 1989, pp. 1-31.

Gilani, Ijaz S. *The four 'R's of Afghanistan*. Islamabad, 1985 (approx).

Gilmartin, David. "Religious Leadership and the Pakistan Movement in the

Punjab", *Middle Eastern and African Studies*, vol. 13, no. 3, 1979, pp. 485-517.

――――. "Shrines, Succession, and Sources of Moral Authority", in B.D. Metcalf, ed., *Moral Conduct and Authority*, op.cit., pp. 221-240.

Gilsenan, Michael. *Recognizing Islam*, London, 1982.

Gilani, S.M.A. *Hindûstân mêñ Musalmânôñ kâ nizâm-i ta'lîm o tarbiyyat*, vols. I and II, Delhi, 1966 (Urdu).

Goldschmidt, D. and H. Melber eds., *Die Dritte Welt als Gegenstand erziehungswissenschaftlicher Forschung*, Weinheim, 1981 (Zeitschrift für Pädagogik 16. Beiheft).

GoP, Auqaf Department, West Pakistan. Manual of Rules and Regulations of the Auqaf Department: *The West Pakistan Jamia Islamia (Bahawalpur) Ordinance, 1964, West Pakistan Ordinance No. XVII of 1964*, Lahore, 1969, pp. 68-97.

GoP, CII. *Annual Report of the Proceedings of the Advisory Council of Islamic ideology for the year 1966*, n. d. (report 3).

――――. *Annual Report of the Proceedings of the Advisory Council of Islamic ideology for the year 1967*, n. d. (report 4).

――――. *Annual Report of the Proceedings of the Advisory Council of Islamic ideology for the year 1971*, n. d. (report 8).

――――. *Consolidated Recommendations of the CII relating to Education system in Pakistan, 1962 to 1982*, Islamabad, 1982 (Urdu/English).

――――. *Constitutional Recommendations for the Islamic System of Government*, Islamabad, 1983.

――――. *Islamic Social Order Report of the CII 1962-1982*, Islamabad, 1982 (Urdu).

――――. Tanzil ur-Rahman, *introduction of Zakat in Pakistan*, CII, Islamabad, n.d.

――――. *Consolidated Recommendations on the Islamic Economic System*, Islamabad, 1983 (Urdu/English).

GoP, *Curriculum for Arabic for grades six to eight*, Islamabad, 1975 (Urdu/Arabic).

――――. Federal Budgets, selected years.

GoP, Federal Ministry of Education. *Pakistan Studies*, Lahore, 1983.

GoP, *International Islamic University Ordinance 1985*, Islamabad, 1985.

GoP, Islamic Research Institute, ed., *Pâkistân mêñ Dînî Mâdâris kâ* (sic!) *fihrist*, Islamabad, 1982 (Urdu).

GoP, LAMEC. *Literacy: A new thrust*, Islamabad, n.d.

――――. *Literacy: A new thrust*, by Dr. A. R. Chaudhary, Chairman LAMEC, Islamabad, n.d.

GoP, Mahkamah Awqâf Punjab, Lahore. *Bujet barâ-e sâl 1985-86*, Lahore, 1986 (Urdu).

GoP, *Manual of Rules and Regulations of the Auqaf Department, West Pakistan*, Lahore, 1969.

GoP, Ministry of Education, Curriculum Wing. *Curriculum and Syllabi for PTC*

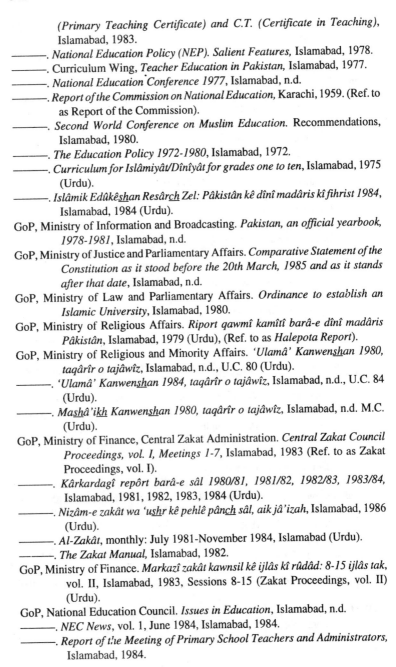

(Primary Teaching Certificate) and C.T. (Certificate in Teaching), Islamabad, 1983.

―――. *National Education Policy (NEP). Salient Features*, Islamabad, 1978.

―――. Curriculum Wing, *Teacher Education in Pakistan*, Islamabad, 1977.

―――. *National Education'Conference 1977*, Islamabad, n.d.

―――. *Report of the Commission on National Education*, Karachi, 1959. (Ref. to as Report of the Commission).

―――. *Second World Conference on Muslim Education*. Recommendations, Islamabad, 1980.

―――. *The Education Policy 1972-1980*, Islamabad, 1972.

―――. *Curriculum for Islâmiyât/Dîniyât for grades one to ten*, Islamabad, 1975 (Urdu).

―――. *Islâmik Edûkêshan Resârch Zel: Pâkistân kê dînî madâris kî fihrist 1984*, Islamabad, 1984 (Urdu).

GoP, Ministry of Information and Broadcasting. *Pakistan, an official yearbook, 1978-1981*, Islamabad, n.d.

GoP, Ministry of Justice and Parliamentary Affairs. *Comparative Statement of the Constitution as it stood before the 20th March, 1985 and as it stands after that date*, Islamabad, n.d.

GoP, Ministry of Law and Parliamentary Affairs. *Ordinance to establish an Islamic University*, Islamabad, 1980.

GoP, Ministry of Religious Affairs. *Riport qawmî kamîtî barâ-e dînî madâris Pâkistân*, Islamabad, 1979 (Urdu), (Ref. to as *Halepota Report*).

GoP, Ministry of Religious and Minority Affairs. *'Ulamâ' Kanwenshan 1980, taqârîr o tajâwîz*, Islamabad, n.d., U.C. 80 (Urdu).

―――. *'Ulamâ' Kanwenshan 1984, taqârîr o tajâwîz*, Islamabad, n.d., U.C. 84 (Urdu).

―――. *Mashâ'ikh Kanwenshan 1980, taqârîr o tajâwîz*, Islamabad, n.d. M.C. (Urdu).

GoP, Ministry of Finance, Central Zakat Administration. *Central Zakat Council Proceedings, vol. I, Meetings 1-7*, Islamabad, 1983 (Ref. to as Zakat Proceedings, vol. I).

―――. *Kârkardagî repôrt barâ-e sâl 1980/81, 1981/82, 1982/83, 1983/84*, Islamabad, 1981, 1982, 1983, 1984 (Urdu).

―――. *Nizâm-e zakât wa 'ushr kê pehlê pânch sâl, aik jâ'izah*, Islamabad, 1986 (Urdu).

―――. *Al-Zakât*, monthly: July 1981-November 1984, Islamabad (Urdu).

―――. *The Zakat Manual*, Islamabad, 1982.

GoP, Ministry of Finance. *Markazî zakât kawnsil kê ijlâs kî rûdâd: 8-15 ijlâs tak*, vol. II, Islamabad, 1983, Sessions 8-15 (Zakat Proceedings, vol. II) (Urdu).

GoP, National Education Council. *Issues in Education*, Islamabad, n.d.

―――. *NEC News*, vol. 1, June 1984, Islamabad, 1984.

―――. *Report of the Meeting of Primary School Teachers and Administrators*, Islamabad, 1984.

————. *Report of the meeting of Public Schools,* Islamabad, 1985.

————. *The good schools: a survey,* Islamabad, n.d.

GoP. *National Education Policy and Implementation Programme,* Islamabad, 1979.

————. *Nazariyyâtî kawnsil kî sâlânah riport 1977-78,* Islamabad, 1979 (Urdu).

————. *Nazariyyâtî kawnsil kî sâlânah riport 1978-79,* Islamabad, 1980 (Urdu).

————. *Nazariyyâtî kawnsil kî sâlânah riport 1980-81,* Islamabad, 1982 (Urdu).

GoP, Pakistan Narcotics Control Board. *National Survey on Drug Abuse in Pakistan,* 1986 (Highlights), Islamabad, 1987.

GoP. Pakistan Statistical Yearbook, 1986.

GoP. Pakistan Tourism Development Corporation. *Journey into Light,* Islamabad, 1985.

GoP. *Report of the Committee set up by the Governor of West Pakistan for Recommending improved Syllabus for the various Darul Ulooms and Arabic Madrasas in West Pakistan,* Lahore, 1962 (Ref. to as Report of the Committee).

GoP, Statistics Division, Population Census Organisation. *1981 Census Report of Pakistan,* Islamabad, 1984 (for several districts).

GoP, Statistics Division. *Pakistan Statistical Yearbook,* 1985, Islamabad, 1985.

GoP. *Ta'âruf al-jâmi'at al-islâmiyyah,* Islamabad, 1984 (Urdu).

GoP, UGC. *A Guide to the Equivalence of Degrees and Diplomas in Pakistan,* Islamabad, 1978.

Gorekar, M.S. *Glimpses of Urdu Literature,* Bombay, 1961.

Gough, K. and H.P. Sharma eds., *Imperialism and Revolution in South Asia,* New York, 1973.

Guraya, Muhammad Yusuf, comp., *Tarîkh-e Tasawwuf* (by Prof. Y. S. Chishti), Awqâf Department, ed., Lahore, 1972 (Urdu).

Gramlich, Richard. *Die schiitischen Derwischorden Persiens,* Teil II, in *Abhandlungen für die Kunde des Morgenlandes,* Wiesbaden, 1976.

Habermas, Jürgen. *Zur Rekonstruktion des Historischen Materialismus,* Frankfurt, 1982.

Halepota, A.W.J. "Islamic Conception of Knowledge", *Islamic Studies,* vol. 14, no. 1, Islamabad, 1975, pp. 1-8.

Haq, Diya al-. *Tashkîl-e naw,* Opening speech, Islamabad, 1981 (Urdu).

Haq, Mazhar-ul. *Civics of Pakistan,* Lahore, 1983.

Haq, Sami al-. *'Aqâ'id wa Sunan,* Peshawar, 1985 (Urdu).

Haq, Zia ul. "Islamic Research: Method and Scope", *Islamic Studies,* Foundation Day Supplement, Islamabad, Summer 1976, pp. 43-50.

————. "Muslim religious education in Indo-Pakistan", in *Islamic Studies,* vol. 14, no. 1, Islamabad, 1975, pp. 271-292.

Hardy, Peter. "Islamischer Patrimonialismus: Die Moghulherrschaft", in W. Schluchter, ed., *Max Webers Sicht des Islam,* op.cit., pp. 190-216.

————. *Partners in Freedom and True Muslims: Political thought of some Muslim scholars in British India 1912-1947,* Lund, 1971.

————. *The Muslims of British India,* Cambridge, 1972.

Harley, Harry. *Mohalla Schools: A Case for Unicef Support,* Karachi, 1979.

Harrison, Selig S. "Ethnicity and the Political Stalemate in Pakistan", in *The State, Religion and Ethnic Politics: Afghanistan, Iran and Pakistan.* Paper presented at the Conference: Islam, Ethnicity and the State in Afghanistan, Iran and Pakistan, Nov. 1982, Tuxedo, N.Y. 1986, pp. 267-298.

Hasan, Mubashir. *Razm-e Zindagî,* Lahore, 1978 (Urdu).

Hasan, Sibte. *Pâkistân mêñ Tahdhîb kâ Irteqâ',* Karachi, 1984 (Urdu).

Hashmi, Bilal. "Dragon Seed", in H. Gardezi and Jamil R. eds., *Pakistan: Roots of Dictatorship,* op.cit., pp. 148-172.

Hazarwi, Muhammad Sadiq. *Ta'âruf-e 'Ulamâ'-e Ahl-e Sunnat,* Lahore, 1979 (Urdu) TUAS.

Hashmi, Ishfaq. *Mawlânâ Muftî Mahmûd,* Lahore, 1980 (Urdu).

Herald, monthly, Karachi (English).

Hobsbawm, E.J. *Die Banditen,* Frankfurt, 1972.

————. *Sozialrebellionen,* Gießen, 1979.

Hollister, J.N. *The Shi'a of India,* London, 1953.

Hopwood, Derek. *Egypt: Politics and Society 1945-1981,* London, 1982.

Hourani, Albert. *Arabic Thought in the Liberal Age 1798-1939,* Oxford, 1962.

Hudhboi, Parvez A. *Sâ'ins kê maidân mêñ Pâkistân kî pasmândegî, samâjî awr nazariyyatî asbâb,* Islamabad, 1984 (Urdu).

Humaira, Ruhi T. *Ta'lîm-e 'âmah mêñ masjid skûl skîm kâ jâ'izah,* M. ed. Arbeit am *IER* der Punjab University, 1984 (nr. 2596) (Urdu).

Hussain, Asaf. *Islamic Movements in Egypt, Pakistan and Iran: An annotated bibliography,* London, 1983.

Hussain, S.S. and S.A. Ashraf. *Crisis in Muslim Education,* Hodder and Stoughton, Jeddah, 1979.

Ibn Khaldun. *Al-Muqaddimah: An introduction to history,* translated by F. Rosenthal. London, 1978 (1st edn. 1967).

Ihsanullah, Lt. Col. Muhammad. *Pashtûn Qabâ'il,* Lahore, 1984 (Urdu).

Ikram, M. *Modern Muslim India and the Birth of Pakistan,* Lahore, 1977.

Imamuddin, S.M. "Mosque as a centre of education in the early Middle Ages", *Islamic Studies,* vol. 23, no. 3, Islamabad, 1984, pp. 159-170.

Index for *fikr o nazr 1963-1978,* IRI, Islamabad, 1980 (Urdu).

Index for *Islamic Studies 1962-1981,* IRI, Islamabad, 1982.

Iqbal, Afzal. *Islamisation of Pakistan,* Lahore, 1986.

Iqbal, Javed. *Ideology of Pakistan,* Lahore, n.d. (1st edn., Karachi, 1959).

Istiqlal. *Mashâ'ikh nambar,* vol. 11/40, Lahore, 1982 (Urdu).

Jam'iyyat al-Mashâ'ikh Pâkistân, monthly, no. 2, Sept. 1984, no. 4, Nov. 1984, vol. II, no. 15, Oct. 1985, Islamabad (Urdu).

Janjua, Zia ul Islam. *The Manual of Auqaf Laws,* Lahore, 1980.

Jansen, J.J.G. "The Creed of Sadat's Assassins", in *Die Welt des Islams,* vol. 25, 1985, pp. 1-30.

Jayawardena, Kumari. "Ethnic Consciousness in Sri Lanka: Continuity and Change", in *Sri Lanka: The Ethnic Conflict,* ed. by Committee for Rational Development, New Delhi, 1984, pp. 160-173.

Johansen, Barber. *Islam und Staat,* Berlin, 1982.

Johnson, B.L.C. *Pakistan,* London, 1979.

Jones, D.E. and R.W. Jones. "Educational Policy Development in Pakistan", in Ahmad, M., ed., *Contemporary Pakistan,* Karachi, 1982, pp. 252-269.

Jones, R.W. "The Military and Security in Pakistan", in C. Baxter, ed., *Zia's Pakistan: Politics and Stability in a Frontline State,* Lahore, 1985, pp. 63-91.

Jong, F. De. "Die mystischen Bruderschaften und der Volksislam", in W. Ende and U. Steinbach, eds., *Der Islam in der Gegenwart,* op.cit., pp. 487-504.

Kandil, Fuad. *Nativismus in der Dritten Welt,* St. Michael, Blaschke, 1983.

Kardar, Shahid. *Political Economy of Pakistan,* Lahore, 1987.

Karpat, Kemal H., ed., *Political and Social Thought in the Contemporary Middle East,* New York, 1982.

Kashif, A. Mohammad. "A Sociological Study of the Response Patterns of the Enforcement of Ushr", Master's Thesis, Faisalabad, 1984.

Keddie, Nikki R., ed., *Scholars, Saints and Sufis,* Berkeley, 1972.

———. *An Islamic Response to Imperialism,* Berkeley, 1983.

Kedourie, Elie. *Afghani and 'Abduh: An Essay on Religious Unbelief and Political Activism in Modern Islam,* London, 1966.

Kennedy, Charles H. *Bureaucracy in Pakistan,* Oxford, 1987.

———. "Rural Groups and the Stability of the Zia Regime", in Craig Baxter, ed., *Zia's Pakistan: Politics and Stability in a Frontline State,* op.cit., pp. 23-46.

Khalid, Detlev. *Reislamisierung und Entwicklungspolitik,* Köln, 1982.

Khalid, Duran. "Pakistan und Bangla Desh", in W. Ende and U. Steinbach eds., *Der Islam in der Gegenwart,* op.cit., pp. 274-307.

Khan, Abdul Wali. *Facts are Sacred,* Peshawar, n.d. (c. 1986).

Khan, Amanullah. "The scientific methodology in Islam", *Journal of Research (Humanities),* Lahore, vol. X, no. 2 and vol. XI, no. 1, July 1975 and January 1976, pp. 67-80.

Khan, Ayub. *Friends not Masters,* Oxford, 1967.

Khan, Hamiduddin. *History of Muslim Education.* vol. 1, Karachi, 1967.

Khan, K.A. *The Mosque Schools in Pakistan: An Experiment in integrating Non-formal and Formal Education,* UNESCO, Paris, 1981.

Khan, Mahmood Hasan and Mahmood Iqbal. "Socio-Economic Indicators in Rural Pakistan: Some Evidence", in Nabi, Ijaz, ed., *The Quality of Life in Pakistan,* Lahore, 1986, pp. 93-108.

———. *Underdevelopment and Agrarian Structure in Pakistan,* Lahore, 1981.

Khan, Masud Husain: "Urdu", in Th. A. Seboek. *Current Trends in Linguistics,* vol. 5, *Linguistics in South Asia,* Mouton, 1969, pp. 277-283.

Khan, Mohammad Asghar. ed., *The Pakistan Experience: State and Religion,* Lahore, 1985.

Khan, Qamaruddin. *The Methodology of Islamic Research,* Karachi, 1973 (1st edn., 1967).

———. *The Political Thought of Ibn Taymiyah,* Islamabad, 1985.

Khan, R., N. Mahmood, and R. Siddiqui. *An Analysis of the School-level Enrolment, Drop-outs and Output in Pakistan, 1970/71-1982/83*, Islamabad, 1984. Mimeograph.

———. "An assessment of the priorities and the efficiency of Pakistan's public sector educational expenditure 1970/71-1982/83", *PIDE*, Islamabad, 1984.

Khan, Wasiullah M. *Education and Society in the Muslim World*, Jeddah, 1981.

Khan, Zafar Iqbal. *Land Tenure System in Mansehra District NWFP Pakistan*, Master's Thesis, Islamabad, 1981.

Khalid, M. *Islâmî nizâm-e ta'lîm awr Pâkistân kê hawâlê sê mashrah kitâbiyyât-e ta'lîm*, IPS, Islamabad, 1984 (Urdu).

Khuro, Hamida. ed., *Sind Through the Centuries*, Oxford, 1982.

King, A.D. *Colonial Urban Development: Culture, social power and environment*, Boston, London, 1976.

Korson, J.H. "Bhutto's Educational Reform", in J.H. Korson. ed. *Contemporary Problems of Pakistan*, op.cit., pp. 119-146.

Korson, J.H. ed., *Contemporary Problems of Pakistan*, Leiden, 1974.

Kotenkar, Arun. *Grundlagen hinduistischer Erziehung im alten Indien*, Frankfurt a.M., 1982.

Kozlowski, G.C. *Muslim Endowments and Society in British India*, Cambridge, 1985.

Kraan, J.D. *Religious Education in Islam with special reference to Pakistan*, Rawalpindi, 1984.

Krbek, J.H.P. Evans-von. *The social structure and organization of a Pakhtun-speaking community in Afghanistan*, Department of Anthropology, University of Durham, 1977.

Kreutzmann, Hermann. "Die Talschaft Hunza (Northern Areas of Pakistan): Wandel der Austauschbeziehungen unter Einfluß des Karakorum Highway", *Die Erde*, Nr. 118, 1987, pp. 37-53.

Kuhn, Thomas S. *Die Struktur Wissenschaftlicher Revolutionen*, Frankfurt a.M., 1973.

Laimer, M., J. Malik and R. Schulze. "Jahresbericht zum Reintegrationsprojekt für freiwillige Rückkehrer in ihre Heimatländer des DRK 1982", Bonn, 1983. Mimeograph.

Lambrick, H.T. *The Terrorist*, London, 1972.

Leitner, G.W. *History of indigenous education in the Punjab since Annexation and in 1882*, New Delhi, 1971 (1st edn., 1883).

Ludhianwi, Muhammad Y. *Dînî madâris kê bârê mêñ wizârat-e ta'lîm kâ mujawwazah mansûbah awr 'ulamâ'-e karâm kâ radd-e 'aml*, ed. by the Wafâq al-Madâris al-'Arabiyyah Pakistan, Multan, 1981 (Urdu) (*radd-e 'aml*).

———. *Repôrt qawmî kamîtî barâ-e dînî madâris Pâkistân awr 'ulamâ'-e ummat kê lî'ê lamhah-e fikriyyah*, hrsg. von Wafâq al-Madâris, Multan, n.d., (*lamhah-e fikr*, Urdu).

Luxemburg, Rosa. *Gesammelte Werke*, vol. 5, Berlin (Ost), 1975.

Mahkamah Awqâf Punjâb, Lahore. *Gâ'id Buk*, Lahore, n.d. (Urdu) (*Gaid Buk*, Urdu).

———. *Ta'âruf 'Ulamâ' Akademî*, Lahore, 1982 (*Ta'âruf*, Urdu).

Mahmood, Shaukat Sh. *The Constitution of Pakistan*, Pakistan Law Times Publications, Lahore, 1969.

Majalla, *Râbitat al-'âlam al-islâmî*, (Mecca) 23 (1405) 5/6 (Arabic).

Maktab Wafâq al-Madâris al-'Arabiyyah Pâkistân. eds., *Fihris al-Jâ'miât wa al-madâris al-mulhiqah bî wafâq al-madâris al-'arabiyyah Bâkistân*, Multan, 1403/1982 (Arabic).

Malik, Din Mohammad. *Philosophical and sociological implication of the report of the Commission of National Education for Pakistan 1953*, Washington State, 1966.

Malik, S. Jamal: "Al-Mashraqi und die Khaksar, Eine religiöse Sozialbewegung indischer Muslime im 20. Jahrhundert", Master's Thesis, Bonn, 1982. Mimeograph.

———. "Islamization of the Ulama and their places of learning in Pakistan 1977-1984", *Asien*, no. 25, Hamburg, October 1987, pp. 41-63.

———. "The Luminous Nurani: Charisma and Political Mobilisation among the Barelwis in Pakistan", in Pnina Werbner, ed., *Person, Myth and Society in South Asian Islam*, Adelaide, *Social Analysis*, no. 28, 1990.

———. "Waqf in Pakistan: Change in traditional institutions", in *Die Welt des Islams*, Leiden, 1990, vol. 30, pp. 63-97.

Masud, Muhammad Khalid. "Islamic Research Institute–An Historical Analysis", *Islamic Studies*, Foundation Day Supplement, Islamabad, Summer 1976, pp. 33-41.

Maududi, Abul Ala. *Islamic Law and Constitution*, Lahore, 1980.

Mawdudi, Abul Ala. *Islâmî iqtisâdî nizâm*, Lahore, 1984 (Urdu).

———. *Ta'lîmât*, Lahore, 1982 (Urdu).

Mayer, Adrian C., "Pir and Murshid; an aspect of religious leadership in Westpakistan", in *Middle Eastern Studies* 3, 1967, pp. 160-169.

Malik, Abdullah. *"Yêh muftî, yêh mashâ'ikh" awr inqilâb-e Afghânistân*, Lahore, 1985 (Urdu).

Memon, Moojan. *An Introduction to Shi'i Islam*, New Haven and London, 1985.

Metcalf, B.D., ed. *Moral Conduct and Authority: The place of ADAB in South Asian Islam*, Berkeley, 1984.

———. *Islamic Revival in British India, Deoband 1860-1900*, Princeton University Press, 1982.

Mitchell, R.P. *The Society of the Muslim Brothers*, London, 1969.

Moazzam, Anwar. *Jamal al-din al-Afghani: A Muslim intellectual*, Lahore, n.d.

Mughal, Ghulam Nabi. *Sindh kîâ sôch rahâ hai*, Karachi, 1986 (Urdu).

Muhammad, Mawlana Nur. *Brêlwî Fatwe*, Lahore, 1983 (Urdu).

Munir, M.N.Q.A. *Constitution of the Islamic Republic of Pakistan*, Lahore, n.d.

Munir, Muhammad. *From Jinnah to Zia*, Lahore, 1980.

Muslehuddin, Muhammad. *Islamic Education: Its Form and Features*, Islamabad, n.d.

Muslim Education: Quarterly, ed. by King Abdulaziz University, Jeddah.

Nabi, Ijaz. ed., *The Quality of Life in Pakistan*, Lahore, 1986.

Nadwi, Sayyid Sulaiman. *Maqâlât-e Shiblî*, vol. 3, n.p., 1955 (Urdu).

Nagel, Tilman. *Staat und Glaubensgemeinschaft im Islam: Geschichte der politischen Ordnungsvorstellungen der Muslime*, vols. I and II, Zürich and Munich, 1981.

Naqwi, Sayyid Hussain Arif. *Tadhkirah-e 'Ulamâ'-e Imâmiyyah Pâkistân*, Islamabad, 1984 (Urdu).

Nasr, Seyyed Hossein. *Science and Civilisation in Islam*, Lahore, 1983.

Niazi, Maulana Kausar. "Reorientation of Islamic Research Institute", in *IS*, Foundation Day Supplement, Islamabad, Summer 1976, pp. 3-7.

Niyazi, Mawlana Kawthar. *Jamâ'at-e Islâmî 'awâmî 'adâlat mêñ*, Lahore, 1973 (Urdu).

Nu'mani, Shibli. *Omar the Great*, vol. II, Lahore, 1981.

Oldenburg, Veena Talwar. *The Making of Colonial Lucknow, 1857-1877*, New Jersey, 1984.

Osterloh, K.H. "Traditionelle Lernweisen und europäischer Bildungstransfer. Zur Begründung einer adaptierten Pädagogik in den Entwicklungsländern", in T. Schöfthaler and D. Goldschmidt, eds., *Soziale Struktur und Vernunft*, op.cit., pp. 440-460.

Pakistan Commentary, Hamburg.

Pakistan: A comprehensive bibliography of books and Government publications with annotations 1947-1980, Islamabad, 1981.

Paret, Rudi, Trans, *Der Koran*, Stuttgart-Berlin-Köln-Mainz, 1979.

Pasha, H.A. and Tariq Hasan. "Development Ranking of Districts of Pakistan", in Nabi, Ijaz, ed., *The Quality of Life in Pakistan*, op.cit., pp. 47-92.

Peters, Rudolph. "Erneuerungsbewegungen im Islam vom 18. bis zum 19. Jahrhundert und die Rolle des Islams in der neueren Geschichte: Antikolonialismus und Nationalismus", in W. Ende and U. Steinbach eds., *Der Islam in der Gegenwart*, op.cit., pp. 91-131.

———. *Islam and Colonialism; The Doctrine of Jihad in Modern History*, The Hague, 1979.

———. "Islamischer Fundamentalismus: Glaube, Handeln, Führung", in Schluchter Wolfgang, ed., *Max Webers Sicht des Islams*, op.cit., pp. 217-241.

Phadnis, Urmila. *Religion and Politics in Sri Lanka*, London, 1976.

Philips, C.H. ed., *Politics and Society in India*, London, 1963.

Prinz, Thomas. *Die Geschichte der United National Party in Sri Lanka*, Heidelberg, 1990.

Provisional Constitution Order 1981, Asmat Kamal Khan, ed., Lahore, 1982.

Qadeer, Mohammad A. *Lahore: Urban Development in the Third World*, Lahore, 1983.

Qasuri, Muhammad Munsha Tabish, *"Tahrîk-e nizâm-e mustafâ' awr Jâmi'ah Nizâmiyyah Ridwiyyah Lâhawr"*, Lahore, 1978 (Urdu).

Qasuri, Muhammad Sadiq, *Akâbir-e tahrîk-e Pâkistân*, vols. I and II, Lahore, 1976 and 1979 (Urdu) (ATP).

Qayyum, A. *Non-Formal Approaches to Revitalize Basic Education: Some stray experiences of Pakistan,* UNESCO; UNICEF, Paris, 1981 (Ref. to as Qayyum).

Qayyum, Abdul. "Revitalization of Rural Mosques as centres of Learning", Islamabad, 1983. Mimeograph.

Qazilbash, Agha K.H. "Authority and Power Structure in Konsh Valley Distt: Mansehra NWFP", Master's Thesis, Islamabad, 1981.

Qadiri, Muhammad Din Kalim. *Tadhkirah-e Maṣ'ld'ikh-e Qâdiriyyah,* Lahore, 1985 (Urdu).

Qasimi, Ahmad Nadim. *Sannâtâ,* Lahore, 1959 (Urdu).

Quraishi, Mansoor A. *Some aspects of Muslim Education,* Lahore, 1983 (finalized 1970).

Qureshi, A.I. *The Economic and Social System of Islam,* Lahore, 1979.

Qureshi, I.H. *Education in Pakistan,* Karachi, 1975.

————. *Ulama in Politics,* Karachi, 1974.

Rahman, Fazlur. *Islam and Modernity,* Chicago, 1982.

————. "The Qur'anic solution of Pakistan's educational problem", in *Islamic Studies,* vol. 4, no. 4, Karachi, 1967, pp. 315-326.

Rahman, Tanzil al. "Islâmî nazariyyâtî kawnsil", *fikr o nazr: nifâz-e sharî'at nambar,* vol. 20, no. 10/9, Islamabad, 1983, pp. 153-162 (Urdu).

————. "Islâmî nazariyyâtî kawnsil", *Hurmat: Nifâz-e Islâm nambar,* vol. 20, no. 25/26, Rawalpindi, 1983, pp. 193ff (Urdu).

Rahman, Tanzil ur. *Introduction to Zakat in Pakistan,* Islamabad, n.d.

Rashid, S. Kh. and S. A. Husain. *Wakf Laws and Administration in India,* Lucknow, 1973.

————. *Muslim Law,* Lucknow, 1973.

Rauf, Abdur. *Renaissance of Islamic Culture and Civilisation in Pakistan,* Lahore, 1965.

Rahi, Akhtar. *Tadhkirah 'Ulamâ'-e Punjâb,* vols. I and II, Lahore, 1980, (Urdu).

————. *Tadhkirah-e musannifîn dars-e nizâmî,* Lahore, 1978, (Urdu).

Register of the candidates for graduation of different Madâris organizations. Mimeograph (Urdu).

Ridwân, Hizb al-Ahnâf, vol. 33, no. 4/5, May 1984 and vol. 38, no. 6, Lahore, June 1984 (Urdu).

Ridwi, Sayyid Mahbub. *Tarîkh Dâr al-'Ulûm Dêôband,* vols. I and II, Delhi, 1977 (Urdu).

Riport barâ-e sâl 1984, ed. by the markaz-e 'ilm wa dânish, Jâmi'at al-Muntazar, Lahore, 1984 (Urdu).

Robinson, Francis. *Separatism among Indian Muslims: The politics of the United provinces' Muslims 1860-1923,* Cambridge, 1974.

————. "The 'Ulamâ' of Farangî Mahall and their Adab", in B.D. Metcalf, ed. *Moral Conduct and Authority,* op.cit., pp. 152-183.

Rosenthal, E.I.J. *Islam in the Modern National State,* Cambridge, 1965.

Rothermund, Dietmar. ed., *Islam in Southern Asia: A survey of current research,* Wiesbaden, 1975.

————. *Europa und Indien im Zeitalter des Merkantilismus*, Darmstadt, 1978.

————. *Grundzüge der indischen Geschichte*, Darmstadt, 1976.

————. "Nationalismus und Sozialer Wandel in der Dritten Welt: Zwölf Thesen", in Otto Dann, ed., *Nationalismus und Sozialer Wandel*, Hamburg, 1978, pp. 187-208.

Roy, Olivier: *Islam and Resistance in Afghanistan*, Cambridge, 1986.

Said, Hakim Muhammad. comp., *Nazariyyah o falsafah-e tal'îm-e islâmî*, 4. Hamdard Sîrat Conference, vol. I, Karachi, 1984 (Urdu).

Sadiqi, Hafiz al-Rahman and Anis Ahmad. *Ta'lîmî palîsî 1979*, Islamabad, 1981 (Urdu).

Said, Edward. *Orientalism*, London, 1979.

Sajjad, Muslim. *Pâkistân meñ nizâm-e ta'lîm kî islâmî tashkîl kî hikmat-e 'amlî*, Islamabad, 1982 (Urdu).

Salim, Sayyid Muhammad. *Hind'o Pâkistân meñ musalmânôñ kâ nizâm-e ta'lîm o tarbiyyat*, Lahore, 1980 (Urdu).

Saqib, Ghulam Nabi. *Modernization of Muslim education*, Lahore, 1983.

Sayeed, Khalid B. *Politics in Pakistan*, New York, 1980.

Schacht, Joseph. *An Introduction to Islamic Law*, Oxford, 1982.

Schimmel, A., ed., *Botschaft des Ostens*, Tübingen, 1977.

Schimmel, A. *Mystical Dimensions of Islam*, Chapel Hill, N.C., 1975.

Schluchter, Wolfgang, ed., *Max Webers Sicht des Islams*, Frankfurt a.M., 1987.

Schmucker, Werner. "Sekten und Sondergruppen", in Ende, W. and U. Steinbach, eds., *Der Islam in der Gegenwart*, op.cit., pp. 505ff.

Scholz, Fred. "Detribalisierung und Marginalität. Eine empirische Fallstudie", in Wolfgang Köhler, ed., *Pakistan: Analysen, Berichte, Dokumentationen*, Hamburg, 1979, pp. 31-68.

————. "Verstädterung in der Dritten Welt: Der Fall Pakistan", in W. Kreisch, W.D. Sick and J. Stadelbauer, eds., *Siedlungsgeographische Studien*, Berlin, 1979, pp. 341-385.

Schöfthaler, T. and D. Goldschmidt. eds., *Soziale Struktur und Vernunft*, Frankfurt a.M., 1984.

Schulze, Reinhard. "Die Politisierung des Islam im 19. Jahrhundert", in *Die Welt des Islams*, vol. XXII, no. 1-4, pp. 103-116.

————. "Islamische Kultur und soziale Bewegung", *Peripherie*, no. 18/19, April 1985, pp. 60-84.

Senghaas, D. *Weltwirtschaft und Entwicklungspolitik, Plädoyer für Dissoziation*, Frankfurt a.M., 1978.

Senghaas, D., ed., *Peripherer Kapitalismus: Analysen über Abhängigkeit und Unterentwicklung*, Frankfurt a.M., 1981.

Shahani, R.G. "Osmania University and the growth of Urdu literature", *Indian Art and Letters*, NS 15, London, 1941, pp. 12-24.

Shahab, Rafi Allah. *Islâmî Rîâsat kâ mâliyyâtî nizâm*, Islamabad, 1973 (Urdu).

Shaikh, Fadl Karum and Asrar al-Rahman Bukhari. *Pâkistân kê idârê*, Lahore: (approx) 1983 (Urdu).

Shalabi, Ahmad. *Tarîkh-e Ta'lîm o Tarbiyyat-e Islâmîyyah*, Lahore, 1963 (Urdu).

Shalaby, Ahmad. *History of Muslim Education*, Beirut, 1954.

Shah, Mufti Anwar. *Manuscript on the Wafâq al-madâris al-'arabiyyah*, Multan, 1986 (Urdu). Mimeograph.

Shakir, Iliyas. *MRD, Kamiyâbîâñ, Nâkâmîâñ*, Karachi, 1985 (Urdu)

Smith, W.C. *Modern Islam in India: A social analysis*, Lahore, 1969.

————. "The 'ulama' in Indian Politics", in C.H. Philips, ed., *Politics and Society in India*, London, 1963, pp. 39-51.

Sufi, G.M.D. *Al-Minhaj: Evolution of curricula in the Muslim educational institutions*, Sh. Muh. Ashraf, Lahore, 1981 (1st edn., 1941).

Suhail, Azhar. *Pîr Pagârô kî kahânî*, Karachi, 1987 (Urdu).

Syed, A. *Pakistan: Islam, Politics and National Security*, Lahore, 1984.

Syed, G.M. *Sindhu Desh: A Nation in Chains*, n. p., 1974.

Syed, Riaz Ahmed. *Pakistan on Road to Islamic Democracy: Referendum 1984*, Islamabad, 1985.

Ta'âruf; Râbitah al-madâris al-islâmiyyah Pâkistân, Lahore, 1984 (Urdu).

Taeschner, Franz. *Zünfte und Bruderschaften im Islam*, Munich, 1979.

Tanzîm al-Madâris al-'Arabiyyah, eds., *Fihrist madâris-e mulhiqah tanzîm al-madâris Pâkistân*, Lahore, 1984 (Urdu).

Tanzîm al-madâris al-'arabiyyah kê sâlânah rûdâd, Lahore, (Urdu).

Tanzîm al-Madâris al-'arabiyyah: Lâ'ihah-e 'aml, Lahore, 1974 and 1983 (Urdu).

Tarin, Abd al-Hamid, *Faqîr Epî*, Karachi, 1984 (Urdu).

The Gazette of Pakistan, Extraordinary.

The Institute of Strategic Studies, ed., *Afghanistan Report*, Islamabad (monthly).

Tibawi, A.L. *Islamic Education*, London, 1972.

Tibi, Bassam. *Die Krise des Modernen Islam*, Munich, 1981.

Tirmizi, Mufti Sayyid Abd al-Shakur. *'Aqâ'id-e 'Ulamâ'-e Ahl-e Sunnat Dêôband*, Lahore, 1984 (Urdu).

Trimingham, J.S. *The Sufi Orders in Islam*, Oxford, 1971.

Troll, C.W. *Sayyid Ahmad Khan: A Reinterpretation of Muslim Theology*, Delhi, 1978.

Tufail, Muhammad. *Nuqûsh Lâhawr Nambar*, Lahore, 1962 (Urdu).

Turner, Brain S. "Accounting for the Orient", in D. Maceoin and A. Al-Shahi, eds., *Islam in the Modern World*, Canberra, 1983, pp. 9-26.

UGC. *Higher Education News*, vol. II, no. 10, October 1982.

UNESCO. *Traditional forms of Education within a diversified Educational field: The case of Coranic Schools*, Paris, Dec. 10-12, 1984.

Viewpoint, Lahore, weekly.

Wafâq al-Madâris al-'Arabiyyah Pâkistân, eds., *Kârwâ'î ijlâs Wafâq al-madâris*, Multan, 1980 (Urdu).

Wafâq al-Madâris al-'Arabiyyah Pâkistân, *Sôlah sâlah nisâb-e ta'lîm, manzûrkardah*, n.p., 1983 (Urdu) (manzûrkandah I)

————. *Sôlah sâlah nisâb-e ta'lîm, manzûrkardah*, Multan, 1984 (Urdu). (manzûrkardah II)

Waseem, Mohammad. *Pakistan under Martial Law, 1977-1985*, Lahore, 1987.

Wright, T.P. (Jr.) "Indian Muslim Refugees in the Politics of Pakistan", *The Journal of Commonwealth Comparative Politics,* vol. XII, no. 2, July 1974, pp. 189-205.

Yazdani, Muhammad Hanif, comp., *Hindûstân mêñ Ahl-e Hadîth kî 'ilmî khidmat* (ed. by Abu Yahya Imam Khan Nawshehrwi), Maktabah Nadhiriyya, Chichawatni, 1970 (Urdu).

Zafar, M.D. *100 Questions on Islamic Education,* Lahore, 1984.

Zahid, N.S. "Ushr: A Theoretical and empirical analysis, Discussion paper no. 39, Applied Economics Research Centre", Karachi, 1980 (unpublished).

Zingel, Wolfgang-Peter. *Die Problematik Regionaler Entwicklungsunterschiede in Entwicklungsländern,* Wiesbaden, 1979.

―――. "Urbanisierung und regionale Wirtschaftsentwicklung in Pakistan", in Hermann Kulke, H.C. Rieger and L. Lutze, eds., *Städte in Süd Asien, Beiträge zur Süd-Asien Forschung,* vol. 60, Wiesbaden, 1982, pp. 233-267.

Ziring, Lawrence. *Pakistan: The Enigma of Political Development,* Dawson Westview, 1980.

UNPUBLISHED DOCUMENTS

Dalil, *Dâr al-'Ulûm al-Haqqâniyyah Akorâ Khattak Madînah Bishâwar, Bâkistân, Taqaddama Idârah al-Ta'lîm,* Peshawar, n.d. (Arabic).

Data from the Pakistan Banking Council.

Extract from "A Brief Account of the Activities of the Advisory Council of Islamic Ideology", January 1964, December 1970.

Fihrist dînî madâris jin kô sâl 1984/85 kê lî'e sûbâ'î Zakât Fund sê mâlî imdâd faraham kî gâ'î, Lahore, 1986, PZC Punjab (Urdu).

File on FSC's Judgement, consulted on 18.2.86 in the Auqaf Department Punjab, Lahore.

GoP, Allama Iqbal Open University. *Arabic Teacher Courses,* Islamabad, 1985 (Arabic)

GoP, CZA. *List of Zakat-receiving DM from the Provincial Zakat Fund,* Islamabad.

GoP, LAMEC: *Dînî Madâris Prôject,* Islamabad, 1985 (Urdu).

GoP, Ministry of Education, Curriculum Wing. *Qurtâs 'amlî. Pâkistân mêñ ta'lîmî nizâm kô islâmî sânchê mêñ dâlnê kâ 'amal,* Islamabad, 1984 (Urdu).

GoP, Ministry of Education, Directorate for Educational Planning and Managment. *Material for Supplementaries (for the mosque schools scheme),* Islamabad, 1985.

GoP, Ministry of Education, Islamic Education Research Cell. *Important statistics of the Deeni Madaris of NWFP,* Islamabad, 1983.

GoP, Ministry of Education: *Data Book,* Islamabad, 1982.

―――. *Dînî madâris Pâkistân kê kawâ'if,* Islamabad, (approx. 1983) (Questionnaire).

GoP, Ministry of Law and Parliamentary Affairs (Law Division). *Draft Shariat Commission Order*, Islamabad, 1978.

GoP, Ministry of Religious Affairs. *Main and Sub-Committee on Deeni Madaris*, 4 August 1980.

―――. "Working paper" from October 1985 about shrines in the Punjab and in Sindh.

―――. *Equivalence of Deeni Sanads*, n.d.

―――. *Madaris-e 'arabiyyah kî muttahidah tanzîm; aik sarsara jâ'izah,* December 19, 1978 (Urdu).

―――. *Report of the Committee on the Eligibility of Religious Institutions and their Students for Zakat*, Islamabad, n.d.

―――. *Sargodha Report of September 28, 1978,* Islamabad, 1978.

Islamic Research Institute, *Qawmî Idârah barâ-e dînî madâris Pâkistân ordînans mujariyyah 1400 hijrah (musawwadah); pîsh kardah Dr. Abd al-Wahid Halepotah,* Islamabad, 1980 (Urdu).

Islamic University Islamabad, *Seminar on Islamization of Knowledge,* January 4-9, 1982, Papers contributed, vol. 1, Islamabad, 1982.

Khan, A.A. *Paper on the Seminar on the management and development of Awkaf Properties at Jeddah 1984.*

Panel Report on Zakat 1978, Islamabad, n.d.

PZC, Peshawar. *Disbursement from Provincial Zakat Funds to Deeni Madris,* June 1985 (stating all the provinces).

PZC, Punjab. *List of Zakat-receiving Dini Madaris in Zila Lahore,* (Urdu).

―――. *Subâ'î zakât Fund se dînî Madâris ko sâlânah imdâd kî frâhamî,* PZC Punjab 1985 (Urdu).

Talal, Yusuf. *Draft chapter on Islamic Education for inclusion in the Report of the president's Task Force on Education,* Islamabad, 1982.

UGC. *Qurtas 'amlî/pîshnamah barâ-e Kamîtî ma' adâlah isnâd dînî wa jamî'i,* August 25th, 1982, Islamabad (Urdu).

Several letters, orders and telegrams concerning the National Committee of religious schools.

DAILY NEWSPAPERS

Anjâm (Urdu)
Daily Ittehad
Dawn
Hurriyat (Urdu)
Imrôz (Imroze) (Urdu)
Jang (Jang) (Urdu)
Jasârat (Jasarat) (Urdu)
Jur'at (Jurat) (Urdu)
Kohistan Times
Mashriq (Urdu)

Military and Civil Gazetteer
Morning News
Musâwât (Musawat) (Urdu)
Nawâ'-e Waqt (Nawa-e Waqt) (Urdu)
New Times
Pakistan Times
Pakistan Observer
Shâhbâz (Shahbaz) (Urdu)
Statesmen
Tam'îr (Tameer) (Urdu)
Tasnîm (Tasneem) (Urdu)
The Muslim
The Sun

INDEX

Abul Ala Mawdudi 7
Administrator Auqaf 60-2
Afghanistan 151, 206ff, 232ff, 241ff,
    251-2, 266-7.
agrarian structures 265-9
Ahl-e Hadith (the people of the
    Prophet's tradition) 6, 24, 42, 45,
    124, 141, 143, 151, 187, 196ff,
    213-16, 229-31, 251, 268, 275,
    304ff
Ahmad Rida Khan 5, 59
Ahmad Said Kazimi (Brelwi) 45
a'imma (prayer leaders) 61
Al-Azhar University (Cairo) 270, 271,
    302
All Pakistan Education Advisory Board
    131
Allamah Ahmad Said Kazimi (Brelwi)
    45
Anjuman-e sajjâdah-nashîn 64
Ansari, Mawlana 45
Arabic 43, 126, 127, 130, 135, 141,
    164, 168, 170, 175, 178, 271ff
army 278
Asia Foundation 125
Auqaf Federal Control (Repeal)
    Ordinance 1979 62
Auqaf Ordinance 1960 59
Awqâf (religious endowments) 1, 3, 10,
    55-74, 120-53, 305ff
    see also Dînî Madâris
Ayub Kahn 34ff, 44, 61, 62, 64, 123-6,
    132, 168, 214, 293

Bahawalpur 71
Baluchistan 108, 111, 142, 150, 151,

178ff, 235, 242, 244, 245
banking 35-6, 46, 298
Benazir (Bhutto) 300
Bengalis 34
Bhutto (Zulfikar Ali) 37-8, 46, 61, 62,
    70, 128, 138, 181, 211, 214, 266-
    7, 271, 291, 293
Brelwis 5, 7, 8, 24, 42, 44, 45, 57, 59,
    64, 69, 124, 143, 151, 153, 172-4,
    196ff, 213-16, 227, 229, 230, 231,
    245, 246, 251, 268, 269, 302ff
Brohi, Justice A.K. 45

Central Council/Fund/Zakat 95, 97,
    100, 102ff, 143, 149, 210ff, 213
clergy 16, 19, 21, 42, 121, 128-9, 140ff,
    168ff, 179
colonial rule 6, 121, 289ff
    its legal system 4
    its values 3-4, 6, 10, 17, 24, 289ff
    opposition to 15ff
colonial sector of society 15, 17-24,
    289ff
comparative religion (school subject)
    169ff
conflict resolution 21, 22, 173
Constituent Assembly 34
Constitution 36, 37, 38, 39, 41, 86, 129
Council of Islamic Ideology (CII) 3, 10,
    24, 33-48, 87-91, 129, 132, 153,
    270, 272, 290, 293, 300ff
cultural complexity of Pakistan 3, 18,
    122-3

Dâr al-'Ulûm (seminaries) 42-3
Dâr al-'Ulûm Ashrafabad 215-16

Dâr al-'Ulûm Haqqâniyyah (in Akora
    Khattak) 202-9, 227ff, 240, 241
dastûr 23
dawla 23
Deobandi 4, 5, 6, 7, 34, 42, 45, 57, 59,
    69, 124, 136, 139, 143, 151, 153,
    164, 169-72, 173, 188, 192, 196,
    197, 198ff, 202-9, 213, 215, 216,
    227, 230, 231, 235-7, 245, 251,
    301ff
democracy 41
Dera Ghazi Khan 124
Dînî Madâris (religious schools) 1, 3, 8,
    10, 19, 43, 62, 66-7, 120-53, 164-
    216, 246-7, 304
    Brelwi graduates of 244-7
    Deobandi graduates of 235-7
    growth in numbers of 179-87, 227
    increasing numbers of graduates
    227-31
    Zakat funds for 143-53, 177-9,
    190-2
Directorate of Religious Education 128

economics (school subject) 169ff
education (traditional Islamic) 2, 7, 17,
    42, 43, 45-6, 66-9, 120-53, 164-
    216
    curricula 122, 125-8, 131, 132,
    133, 164-76, 271ff
    drop-outs from 252ff
    eight- vs sixteen-year curriculum
    164, 171-2, 176, 253
    nationalization of 129
    privatization 167ff, 181, 184
    teacher-student numbers 177-9
    teachers 177-9, 252ff
employment (problem of) 265-79, 304
endowments, religious see Auqâf,
    Awqâf, Dînî-Madâris
English 126, 127, 164, 167, 168, 169,
    170, 172, 173, 175, 252-3, 270,
    305ff

Fadl al-Rahman, Dr. 44
Federal Council 41
Federal Shariat Court, 23, 59, 65, 293

Hafiz Nadhr Ahmad 121, 125, 133
Halepota Report 133-6, 138, 139, 140,
    164ff, 188, 271
Hamoodur Rahman 37
Hanafi legal system 4, 5, 7
Hizb al-Ahnaf 153
holidays 45
hospitals 61, 144
hudûd regulations 38

Ibn Khaldun 166-7
ijmâ' 23
ijtihâd 7, 16
industrialization 269-70
Institute for Islamic Research (IIR) 35,
    36, 44, 69
Institute for Shariah 250
integration (of Islam to colonial sector)
    23-4, 37-9, 39-44, 47, 123ff 134,
    164-76, 289ff, 297ff
interest 35
International Islamic Conference 1968
    86
Iqra Centres 274ff
Iran 6
Islam: theology to ideology 15, 16, 17,
    35, 42, 122-8, 289-96
Islamic Advisory Council 35
Islamic Democratic Alliance 298ff
Islamic economics 45-6
Islamic University Bahawalpur 66, 140
Islamic University Islamabad 301
Islamization, agents of 10, 15ff, 289ff
    policy of 8-10, 15-24, 42, 44, 45-
    8, 289ff
    process 20-4, 62ff, 289ff
    see also Islam: theology to
    ideology
Ismailis 6

ithnâ 'ashar ('twelver Shias) 6
Ittihâd al-Madâris 132

Jama'at-e Islami (Sunnis) 6-7, 24, 41,
    45, 90, 104, 151, 166, 176, 196,
    203ff, 208ff, 213-16, 301, 304
Jamal ad-Din al-Afghani 16
Jâmi'ah 'Abbâsiyyah 66
Jâmi'ah al-Ahnâf 153
Jâmi'ah al-Muntazar 229
Jami'ah Islamia 62, 66
Jâmi'ah Madaniyyah 153
Jam'iyyat al Mashâ'ikh Pakistan (JMP)
    5, 8, 64
Jam'iyyat al 'Ulama'-e Hind 5
Jam'iyyat-e 'Ulama'-e Islam (JUI) 5,
    57, 153, 303
Jam'iyyat-e 'Ulama'-e Pakistan (JUP)
    5, 57, 303
Javed Iqbal 59
jihâd 202-9, 232ff, 304ff
Jinnah 55-6
Joint Stock Companies 184ff
Jurisprudence 167ff

Kashmir 142, 178ff, 244, 247
Khair al Madâris 241
khânqâh (hospice) 7, 8, 121
khutabâ (preachers) 61-2
Koran studies (including exegesis)
    166ff, 273ff

labour 21, 265-79, 304
land ownership 265-6
land reforms 65, 268
landlords 58, 185, 213, 243-4, 246, 251,
    265ff, 268
law and legal system 4, 8, 23-4, 37ff, 45
    see also Hanafi, Sharî'a-e Islam
legitimation 10, 16, 18, 24, 33-48, 112-
    13, 172, 232, 292, 297ff
Liaqat Ali Khan 86
libraries 135
literacy campaign 274

Local Zakat Committees/Funds 92, 95,
    100, 101, 107-11, 274
logic (school subject) 171ff

madrasas see Dînî Madâris
Madrasah Arabiyyah Islâmiyyah 241
Majlis-e nazârât-e, shî'ah Madâris-e
    'Arabiyyah 124
Markaz-e Jam'iyyat Ahl-e Hadith 124
mathematics (school subject) 166ff
Mawdudi, A.A. 8, 17, 166
migration 267ff
millenaristic movements 58
modernizaton
    agents of 2-3, 8-9, 123ff, 166ff
    modes of 2, 59-64, 123ff
    of education 42ff, 66-9, 122-8
    perceptions of 1ff, 8, 165-6, 305ff
    see also colonial sector,
    secularism, universalization of
    culture
Moghul period 121
mosques as literacy centres 274ff
    as schools 276ff
    employment in 270ff
Mufti Anwar Shah 215
Mufti Mahmud 138ff, 211ff, 294
Mufti Muhammad Husain Naimi
    (Brelwi) 44-5, 112-13
Muhammad Afzal Cheemah 38, 45, 90
Muhammad Iqbal 59
Muhammad Qasim Nanotawi 137
Muhammad Yusuf Ludhianwi 136-8
Mujâhir Qawmî Mahâz (MQM) 303
Muslim League 56-7
Mussalman Wakf Validating Act (1913)
    56, 73
Mu'tamar al-âlam al Islâmî 37
mystics, mysticism (mashâ'ikh) 8, 16-
    17, 57, 65, 68, 122, 140ff, 290

Naqshbandiyyah order 5, 64
National Assembly 37, 46, 129
National Committee for Dînî Madâris

132, 133, 164, 176, 295
National Book Foundation 135
National Education Policy 1979 271, 272, 276
National Institute for Dînî Madâris 134, 139ff
National Zakat Foundtion 95
nationalism 15, 24
Nawaz Sharif 298ff
Nizam al-Din, Mulla 122
non-Muslims 88, 104, 292
NWFP Í08, 109, 111, 142, 150, 151, 177, 178ff, 206ff, 235-8, 239ff, 244, 245, 247

Pakhtuns 214
Pakistan Muslim League 299, 306
Pakistan National Alliance 120, 130, 138
Pakistan People's Party (PPP) 37, 128-9, 130, 266, 298, 300-6
Pakistan Studies (school subject) 167ff
peasantry see rural society
persian 130, 141
Peshawar region 202ff, 239ff, 242, 251
philosophy (school subject) 168ff
pîrs (saints) and their cults 4-5, 7-8, 39, 55-74, 173, 245, 250-1, 270ff, 291
Planning commission 90, 91
popular (folk-) Islam 7-8, 55, 57, 68ff, 290ff
population density 266ff
prayer 45, 167ff
Provincial Assembly 37
Provincial Zakat Councils/Funds 95, 100, 108, 143, 147-8, 150, 152, 177, 191ff, 206ff

Qadiriyyah 5, 64

rational sciences 166-7
reform, social 35
religious education see Dînî Madâris
Report of the Commission on National

Educaiton (1959) 125
Report of the Committee for...improved syllabus for...Madrasah (1960-61) 127
Report on Islamic System of Government and Elections (1983) 41
ribâ (interest) 35
rural society 7-8, 17, 58, 85, 88-90, 91, 97, 98, 128, 131, 185, 186, 213-14, 246, 250, 252-3, 265-70

saints see pîrs
Saudi Arabia 64, 206, 229, 230, 303
Sayyid Ahmad Khan 8, 16, 17, 55-6
Sayyid Muhammad Radi 44
science (school subject) 167ff
sectarianism 303ff
secularism 15-24, 35, 42, 45, 59-62, 63, 64, 66-74, 125-6, 140, 270ff, 278, 290ff
Shabbir Ahmad Uthmani 34, 57
Sharî'a-e Islam 8, 37, 38, 166ff, 210-12, 250, 270, 298, 299
shaikhs see mystics
Shias 4, 6, 24, 41, 42, 44, 45, 47, 98, 104, 124, 141, 143, 188, 196ff, 213ff, 229-30, 231, 247-9, 251, 301ff
Shibli Numani 55-6
shrines 19, 55, 57, 58, 63, 68-9, 131, 291, 292
Sindh 24, 109, 110, 142, 149, 150, 151, 152, 178ff, 213ff, 235ff, 242, 244, 247, 251
    nationalism in 213-26, 303ff
social sciences 167ff
Special Welfare Tax 88
Sûfîs 5, 57, 63, 68, 122
Sunnis see Jama'at-e Islami
Supreme Council of Islamic Affairs 41
Syed, G.M. 214

Ta'limat-e Islamiyyah 33, 34, 40, 42

Tanzil al-Rahman 40, 41, 45, 91
Tanzîm al-Madâris al-'Arabiyyah 124,
129, 141
Tanzîm al-Madâris (Brelwi) 141, 164,
167, 169, 172-4, 176ff, 188, 213,
227, 244
taqlîd 7, 16
taxation *see* Zakat

UGC 43, 68, 129, 134, 141
'ulamâ' (Islamic scholars, theologians)
4, 7, 10, 34, 35-40, 42-4, 47-8, 63,
65, 122ff, 130, 140ff, 144, 164-
216, 227-31
Brelwi 244-7
Deobandi 235-41
parentage 241-7
'Ulamâ' Akademî 67-8
'Ulamâ' Board 33
'Ulamâ' Convention (1980) 45-6
universities 133, 172
urban society 6, 7, 17, 19-22, 185ff,
246-7, 250, 269-70, 300
Urdu 121, 126, 127, 132, 141, 253, 274
'urs (feasts) 61, 64
ushr (tithe) 66, 85, 86-113, 291ff, 300ff

Wafâq al-Madâris al'Arabiyyah 124,
129, 132, 138, 176, 205, 211ff,
237, 238
Wafâq al-Madâris (Deobandi) 141, 151,
169ff, 188, 273, 302
Wafâq al-Madâris al-Salafiyyah 188,
229, 249-50
Wafâq al-Madâris Shia 229, 248-9
Waqf Ordinance (1979) 65, 293

Waqf Properties Ordinance (1961) 60,
124
World Conference on Islamic Education
165-6

Yusuf Guraya, Dr. 68
Yusuf Talal Ali 141

Zafar Ahmad Ansari 40, 42
Zakat 3, 10, 24, 38, 45, 66, 85-113, 142-
53, 230ff, 290ff, 300ff
administration 92-113, 144, 177ff,
210ff, 292ff, 301ff
boycott of 210-13
changes in 87ff
disbursement of 87, 89, 90-2, 99-
113, 135, 142-53, 206ff
entitlement 85
evasion 88, 102-7, 292
exemption 88-90, 98, 211ff
levies 85-6, 89, 92-113
rates 87, 89-91, 104
as state revenue 97ff
voluntary 102
Zakat and Ushr Order 1979 90, 292ff
Zakat and Ushr Ordinance 1980 44-5
Zakat and Ushr system 85-113
Zakat Regulation of 1980 92, 100,
211, 230
Zakat 'Ulamâ' Committees 39-40
Zia ul Haq 8, 24, 33, 38ff, 44ff, 62ff, 67,
70, 87, 120, 124, 130, 132, 138,
139, 147, 151, 172, 178, 181, 188,
192-3, 214, 227, 230, 242, 271,
290-1, 297ff